The Johnson Years, Volume Three

The Johnson Years, Volume Three

LBJ at Home and Abroad

Edited by Robert A. Divine

University Press of Kansas

Published by the University Press of Kansas (Lawrence, Kansas 66049),
which was organized by the Kansas Board of Regents and is operated and
funded by Emporia State University, Fort Hays State University, Kansas
State University, Pittsburgh State University, the University of Kansas,
and Wichita State University

Library of Congress Cataloging-in-Publication Data

The Johnson years.

 Vol. 1 originally published: Exploring the Johnson
years. Austin, Tex. : University of Texas Press, © 1981.
 Includes bibliographies and indexes.
 Contents: v. 1. Foreign policy, the Great Society,
and the White House — v. 2. Vietnam, the environment,
and science — v. 3. LBJ at home and abroad.
 1. Johnson, Lyndon B. (Lyndon Baines), 1908–1973.
 2. United States—Politics and government—1963–1969.
 I. Divine, Robert A.   II. Exploring the Johnson years.
 E846.J64 1987   973.923   86-32443
 ISBN 0-7006-0326-3 (pbk. : v. 1)
 ISBN 0-7006-0327-1 (v. 2)
 ISBN 0-7006-0655-6 (v. 3)

Printed in the United States of America
10 9 8 7 6 5 4 3 2 1

The paper used in this publication meets the minimum requirements of
the American National Standard for Permanence of Paper for Printed
Library Materials Z39.48-1984.

Contents

Preface

THIS IS THE THIRD VOLUME of essays that I have edited on the Johnson years. Like the first two, *Exploring the Johnson Years* (1981) and *The Johnson Years, Volume Two* (1987), the collection offers the insight of seven scholars who have used materials at the Lyndon Baines Johnson Library and have related their archival findings to the existing body of scholarly writing on their respective topics. The essays serve both to demonstrate the richness of the Johnson Library and to explore important aspects of the history of the 1960s.

This group of essays is more heavily weighted toward foreign policy than those in the earlier volumes. This emphasis marks a deliberate attempt to redress an earlier imbalance; it also reflects the increasing availability of previously security-classified material at the Johnson Library. Only one of the four foreign policy essays deals with Vietnam, undeniably an important topic but one that too often overshadows other significant foreign policy issues of the Johnson years. Three essays focus on domestic issues, with special emphasis on political themes.

In the preface to the second volume, I commented on how difficult it was to find documents in the Johnson Library bearing the imprint of Lyndon Johnson himself. In this collection, there is a wide divergence, with some of the authors focusing directly on the president's personal role in shaping policy while others deal more broadly with the Johnson administration.

The three essays in which LBJ is on center stage most often are those by Lewis L. Gould, Steven F. Lawson, and Douglas Little. Gould shows how Johnson took personal charge of political issues in the 1960s to the detriment of the Democratic party. He argues that Johnson's attempts to rise above partisan considerations contributed significantly to the long-term decline in Democratic presidential fortunes that began in 1968. Lawson is equally intent on exploring LBJ's personal relationship with representatives of the major black-protest organizations. His account reveals a president who tended to identify with those African-American leaders who sought reform along traditional lines; LBJ had little rapport with those like Martin Luther King and the SNCC leaders who championed more radical efforts at change. In foreign policy, Douglas Little reveals a surprising side of Lyndon Johnson—a president who not only was personally involved in conducting Middle Eastern policy but who guided a major shift away from John F. Kennedy's efforts to woo radical Arab leaders like Gamal Nasser in favor of developing close ties with both Israel and conservative Muslim regimes in Iran and Saudi Arabia.

In contrast, Susan M. Hartmann and Lawrence S. Kaplan cover areas in which Johnson largely delegated authority to others within his administration. Hartmann shows that LBJ gave the emerging women's movement much less attention than he accorded civil rights, except for two areas that he deemed sensitive politically—family planning and the appointment of women to high federal positions. Kaplan reveals that Johnson was even more detached from NATO policy, allowing the Pentagon and the State Department to have a free hand in dealing with such issues as the multilateral force and the French withdrawal from military participation in NATO. Kaplan does give LBJ high marks, however, for avoiding a personal confrontation with Charles de Gaulle over the French challenge to NATO in the mid-1960s.

The final two essays show a president somewhere between the poles of intense personal involvement and aloof detachment. Lloyd Gardner focuses on the struggle in 1968 between two groups of presidential advisers over the degree and pace of the American withdrawal from Vietnam from the time of LBJ's March 31 speech to the October 31 announcement of American willingness to begin the Paris peace talks. Johnson presided over the contest between the doves, led by Clark Clifford, and the hawks, headed by Dean Rusk, as he moved reluctantly but inexorably toward deescalation in Vietnam. My essay on the origins of the SALT talks reveals a similar presidential aloofness. It was Robert McNamara and Dean Rusk who took the initiative in seeking arms control talks with the Soviets, with Johnson showing little enthusiasm at the outset. Only after he had become a lame duck in the spring of 1968 did LBJ develop a strong interest in arms control talks with the Soviet Union, seeking SALT as a way to balance the failure in Vietnam, but then it was too late. The Soviet invasion of Czechoslovakia denied Johnson his final hope of taking a memorable step toward world peace before he left office.

I wish to acknowledge the heavy debt this volume owes to the Lyndon B. Johnson Foundation and the dedicated members of the staff of the Johnson Library. The foundation provided generous financial support, which made it possible for the contributors to conduct their research in the files of the presidential library. The staff members, especially Director Harry Middleton, who has been a steadfast and enthusiastic supporter of all three volumes, and David Humphrey, who served as the library's liaison with the authors and editor, offered assistance and guidance that was vital to the completion of this project.

Introduction

1 | The Maturing Johnson Literature

Robert A. Divine

THE RENEWED INTEREST in the life and times of Lyndon Johnson that began in the 1980s continued into the early years of the next decade. Scholars probed more deeply into the Great Society and the Vietnam War, seeking explanations for Johnson's relative success at home and failure abroad. The passage of time added new perspective and dampened some of the controversy that had marred the early work on the Johnson administration, and greater access to manuscript sources offered more insight into the dilemmas of the 1960s.

One issue, however, remains as much in dispute in the 1990s as in the 1960s—the political career and achievements of Lyndon B. Johnson. Biographers and memoir writers have failed to reach a consensus on such disputed topics as the simplicity or complexity of Johnson's personality, the depth of his political ambition, and the nature of his ideological beliefs. Was he a supreme egotist driven solely by the desire to achieve and hold power, or did he embody political goals that transcended his own personal ambition? The failure to achieve a scholarly consensus on LBJ's role in twentieth-century American politics, beyond a recognition that he was a major figure, raises interesting questions that continue to enliven the Johnson literature.[1]

I

The appearance of two major biographical volumes about Lyndon Johnson within a year of each other highlighted the contrasting view that each offered. In 1990 Robert Caro published the second volume of *The Years of Lyndon Johnson*, originally planned as a trilogy but now expected to be at least four volumes. A year later Robert Dallek published *Lone Star Rising*, the first of a two-volume biography of LBJ. Caro's book covered only seven years in the 1940s, and Dallek traced Johnson's career through his election to the vice-presidency in 1960, but neither author has yet touched on LBJ's crucial presidential years. The only recent biographer to cover Johnson's entire life, including the White House period, is Paul K. Conkin in his relatively brief one-volume treatment, *Big Daddy from the Ped-ernales.*[2]

Robert Caro's work offers the most clear-cut portrait of LBJ. Al-though Caro sees two threads running through Johnson's life—a bright thread that culminated in his contributions to the civil rights movement and a dark thread that led to disaster in Vietnam—the au-thor readily admits that in his second biographical volume, ''the bright one is missing.''[3] Covering the years from the time LBJ lost his first race for the Senate until his dubious triumph in 1948, Caro focuses on the means Johnson used to fulfill his ultimate goal of reaching the White House. He used World War II to advance both his political career and the wealth of his benefactors, he exploited his political position to acquire the radio station that became the basis of his fortune, and he defeated Coke Stevenson by ruthless and un-derhanded means to reach the Senate, a vital stepping-stone.

It is this last quest that dominates the book and gives it both its power and its distortions. Caro offers the fullest account yet of how Johnson benefited from the 200 additional votes from Box 13 in Jim Wells County. Although the author is unable to show that LBJ par-ticipated personally in the fraud, he presents a detailed and convinc-ing account of how the people working for Johnson were able to pro-vide enough votes to give him the 87-vote margin over Stevenson. Caro is equally persuasive in showing how Johnson, through great effort and careful maneuvering, was able to win the subsequent po-litical and legal effort to keep his name on the ballot in the fall elec-tion.

Where Caro fails, however, is in his effort to demean Johnson by portraying his 1948 opponent as a saintly figure. In Caro's pages, Coke Stevenson is endowed with all the qualities Johnson lacked— integrity, rugged individualism, and the respect of his fellow citi-zens. The result is a striking contrast between a corrupt and an hon-est politician but one that is so overdrawn as to be a caricature. In presenting Stevenson as a flawless candidate who represented true Texas values, Caro ignores the candidate's racism, his isolationism, and his reactionary political views.

Equally important, Caro fails to probe the dynamics of Texas politics in the 1940s. A crucial change was taking place within the Democratic party, one that would lead to the emergence of Texas as a two-party state toward the end of the century. Johnson and his men-tor, Congressman Sam Rayburn, were aligned with the New Deal, pro-Roosevelt wing of the party in contrast to Stevenson, who was supported by the Texas regulars who had led a conservative rebellion in 1944 against a national party they believed was too liberal, too favorable toward organized labor, and too sympathetic to the aspirations of blacks. Rather than symbolizing the conflict between the old Texas politics of personal values against the new techniques of electronic manipulation of the electorate, as Caro claims, the 1948 contest foreshadowed the struggle Johnson and Rayburn would fight in the 1950s against Allan Shivers, who helped the Republicans carry Texas for Eisenhower in both 1952 and 1956.

Caro's account owes its strengths and its weaknesses to the author's background as an investigative journalist. He relies heavily on personal interviews, an approach that works well in helping unravel the mystery behind the disputed Box 13 from Jim Wells County in 1948 but that fails to set events in their proper historical setting. To a considerable extent, the author becomes the prisoner of people's memory, which often means he is recounting not what happened but what the people he talked with believed or wished to have happened. At the same time, he neglects the documentary record that offers a more sober and accurate but less sensational account of the historical process. The result is a compelling narrative with high moral drama but with inevitable distortions of the truth. Caro's LBJ becomes a figure larger than life, a man driven by relentless ambition with little concern for the people he must crush in his pursuit of the ultimate goal—the White House.

In contrast, Robert Dallek tries to place Lyndon Johnson within the context of the major forces shaping the history of twentieth-century America; it is no accident that his work is subtitled, ''Lyndon Johnson and His Times.'' Two themes stand out sharply—LBJ's commitment to moderate reform at home and to international cooperation for peace abroad. Relying primarily on the documentary record from the files of the Johnson Presidential Library and a wide range of other manuscript sources, Dallek presents Johnson as a politician who subordinated states' rights to federal action on domestic issues and supported a strong international role for the United States in world affairs.

The term Dallek uses to describe Johnson's ideological position is ''liberal nationalist.'' He was liberal in his support for New Deal measures and nationalist in seeking ''to integrate the South into the mainstream of American economic life.''[4] Though Dallek makes a good case for the overall ideological consistency of Johnson's political career, he has difficulty with LBJ's willingness to cater to compromise in order to advance that career. He bridges this gap by claiming that Johnson was a ''self-serving altruist.''[5] Thus he argues that

Johnson served both the interests of rural constituents and the fortunes of the Brown and Root construction company by championing the building of dams on the Colorado in the 1930s. And Dallek later sees Johnson again, as Senate majority leader, combining political opportunism with genuine idealism in achieving the Civil Rights Act of 1957.

Yet it seems clear that in both cases Johnson was more concerned with advancing his political career than in serving his fellow Americans. The alliance he forged with Herman and George Brown in supporting their building of the Mansfield Dam and later of many defense installations during World War II gave him access to a major source of funds for his Senate races. And as Dallek notes, the modest provisions of the 1957 Civil Rights Act, although an important precedent, did little to gain blacks the right to vote in the 1950s. But by taking the lead in passing the first civil rights law since Reconstruction, Johnson transformed himself from a regional into a national political leader who could be considered a legitimate contender for the presidency.

It is precisely the question of Johnson's presidential ambition that provides the sharpest contrast between Caro's and Dallek's treatment of LBJ. Caro's approach is based on the premise that from the outset of his political career, Johnson had his eye on the White House. The very titles of his two volumes, *The Path to Power* and *Means of Ascent*, reveal Caro's conviction that LBJ was driven by "the great ambition beyond the Senate of which he always dreamed but almost never spoke."[6] Dallek, on the other hand, indicates that Johnson's political goals were more limited and pragmatic and sees LBJ advancing step by step without any clear final destination in mind. On Johnson's entering the Senate in 1949, Dallek writes, "He aimed to build a long Senate career on a reputation as one of the most effective senators Texas, the Southwest, and the nation had ever seen." It is only after he became majority leader that Dallek begins to detect LBJ's "presidential ambitions," and even then Dallek is vague about how long Johnson had his eye on the White House.[7]

It is impossible to decide conclusively which author is right about Johnson's ambition. Neither a search of the documentary record nor a recording of reminiscences by those people who knew LBJ can provide insight into his innermost thoughts and desires—nor is this issue decisive in reaching an understanding of Lyndon Johnson's political career. Both authors view him as a highly ambitious politician who used every available means to advance his fortunes. The difference is that while Caro sees LBJ as purely self-seeking, Dallek presents a more complex leader who combined ambition with a genuine desire to help others—whether rural residents of the Texas hill country or southern blacks who had been unfairly denied the right to vote for too long. By stressing Johnson's relationship to New Deal liberalism, Dallek makes a convincing case that LBJ was a man driven not just by personal gain but by a sense of furthering a worthy cause.

Unfortunately, it is likely to be another decade before either Caro or Dallek reaches the crucial years when Johnson finally achieved the pinnacle of power. As indicated, the only recent biography that deals with Johnson's presidency is Paul Conkin's brief volume. Although he makes no effort to duplicate the detailed research of Caro and Dallek, Conkin skillfully uses the existing Johnson literature and some of the files of the Johnson Library to offer considerable insight into Johnson's life.

Two themes stand out in Conkin's biography. The first is his analysis of Johnson's relationship to the people around him. Conkin probes the familiar LBJ tactic of ingratiating himself with older men of power, from Pres. Cecil Evans at Southwest Texas State Teachers College to Richard Russell in the Senate. Yet instead of seeing this tactic as merely a crude means of self-advancement, Conkin perceives Johnson as always wanting to be part of an extended family. LBJ would begin by playing the role of the dutiful son, loyally and faithfully carry out the most menial and unpleasant duties but then gradually gaining power and influence. Ultimately he would become, in Conkin's term, "the big daddy of American politics," ready to dispense favors and help others in this new extended family.[8] Johnson could be a dedicated follower and a generous leader, Conkin claims, but he "had great difficulty relating to social equals." He could not be simply a member of the club; instead, according to Conkin, "He had to lead, to dominate, to be the great benefactor or the center of attention, else he usually dropped out."[9]

This trait explains in part why Johnson was so successful as Senate majority leader but why he ultimately failed as president. The Senate was a small body, one which Johnson could treat like an extended family. By cultivating the support of leaders such as Richard Russell at the outset, LBJ was soon able to gain mastery over this body, keeping a close personal relationship with its members and serving as their "big daddy." But once in the White House, he no longer could be on intimate terms with those people he attempted to serve. He never succeeded in making the press part of his intimate family, and his efforts to control and manipulate public opinion led only to the credibility gap. One reason for Johnson's ultimate failure in the White House was that the presidency was not suited to his personal style of leadership.

Conkin also discerns in Johnson's political career a recurring cycle. LBJ entered each new political arena with great energy and ambition, yet he soon exhausted his initial enthusiasm, became frustrated with the course of events, and finally wanted to withdraw until a new challenge began the process again. His career in the House followed this pattern as he slipped from an outburst of great activity and zest at first to a sense of growing despair over the lack of opportunity to exercise leadership in this large body. Then his election to the Senate gave him a new world to conquer; he quickly rose to the position of majority leader and transformed it into a powerful office by serving as the mediator between a Democratic legislative majority and a Republican president. But after the sweeping Democratic victory in the 1958 congressional elections, his more liberal colleagues began to chafe at his tactics of accommodation to the Eisenhower administration and moved to curb his power.

Conkin argues that this cycle reached its culmination when LBJ arrived in the White House. "In his five years as president," he observes, "Johnson moved from brilliant early success and from intense but fulfilling engagement to galling frustration, a sense of failure, and then to a characteristic withdrawal."[10] This pattern of behavior suggests that it was not just Vietnam that brought about Johnson's downfall. LBJ seemed to understand his own tendencies when he insisted on gaining as many legislative victories as possible in 1965. Like a gambler on a roll, he knew he had to achieve as much as possible before his luck began to turn and the inevitable obstacles arose to thwart his efforts.

The strength of Conkin's book is that it offers insight into how Johnson's personal traits may have affected his performance in the White House. Conkin presents a brief and unexceptional account of the Great Society programs and of LBJ's growing obsession with Vietnam, culminating in his decision to withdraw from the 1968 presidential contest in an effort to begin the peace process. But by suggesting that the explanation of Johnson's uneven performance as president was rooted in distinctive personal traits, Conkin provides a challenge to both Caro and Dallek; when Johnson's definitive biographers address the presidential years, they will need to take Conkin's insights into account. Clearly there is more to the Johnson presidential performance than can be explained by reference to ruthless ambition or commitment to the creed of liberal nationalism.

LBJ's successes and failures in the White House were the product of the interaction between the circumstances of the 1960s and the unique personal qualities that made him such an unusual leader.

II

The memoirs of three key figures in the Johnson administration offer insight into the White House years that Caro and Dallek have not yet covered. Richard Goodwin, a gifted speechwriter who was one of the main architects of the Great Society, wrote a 1988 memoir of his experiences in the 1960s that included a highly controversial view of Johnson's mental stability. Joseph A. Califano, who joined the White House staff just before Goodwin left, chronicles many of LBJ's eccentric traits from a more sympathetic perspective in a memoir published in 1991. And Clark Clifford described his service as an informal adviser and later as a cabinet member in the Johnson administration in the account of his life that he wrote with Richard Holbrooke.[11]

Despite his close ties to John F. Kennedy, Richard Goodwin developed considerable respect for Lyndon Johnson while he served as his main speechwriter during the passage of most of the key Great Society measures. Goodwin is especially complimentary toward LBJ in regard to civil rights, claiming that "no president—before or since—acted more firmly or with greater commitment to the cause of black equality than Lyndon Johnson."[12] He is more grudging in assessing LBJ's legislative skills, attributing them to an "incredible intuition" that enabled Johnson to measure how best to appeal to or to intimidate legislators. It was this instinct that Goodwin believes was "the heart of Johnson's genius—that capacity for manipulation and seduction bred by his extraordinary intuition of other men—their ambitions, needs, weaknesses, pride."[13] Although he admired the legislative results, Goodwin found many of LBJ's actions to be personally distasteful. He especially resented Johnson's determination to maintain control over his staff members and at times over members of Congress by using tactics designed to "divide and dominate."[14] By making each subordinate think that he or she alone had the president's favor, Johnson sought to ensure that his own will prevailed.

Goodwin, enthusiastic over the Great Society measures but appalled by LBJ's Vietnam decisions, believes that a dangerous change took place in the president in 1965. As Johnson embarked on a carefully disguised escalation of the American military effort in Vietnam designed not to jeopardize his legislative victories, his behavior became extreme. Goodwin argues that certain actions he had viewed as LBJ's eccentricities "had taken a huge leap into unreason."[15] Although Johnson always was able to maintain a calm and reasonable demeanor in his public statements, Goodwin claims that the president often became irrational in private. He would blame criticism of his Vietnam policy on "the Kennedy crowd" or on the Soviets, claiming that Ambassador Dobrynin's car had been spotted at the homes of the columnists who condemned Johnson's Southeast Asian policies.[16] Goodwin sees a pattern of paranoid behavior in these outbursts against liberals, intellectuals, and Communists. Fearing that he was losing control, Johnson tried to substitute his beliefs for reality; by blaming his difficulties on his enemies at home and abroad, LBJ sought to justify his actions. Goodwin compares him to a volcano: Crops and cities flourished on its slopes, but beneath the surface dangerous pressures were building up, ready to explode.

Goodwin castigates himself for failing to go public with his growing conviction that the president was mentally ill. He shared his views with Bill Moyers, and both men independently consulted psychiatrists who seemed to confirm their layman's diagnosis of paranoia. But Goodwin explains that Johnson had sufficient control to have made them look like fools had they challenged his sanity openly. (Goodwin might have asked himself how fair it was to make these accusations more than twenty years later when Johnson was no longer alive to defend or explain his behavior.)

Much of the behavior Goodwin describes seems consistent with Johnson's personality and with his tendency to let off steam at people around him. As Goodwin notes, LBJ never exposed this side of himself in public despite the many provocations as the growth of antiwar sentiment gradually made him a prisoner in the White House. A leader under pressure, especially one as dynamic and as hypersensitive as Lyndon Johnson, was bound to blame his difficulties on his political opponents. Harry Truman wrote letters he never sent to give vent to his wrath and frustration; Eisenhower would generally keep his feelings bottled up, but aides would testify to the throbbing veins and high color that accompanied his silent rages. Actions that Goodwin believes were evidence of paranoia can just as easily be seen as the healthy process of a leader under great stress using his private moments to say the things he knew he could not voice in public. Johnson was a strange and eccentric individual, filled with great energy and great self-doubt. But these traits led to the triumphs of the Great Society that Goodwin applauds as well as to the disaster in Vietnam.

Joseph Califano, like Goodwin, notes many of LBJ's characteristics in his memoir, but Califano does so with awe and admiration rather than with distaste and disgust. He gives abundant examples of Johnson's often bizarre behavior, ranging from his excessive demand for secrecy to his insistence on total control of his staff. Yet Califano treats these episodes as the product of Johnson's frustration and stress, traits in his character that are more than redeemed by LBJ's genuine commitment to the Great Society programs.

There is much in Califano's book that contributes to a negative view of Lyndon Johnson. The president dominated the lives of his aides, making them work long hours, keeping in touch with them by telephone constantly, and rarely allowing them time to relax or unwind. He could be cruel, as Hubert Humphrey, his long-suffering vice-president, discovered. At one point, LBJ not only deprived Humphrey of his position as head of the administration's civil rights efforts but had Califano force Humphrey to announce his own demotion publicly. LBJ's behavior was often purposefully crude. He regularly referred to having cut off someone's pecker to symbolize his degree of control; once, when Califano made a deal with Sen. John McClellan of Arkansas, Califano recalls Johnson rising from his green chair and saying: "Unzip your fly, because there's nothing there. John McClellan just cut if off with a razor so sharp you didn't even notice it."[17]

Califano's portrait of Johnson is filled with contradictions. "The Lyndon Johnson I worked with was brave and brutal," he writes, "compassionate and cruel, incredibly intelligent and infuriatingly insensitive. . . . He could be altruistic and petty, caring and crude, generous and petulant, bluntly honest and calculatingly devious—all within the same few minutes."[18] Yet above all Califano saw LBJ as committed passionately and completely to the cause of reform and to the improvement of American society. The theme of his account, implicit in the title, reveals that Johnson struggled to complete his Great Society programs in the face of the growing involvement in what proved to be the Vietnam fiasco.

From 1965 onward (Califano had joined the White House staff in July of that year), the president tried incessantly to persuade Congress to pass his reform measures. Medicare, federal aid to education, civil rights measures, the War on Poverty—these early victories only whetted Johnson's appetite. As Califano worked with the president on new proposals to be included in the 1967 State of the Union address, Califano marveled at LBJ's ambitions for the nation. "There will never be enough for this man," Califano thought; "he adopts programs the way a child eats rich chocolate-chip cookies." What impressed Califano most was Johnson's sense of urgency; the president always seemed to be "in a race against time," "always conscious that his days were numbered and that his political capital, however enormous as he began his presidency, was limited." Califano soon realized that despite Johnson's decision to escalate the Vietnam War in 1965, the president intended to go "full-steam-ahead fighting for the Great Society."[19] Even as he gave up on victory in Vietnam and announced that he would not run for reelection in 1968, he kept pressing Califano for new legislative proposals to send to Congress. When Califano cautioned against this "whirl of desperate haste," LBJ refused to let up, saying, "I want to get them up there so I can get my program passed."[20] Johnson's judgment was vindicated with the passage of his last two major proposals—the fair-housing bill and a 10-percent income tax surcharge—in spring 1968.

The "tragedy" of Califano's title is the Vietnam War that finally wore Lyndon Johnson down. Yet in a way the real source of Johnson's sorrow was more personal. The Great Society was his attempt, by the sheer weight of his will, to eradicate poverty and to make life better for all Americans. "There was no child he could not feed," Califano writes; "no adult he could not put to work, no disease he could not cure." Johnson's reform program, which Califano describes as "a reflection of his immense ego," was LBJ's gift to the nation.[21] Yet he never received the praise he felt he deserved. On the eve of the 1966 congressional election, sensing his party's forthcoming defeat, LBJ asked if any "objective historian" could deny that he had done more "to help my country" than any other president. According to Califano, Johnson "ached over the lack of appreciation from the people for his achievements."[22] Even more than his defeat in Vietnam, Johnson was haunted by his failure to win the nation's undying love and gratitude for the Great Society.

Despite his insight into Johnson's commitment to his reform agenda, Califano was too close to LBJ to perceive the reasons for the president's failure. In part it was simply that Johnson was not lovable—the American people were repelled by his crudity, his fondness for deception, and his monumental ego. More important, Johnson was betrayed by his belief that the passage of legislation alone guaranteed the solution to all national problems. His passion for congressional victories blinded him to the need for imaginative and sustained governmental action to deal with poverty, ignorance, and racial injustice. As Califano reluctantly admits, "His own singular capacity to enact so many laws and programs led him to overestimate the capacity of the government to administer and the nation to absorb so much so fast."[23] Johnson gloried in the vast number of laws he enacted; the Great Society might have been far more effective if he had been more selective and had tried to remedy a more limited number of national ills.

Clark Clifford's memoir is more disappointing than Goodwin's or Califano's in terms of the light it sheds on Lyndon Johnson. In recalling his services as LBJ's confidential adviser and later as secretary of defense during the climax of the Vietnam War, Clifford is primarily concerned with explaining his own role. His self-serving account thus offers only an oblique view of Johnson yet one that confirms many traits noted by other observers—LBJ's complexity, his fondness for indirection, and his enormous energy. "On occasion," Clifford comments, "he reminded me of a powerful, old-fashioned locomotive roaring unstoppably down the track."[24]

Johnson's great failing, Clifford believes, was his desire to be loved by everyone. Accordingly, LBJ preferred devious tactics designed to play down disagreements and to avoid confrontations. Fearful always of being rejected, Johnson repeatedly tried to entice Clifford into taking a position in his administration without ever making a specific offer. And when Clifford finally did accept the job of secretary of defense in early 1968, he believed that the only way he could persuade LBJ to reverse course on Vietnam was to avoid a showdown. "I decided," Clifford explains, "I could be most effective if I moved gradually." Even so, Clifford's insistence on seeking peace in Vietnam altered his relationship with the president: "Our long friendship," he writes, "would never be the same again."[25]

It was the quiet campaign that Clifford waged from the Pentagon after the Tet Offensive that finally convinced Johnson to begin the process of deescalation in Vietnam. Yet Clifford's own refusal to confront Johnson directly helped block the defense secretary's primary goal—a broad effort to end the fighting and achieve peace before LBJ left the White House. Instead of urging a complete halt in the bombing, Clifford settled for the limited bombing that Rusk favored and that Johnson announced when he made his March 31 speech declaring that he was dropping out of the 1968 presidential contest. To Clifford's dismay, Johnson continued to cling to elusive hopes for victory in Vietnam through fall 1968 and only grudgingly agreed to a complete bombing halt on October 31, too late to achieve a breakthrough in peace negotiations during his presidency.[26]

Clifford blames Johnson for refusing to tell his advisers in advance about his plans to end his political career in the March 31 speech. By calling for only a limited bombing halt and by not facing the reality of defeat in Vietnam, Johnson created a split between those people around him who wanted to achieve an honorable end to the war and those who simply wanted "to shore up domestic support . . . without changing our objective in Vietnam." As a result, "He sent conflicting signals and possibly lost the opportunity to end the war during his term in office." Clifford contends that if he had known that Johnson planned to give up the presidency, " I would have argued for a full bombing cessation despite the difficulty of gaining his approval."[27]

The fault would seem to lie more with Clifford than with Johnson. The ultimate insider, Clifford hoped to use indirect means to gain his goal of extracting the United States from the Vietnam quagmire. He thought he knew how best to manipulate Lyndon Johnson, yet he achieved only a partial success, getting LBJ to begin a new peace initiative but without making the full effort that might have been successful. Had Clifford been willing to place his own career on the line by forcing Johnson to choose between a partial or a total bombing halt in spring 1968, Clifford might have prevailed. Such an outcome not only would have reflected well on Clifford but also would have served what he claims was his real purpose, enabling Johnson to end the Vietnam War before he left the White House. For a man who prides himself on his dedicated service to presidents, Clifford is strangely unwilling to accept responsibility for his failure at a time when, as he claims, "the stakes were transcendentally important."[28]

III

The most revealing book on the Johnson presidency is a photographic history compiled in 1990 by Harry Middleton, *LBJ: The White House Years*. Middleton, a former LBJ speechwriter who has served as director of the Johnson Presidential Library for more than two decades, draws on the library's vast photographic archives to present a sympathetic view of the Johnson presidency. For five years, a staff of photographers led by the late Yoichi Okamoto was given an unusual opportunity to record not only the official activities of the president but many informal ones as well. The result is a fascinating portrait of Lyndon Johnson in office.[29]

The photographs cover a wide range of presidential scenes, ranging from cabinet meetings to posed pictures with White House visitors. A few are quite familiar—Lyndon flanked by Lady Bird and Jacqueline Kennedy at the swearing-in on board Air Force One just after the Dallas assassination, LBJ holding his beagle up by the ears on the White House lawn, and the president baring his belly to show the media the scar from his gall bladder operation. But a surprisingly large number are fresh and insightful, showing Johnson in action and apparently unaware of the photographer's presence.

In the accompanying text, Middleton makes no effort to disguise his bias. He offers a friendly account of the Johnson presidency, praising LBJ's efforts to enact the Great Society measures and to advance civil rights and bemoaning the growing cancer of the Vietnam War. He also uses apt quotations from the oral histories of people close to Johnson to complement the pictures. Thus Wilbur Cohen, then serving as assistant secretary of health, education and welfare, comments on the hectic pace Johnson set for his legislative program: "I never worked so hard in my life," Cohen recalls, "as I did between February and June of 1965."[30] Yet even then Vietnam was looming as what Middleton terms Johnson's "nemesis." The war in Southeast Asia, he writes, was "the dark beast he would wrestle for the rest of his time, which would grow to horrifying size and finally overpower him."[31]

One aspect of the Johnson years missing from this account is the sense of turmoil created by the antiwar protests and the riots in the cities. Johnson is seen repeatedly meeting with civilian and military advisers on Vietnam and even traveling there, but Middleton includes little evidence of the growing national resistance to the Vietnam War. One curiously sedate picture of a group of protesters led by Coretta Scott King and Dr. Benjamin Spock at the White House gates hardly conveys the depth of public feeling. There are no photographs of urban rioting; we see only the gathering of worried officials in the White House. There is, however, one remarkable picture of LBJ aboard a helicopter viewing the destruction in Washington following the assassination of Martin Luther King, Jr., in 1968.

Some of the most effective passages in the book are the comments by Johnson aides that Middleton uses to explain the pictures. An observation by Douglass Cater accompanies a picture of LBJ opening the bottom of the frame around the teletype machine in the Oval Office to peer inside. The president "would disappear down into the bowels of the thing to read it as it was actually being typed out on the spindle. He wanted to get even farther ahead of the news before it could surface," Cater remarks, calling this practice LBJ's "obsessive communications system."[32] Harry McPherson's words help illuminate a marvelous pair of pictures of Johnson gesticulating with outstretched arms to a small group of listeners. Contrasting Johnson's woodenness on television to his effectiveness in person, McPherson summarized LBJ's whirlwind style:

> Sometimes, after touching first base, he goes to left field, climbs into the bleachers, sells hot dogs, runs back down on the field, and circles the bases and comes home. You think he's never going to get to the point. But it all comes back with tremendous force and with great comprehensive power when he ends his argument, and it's damned near irresistible when he's at his best. This can't be done on television.[33]

Three images stand out in the photographs of the Johnson White House. The first is the omnipresent telephone. In nearly all the Oval office scenes, either the president or one of his aides is seen talking on the phone. A candid shot of Thurgood Marshall just after LBJ informed him of his Supreme Court nomination shows Marshall telephoning the good news to his wife with an expansive Johnson beaming in the background. A solemn LBJ is shown calling the Kennedy family with condolences after Bobby Kennedy's assassination as Lady Bird looks on sadly. There is even a picture of Johnson talking on the phone while reading the news ticker. "If there was a phone call for him," comments Marie Fehmer, a secretary, "and there wasn't a phone beside wherever he was sitting, he'd say, 'Have one put in.'"[34] The happiest photograph shows Johnson beaming at his grandson playing with the telephone on the White House desk.

Pictures of Johnson in bed are almost as common as photographs of him on the telephone. He and Lady Bird are seen in bed at the ranch watching the turbulent scenes from the 1968 Democratic convention, with members of their family surrounding them. More often he is shown in the four-poster in his White House bedroom that was as much command post as a place to sleep. There is a photo of the thick bundle of papers labeled "night reading" that he went through every evening as well as a picture of Johnson in pajamas conferring with four aides in their business suits. These scenes confirm Califano's depiction of LBJ spending his first few hours every morning reading through several newspapers, watching the morning television programs, talking with cabinet officers by telephone, and barking out orders to one of his aides. Lady Bird often "would patiently lie there next to him, bed jacket on," waiting for a chance to slip away quietly to her nearby dressing room.[35]

The most surprising aspect of the photographs is the frequency with which Johnson is shown listening to someone else speaking. The image of LBJ as always in command, telling people what to do, gives way to a portrait of a leader besieged by difficulties, seeking advice and information from others. Often with his brow furrowed and his hand holding his head, here he is seen listening intently to such different men as Sen. Russell Long, cellist Pablo Casals, Secretary of Defense Robert McNamara and his successor, Clark Clifford, or to Gen. William Westmoreland, during a trip to Vietnam. There is an extraordinary picture of Johnson meeting with presidential candidate Richard Nixon at the White House in 1968; LBJ is peering across a conference table as Nixon is speaking. Even more dramatic is the photo of Johnson alone in a large conference room, his head bowed, listening to a tape sent from Vietnam by Charles Robb, his son-in-law. Robb explains that Johnson had given him a tape recorder when he left for Vietnam as a marine captain; he sent back reports of operations he had taken part in to give LBJ "some of the texture of the war at company levels—without all the gory details."[36]

The last photographs in the volume, taken after Johnson left the White House, reveal the toll the presidency had taken. Middleton recalls how even then Johnson insisted that the presidential library cover Vietnam in its displays and that the exhibits include the "meanest letter I ever got." LBJ himself rummaged through boxes of hate mail to find a postcard whose sender described Johnson as "a gutless sonofabitch" and demanded that he "resign as President of the United States." "You can't get much meaner than that," Johnson commented as he selected the postcard for public display.[37]

In mid-January 1972, sensing he would die soon, LBJ told Lady Bird to be sure that the people attending his funeral include not just the wealthy and powerful few who could fly to Texas in their private planes. "I want the men in their pickup trucks," he insisted, "and the women whose slips hang down below their dresses to be welcome, too." There is a picture of his burial in the family graveyard beside the Pedernales ten days later. Middleton says, "They were all there, the men who landed their planes on the runway and the neighbors from the ranches and towns around who brought their families by truck."[38] Despite his flaws, LBJ tried to fulfill the hopes and dreams of all the American people. He did not always succeed, but these pictures capture the vitality and the poignancy of that effort as well if not better than the words of the people who have written about him.

Notes

1. For earlier evaluations of writing on LBJ, see Robert A. Divine, "The Johnson Literature," in *Exploring the Johnson Years*, ed. Robert A. Divine (Austin: University of Texas Press, 1981), pp. 3–23, and "The Johnson Revival: A Bibliographical Appraisal," in *The Johnson Years, Volume Two*, ed. Robert A. Divine (Lawrence: University Press of Kansas, 1987), pp. 3–20.

2. Robert A. Caro, *Means of Ascent* (New York: Alfred A. Knopf, 1990); Robert Dallek, *Lone Star Rising: Lyndon Johnson and His Times, 1908–1960* (New York: Oxford University Press, 1991); Paul K. Conkin, *Bid Daddy from the Pedernales: Lyndon B. Johnson* (Boston: Twayne Publishers, 1986).

3. Caro, *Means of Ascent*, pp. xxvii–xviii.

4. Dallek, *Lone Star Rising*, p. 167.

5. Ibid., p. 174.

6. Caro, Means of Ascent, p. xxviii.

7. Dallek, *Lone Star Rising*, pp. 379, 492.

8. Conkin, *Big Daddy*, p. xi.

9. Ibid., p. 46.

10. Ibid., p. 173.

11. Richard N. Goodwin, *Remembering America: A Voice from the Sixties* (Boston: Little, Brown, 1988); Joseph A. Califano, Jr., *The Triumph & Tragedy of Lyndon Johnson: The White House Years* (New York: Simon and Schuster, 1991); Clark Clifford, with Richard Holbrooke, *Counsel to the President: A Memoir* (New York: Random House, 1991).

12. Goodwin, *Remembering America*, p. 311.

13. Ibid., pp. 252, 271.

14. Ibid., p. 255.

15. Ibid., p. 393.

16. Ibid., pp. 396, 406.

17. Califano, *Triumph & Tragedy*, p. 126.

18. Ibid., p. 10.

19. Ibid., pp. 11, 52, 180.

20. Ibid., p. 260.

21. Ibid., pp. 338–39.

22. Ibid., pp. 151–52.

23. Ibid., p. 338.

24. Clifford, *Counsel*, p. 385.

25. Ibid., p. 488.

26. Johnson might well have halted the bombing sooner had not the South Vietnamese government, encouraged by Richard Nixon, resisted this move so strongly (see Lewis L. Gould, *1968: The Election That Changed America* [Chicago: Ivan R. Dee, 1993], pp. 151–61).

27. Ibid., pp. 525, 528.

28. Ibid., p. 527.

29. Harry Middleton, *LBJ: The White House Years* (New York: Harry N. Abrams, 1990). For a full discussion of the rich audio-visual archives at

the LBJ Library, see David Culbert, "Johnson and the Media," in Divine, ed., *Exploring the Johnson Years*, pp. 214–48.

30. Middleton, *LBJ*, p. 77.

31. Ibid., p. 43.

32. Ibid., p. 118.

33. Ibid., p. 121.

34. Ibid., p. 189. Califano recalls that the second time the president tried to reach him by phone when Califano was using the bathroom adjoining his White House office, LBJ had the Army Signal Corps install a telephone next to his toilet within an hour (Califano, *Triumph & Tragedy*, p. 26).

35. Ibid., p. 27. For a photographic history focusing on Mrs. Johnson, see Harry Middleton, *Lady Bird Johnson: A Life Well Lived* (Austin, Tex.: Lyndon Baines Johnson Foundation, 1992).

36. Middleton, *LBJ*, p. 247.

37. Ibid., p. 260.

38. Ibid., p. 264.

Part 1 | LBJ at Home

2 | Never a Deep Partisan: Lyndon Johnson and the Democratic Party, 1963–1969

Lewis L. Gould

FEW PRESIDENTS HAVE A reputation for political adroitness that exceeds that of Lyndon Johnson. Every biographer notes that Johnson was above all else a political animal, but the exact nature of Johnson's political ability remains in dispute. His success as a legislative leader in the Senate and as president is unquestioned; there is more doubt about his capacity as a national political figure and as a leader of the Democratic party. On the one side, his success in Texas politics took him from a position as the congressman from the Tenth District to the United States Senate. He was also an important element in John F. Kennedy's presidential victory in 1960. Beyond that, of course, there was Johnson's own electoral landslide in 1964 when he defeated Sen. Barry M. Goldwater, the Republican nominee.

Even with these positive achievements in mind, aspects of Johnson's political career raise questions about his national skills. His attempts to gain the Democratic presidential nomination in 1956 and 1960 were unsuccessful. Moreover, the Democrats suffered serious losses in the 1966 elections when he was president. Two years later his vice-president, Hubert H. Humphrey, was narrowly defeated by Richard M. Nixon and the Republicans. After Johnson left office in 1969 the Democrats won only one of the next five presidential contests. To the extent that the Democrats become a congressional party that was less competitive in presidential races from 1972 to 1988, how much of the responsibility belonged to Lyndon Johnson and his stewardship of the Democrats between 1963 and 1969? How correct was Humphrey's assessment of Johnson: "Legend to the contrary notwithstanding, when it came to party politics, he was not good"?[1]

Lyndon Johnson spoke often of his Democratic background. It was, he wrote in 1956, "my heritage and my legacy from my forebears." But he stressed that his party allegiance was also a matter of conviction: "The Democratic party has more to offer to the successive generations of this nation than has the other party." It was, he asserted, ''the party of all America'' and, unlike the Republicans, ''not the tool of any one section, any one class, any one group.'' He did not believe in an aggressive partisan stance, however. ''Partisanship,'' he said, should be based upon ''sincere disagreement as to the course that is best for our nation.''[2]

Johnson's vision of the Democrats and his attitude toward partisan politics were direct results of his political apprenticeship in Texas. The Democratic party in Texas for most of Johnson's formative years did not face any serious challenge from the Republicans. There were factions within the party in Texas as the dominant conservatives battled a smaller minority of liberals from the late 1930s to the 1950s, and while these battles could be intense and bitter, they were largely personal and internecine in character. More important, they insulated Johnson from contact with the Republican party as an electoral force nationally. He had little sense of the roots of Republican allegiance across the country and even less grasp of how that party conducted its campaigns.[3]

Johnson's view of the national Democratic party was also skewed. Negative in his appraisal of the party leaders in northern states, he believed, said James Rowe, ''that those bosses up North are a bunch of damm crooks.'' The labor unions that were so influential in the industrial states also came in for Johnson's scorn: ''They are a bunch of racketeers,'' he said in the 1950s.[4]

His view of the Democratic National Committee (DNC) was equally corrosive; Johnson did not believe that it performed any important functions. A formative episode in Johnson's perception of the national Democratic party took place in 1940 when he ran the House Democratic Campaign Committee in the months just before the presidential election. Faced with the prospect of Republican gains in the House, Johnson, in conjunction with Sam Rayburn, raised money from Texas oilmen and other constituents and provided the resources to enable the Democrats to retain control of the House. For Johnson the lesson was that the national Democrats lacked the will and the energy to survive on their own without the help of energetic operatives like himself.[5]

During the 1950s, with Republican Dwight Eisenhower in the White House, Johnson approached his task as Senate majority leader with a similar suspicion toward intense partisanship. Having only a narrow Democratic majority in the Senate, Johnson stressed the values of bipartisan cooperation as an approach to public policy. Cooperation with the president succeeded as a legislative strategy and helped to build Johnson's reputation as the Senate leader. But the collegial atmosphere of the Senate gave Johnson an inadequate perception of the extent to which partisanship operated in the electoral process. Because he was able to win converts among the Republicans on particular issues in the Senate, he came to believe that a similar act of persuasion might occur among members of the GOP nationally. As president he would invoke bipartisanship repeatedly in an effort to win over Republicans to his side. After his landslide victory in 1964, he told reporters privately that "I want a stronger Republican party so that it can do more to help me and the country."[6]

Johnson's strategy for dealing with Eisenhower and the Republicans brought him into conflict with the Democratic National Committee and its chairman, Paul Butler of Indiana, at the end of the 1950s. Butler believed that the Democrats should emphasize their differences with the Republicans. "We can't let the Republican President set a pattern for us to follow," he said in 1959, and he disliked the way that Johnson and Sam Rayburn accepted so many of Eisenhower's policies. Johnson disagreed with the premise of Butler's ideas. He resisted the chairman's attempts in 1956 and his later efforts to establish the Democratic Advisory Council (DAC), created after the presidential election, as a strong voice in Democratic affairs. By February 1958 Johnson was complaining "incessantly" to Adlai Stevenson "about Butler, DNC [Democratic National Committee], DAC, his health, his trials."[7]

Lyndon Johnson had an innate aversion to extremes in politics. He often referred to liberal Democrats as "bombthrowers" whom the more moderate party members had to restrain. And in Johnson's mind, Republicans on the Right who believed that all Democrats were part of a liberal effort to subvert American values were part of a comparable pattern of foolishness. The wise statesman stood in the center of politics and assembled a consensus of like-minded individuals irrespective of party. To a significant degree Johnson did not understand the powerful allegiance and the emotional commitment of Republicans to their party during his political career.[8]

The first year of Johnson's presidency reinforced most of the assumptions about the Democratic party that he brought with him to the White House. It was a simple matter to deal with the formal structure of the party in 1964. He built on the legacy of John F. Kennedy by leaving the officials whom his predecessor had named on the Democratic National Committee. No Johnson man replaced Chairman John Bailey of Connecticut; instead, a Johnson ally, Clifton Carter, was added to the committee's staff. Similarly, other Johnson men such as Walter Jenkins and Jack Valenti cooperated with

Kennedy holdovers Lawrence O'Brien, Kenneth O'Donnell, and others. Any kind of wholesale purge of the party would have imperiled Johnson's carefully constructed image of Democratic consensus and harmony.[9]

The election year of 1964 presented Johnson with some problems in managing the Democrats, but he surmounted the obstacles with little apparent damage to his political standing. The most crucial challenge to his presidential chances was the problem of Robert F. Kennedy and the vice-presidential nomination; the two men loathed each other, and it was unthinkable that the president would have chosen the attorney general as his running mate. Johnson's solution was to rule out all cabinet members as potential vice-presidential choices, which eliminated Kennedy without seeming to make him the target of the action. Of course, the animosity between Johnson and Kennedy remained and grew.[10]

The selection of Hubert Humphrey as the vice-presidential choice won general praise from Democrats. He and Johnson had come to the Senate at the same time, and Humphrey seemed a northern liberal balance to Johnson's perceived southern conservatism. The choice was made, however, with the typical Johnsonian intrigue and secrecy. In the process Johnson alienated Sen. Eugene McCarthy of Minnesota, rival to Humphrey, with consequences that would emerge three years later. As for the Democratic National Convention in Atlantic City, Johnson scrutinized every aspect of the event, especially the party's platform. Offstage the president went through a familiar ritual of considering whether he ought to run at all and showed his wife a draft statement of withdrawal. Mrs. Johnson responded with a deftly written comment that reminded him of his duty to the country and the charges of cowardice that his enemies would level against such a decision. The president put aside any ideas about withdrawing and prepared to accept his party's nomination.[11]

One episode during the Democratic National Convention did test Johnson's capacity as a party leader. The Mississippi Freedom Democratic Party (MFDP) challenged the regular Democratic delegation and asked that it not be seated. Their reasons were solid: The white Democratic party had long excluded blacks from party affairs. But Johnson feared a walkout by southern Democrats if a black delegation was seated and a white delegation ousted. After a protracted series of negotiations, the black challengers received two at-large seats, nonvoting seats for the rest of the delegation, and a promise to see that in 1968 delegates would be chosen fairly in Mississippi. The

MFDP members rejected the Johnson compromise, but it mollified enough southerners to block the regional bolting that Johnson had feared. Civil rights advocates were disillusioned with the president's actions, but the episode did not overshadow the generally harmonious tone of the convention. More lasting consequences for the party arose from the related decision to begin revision of the party rules for the 1968 convention.[12]

In the general election campaign, Johnson knew that victory over Goldwater and the Republicans was almost ensured from midsummer onward. He tried to capitalize on his electoral advantage with a strategy that stressed inclusiveness and nonpartisanship. Accepting the presidential nomination, he described the Democrats "as a party for all Americans, an all-American party for all Americans." He gave his old friend James Rowe the assignment of cultivating the Republicans and Independents whom Barry Goldwater had frightened; dozens of committees were formed to allow these converts to join the Johnson coalition. The president told the members of the National Independent Committee for Johnson and Humphrey that "our American system was not intended to be controlled by rigid discipline of party." When he spoke in Vermont in late September, he declared that "my own party does not believe in partisanship for the sake of partisanship."[13]

In 1964 the Democrats had the financial resources to conduct the kind of consensus-style campaign that Johnson wanted. At the start of the campaign, the president was told that the Democrats would raise $15 million, and there were predictions of a surplus that would enable the party to pay off its debts. Johnson used the money in an expansive way for elaborate (and often redundant) polls and for a welter of advertisements and billboards across the country. During the heady days of the campaign, with Johnson so far ahead, it seemed as if the Democrats might achieve an electoral rout of historic proportions. The frenetic Johnson, campaigning headlong across the country, made commitments for billboards and advertising with abandon during October 1964.[14]

The results on election night were all that Lyndon Johnson could have wished. His candidacy rolled to a landslide victory over Goldwater, with Johnson receiving 61 percent of the vote to 38.5 for Goldwater. The electoral vote total was equally one-sided: Johnson carried forty-four states with 486 electoral votes; Goldwater won Arizona and five states in the Deep South for 53 electoral votes. The Democrats controlled the Senate 68 to 32 and won 295 House seats to 140 for the GOP. As Hubert Humphrey recalled, Johnson "reveled in his success" during the campaign, "no longer President by accident, but soon to be overwhelmingly elected in his own right."[15]

Such a landslide prompted few of the happy Democrats to look for ominous portents, but troubling signs were present that would vex Johnson during his second term. Goldwater's success in the South reflected a deep alienation of white voters from the Democratic party. During the spring primaries of 1964, Gov. George Wallace had first exploited evidence of a reaction that commentators called the "backlash" among white voters in their response to civil rights and black gains. Wallace's strong showings in such northern bastions as Wisconsin, Indiana, and Maryland revealed the latent possibilities of an assault against programs to aid blacks in the North and the South. The phenomenon seemed to fade after summer 1964, but it was present in Goldwater's victories in Alabama, Georgia, Louisiana, Mississippi, and South Carolina. When the Republicans rebounded after 1964, they built on the strong base that Goldwater had established in the South. The region was moving from its historic Democratic allegiance to an alignment wherein the Republicans would be ascendant in presidential races.[16]

Another problem was less tangible. By stressing the nonpartisan appeal of his candidacy and by courting wavering Republicans unhappy with Goldwater, Johnson did little to arouse intense feelings on his own behalf among committed Democrats. The victory that he secured was very much a personal one in which his Democratic colleagues had little emotional stake. The campaign "did not evoke fierce loyalty from partisan Democrats," an aide told him three years later in trying to explain why Democrats did not rally to his defense.[17]

Johnson and the Democrats faced still another problem, this one of their own making. During the 1964 campaign, with ample financial resources apparently available, the party had spent lavishly; in particular the president himself had authorized television commercials and billboard advertising at the end of the campaign that had run up expenses. The original budget for the campaign had been projected "to come through the election with a small surplus." In fact by March 1965 internal reports by the Democratic National Committee indicated that debts and bank loans of $3 million were outstanding from 1964. The largest bill was owed to the New York advertising agency Doyle, Dane & Bernbach, which the Democrats had hired to frame some of the most effective anti-Goldwater commercials of 1964. The most notorious of course was the ad that depicted a young girl "plucking petals from a daisy" that segued into a mushroom cloud. When the campaign was over the Democrats owed the agency $427,000. Telephone bills ran another $384,000, and the party owed American Airlines $262,000.[18]

Johnson had inherited from John F. Kennedy a fund-raising strategy for the Democrats that emphasized large donors as the backbone of the party's finances. The mechanism for this effort was the President's Club; consisting of donors who gave at least $1,000 each, the club offered its members a round of fund-raising dinners and the promise of social gatherings with the president and easier access to the White House staff. Under Kennedy, the President's Club raised almost $2 million for the Democrats. Both Kennedy and Johnson saw the President's Club as a way to counter the financial advantages that the Republicans enjoyed in the business community and to soften the image of the Democrats as antagonistic to free enterprise. During 1964, with Johnson at the height of his influence and popularity, the fund-raising bonanza continued, and some $2,271,000 was collected at President's Club events during the election year.[19]

Naturally Johnson and his aides assumed that the president's drawing power as a source of contributions would continue unabated during the administration to come, and they gave little thought to broadening the base of potential donors for the party or to attracting small givers in large numbers. The strategy made sense in late 1964 and early 1965, but it left Johnson and his party at the mercy of unexpected events. It also exposed Johnson and the President's Club to plausible charges of selling political access and influence since the main drawing card of the club was the promise of "inside-dopesterism" and the relative cloak of secrecy that Republican donors enjoyed. Should the fortunes of the president decline, the President's Club strategy had potential liabilities, but these did not become evident until after 1965.[20]

The chairman of the President's Club was Arthur Krim, the president of United Artists. President and Mrs. Johnson had become close friends with Krim and his wife Mathilde, who shared the president's interest in health issues. "I am always cheered when there is a Krim around," the president wrote to Krim in August 1965, and the movie executive became an informal but influential political adviser. His phone calls received a quick response from the White House, he was consulted about national politics, and he could propose candidates for federal appointments. More than anyone else during this period, Krim served as Johnson's working link with the Democratic National Committee and its affairs.[21]

In the aftermath of the landslide election, the committee had launched an ambitious effort to ensure the reelection of the sixty-eight new Democratic members of the House of Representatives whom Johnson's coattails had pulled into office. There was a "Congressional Support Program" that sought to "work with these freshmen to win popular recognition at home." Among the services provided to the new congressman were briefings about how to get reelected, liaison meetings with the administration, audio-press releases to be sent to home districts, and computerized mailing lists for targeted mailings to constituents. The newly elected politicians appreciated these services, but the program conflicted with long-standing Democratic committees on Capitol Hill that oversaw the election campaigns of congressmen and senators. Moreover, in order to work, the program had to be sustained through 1966 in an effective manner.[22]

Support for elected officials required money, and over this issue the relations between Lyndon Johnson and his party grew increasingly difficult in 1965 and 1966. The party treasurer, Richard A. Maguire, was a Kennedy holdover who operated in persistent secrecy. After the 1964 election, the only information that the Democratic National Committee received about its financial condition was a single sentence from Chairman Bailey that disclosed for 1964 "a great vote surplus and a sort of a little financial deficit."[23]

In response to the existence of such financial problems, the DNC began cutting back its staff as early as April 1965. Ten people were let go, and the president was told that "we will find still others that can be discharged." Johnson then received an official statement of the size of the party's debt on May 20, 1965. It stood at $3,615,536 and was "some larger than had been anticipated." Eleven days later the president instructed Bailey to give him a plan "that will completely eliminate the Democratic National Committee debt by September 1, 1965" and to reduce monthly expenditures from $69,000 to $50,000. Johnson asked for monthly reports of all DNC expenses, which were to be forwarded through Marvin Watson, the administrative chief of staff at the White House. Richard Maguire decided that he would leave the committee at the end of 1965.[24]

The economy drive continued through 1965. By the end of the year, Johnson had recommendations for paring back most of the substantive programs in which the DNC had been engaged, including voter registration drives that would be shifted to "existing or ad hoc groups formed for the purpose in the various local areas," congres-

sional relations, the women's division, the youth division, and ethnic relations. The duties of the party chairman would be much re-
stricted and a new person named "who has the complete confidence
of the President."[25]

Johnson decided not to let Bailey resign, but otherwise the
budget ax fell on the committee. With the staff already pared down
to eighty-five people, another forty were dismissed on December 17,
1965, putting the size of the staff well below the usual level of non-
presidential years. Most of those people who conducted voter registration and congressional support programs were let go, and the
number of employees who had links to the Kennedy years was dramatically reduced. These decisions caused some resentment among
Democratic professionals; one of them wrote in a memorandum
that was leaked to the press, "A National Committee has no claim
to existence if it abolishes voter registration. The very willingness to
even suspend it for any period of time is appalling."[26]

For Lyndon Johnson, however, the situation at the DNC accorded with his view of how the party should operate. Throughout
1965 he relied on the President's Club for Democratic fund-raising.
When Richard Maguire stepped down, Clifton Carter became acting
treasurer as well as executive director, but increasingly, Marvin Watson was the chairman of the Democratic National Committee in all
but name. A conservative Democrat from East Texas, Watson had
management skills but little sense of how Washington worked. His
knowledge of the Democratic party was sketchy, and his imperious
manner made more enemies than friends. Then in April 1966, Arthur Krim became finance chairman with supervisory authority over
the President's Club and other fund-raising activities.[27]

By the early part of 1966 the general political situation for the
Democrats was shifting. During 1965 the majorities that Johnson
and the party held in Congress had allowed for the passage of an impressive amount of Great Society legislation. In foreign policy the
nation's involvement in South Vietnam had increased dramatically
with the introduction of large numbers of American ground forces.
The economy remained strong and the nation was prosperous. Despite these favorable indicators, Democratic strategists in the White
House expected the Republicans to rebound in the 1966 congressional contest. As Charles Roche told Marvin Watson in late January,
"The Democratic party structure generally is in bad shape," and the
party had "several exposed flanks which are vulnerable to Republican attack."[28]

Throughout the year there were portents of the party's weakening position. In May a California congressman reported "some rather disturbing signs that do not look well for the fall elections," including a rise in Republican registration in his state. More worrying were the poll results that indicated growing popular unhappiness with the failure of the Vietnam War to bring a speedy victory. A pollster close to the White House, Lou Harris, summed up the mood for Johnson's aide Bill Moyers: "The people are in a foul mood over Vietnam; there is no getting around that fact. The overwhelming sentiment is not for the United States to withdraw; it is, rather, 'why can't we get it over with?'" Surveys in Iowa and New Hampshire showed similar results. By late June 1966 Johnson was showing his "greatest weaknesses according to the polls" in "Vietnam, inflation, and farm." Since the president knew that the Democrats would have faced losses in Congress in any case, the decisions that he made about party finances and support for Democratic candidates undercut his earlier commitment to helping the freshman congressmen swept into office during the 1964 landslide.[29]

Another serious issue that eroded Democratic strength in 1966 was racial unrest. Outbreaks of urban rioting in major cities, first in summer 1965 and then again during summer 1966, had an immediate impact on white voters who had previously voted Democratic. Candidates favorable to the position of organized labor, for example, lost in primaries in Maryland and Louisiana. Several British politicians who toured the United States just after the elections told the staff of Vice-President Humphrey that "they found an undercurrent of resentment concerning civil order and gains made by the Negro population."[30]

Throughout 1966 Johnson and the administration endeavored to instill some energy into the party and to revitalize the president's position but without much visible success. As Johnson's ratings in the public opinion polls declined, he became more and more interested in reversing the perception of unpopularity that the trend revealed. He told aides to "get up statements for members of Congress to make on the good portions of the polls" in June.[31]

The continuing difficulties with the organization of the Democratic party undercut much of what Johnson wanted the White House to accomplish. During spring and summer 1966, the Republicans in Congress began to focus on whether there were conflicts of interest between the administration and members of the President's Club. Their purpose, one said, "was to make the President repudiate the President's Club. If we can do this, we believe the funds will be dried up for the Democratic Party effort."[32]

The GOP capitalized on some instances of apparent favoritism. In the case of August Busch of the Anheuser-Busch Brewing Company, it seemed a suspicious coincidence that his membership in the club and a Justice Department decision to drop an antitrust prosecution against his firm occurred almost simultaneously. Another case involved a contract awarded to Johnson's old business associate, George R. Brown, of Houston, Texas. When reporters asked the president about "suggestions that contributions to the President's Club of the Democratic Party may influence the award of Government contracts," he responded that "periodic political charges were to be expected "from the party that has been rather strongly rejected by the people."[33]

By September, however, the issue of the President's Club had become sufficiently sensitive that the president decided to cancel most of the large fund-raising activities planned for the organization. In the case of Frank O'Connor, who was running for governor of New York, Johnson disapproved the projected appearance of Vice-President Humphrey at a fund-raising dinner in late October. Other party fund-raising efforts were also quietly shelved to stave off further Republican criticism.[34]

Johnson proved equally reluctant to funnel money to Democratic candidates during the 1966 election season. He balked at contributions for a Democratic congressman in Louisiana whom Lawrence O'Brien wanted to help through "a very difficult primary campaign." When the name of a Maryland congressman, Edward Garmatz, was proposed for a $2,000 contribution on behalf of the president, Johnson scribbled on the memorandum, "We don't have a dime & why do we help Garmatz?" To a suggestion from Edmund Muskie of Maine that Humphrey appear at a fund-raiser in that state, Johnson responded, "I believe this is bad, very bad."[35]

Johnson did make an appearance at the Dollars for Democrats luncheon in late August where he gave a tepid plea for party contributions from small donors. He said that even Republicans should participate in their party's affairs, and he praised GOP support for his legislative program. He reviewed his administration's record in Congress and asserted that "most of the legislation in behalf of the people has been sponsored and supported by the Democratic party." Plans for a five-minute televised speech on behalf of the party's money-raising program were shelved. Unlike later Republican presidents, Johnson did not see himself as a fund-raising instrument for strengthening his partisan base; his language continued to reflect his emphasis on consensus and nonpartisanship. As he said in a speech in Tulsa on August 26, "This is no time to play politics with the problems that all of us face, Democratic Presidents, Republican Congressmen, Democratic Senators, Republican Mayors."[36]

By 1966 an undercurrent of resentment was growing among Democratic loyalists toward the nonpartisan policy that the Johnson White House followed on appointments. In Ohio there were complaints that Republican fund-raisers were named to federal panels; similar remarks were being made about Pennsylvania and other states. Anger surfaced because the president allowed his appointments chief, John Macy, to recommend Republicans for prominent positions in key states, and an equal amount of discontent arose over the failure to clear some appointments with Democratic politicians before an announcement was made. An irate Ohio Democrat said that these policies reflected the president's wishes: Johnson's approach was to "pay no attention to the Party as such. Take it for granted and cultivate Republicans, businessmen, newspapers, and ethnic groups."[37]

The possibility that Johnson might campaign for his fellow Democrats during the fall was a topic of much interest at the White House during the spring and summer. In early July Johnson told reporters that "I think you will see a good deal of me this year" and that "as time permits, I will be traveling around the country." Two weeks later he said again that he expected to "take advantage of every opportunity to go out into the country and discuss our program, our convictions; tell them what we stand for, and ask for their support." In August he dismissed talk of large Democratic losses in the election; he did not think that there would be "any substantial turnover in either the House or the Senate." Yet when he made speaking tours through the Northeast in August, he had Republicans such as Sen. Margaret Chase Smith of Maine as well as Democrats with him on the platform. He told audiences, "We haven't been talking party matters. We have been talking people matters; problems of people." Local Democrats bristled at this language.[38]

By mid-September he began to back away from any implied commitment to travel extensively for his party's candidates. "We have no plans" to visit any set number of states during the fall, he told reporters on September 21. Two weeks later he announced a wide-ranging Asian tour that would take him to Vietnam, the Philippines, and a number of other countries between October 17 and the week before the elections. When asked about possible campaigning four days before his departure, he said, "We don't have any more plans at this moment." Before he left for Asia, he did make one speaking stop on behalf of Democrats in New Jersey. The Republican platform in 1966, he said, "is made up of one word—fear," but his language did not strike a strongly partisan note.[39]

By the time Johnson had departed for Asia, it was evident that the Republicans were going to do well in the congressional and state elections of 1966. The Republicans were stressing the issue of inflation at the behest of their national chairman, Ray Bliss of Ohio, who had rebuilt the party after the Goldwater debacle. Richard Nixon actively campaigned for Republicans, and in California a political newcomer, Ronald Reagan, presented a strong challenge to the incumbent governor, Edmund G. "Pat" Brown. Riots in the cities during the summer had revived talk of the backlash, helping the Republicans to gain white voters who had supported Johnson in 1964. "High officials of this Administration had condoned and encouraged disrespect for law and order," said the Republicans after Hubert Humphrey had told the NAACP convention that ghetto conditions might prompt him to "lead a mighty good revolt."[40]

While the president was traveling in Asia, he decided to make a campaign swing upon his return during the four days that would be left before the election. Arrangements were made and candidates notified of his plans; having second thoughts, however, Johnson abruptly reversed himself and canceled the trip. This decision left the Democratic candidates upset, and Johnson's denials that his plans had changed became another example of presidential deception. Meanwhile, a controversy with Richard Nixon further wounded Johnson. Nixon had criticized Johnson's communique from the Manila conference on Vietnam, and Johnson struck back at a press conference on November 4, saying that he did not wish to "get into a debate on a foreign policy meeting in Manila with a chronic campaigner like Mr. Nixon." This jab, and others that Johnson made, redounded to Nixon's credit and helped establish him as a credible rival to the president. It was the last mistake of an ill-starred Democratic campaign. On November 6 Johnson tried to take the sting out of the "white backlash issue," which he believed "divides this Nation at a very critical time—and therefore weakens us as a united country."[41]

The election returns showed sizable Republican gains. The GOP added forty-seven House seats to its total, picked up three seats in the Senate, elected an additional eight governors, and ran well in state legislatures. Nelson Rockefeller won a large victory in New York, Spiro Agnew was elected governor of Maryland, and Ronald Reagan trounced Pat Brown. "We've beaten hell out of them,"

Nixon said, "and we're going to kill them in '68." Johnson told the press that the elections would probably make it "more difficult for any new legislation we might propose," but he struck a philosophical note: "As a good American, I think we are all glad to see a healthy and competent existence of a two-party system."[42]

Nevertheless, among Democrats the election results produced gloom and foreboding. Reporters said that the Democrats were in a "state of near collapse" as far as the party organization was concerned. Complaints against Marvin Watson and other aides to the president proliferated. "The National Committee is a farce; it has no money, no manpower, no direct pipeline into the [White] house, and absolutely no control over political appointments." wrote one journalist a week after the elections. A White House aide said that a "National Chairman of stature and a recognized Johnson-man is needed." After much internal White House debate, the consensus was to keep John Bailey. A logical alternative was Postmaster General Lawrence O'Brien, but he was flawed because the president perceived him as a potential Kennedy ally. Reporters said that Johnson was following a familiar policy: "He wants no potential rival political power base in the party."[43]

In this respect Johnson's attitude resembled that of other presidents who did not wish to see rivals flourish while they were in office. The presence of Robert F. Kennedy as the leader of a party-in-exile no doubt reinforced Johnson's predilections about maintaining his unquestioned dominance. Yet the problem for Johnson was that in choking off possible opposition he also strangled party-building efforts that might have helped the Democrats compete better against the resurgent Republicans. Moreover, an absence of intense emotional loyalty to the Democratic party influenced Johnson's calculations.

John Bailey became a kind of standing political joke, telling friends of his inability to get Marvin Watson to respond to his phone calls. Democrats wanted Johnson to devote time to rebuilding the party apparatus after the debacle of 1966, and there were some efforts in that direction during the first half of 1967. The president lifted the hiring freeze that had hobbled the party during 1965 and 1966. The National Committee added some personnel to strengthen its political operations, including the addition of former congressman Charles Weltner of Georgia to conciliate young Democrats. Still, resentment among party activists persisted. When the Democratic National Committee met in Washington in mid-March, some members complained about how little help the party had been to candidates in 1966 and asked if Johnson wanted "an active National committee."[44]

The immediate financial situation of the Democratic National Committee had improved by early 1967 because of the cost-cutting measures that Johnson had imposed during 1965 and 1966. At the end of 1966 the party's outstanding debt stood at $1.5 million; the goal in 1967 was to retire the remainder of the debt and to raise another $1.5 million for current operations. Using the fund-raising talents of Arthur Krim and the still-potent appeal of presidential access, the party raised enough money to eliminate the debt and to pay running expenses for 1967. At a dinner in Los Angeles on June 23, 1967, Johnson told the guests: "You have made the Democratic Party debt free tonight." Unfortunately, these activities did not build up a war chest for 1968, and the Democrats lagged well behind the Republicans in attracting small, consistent donors. Once Johnson left the scene in March 1968, the main basis for party fund-raising vanished. In essence, the Democrats had simply run in place during the Johnson years and had done little to address their long-range money needs.[45]

The president faced a litany of other political problems during 1967. His support in the nation's farm belt eroded badly, and his secretary of agriculture, Orville Freeman, became a symbol of the discontent among farmers. Renewed outbreaks of racial violence in the cities during the summer, particularly in Detroit, revived voter backlash and added fuel to Republican charges about the lack of law and order. Although the nation was prosperous, voters showed increasing concern about inflation and its impact on their pocketbooks. One of Johnson's pollsters, however, summed up the president's "number one obstacle to—higher popularity—reelection," in a single word: "Vietnam." The continuation of the war, the mounting casualty lists, and the open-ended nature of the struggle ate away at the president's standing with the American people. Moreover, by 1967 there was growing disenchantment with Johnson personally; one Democratic woman in Idaho told *Newsweek*: "I'm beginning to hate that man."[46]

As the war continued and the president's popularity sank, Democrats began to consider a possibility that would have seemed unthinkable in 1964—an overt challenger to Johnson for the Democratic nomination in 1968. The first name that came to mind among dissident Democrats was Sen. Robert F. Kennedy of New York. Never friendly, Robert Kennedy and Lyndon Johnson had submerged their personal differences in the interest of their individual election campaigns in 1964, but once Kennedy was in the Senate, the strains between the two men grew as the senator moved toward opposition to the Vietnam War.[47]

Johnson and Kennedy hated each other with a mutual intensity that governed their responses to whatever the other did. Kennedy believed that Johnson was a cowardly liar who had betrayed the heritage that John F. Kennedy had left to him. Johnson thought of Robert Kennedy as a ruthless enemy whose every move was directed toward the president's political defeat. Each in their own way did much to confirm these impressions. When someone who had been aligned with Kennedy or who might possibly help the senator's political career was proposed for a government post, Johnson often took steps to block the appointment. On the other hand, Kennedy and the people around him encouraged the formation of a coalition that was in effect a "government-in-exile" within the Democratic party. Rumors floated back to Johnson of Kennedy statements that the president might not run in 1968. One reason for Johnson's suspicion of the Democratic National Committee was that he saw it as a means through which Kennedy might challenge his power.[48]

Relations between the two men worsened behind the scenes during 1966 and then shattered dramatically in early 1967. An interview with *Newsweek* that Kennedy gave during a European trip angered the president, who blamed the senator for undercutting the government's negotiating position on Vietnam. A meeting was arranged, and Johnson and Kennedy exchanged angry words and some profanity; friends of both men called it "the final break between Bobby and LBJ."[49]

Meanwhile, there was gathering support within the Democratic party for a less bellicose policy toward Vietnam. In California, anti-Vietnam Democrats talked about running a "peace" delegation for the national convention in 1968 that would support a candidate who favored "an immediate halt to the bombing of North Vietnam" and a negotiated settlement of the conflict. Among the Young Democrats several peace candidates endeavored to gain the support of that organization for an antiwar position. In Wisconsin, Minnesota, Massachusetts, and Connecticut there were stirrings of dissent against the administration. Congressmen such as Morris Udall (D.-Ariz.), brother of the secretary of the interior, came out against the war during autumn 1967; Sen. George S. McGovern of South Dakota moved toward the peace position as did other Democratic senators.[50]

The political problems that Lyndon Johnson faced in 1967 were well illustrated in a state with a large bloc of electoral votes: Johnson had carried California in 1964 by more than 1.2 million ballots; two years later Ronald Reagan defeated Gov. Edmund G. "Pat" Brown by almost 1 million votes. Democratic registration in the state fell off by 1 million voters after the 1966 campaign. Moreover, the Democrats were divided among the supporters of Brown, those voters who flavored the erratic mayor of Los Angeles Sam Yorty, the faction controlled by Speaker of the California House of Representatives, Jesse Unruh, and other shifting alignments of liberals, conservatives, friends of Robert F. Kennedy, and anti-Vietnam peace candidates. A White House aide summed up the confusion in March 1967: "The California situation is bad now but it will be hopeless if the factions cannot be united in a common effort behind the President."[51]

Johnson's political position steadily worsened during the remainder of 1967. By August 1967 a Louis Harris poll showed his favorable rating at 39 percent, "the lowest since [he] took office." His old friend James Rowe wrote him in October 1967 that "it is necessary and desirable for you to speak as the Democratic party Leader." Rowe was typically candid about Johnson's perceived shortcomings among Democrats: "The Democratic Party people I see from all over the country really believe (a) you do not understand them or (b) if you do, couldn't care less about them." Efforts to have Johnson exert himself as a party leader generally went unheeded as 1967 wore on. The White House did keep files on its potential rivals within the Democratic party, among the Republican challengers, and on possible third-party candidate Gov. George C. Wallace of Alabama, but in other respects, the president seemed to be fairly listless about gearing up for a possible nomination fight and reelection campaign.[52]

Anti-Johnson Democrats searched for an alternative candidate to the president during the latter half of 1967. Robert Kennedy gave much thought to challenging Johnson but decided that he could not run against the president without reviving charges of his own "ruthlessness" as a politician. The agents of the campaign against Johnson, most notably Allard Lowenstein and Curtis Gans, then turned to other senators as potential candidates. They found Eugene McCarthy to be receptive to their invitation, and the Minnesota senator announced on November 30 that he would enter several primaries to "challenge the President's position" on Vietnam. Arguing that his campaign did not pose "any great threat to the unity and strength of the Democratic party," McCarthy criticized Johnson's conduct of the war, his exercise of presidential power, and his treatment of the Democratic party generally.[53]

When McCarthy announced his candidacy, the political consensus was that he did not pose a serious threat to Lyndon Johnson's re-nomination. How could a relatively obscure senator from a mid-western state defeat an incumbent president? The slow start of the McCarthy campaign reinforced the conventional wisdom around Washington. Antiwar Democrats complained that the McCarthy campaign was "a disaster"; the candidate's speeches were "dull, vague, and without either balls or poetry." A White House aide, John P. Roche, informed the president in mid-December that "Eugene McCarthy is doing so badly that I am tempted to float a rumor that he is actually working for you to dispirit the 'peace movement.' " Reports from other Democrats reinforced this opinion and con-firmed the tendency within the White House to underrate the seri-ousness of McCarthy's challenge.[54]

The attention of the White House was devoted to planning for the general election in 1968, and the dimension of that task was re-vealed in a memorandum that Lawrence O'Brien prepared for John-son in late September. The tone of the O'Brien "White Paper," as it came to be known, was pessimistic: "This is not an election that can be easily won. Our effort must be massive." O'Brien, pointing to some of the obstacles that a Johnson campaign would confront, observed that the Democratic state parties were "flabby and wedded to techniques which are conventional and outmoded." As for the Democratic National Committee, it was "not staffed or equipped to conduct a successful Presidential election." Most ominously, "the Democratic Party, to a greater or lesser extent, has lost contact with the voters." The party was weak in the suburbs, out of touch with the middle class, and losing ground with the young. Moreover, O'Brien's analysis failed to address the question of how the Johnson campaign and the Democrats would assemble a majority of the elec-toral votes for a presidential victory. The party's hold on the cities was loosening, and the former bastion of the South was moving to-ward the Republicans. In many respects, O'Brien's essay was a diag-nosis of the state of the Democrats after four years of Lyndon John-son and an uncanny forecast of the problems that would confront the party during the twenty years that followed.[55]

Underrating McCarthy's challenge as they did, the president and his aides committed some political blunders that helped the Minnesota senator in his quest for a primary victory in the first test against Johnson in New Hampshire. The White House relied on the existing Democratic organization in the state, including Gov. John King and Sen. Thomas McIntyre, but a prominent businessman ran the actual campaign. Since the president was not yet an "official" candidate, his campaign was aimed at securing write-in votes. As a means of tracking the allegiance of Johnson voters, the campaign used "pledge cards" that registered voters could fill in; each card was numbered, and one went to the White House and another to the Johnson headquarters. The McCarthy campaign charged that the pledge cards interfered with a secret ballot. The Johnson camp further overreached itself when campaign ads claimed that a vote for McCarthy was a vote for the North Vietnamese leader, Ho Chi Minh. Finally, the proposed Johnson delegation had more candidates than places available, but the more focused McCarthy campaign had just the right number of delegate candidates.[56]

By the early months of 1968 Johnson was in deep political difficulty. The Vietnam War, which had seemed stalemated at best, took a surprising turn with the outbreak of the Tet Offensive at the end of January. The North Vietnamese suffered a military setback; the Johnson administration sustained a serious political defeat with the electorate. When the White House tried to convince people that the offensive had been a military success, Sen. George Aiken (R.-Vt.) responded, "If this is a failure, I hope the Viet Cong never have a major success." The prospect of further escalation of the war loomed in early March. At the same time, the Kerner Commission, named to probe the causes of urban rioting, reported that the nation was "moving toward two societies, one black, one white, separate and unequal."[57]

Then came the results of the New Hampshire primary. The president won the popular vote with 27,243 ballots (49.4 percent) to 23,280 (42.2 percent) for McCarthy. Since it was widely assumed that Johnson would win easily, the extent to which McCarthy exceeded the press's expectations of his performance translated into a "victory" for the senator. And in the race for delegates, the McCarthy campaign won the larger share. The challenger, running as an underdog with the help of college students and antiwar activists, had punctured the myth that Lyndon Johnson was an unbeatable, inevitable choice for the Democratic presidential nomination. Analysis of the votes later revealed that as many Democrats who were for escalation of the war voted for McCarthy as did those who opposed the conflict. One thing seemed clear: There was a deep suspicion of Lyndon Johnson within the Democratic party.[58]

Four days after the New Hampshire primary, Robert F. Kennedy entered the presidential contest. The New York senator had begun reassessing his position before the New Hampshire primary, and he later maintained that his decision to run had been made before Mc-

Carthy's victory. For Johnson, Kennedy's candidacy confirmed his worst fears that his presidency would be only an interruption between two Kennedy administrations. There was an abortive attempt to arrange a deal between the two men over Vietnam before Kennedy announced, but the arrangement fell through because of its inherent assault on Johnson's authority as president.[59]

Once Kennedy announced, Johnson reacted in strident terms. In public speeches in mid-March he proclaimed, "There is no cheap or no easy way to find the road to freedom and the road to order. Both danger and sacrifice built this land and today we are the number one nation. And we are going to stay the number one nation." Johnson's friends warned him that such language would not work; James Rowe told him that "everyone has turned into a dove." If the president increased the number of troops for Vietnam, the political impact would be devastating. "The prospects of a large scale escalation are threatening to bring down the house," warned a California leader. From Wisconsin came the verdict that unless the war was wound down, "this Administration cannot survive politically."[60]

By the end of March, the president's political position had deteriorated badly. James Rowe informed his old friend that in talking with Democrats Rowe now faced the question, "Is the President running?" The Kennedy forces were telling people that Johnson would pull out and that their best course was to "stay loose and stay uncommitted." In Wisconsin the prospect of a demoralizing defeat seemed evident as the McCarthy supporters gained momentum among the antiwar forces in that state.[61]

Johnson in fact was on the verge of withdrawing from the presidential race. The reasons that impelled him to make his dramatic announcement on Sunday, March 31, 1968, have remained controversial ever since he delivered the speech. His health, the importunings of Lady Bird Johnson, and the quest for a settlement to the Vietnam conflict played their part in his decision, but his collapsing political situation had an important effect on the outcome. If he suffered a devastating defeat in the Wisconsin primary, his withdrawal would have seemed an admission of his repudiation; if he were going to step aside he had to do it before April 2. Had he beaten McCarthy soundly in New Hampshire and had Kennedy not entered the contest, it is doubtful, even with the events of the war in Southeast Asia, that Johnson would have felt the same urgency about ending his presidential ambitions in 1968.[62]

Once he had withdrawn as a candidate, Johnson was in the nonpartisan position that he had long espoused as a principle of governance. "I have never been a deep partisan," he told the press after his speech on March 31, and "I am not going to spend much of my time on partisan politics" during the remaining months in the White House. When he met with Robert Kennedy and then with Hubert Humphrey, he told each of them that "except for a few fund-raising dinners, he planned to keep out of campaign politics." There was, of course, no chance that he would endorse Kennedy's candidacy, but he also withheld any formal support for his vice-president. It was the beginning of a long and difficult period for Hubert Humphrey in his political relations with Lyndon Johnson.[63]

During the two months after his withdrawal, Johnson had an apparent stake in seeing that Humphrey prevailed over McCarthy and Kennedy. Yet during April 1968 he quietly encouraged Nelson Rockefeller to announce for the Republican nomination. As for his vice-president, although Johnson extended no blessing as such, the pro-Johnson forces within the Democratic party, especially the large contributors, amply funded the Humphrey search for convention delegates. After the death of Robert Kennedy in early June, however, Johnson's need to help Humphrey receded. During the rest of the campaign, the president's priority was to ensure that his policy on Vietnam received the endorsement of his party. Since many Democrats believed that Vietnam was the issue on which Humphrey had to demonstrate his independence from the president, the inherent political conflict between the two men shaped the fate of the party in 1968.[64]

Johnson put a number of obstacles in Humphrey's path to the nomination, refusing to move the Democratic National Convention from Chicago to Miami and turning down Humphrey's suggestions about the operation of the convention itself. Johnson's decision to schedule the convention in late August, the better to celebrate his birthday, deprived Humphrey of valuable time during the fall campaign. Most important, Johnson exercised personal control over the workings of the convention to ensure that the Democratic platform reflected his views on foreign policy.[65]

The Humphrey camp had tried to devise language about the Vietnam War for the Democratic platform on which the partisans of Eugene McCarthy and the vice-president's delegates could agree. After protracted negotiations, acceptable language was found that both sides could accept. Humphrey even won grudging acceptance from Secretary of State Dean Rusk. For Johnson, however, the wording of the proposed plank was out of the question because it proclaimed a halt in U.S. bombing without allowing for sufficient protection for the army in the field. Humphrey and his aides saw the issue as one of semantics and believed that the plank "was acceptable and not offensive." In a phone conversation, Johnson told Humphrey "this plank just undercuts our whole policy and, by God, the Democratic party ought not to be doing that to me and you ought not to be doing it, you've been a part of this policy." At a key point in his presidential candidacy, Humphrey wavered and gave in to Johnson's demand.[66]

Did Johnson's desire to preserve his own historical legacy include the possibility of securing a draft nomination in 1968? John Connally and Joseph Califano have suggested that the president was interested in a draft that he could then decline, his aim being to "validate his presidency in the eyes of fellow Democrats." Given the weakness of Humphrey as a national candidate in the summer, Johnson may have even briefly contemplated a serious race. Was a Johnson nomination ever possible at the convention in August 1968? It might have been theoretically feasible to have assembled a majority of the delegates for the president, but the political cost would have been severe. Hubert Humphrey would have been repudiated, the liberals would probably have formed a third party, and the old animosities toward Johnson would have reappeared among Democrats and elsewhere. If Johnson had engineered a draft, he would have been defeated in the elections and in the process lost whatever goodwill his March 31 announcement had gained for him.[67]

The Democratic National Convention was a disaster for the party. Humphrey received the presidential nomination, and the selection of Edmund Muskie as his running mate was widely applauded. On the negative side, however, the violence and riots that raged in the streets of Chicago, the confrontations between demonstrators and the city's police force, and the turbulence that spilled over on to the convention floor left the Humphrey campaign trailing in the public opinion polls, out of money, and hounded by angry protestors at every campaign stop.[68]

Johnson did not help his vice-president much in the early stages of the campaign. During August he had brought Richard Nixon to his ranch in Texas publicly in a manner that at least suggested neutrality in the campaign; the president also refused to release as much as $600,000 in President's Club money that might have boosted the Humphrey campaign at its most desperate time. When Humphrey mistakenly suggested that troops might be brought home from Vietnam soon, Johnson corrected the mistake in a speech and emphasized that "nobody can predict" when troop withdrawals might occur. Johnson resented the efforts of people around Humphrey to put distance between their candidate and the White House; the president apparently wanted Humphrey to ask him directly for help in the campaign. Some observers thought that Johnson preferred Nixon in 1968, whose election would reflect "a deep turn of national sentiment and a rejection of the Democratic party as a whole, rather than the victory of another Democrat, which would suggest merely a repudiation of Johnson personally."[69]

With his campaign floundering, Humphrey decided during the latter part of September to move away from the president on the issue of Vietnam. He gave a speech in Salt Lake City on September 30, 1968, in which he said he would "stop the bombing of the North [Vietnam] as an acceptable risk for peace." Johnson was not pleased with what Humphrey had said, but the speech revived the vice-president's candidacy, and during October Humphrey closed the gap between himself and Richard Nixon. Meanwhile, organized labor threw its weight into the campaign to turn back the third-party threat of Gov. George Wallace of Alabama.[70]

As Humphrey's prospects improved, his advisers hoped that Johnson would take a more active role. James Rowe told the president that he and Gov. Terry Sanford of North Carolina "have come to the conclusion that President Johnson should be working harder!" Would he go into West Virginia, Kentucky, and Texas on behalf of Humphrey? Johnson agreed to do so and made some attacks on Nixon and the Republicans. He also appeared with Humphrey at the Astrodome in Houston two weeks before the election.[71]

Johnson took one significant step to help Humphrey in the days before the voting. On October 31 the president announced that he was ordering the cessation of air and naval action against North Vietnam; he believed that he had assurance from the North Vietnamese that serious negotiations would follow this move. Unfortunately for Humphrey, the South Vietnamese, prodded by the Nixon campaign, declined to attend the talks scheduled for Paris; their announcement undercut the positive impact of the bombing halt on Humphrey's candidacy.

On November 5, 1968, Richard Nixon was elected as president of the United States, but the closeness of the race underscored the divisions within the nation. Nixon received 31,770,000 popular votes and 301 electoral votes; Humphrey polled 31,270,000 ballots and garnered 191 electoral votes; George Wallace carried five states with 46 electoral votes. In some respects the outcome of the election masked the dimensions of the defeat that the Democrats had suffered. Humphrey received 42.7 percent of the total vote, almost 19 percent below the number Johnson had amassed in 1964. Had it been a two-man race between Humphrey and Nixon, it seems clear that the Republican would have won more decisively, and the election results would have resembled the later Republican triumphs of 1972, 1980, 1984, and 1988.

The Democratic National Committee emerged from the 1968 election in a bad financial condition. The party's debt stood at $6.2 million, and it worsened during the years that followed, reaching a total of $9.3 million by 1970. The money problems of the 1960s became a recurring drag on the ability of the Democrats to compete with the Republicans in presidential races, even with federal financing of those contests.[72]

After he left office, Lyndon Johnson's connections with the Democratic party rapidly frayed. He rebuffed efforts requesting him to speak for party candidates. In 1972 he gave the Democratic presidential ticket, headed by George McGovern, his formal support, but he also assured Democrats who might favor Richard Nixon that "what an individual does in a presidential campaign is a matter of conscience, and I'm not going to interfere with that decision." He told a CBS producer that he was not going to get involved in the campaign because "all I could accomplish would be to make a fool of myself." Lingering bitterness surfaced: "The only thing more impotent than a former president is a cut dog at a screwing match," Johnson said.[73]

The causes of the Democratic party's decline during the 1960s are many and complex. The Vietnam War, racial conflicts, popular resistance to Johnson's Great Society, and changing population patterns that favored the Republicans all contributed to the resurgence of the GOP after Goldwater's defeat in 1964. The leaders of the party—Robert Kennedy, Eugene McCarthy, and Hubert Humphrey—each displayed weaknesses as politicians that further intensified the Democratic predicament. Moreover, the party was running out of new ideas by the 1960s; as the agenda of the New Deal was achieved, the creative energies of the Democrats ebbed for a generation.

It would be unfair to lay all the blame for the downturn of the Democrats during the 1960s at the door of Lyndon Johnson. Yet the president bore a large share of the responsibility for the weakening of the party's structure. He allowed the institutional framework of the Democrats, never very strong, to erode drastically while he was president. At a time when the Republicans were establishing a strong base of small donors, Johnson turned to wealthy contributors whose donations were premised on access to the White House rather than on loyalty to the party. Decisions to cut off the party's voter registration programs, to weaken its issue-oriented staff, and to pay little attention to strengthening state parties were mistakes that would be difficult for the Democrats to overcome during the twenty years that followed.

Johnson's efforts to be a consensus president rather than a partisan leader also proved misdirected in that this strategy allowed the Republicans to attack his administration without evoking a sustained response from the Democrats. Moreover, the policy of nonpartisan patronage that the White House followed on numerous federal appointments undercut Democratic morale. By making loyalty to himself and to the White House the main standard for political reward, Johnson gave other Democrats few reasons to support him when they disagreed with his foreign policy decisions or his domestic policies.

Despite his cynicism and his sophistication about politics, Johnson operated from a view of the two-party system that limited his effectiveness. He genuinely believed that the president should appear to be above partisan considerations in carrying out the duties of his office. Having seen Republicans only in Texas and in the Senate, he was not attuned to the divisions between the parties that characterized politics in the rest of the nation. Above all, his emotional loyalty to the Democratic party was thin. When he put it in fourth place in his famous litany, "I am a free man first, an American second, a public servant third, and a Democrat fourth—in that order," he was speaking more truly than perhaps even he realized. As Joseph Califano recalled, "In my years on Lyndon Johnson's White House staff, never once did I hear him say that he wanted to leave behind a strengthened Democratic party." Lacking any strong identification with the future of the party, Johnson felt little responsibility for its welfare and growth. In that respect he differed from the strongly partisan Republicans who followed him, especially Ronald Reagan and George Bush.[74]

As the 1968 election approached, a shrewd journalist sought an explanation for the dramatic collapse of the Democrats during the 1960s. John Steele of *Time* concluded that "the abrupt, precipitous decline of Democratic fortunes" resulted from the way Johnson had conducted his presidency. Steele said that Johnson had "pushed into disuse and ruin the powerful organizational arm of his party, its national committee." He has also "horribly neglected the political mechanisms in the critical states save for tenuous and erratic per-

sonal relations with a few outmoded political bosses, relics of a bygone past." These errors, which could be repaired, Steele saw as symptoms of a larger failure on Johnson's part. The president had lost the confidence of the people and was "totally out of touch. He neither listens nor is heard. His vanity, myopia, his secrecy, his father-knows-best, his avuncularism has been his ruin and temporarily at least, his party's ruin."[75]

Steele's judgment has proved to be one of enduring merit. It indicates that Johnson's leadership of the Democrats during his presidency was much of a piece with the other difficulties that his administration encountered. An examination of Johnson's actions as a party leader, based on the ample and informative record in the Johnson Library, is thus another avenue to understanding the political impact of one of the most interesting and important presidents of this century.

Notes

1. Hubert Humphrey, *The Education of a Public Man: My Life and Politics* (Garden City, N.Y.: Doubleday, 1976), p. 366; this book offers an insightful critique of Johnson as a party leader. A contemporary assessment is Meg Greenfield, "LBJ and the Democrats," *Reporter*, June 2, 1966, pp. 8–13. David S. Broder, *The Party's Over: The Failure of Politics in America* (New York: Harper and Row, 1972), pp. 58–77, is also critical of Johnson's performance as a party leader. Herbert S. Parmet, *The Democrats: The Years after FDR* (New York: Macmillan, 1976), pp. 228–29, examines the limits of Johnson's partisanship.

2. See Lyndon B. Johnson, "Foreword," in Booth Mooney, *The Lyndon Johnson Story* (New York: Farrar, Straus and Cudahy, 1956), pp. ix (first and second quotations), 169 (third quotation), 168–69 (fourth quotation). Lyndon Johnson, "My Political Philosophy," *Texas Quarterly* 1 (Winter 1958): 15, contains the formulation of his attitude toward partisan politics: "I am a free man, an American, a United States Senator and a Democrat—in that order." He never tired of quoting variations of this remark. See, for example, "Remarks at a Democratic Party Rally in Newark, October 7, 1966," in *Public Papers of the Presidents of the United States: Lyndon B. Johnson, 1966*, 2 vols. (Washington, D.C.: Government Printing Office, 1967), 2:1131 (hereafter cited as *Public Papers*).

3. The best account of Johnson's rise to prominence in Texas politics is Robert Dallek, *Lone Star Rising: Lyndon Johnson and His Times, 1908–1960* (New York: Oxford University Press, 1991).

4. James H. Rowe Oral History, September 16, 1969, Lyndon B. Johnson Library (hereafter cited as LBJL), Austin, Texas, p. 46 (both quotations). See also George L-P. Weaver Oral History, January 6, 1969, LBJL, p. 29. All citations to primary sources are from LBJL.

5. Dallek, *Lone Star Rising*, pp. 199–206, is an excellent treatment of these events.

6. Johnson's speech at Whitney, Texas, his first public appearance after his 1955 heart attack, is a good statement of his attitude toward Eisenhower (see *Congressional Record*, 84th Cong., 2d sess., January 17, 1956, pp. 629–30). For discussions of Johnson's Senate leadership during the 1950s, see Doris Kearns, *Lyndon Johnson & the American Dream* (New York: Harper and Row, 1976), pp. 135–59. The quotation is from John L. Steele's interview with Johnson, December 17, 1964, John L. Steele Papers, LBJL.

7. George C. Roberts, *Paul M. Butler: Hoosier Politician and National Political Leader* (Lanham, Md.: University Press of America, 1987), p. 68. For Johnson's reluctance to take part in the Democratic Advisory Council, see Lyndon B. Johnson (hereafter LBJ) to Paul M. Butler, December 11, 1956, Paul M. Butler File, Lyndon B. Johnson Archives, box 2, LBJL.

8. Humphrey, *Education of a Public Man*, p. 164. Bobby Baker, with Larry L. King, *Wheeling and Dealing: Confessions of a Capitol Hill Operator* (New York: W. W. Norton, 1978), p. 61, says that another Johnson term for liberals was "the red hots."

9. Clifton Carter Oral History, October 30, 1968, p. 5; Theodore H. White, *The Making of the President—1964* (New York: Atheneum, 1965), pp. 245–46.

10. Paul R. Henggeler, *In His Steps: Lyndon Johnson and the Kennedy Mystique* (Chicago: Ivan Dee, 1991), pp. 76–85.

11. Lewis L. Gould, *Lady Bird Johnson and the Environment* (Lawrence: University Press of Kansas, 1988), p. 45; Humphrey, *Education of a Public Man*, pp. 297–304; Abigail McCarthy, *Private Faces, Public Faces* (Garden City, N.Y.: Doubleday and Company, 1972), pp. 264–76.

12. The Mississippi Freedom Democratic Party episode has been extensively examined. See Harold F. Bass, Jr., "Presidential Party Leadership and Party Reform: Lyndon B. Johnson and the MFDP Controversy," *Presidential Studies Quarterly* 21 (Winter 1991): 85–101, and Steven F. Lawson, *Running for Freedom: Civil Rights and Black Politics in America since 1941* (New York: McGraw-Hill, 1991), pp. 100–102.

13. *Public Papers, 1963-1964*, 2:1010, 1034, 1154.

14. Richard Maguire to Walter Jenkins, May 25, 1964, White House Central Files (WHCF), Executive/Political (EX/PL) 3, April 20, 1964–July 25, 1964, box 110, Kenneth O'Donnell to LBJ, October 3, 1964, WHCF, EX/PL 2, October 2, 1964–October 4, 1964, box 84. Bruce E. Altschuler, *LBJ and the Polls* (Gainesville: University of Florida Press, 1990), pp. 7–16. Milton Viorst, "Johnson's Campaign Machinery," *New Republic*, September 5, 1964, pp. 9–10.

15. Humphrey, *Education of a Public Man*, p. 309.

16. For the backlash issue in 1964, see Henry H. Wilson, Jr., to Lawrence F. O'Brien, July 8, 1964, WHCF, EX/PL 2, June 15, 1964–July 23, 1964, box 83; White, *Making of the President—1964*, pp. 233–37; Jody Carlson, *George C. Wallace and the Politics of Powerlessness* (New Brunswick, N.J.: Transaction Books, 1981), pp. 27–44.

17. Henry H. Wilson, Jr., to LBJ, January 21, 1967, WHCF, EX/PL 2, December 23, 1966–February 2, 1967, box 87; Broder, *Party's Over*, pp. 46–47.

18. Financial Report as of March 25, 1965, Democratic National Committee, Financial Reports, Marvin Watson Files (hereafter MWF), box 19; White, *Making of the President—1964*, p. 322; Altschuler, *LBJ and the Polls*, p. 12. Three-and-a-half years later James Rowe was still fuming about the "royal financial clipping" that he believed Doyle, Dane and Bernbach had given the Johnson campaign (Rowe to LBJ, March 15, 1968, James Rowe Memos, MWF, box 30).

19. For background on the President's Club, see Herbert E. Alexander, *Money in Politics* (Washington, D.C.: Public Affairs Press, 1972), pp. 96–107, and Alexander, *Financing the 1968 Election* (Lexington, Mass.: D. C. Heath, 1971), pp. 151–52. See also Walter Pincus, "Democrats Expect to Gross over $3 Million This Week," *Washington Evening Star*, May 26, 1964.

20. Alexander, *Money in Politics*, p. 96.

21. LBJ to Arthur Krim, August 25, 1965, White House Name File (WHNF), Krim, 1965, box 252 (quotation); for evidence of Krim's activities, see Krim to Marvin Watson, May 6, 1965, Krim to Jack Valenti, October 6, 1965, Jack Valenti to LBJ, November 12, 1965, Watson to LBJ, February 15, 1966, WHNF, Krim, 1965, 1966, box 252. Information on Krim's background is available in Tino Balio, *United Artists: The Company That Changed the Film Industry* (Madison: University of Wisconsin Press, 1987), pp. 16–17, 311–12; Ronald Brownstein, *The Power and The Glitter: The Hollywood–Washington Connection* (New York: Pantheon Books, 1990), pp. 188–202. Jack Valenti, *A Very Human President* (New York: W. W. Norton, 1975), pp. 368–69, discusses the Krim-Johnson friendship.

22. Charles Bartlett, "Johnson Aims at Extinction of GOP," undated clipping enclosed with Watson to LBJ, April 3, 1965, Democratic National Committee, Salaries, MWF, box 21; "Democrats Face Elections with Staff, Money Problems," *Congressional Quarterly*, May 27, 1966, pp. 1074–77. See also Clifton Carter to LBJ, October 14, 1965, WHCF, EX/PL, June 29, 1965–October 18, 1965, box 1.

23. "Democrats Face Elections with Staff, Money Problems," *Congressional Quarterly*, p. 1078.

24. Watson to LBJ, April 3, 1965, Democratic National Committee, Salaries, MWF, box 21; Watson to LBJ, May 20, 1965, November 18, 1965, LBJ to John Bailey, May 31, 1965, four memos of that date, Democratic National Committee, Financial Reports, MWF, box 19.

25. Report and notes attached to Watson to LBJ, November 18, 1965, Democratic National Committee Financial Reports, MWF, box 19. As early as February 1965, the president rejected efforts to emphasize registration of African-American voters through the Democratic National Committee. Hubert Humphrey to John Bailey, February 11, 1965, Watson to Humphrey, February 15, 1965, WHCF, EX/PL 2, December 26, 1964–April 7, 1965, box 86.

26. "Democrats Face Elections with Staff, Money Problems," *Congressional Quarterly*, p. 1078; Rowland Evans and Robert Novak, "Disarray among the Democrats," column enclosed with Albert S. Porter to Clifton Carter, March 17, 1966, WHCF, EX/PL 6-1, Democrats, box 116.

27. For Watson, see "The White House at Work—A Mystery Explained," *U.S. News & World Report*, February 7, 1966, 36–37; Evans and Novak, "Disarray among the Democrats"; Greenfield, "LBJ and the Democrats," pp. 8–13.

28. Charles D. Roche to Watson, January 27, 1966, WHCF, EX/PL 2, January 18, 1966–May 23, 1966, box 86. Roche to LBJ, February 14, 1966, Memos to the President, Charles Roche Files, box 3.

29. William Connell to Clifton Carter, May 12, 1966, Congress-California, MWF, box 2; Moyers to LBJ, June 9, 1966, WHCF, Public Relations (PR)16, box 82; James R. Jones to Watson, June 24, 1966, Correspondence, June 1966, MWF, box 38.

30. Ted Van Dyk to Hubert Humphrey, November 14, 1966, enclosed with Humphrey to Watson, November 28, 1966, WHCF, EX/PL, September 1, 1966–January 19, 1967, box 1; Alan Draper, "Labor in the 1966 Elections," *Labor History* 30 (Winter 1989): 76–92.

31. LBJ comment, June 22, 1966, attached to Robert E. Kintner to LBJ, June 22, 1966, WHCF, PR 16, Confidential, box 81.

32. Watson to LBJ, July 21, 1966, President's Club/Democratic National Committee, MWF, box 20.

33. *Public Papers, 1966*, 2: 877–78 (quotation); U.S. House, *Congressional Record*, 89th Cong., 2d sess. July 14, 1966, pp. 15754–55 August 30, 1966, pp. 21298–303 September 2, 1966, pp. 21717–21722, are examples of the Republican attacks. For the Busch episode, see Peter Hernon and Terry Ganey, *Under the Influence: The Unauthorized Story of the Anheuser-Busch Dynasty* (New York: Simon and Schuster, 1991), pp. 237–39.

34. Marianne Means column, dated September 24, 1966, WHCF, EX/PL 7, August 30, 1966–June 5, 1967, box 122.

35. LBJ comments on Charles D. Roche to Watson, September 6, 1966, WHCF, EX/PL 2, August 31, 1966–November 1, 1966, box 86; John Criswell to Watson, September 30, 1966, WHCF, Federal Government (FG) 440, September 22, 1966–December 31, 1966, box 347.

36. *Public Papers, 1966*, 2: 886, 889, 913.

37. Albert S. Porter to Clifton Carter, March 17, 1966, WHCF, EX/PL 6-1, Democrats, Marianne Means column, November 15, 1966, WHCF, EX/PL 6-2, Democrats, both in box 116. John Criswell to Marvin Watson, December 5, 1966, Democratic National Committee, Salaries, MWF, box 21; Greenfield, "LBJ and the Democrats," p. 13; Frank Mensel to David Brown, September 30, 1966, Irvine Sprague Files, Patronage 1966, box 8, complains about the appointment of a "dyed-in-the-wool" Republican to an advisory panel in Utah.

38. *Public Papers, 1966*, 2: 711, 749, 869, 880.

39. Ibid., 2: 1047, 1135, 1169.

40. Carl Solberg, *Hubert Humphrey: A Biography* (New York: W. W. Norton, 1984), p. 297 (both quotations); Alan L. Otten and Charles B. Seib, "The Minor Masterpiece of Ray C. Bliss," *Reporter*, February 10, 1966, pp. 35–38; "How Ray Bliss Plays the Cards for GOP," *Business Week*, March 9, 1968, pp. 28–30.

41. *Public Papers, 1966*, 2: 1323, 1340. For the Johnson-Nixon episode, see Stephen E. Ambrose, *Nixon, Volume Two: The Triumph of a Politician, 1962–1972* (New York: Simon and Schuster, 1989), pp. 93–99. On Johnson's shift in his travel plans in 1966, see Joseph Califano, *The Triumph & Tragedy of Lyndon Johnson: The White House Years* (New York: Simon and Schuster 1991), pp. 150–53.

42. Ambrose, *Nixon*, p. 100; *Public Papers, 1966* 2: 1358.

43. Rowland Evans and Robert Novak, "Inside Report: The John Bailey Blues," *Washington Post*, January 25, 1967; Marianne Means column, November 15, 1966, WHCF, EX/PL 2, Democrats, box 116; "Meaning of 1966 Elections," no date but received at Central Files, May 2, 1968, in WHCF, EX/PL 2, April 5, 1968–May 7, 1968, box 89. This memo was written shortly after the 1966 elections.

44. Rowland Evans and Robert Novak, "Inside Report: The Democrats Meet," *Washington Post*, March 13, 1967; John Bailey to LBJ, February 10, 1967, Democratic National Committee/Miscellaneous, MWF, box 19; David S. Broder, "Political Parade: The Power of Positive Boredom," *Washington Post*, March 7, 1967.

45. *Public Papers, 1967*, 1: 645; memorandum attached with John B. Criswell to William S. White, November 16, 1967, Democratic National Committee/Financial Reports, MWF, box 19.

46. Fred Panzer to LBJ, June 16, 1967, WHCF, EX/PL 2, June 3, 1967–August 22, 1967, box 87; "The President in Trouble," *Newsweek*, September 4, 1967, p. 17. Johnson's troubles in the farm belt were complex. See Rowland Evans and Robert Novak, "LBJ Down on the Farm," *Washington Post*, June 23, 1967, and William Connell to Marvin Watson, May 2, 1967, Agricultural/Political, DeVier Pierson Files, box 16.

47. Henggeler, *In His Steps*, pp. 175–210, offers the most recent interpretation of this tense relationship.

48. For evidence of Johnson's ongoing concerns about Robert Kennedy, see Watson to LBJ, June 6, 1966, MWF, June 1966 Memos, box 38; Hayes Redmond to Bill Moyers, James Rowe to LBJ, January 16, 1968, MWF, Robert Kennedy, box 25; John P. Roche to LBJ, January 26, 1968, MWF, John Roche, box 29.

49. Henggeler, *In His Steps*, pp. 208–10; Arthur M. Schlesinger, Jr., *Robert Kennedy and His Times* (Boston: Houghton Mifflin, 1978), pp. 767–69.

50. Irvine Sprague to Marvin Watson, September 16, 1967, WHCF, EX/PL/ST5, April 9, 1967–October 7, 1967, box 33; Charles DeBenedetti and Charles Chatfield, *An American Ordeal: The Antiwar Movement of the Vietnam Era* (Syracuse, N.Y.: Syracuse University Press, 1990), pp. 194–95, 200–201.

51. Irvine Sprague to Lawrence F. O'Brien, March 8, 1967, attached with O'Brien to LBJ, March 29, 1967, MWF, California-B, box 2. Watson's files on California in box 2 are extensive and informative on the shifting coalitions among the Democrats in California.

52. Fred Panzer to LBJ, August 11, 1967, WHCF, EX/PL 2; June 3, 1967–August 22, 1967, box 87; James Rowe to LBJ, October 2, 1967, WHCF, EX/PL 3, September 16, 1967–October 6, 1967, box 111; Fred Panzer to Watson, October 4, 1967, WHCF, EX/PL 2, September 19, 1967–October 20, 1967, box 88.

53. Eugene J. McCarthy, *The Year of the People* (Garden City, N.Y.: Doubleday and Company, 1969), pp. 96, 156–57, 265, 267. The events of late 1967 have been covered in numerous accounts. See Lewis Chester, Godfrey Hodgson, and Bruce Page, *An American Melodrama: The Presidential Campaign of 1968* (New York: Viking Press, 1969), pp. 51–77; Dennis Dean Wainstock, "The 1968 Presidential Campaign and Election," (Ph.D. diss.,

West Virginia University, 1984), pp. 43–57; and Lewis L. Gould, *1968: The Election That Changed America* (Chicago: Ivan Dee, 1993), pp. 17–25.

54. John P. Roche to LBJ, December 18, 1967, MWF, Eugene McCarthy, box 26; Jack Newfield, "A Time of Plague, A Season for Courage," *Village Voice*, December 28, 1967; Marvin Watson to LBJ, November 21, 1967, MWF, Arthur Krim, box 26, showing McCarthy with 6 percent of the vote in a race with Johnson and Robert Kennedy, and Marty Underwood to James R. Jones, December 4, 1967, MWF, McCarthy, box 26.

55. Lawrence F. O'Brien, "A White Paper for the President on the 1968 Presidential Campaign," September 29, 1967, MWF, Democratic National Committee/Rowe-O'Brien-Crocker-Criswell Operation, box 20.

56. For the problems of the Johnson campaign in New Hampshire, see Charles D. Roche to LBJ, January 8, 1968, Charles Roche Files, Memos to the President, box 3; Watson to LBJ, February 3, 1968, MWF, Labor Bloc, box 26; LBJ to Charles Bartlett, March 4, 1968, Bartlett to LBJ, February 26, 1968, WHCF, EX/PL 2, February 19, 1968–March 4, 1968, box 89.

57. Larry Berman, *Lyndon Johnson's War: The Road to Stalemate in Vietnam* (New York: W. W. Norton, 1989), p. 151; Charles Kaiser, *1968 in America: Music, Politics, Chaos. Counterculture, and the Shaping of a Generation* (New York: Weidenfeld and Nicolson, 1988), pp. 141–42.

58. On the outcome of the New Hampshire primary, see Al Barkan to Lane Kirkland, March 14, 1968, MWF, Labor Bloc, box 26; Wainstock, "1968 Presidential Campaign," pp. 65–72; Michael Barone, *Our Country: The Shaping of America from Roosevelt to Reagan* (New York: Free Press, 1990), p. 432.

59. Weinstock, "1968 Presidential Campaign," pp. 81–93; Clark Clifford, with Richard Holbrooke, *Counsel to the President: A Memoir* (New York: Random House, 1991), pp. 501–5; Henggeler, *In His Steps*, pp. 234–38.

60. *Public Papers, 1968–1969*, 1: 415; James Rowe to LBJ, March 19, 1968, MWF, Jim Rowe, box 30; Richard Cudahy to LBJ, March 19, 1968, MWF, Wisconsin-B, Primary, box 18; William Connell to Hubert Humphrey, March 19, 1968, MWF, California Convention, box 2.

61. Rowe to LBJ, March 28, 1968, MWF, Jim Rowe, box 30; Marvin Watson telephone conversations, March 29, 1968, MWF, Wisconsin Primary, box 18; George Christian to LBJ, March 29, 1968, WHCF, EX/PL, March 26, 1968–April 4, 1968, box 89.

62. Johnson's decision to withdraw is still a hotly debated topic. For some of the recent writing on the issue, see George Christian, "The Night Lyndon Quit," *Texas Monthly*, April 1988, pp. 109, 168, 170; James R. Jones, "Behind LBJ's Decision Not to Run in '68," *New York Times*, April 16, 1988; Califano, *Triumph & Tragedy*, pp. 253–72; Gould, *1968*, pp. 33–52.

63. *Public Papers, 1968–1969*, 1: 477, 478; Lyndon B. Johnson, *The Vantage Point: Perspectives of the Presidency, 1963–1969* (New York: Holt, Rinehart and Winston, 1971), pp. 539–42.

64. For the Johnson-Humphrey relationship in 1968, see Solberg, *Humphrey*, pp. 325–38, Califano, *Triumph & Tragedy*, pp. 289–94, and Gould, *1968*, pp. 94–95, 115–21.

65. Walt Rostow, "Memorandum of Conversation," April 3, 1968, White House Famous Names, Robert F. Kennedy, 1968 Campaign, box 6; James Jones to LBJ, July 18, 1968, WHCF, EX/FG 440, July 1, 1968–August

31, 1968, box 349; Califano, *Triumph & Tragedy*, pp. 318–19; Solberg, *Humphrey*, pp. 355–57.

66. Humphrey, *Education of a Public Man*, p. 389.

67. Califano, *Triumph & Tragedy*, pp. 320–22, reviews these events.

68. Charles D. Roche to LBJ, September 5, 1968, Charles Roche Files, Memos to the President, box 3. The best study of the Chicago convention is David Farber, *Chicago '68* (Chicago: University of Chicago Press, 1988).

69. For the interaction between Johnson and Humphrey during the fall campaign, see Solbert, *Humphrey*, pp. 375–76; Weinstock, "1968 Presidential Campaign and Election," p. 462; Gould, *1968*, 142–46, 159–60.

70. Humphrey, *Education of a Public Man*, p. 493; Charles S. Murphy to LBJ, October 1, 1968, WHCF, GEN/PL, Hubert Humphrey, box 25; Clifford, *Counsel to the President*, pp. 572–73.

71. James Rowe to LBJ, October 10, 1968, WHCF, GEN/PL, Hubert Humphrey, October 10, 1968–, box 25; Weinstock, "1968 Presidential Campaign," p. 485.

72. Alexander, *Financing the 1968 Election*, pp. 216–21.

73. Ambrose, *Nixon, Volume Two: Triumph*, p. 586; Robert L. Hardesty, "With Lyndon Johnson in Texas: A Memoir of the Post-Presidential Years," in *Farewell to the Chief: Former Presidents in American Public Life*, ed. Richard Norton Smith and Timothy Walch (Worland, Wyo.: High Plains Publishing, 1990), p. 106.

74. Johnson, "My Political Philosophy," p. 15; Joseph A. Califano, Jr., *A Presidential Nation* (New York: W. W. Norton, 1975), p. 159.

75. John Steele, "The Shape of the Democratic Party," October 1, 1968, box 1, Steele Papers.

3 | Women's Issues and the Johnson Administration

Susan M. Hartmann

LYNDON JOHNSON DID NOT consider women's issues or gender inequities to be among the "most important problems, the most pressing goals, and the most historical accomplishments" of his presidency. In nearly 600 pages of memoirs, except for brief comments on his promotion of family planning—and that couched in terms of fighting poverty rather than of championing women's rights—Johnson discussed neither the policy initiatives of his administration nor the intensifying demands of women for governmental action to mitigate their disadvantaged position in American society.[1]

Yet the Johnson years formed an important transition period leading toward what would amount to a revolution in public opinion and government policy concerning women.[2] The increasing participation of women in employment and in higher education had begun to expose the anomalies between policy and popular attitudes on the one hand and the actual experiences and aspirations of growing numbers of women on the other. Official recognition of sex discrimination by the Kennedy and Johnson administrations encouraged women to become more active on their own behalf. In turn, their pressure, combined with developments not directly related to feminist goals, moved the Johnson administration to foster a series of policies that began to reduce sex discrimination and to widen women's opportunities.

In this chapter, I can only begin to explore the policy turning points and the range of sources in the Johnson Library that illuminate these changes. The policy innovations included advancement of women in government and military positions, equal opportunity in private employment, equality in jury service, federal promotion of birth control and family planning, and gender-specific programs in the administration's war on poverty. Only in the areas of family planning and government appointments of women did Johnson take the initiative, and only the latter effort represented a specific intention to advance women's opportunities as women. Most of the reforms grew out of their expedient relationships to other needs of the administration, and they manifested the growing determination of women to alter policy in their favor. Yet, whatever the origins of policy changes that benefited women, Johnson ultimately gave those policies his blessing and often made specific efforts to identify them as his own. In helping to legitimize women's interests, Johnson contributed to the resurgence of feminist activism in the late 1960s.

Women in Johnson's Circle

The president's willingness to support such policy initiatives arose in part from his relationships with and respect for a number of women who had his ear. Although the inner domain of presidential advisers was an exclusively male preserve, several women who were sensitive to gender inequities were able to gain a hearing within the administration. Some were social as well as political friends of the Johnsons, and others had worked with Johnson during his congressional career. Aware of their contributions to his career and to his party, Johnson respected their advice. In addition, his admiration of Lady Bird's business and political skills inclined him to appreciate political views expressed by other women within his circle.[3]

Fellow Texan Elizabeth Carpenter became friends with the Johnsons during her sixteen-year career as a journalist in Washington. Although not an active feminist until the 1970s, as early as 1955 Carpenter complained to Johnson about the all-male character of the National Press Club and urged him to work for tax reform that would allow employed mothers to deduct child-care expenses. In 1960 she abandoned journalism to work on the vice-presidential campaign and then served as executive assistant to Vice-President Johnson. From 1963 to 1969, Carpenter occupied the post of press secretary and staff director for the First Lady.[4]

As Lady Bird Johnson's chief aide, Carpenter's official duties revolved around the president's family and social life. Yet she had ample opportunity to present her views on policy issues and when necessary could get word to Johnson through Lady Bird. Only partly joking, Johnson himself acknowledged that Lady Bird and Carpenter "put questionnaires to me nearly every day about what I have done for women lately." Nor did Carpenter hesitate to nudge presidential staff members, suggesting on one occasion that Jack Valenti get Sargent Shriver to include women among his poverty advisers.[5]

At the same time, the president recognized Carpenter's usefulness in the policy realm, when, for example, he needed her to work on his project to increase the number of women in high-level positions in the federal government. Although delegation of such a task to an East Wing aide suggested that the assignment was not high among presidential priorities, it demonstrated Johnson's confidence in Carpenter and indicated her active role in many aspects of his administration as well as her interest in women's issues.[6]

Johnson's unparalleled attention to the cultivation of Congress opened another avenue for women's claims to reach the White House. During the 1960s the handful of women in Congress became more assertive on policy issues concerning sex discrimination. Congresswoman Edith Green (D.-Oreg.), for example, championed equal pay legislation and greater attention to women in the antipoverty programs. Another congresswoman, Patsy Mink (D.-Hawaii), challenged John Bailey, chairman of the Democratic National Committee, over discriminatory practices at the National Capital Democratic Club. Martha Griffiths (D.-Mich.), the most determined feminist in Congress, pressured the White House on a variety of issues, including sex discrimination in employment, jury service, federal tax policies, and civil service pensions.[7]

Some of Johnson's aides viewed such demands as a necessary burden if not a pain in the neck. After meeting with Griffiths on a number of sex discrimination issues, Johnson's legislative liaison, Henry H. Wilson, Jr., made light of her and her concerns with the remark, "Martha was typically foggy." In transmitting to another official a list of Griffiths's demands, Wilson sarcastically concluded, "I am happy to contemplate this memorandum will generally brighten up your day." Yet, whether the president appreciated congresswomen's views and determination or if he simply needed to have them on his side, he could not easily dismiss their concerns. Referring to an Equal Employment Opportunity Commission report on controversial issues concerning sex discrimination, Johnson wanted to know, "Does this interest Martha Griffiths?"[8]

Anna Rosenberg Hoffman was connected to Johnson in three ways: political supporter, trusted associate, and social friend. She provided financial assistance to his political career as early as 1937 in his first congressional campaign. In the 1950s, when Johnson served on the Senate Armed Services Committee and Rosenberg was assistant secretary of defense for manpower, their mutual esteem grew despite differences over policy. After Rosenberg married Paul Hoffman in 1963, the couple became part of the Johnsons' social circle. Shortly after becoming president, Johnson called on Anna Rosenberg Hoffman for advice and almost immediately began to implement her suggestion to increase the numbers of women in high government positions.[9]

Similar ties connected Mary Lasker to the Johnsons. A successful businesswoman and widow of philanthropist Albert D. Lasker, Mary Lasker worked closely with Mrs. Johnson on her special project, beautification and environmental reform. Lasker's primary concern, however, involved health issues, and she was also an advocate of family planning. With considerable access to the president, she prodded Johnson and organized support for his pathbreaking initiatives in the control of cancer, heart disease, and strokes.[10]

The highest ranking woman within the administration was Esther Peterson, whom Kennedy had appointed assistant secretary of labor and head of the Women's Bureau. After Johnson made her his special assistant on consumer affairs, Peterson relinquished her position in the Women's Bureau to Mary Keyserling, but she continued to play a key role in women's issues. Although Peterson had nothing but praise for Johnson's efforts to advance women, she also noted that his locker-room language in informal situations created discomfort for women around him. Peterson found his risqué jokes ''fun and not fun,'' recalling that she ''had to bend a lot.'' Peterson believed that she had to put up with Johnson's propensity for humor based on women's sexual features, a situation that a later generation of women would label ''sexual harassment.''[11]

The conflict between Peterson's admiration for Johnson's public stance on women's issues and her uneasiness about his informal treatment of women deepens the contradictions that so many associates and scholars have found in the man. Johnson's enormous admiration of Lady Bird and his gratitude for her unfailing support did not prevent him from conducting affairs with other women and bragging to associates that he ''had more women by accident than Kennedy had on purpose.''[12] It is ironic that Johnson helped raise public awareness of sex discrimination but that in private he reduced women to sexual objects. When, for example, an aide reported that Congresswoman Green was giving the administration trouble on one of its education programs, an exasperated Johnson suggested that he take her out for brunch and drinks: ''Tell him to spend the afternoon in bed with her and she'll support any Goddamn bill he wants.'' In response to unfavorable coverage by a female reporter, Johnson proposed a similar approach.[13]

Early Initiatives on Sex Discrimination

The public Johnson, however, aligned himself with women's concerns even before he became president. As the Kennedy administration began to shift government policy from neglect and even support of sex discrimination to active intervention on behalf of equal opportunity, Esther Peterson led the way, and Johnson lent his assistance. Acknowledging that the vice-presidency created a vacuum in the life of the enormously energetic Johnson, Peterson also believed that he was motivated by ''a sensitivity [to women's issues that] I didn't get from Kennedy.''[14]

When Peterson persuaded Kennedy to appoint the President's Commission on the Status of Women (PCSW) in 1961, it was Johnson who suggested that she could give it force by insisting that it include cabinet officials as well as nationally prominent private citizens. Hosting a reception at the vice-presidential home on the occasion of the commission's first meeting, the Johnsons gave it an ''official stamp of approval.'' To commission members Johnson asserted, ''I believe a woman's place is not only in the home, but in the House, and in the Senate and at the conference table.''[15]

The report of the PCWS, issued in 1963, presented the first official systematic examination of the status of women and a series of recommendations to address inequities. Aided by Peterson's staff in the Women's Bureau, the commission quickly generated parallel activities on the state and local levels and energized a small but growing network of women committed to reform. Their increasing impatience with the government and particularly with the failure of the Equal Employment Opportunity Commission to take sex discrimination seriously led some of the women in this network to found the National Organization for Women (NOW) in 1966, the first organizational manifestation of the new feminist movement.[16]

Johnson's position on the proposed equal rights amendment (ERA) to the Constitution reflected his respect for Peterson's views and the report of the PSCW. In an effort to resolve the long-standing disagreement among activist women over the ERA, the PSCW urged an equal rights strategy based on the Fourteenth Amendment's equal protection clause rather than through a new amendment specifically banning sex discrimination. Although he had endorsed the ERA as senator, Johnson quickly adjusted his position to coincide with that of the PSCW and held to that approach even after NOW made passage of the ERA a top priority in 1967.[17]

Passage of equal pay legislation was the Kennedy administration's second important break with tradition regarding women's status, and here too Johnson played a role. Peterson made this objective, long sought by women's organizations and several labor unions, a top priority, and again Johnson came to her aid, not only by helping to plan legislative strategy but by giving it his personal sanction and helping to get it through Congress. According to Peterson, Johnson—ever aware of the importance of publicity—had a photograph taken of Peterson handing him the administration's draft bill, which he then took to Congress. Enacted in 1963, the Equal Pay Act made illegal the centuries-old custom of paying women less than men for the same work, marking the first federal action against sex discrimination in private employment.[18]

After becoming president, Johnson continued to identify himself with these two initiatives. When the Equal Pay law went into effect in 1964, he did not let the occasion go unnoticed: He invited members of women's organizations and labor unions to the White House, where he lauded their efforts on behalf of the measure. Likewise, Johnson sustained his identification with the President's Commission on the Status of Women. With Mrs. Johnson he attended the first meeting of its successor, the Citizens' Advisory Council on the Status of Women (CACSW), created to fulfill the agenda that had been set out by the PCSW. In 1965 and 1966, when representatives from CACSW and parallel state and local bodies met in Washington, Johnson addressed their gatherings at the White House.[19]

Appointments of Women to Government Posts

Despite Johnson's contributions to the PCSW and equal pay legislation, these measures were associated with the Kennedy administration, and Johnson moved quickly to claim his own ground on women's issues. He made the appointment of women to government office the keystone of his efforts, and it was the only women's issue that sustained his interest for any length of time. In choosing to remedy the dearth of women in high-level government positions, Johnson responded to a persistent concern of Democratic women, to advice from Anna Rosenberg Hoffman, and to his own need to distinguish his presidency from the Kennedy administration. Calling a press conference in January 1964, Johnson announced the goal of appointing fifty women to high-level posts within a month and instructed cabinet and agency heads to fulfill that goal. Thereafter, the president made the most of this campaign, occasionally getting carried away by his eagerness for attractive press coverage and announcing an appointment before the woman had accepted or the exact position had been defined. For several months he referred repeatedly in public addresses to his program, and Lady Bird credited her husband with starting a ''women's revolution.''[20]

With few exceptions, the president's interest in women's appointments faded after 1964 and was never integrated into general policies concerning federal personnel. One of this exceptions occurred in 1965, when Johnson addressed a ceremony honoring ten recipients of the National Civil Service League's Career Service Awards. Chiding the selection committee, which "apparently confined their judgment to stags," the president expressed incredulity "that the odds are 10 to nothing in favor of the men when it comes to making awards based on merit" and called for an end to "bias" and "prejudice" against women. Yet one year later when Johnson established a task force on federal programs for career advancement, no women were mentioned and not one was named to the task force.[21]

Johnson's female appointments were impressive but only when compared to the past. He appointed twenty-seven women to offices requiring Senate confirmation, increasing the number of women in such positions from thirty to fifty-two between 1963 and 1968, and recorded advances for women in civil service posts. More important, he raised expectations that went unfulfilled. After initially receiving accolades from numerous women's organizations, by 1966 Johnson began to be pressured to do more. That year the newly organized National Organization for Women wrote to Johnson of its concern "with the merely token number of women holding positions in the federal judiciary." A year later, NOW stressed the "startlingly low number of women in key policy-making jobs" and the need for "more high-echelon women on your own staff in the White House." Even Johnson's admirers conceded their disappointment that he seized few opportunities to appoint women to the federal bench.[22]

Employment Discrimination

A much more important policy development of 1964, one long sought by women activists but enacted independently of administration designs, was Title VII of the Civil Rights Act, banning sex discrimination in all aspects of employment. As several historians have explained, the inclusion of sex discrimination in Title VII resulted from efforts of individuals representing a complex configuration of forces: advocates of gender equality; civil rights opponents hoping that the sex-discrimination ban would kill the entire bill; and supporters of the civil rights bill who wanted it passed in the most expedient way possible. The president was among the latter. Once the bill passed the House with the amendment banning sex discrimination, the president—whose highest priority was to get his civil rights measure as quickly as possible—urged Senate passage of the bill in its current form. Although the Senate did pass a different version of the measure, the sex discrimination proviso remained intact in the bill Johnson signed in July 1964.[23]

In addition to furnishing powerful legal support for equal employment opportunity, Title VII helped spark the resurgence of feminism. Their discovery that they would have to fight to get the Equal Employment Opportunity Commission to enforce the ban on sex discrimination led women activists to found NOW and galvanized traditional women's groups to pressure the administration on other equity issues. Responding to lobbying from NOW, the National Federation of Business and Professional Women, and other women's groups, Johnson issued Executive Order 11375 in October 1967, extending to women additional civil rights protections, most notably affirmative action mandates.[24]

The president's special counsel, Harry McPherson, viewed the executive order as ''not a really major action'' and advised that it ''should not be overplayed,'' revealing continuing myopia among administration officials concerning women's grievances. The directive in fact represented substantial progress, by adding sex discrimination to an earlier executive order banning discrimination by federal agencies and contractors and requiring them to adopt affirmative action policies. In contrast to the views of McPherson, letters of appreciation to Johnson from African-American sororities, the National Association of Media Women, the American Association of University Women, and other women's groups testified to the major importance women attached to the executive order.[25]

Women in the Military

One month following the issue of the executive order, Congress chipped away at another barrier, this one involving women in the military. During his campaign for women's appointments in 1964, Johnson spoke to the Defense Advisory Committee on Women in the Services (DACOWITS), a body of fifty prominent women formed during the Korean War to advise the Department of Defense (DOD) on issues concerning military women. Johnson thanked the members of DACOWITS for their service and no doubt at the same time garnered additional publicity for his appointments program. Blithely discounting the overwhelming and deliberate concentration of servicewomen in clerical or medical assignments, Johnson stressed their contributions as scientists, engineers, lawyers, and managers, urging DACOWITS to encourage "more women to play even more important roles." As was often the case with Johnson's symbolic gestures, the president's remarks encouraged these women to push harder with their agenda.[26]

Since the 1950s DACOWITS had been concerned with barriers to women's career opportunities in the military. The 1948 legislation making women a permanent part of the peacetime military establishment had limited women to the highest rank of colonel (captain in the navy). Only the director of the women's component in each branch could hold that rank, and only for a four-year period, after which former directors were forced to accept temporary demotions to remain in the service. Additional ceilings set at middle ranks and separate promotion lists for men and women further barred women from positions for which they were fully qualified and frequently forced them into early retirement.[27]

DACOWITS' push for elimination of the restrictions on female officers found support in the recommendations of the PCSW in 1963, and military leaders themselves began to recognize the irrationality of the limitations. By 1966 the war in Vietnam added further justification for a policy change, but only with great hesitation did officials turn to women as even a partial solution to the rising demand for personnel. The urgent need for medical specialists and the lack of male nurses ensured a warm welcome in Southeast Asia for female nurses, who constituted the vast majority of the 7,500 military women who served there. But other women who requested assignments to Vietnam met nearly total opposition.[28]

No doubt fearing that deploying large numbers of women near arenas of combat would add fuel to the antiwar movement, Johnson himself dismissed the issue with a joke. To a reporter who noted that women were "distressed" at the lack of opportunity to serve in Vietnam and asked whether "there is any chance that this might take place," Johnson retorted, "Well, there is always a chance of anything taking place when our women are sufficiently distressed."[29]

The services were reluctant to turn to women even to relieve personnel shortages at home or at stations far removed from Vietnam. Instead, the Defense Department resorted to converting military assignments to civilian positions and lowering enlistment standards for men. The first official recognition that women could help to meet the rising demand for military personnel came in 1967. In 1966, with opposition to the draft mounting (it was due to expire in June 1967), Johnson had appointed a National Advisory Commission on Selective Service, chaired by Burke Marshall. The commission recommended extension of the draft but also called for greater efforts to encourage voluntary enlistments. Noting that "women willing to volunteer for military duty exist in far greater numbers than the services will accommodate," the Marshall Commission recommended providing opportunities for more women to serve, "thus reducing the number of men who must be involuntarily called to duty."[30]

Responding to DACOWITS' prodding to recruit more women, in 1966 the DOD established an interservice group to study the utilization of women, and the services agreed to expand their female components by a modest 6,500. That same year, with measures already introduced in Congress to remove the barriers to women's advancement, the DOD submitted its own draft bill, which became the basis for legislative action. Defense officials, Democratic Congresswomen Edith Green (Oreg.) and Patsy Mink (Hawaii), and representatives of DACOWITS, veterans' organizations, the American Nurses Association, and the American Civil Liberties Union testified in support of the measure, and DACOWITS organized an intense letter-writing and lobbying campaign. The bill, which became law in November 1967, made retirement regulations more equitable, removed the middle-grade ceilings on women, and opened the door for women's promotion above the rank of colonel/navy captain. Interestingly, a more far-reaching provision in PL 90-130 received virtually no attention; yet, in abandoning the limit of women to no more than 2 percent of total military strength, that provision laid the grounds for the transformation in women's military service that would result from the move to an all-volunteer military in the 1970s.[31]

In addition to emphasizing the irrationality of the limitations on female officers, the legislative discussion that preceded passage of PL 90-130 reflected two factors converging to produce the new policy: demands for gender equity and expediency. The growing climate of concern about sex discrimination, the model set by the president's campaign to appoint more women to high-level positions, and the increasing activism of women themselves were manifest in the remarks of Congresswomen Green and Mink and representatives of DACOWITS and the American Nurses Association. Congressman Richard S. Schweiker (R.-Pa.), who had anticipated the DOD with his own bill, stressed the need to eliminate "one more pattern of discrimination against women in American government and national life'' and linked his support of the bill with his advocacy of an equal rights amendment to the Constitution.[32]

Congressional debate also tied the bill to the exigencies of the war in Vietnam. Like the Marshall Commission, some legislators argued that the more women recruited, ''the smaller the number [of men] that will have to be drafted.'' Of pressing importance was recruitment of nurses ''because of our commitment in Vietnam.'' Because all nurses were officers, removal of the gender inequities in promotion and retirement regulations was essential to their recruitment and retention.[33]

Military officials and most congressmen who spoke in favor of the measure went to great lengths to diminish its potential to transform women's place in the military. Again and again they insisted, ''This is not a promotion bill.'' It was not designed to quicken promotions of women, and although the bill made possible the elevation of women to the rank of general or admiral, the DOD would not predict when, if ever, that would occur. Congressmen and spokesmen for Defense also were quick to acknowledge that ''there cannot be complete equality between men and women in the matter of military careers'' and to promise that restrictions protecting women from dangerous situations would remain.[34]

The potential of PL 90-130 to transform women's military service lay in a future anticipated by few if any of the measure's supporters. Yet it was of great importance to many female officers and to DACOWITS and its allies, who fought for it for seven years. And Johnson made the most of it. He invited more than 100 women and men to the White House for the signing ceremony, where he paid tribute to all servicewomen and awarded medals to two Vietnam nurses. Asserting that ''we have come here . . . to strike another blow for women's rights,'' Johnson capitalized on the opportunity to gain public attention and to identify his administration with women's aspirations.[35]

Jury Service

The administration's civil rights program opened an avenue for women to attack sex discrimination in jury service. In 1957 women had won the right to serve on federal juries, but procedures for juror selection continued to place them at a disadvantage. Moreover, women continued to face differential treatment in jury selection in state courts. In 1966 only twenty-two states made no gender distinctions; three excluded women entirely from jury service, and twenty-five others established procedures or exemptions that applied to women only. That discrimination had been recognized in 1963 by the President's Commission on the Status of Women, which recommended "equal jury service without distinction as to sex."[36]

The demand for equity in jury service was taken up by the National Federation of Business and Professional Women, the Women's International League for Peace and Freedom, state commissions on the status of women, and other women's organizations as well as the American Civil Liberties Union. Following the precedent set in the area of employment discrimination, advocates of equity in jury selection seized the opportunity to attach women's rights to civil rights legislation when the administration sent to Congress an omnibus civil rights bill in April 1966. Dealing primarily with racial discrimination in housing and other areas, the draft bill included a provision that no person be denied the right to serve on federal or state juries on account of sex.[37]

To women's advocates, however, the bill did not go far enough. It was necessary, they insisted, to go beyond a simple ban on sex discrimination and to eliminate all forms of gender distinctions in juror selection procedures, especially those allowing women to refuse just because they were women. Their pleas feel on deaf ears. Testifying on the bill before a House Judiciary subcommittee, Attorney General Nicholas Katzenbach defended the position that states should have the option of permitting women to claim exemptions from jury service solely on the basis of sex. The rebuff galvanized congresswomen to act as a group and to cross party lines. Republican senator Margaret Chase Smith, along with three Republican congresswomen and Democrats Griffiths, Mink, and Julia Butler Hansen (Wash.), expressed their displeasure and urged Johnson to support an amendment banning any distinctions on the basis of sex.[38]

Taking the matter into their own hands, congresswomen Griffiths and Florence P. Dwyer (R.-N.J.) introduced an amendment that would eliminate the special exemptions for women in state jury service. As was typical during debates about women's issues in the 1960s, congressmen could not let the occasion pass without resort to humor. While expressing support for the amendment, Emanuel Celler (D.-N.Y.) recited a limerick about a man whose "wife likes to roam" and commiserated with the "male constituent, who expects a hot meal on the table when he returns from work." To Sen. Maurine Neuberger (D.-Oreg.), Celler's efforts at merriment demonstrated that "women have to stand up and defend their rights as the men would never think of doing it on their own." She also noted that the jokes were "an attempt to cover up their self-consciousness about the inequities." After they had had their laugh, House members passed the amendment, but the entire civil rights bill, with its controversial open-housing provisions, was filibustered to death in the Senate.[39]

Nevertheless, the advocates of gender equity had made their point. When the administration resubmitted its civil rights bill in 1967, it included a ban on jury-service exemptions based solely on sex. Under pressure from Sen. Sam Ervin (D.-N.C.) to allow states a general exemption for mothers and housewives, Attorney General Ramsey Clark insisted on women's "equal right to jury service."[40]

After congressional leaders split the administration draft into separate bills, reform in state juror selection died in the Senate, but women achieved a partial victory when the Senate passed a measure for federal jury reform. The bill's most important provision eliminated the traditional practice whereby leading citizens—usually white, elite men—drew up federal juror lists, whose members tended also to be white, privileged men. The new bill expressly forbade exclusion on the basis of race, color, religion, sex, national origin, or economic status and mandated the creation of juror lists by random selection from a representative cross-section of the community. House passage of the bill in 1968 ensured women equal access to federal jury service, but the gender distinctions in procedures for state juror selection remained until a Supreme Court decision in 1975.[41]

Family Planning and Birth Control

The administration's new family planning policies differed from other advances for women in that the measures were not informed by a concern for women's rights, and the initiatives did not arise from feminist pressure. Yet governmental endorsement of birth control was an advance of particular importance to poor women, and it helped create a more favorable climate for feminists who would soon seize the issue and leave the administration behind, demanding even greater freedom for women to control their reproductive lives.

Moreover, a role for the federal government in family planning represented a sharp break with the past. Queried in 1959 about promoting birth control abroad through economic aid programs, President Eisenhower's response was a blunt no: "I cannot imagine anything more emphatically a subject that is not a proper political or governmental activity." Less than seven years later, President Johnson insisted that every family "have access to information and services that will allow freedom to choose the number and spacing of their children." When he left office, the federal government was firmly committed to promoting birth control and backing the commitment with increased expenditures for research and the provision of services.[42]

Before the shift in federal policy, a number of constituencies had been urging greater public support of family planning services, which at that time depended on decisions made by public health services in individual states. In 1959 the American Public Health Association defined birth control as an essential foundation for the solution of major social problems; in 1962 the National Urban League deemed it the right of every family to "know about family planning, birth control and the various approved methods." The 1963 report of the President's Commission on the Status of Women also mentioned birth control, endorsing instructions in family planning in public schools, health, and welfare agencies. Even the PCSW, however, did not define access to birth control as a woman's right, connecting it instead to the solution of social problems and the need for all women to "develop moral values" and to "make wise decisions."[43]

The president's interest in the issue of birth control developed primarily from concerns about the impact of global overpopulation on international stability and from his determination to defuse racial unrest and eradicate poverty at home. International affairs formed the context for Johnson's first public statement, when he promised in his 1965 State of the Union message to "seek new ways . . . to help deal with the explosion of world population and the growing scarcity of resources." As the Agency for International Development began to fund family planning programs abroad, Johnson continued to reiterate the importance of American assistance to nations in "the grim race between food supplies and population."[44]

Presidential aides were relieved when no significant controversy greeted Johnson's first public reference to population control, but several were wary about going much further. Special Assistant Horace Busby, for example, advised against a message from the First Lady to the Planned Parenthood Federation of America that might signal the administration's interest in promoting family planning in the United States. "Some of the more sensitive Church people," Busby warned, "would misconstrue such a telegram as the signal for a family crusade, Eleanor Roosevelt style." Another White House aide, Jack Valenti, cautioned against a presidential meeting with

John D. Rockefeller III, one of birth control's most prominent advocates. In a move reflecting Valenti's judgment that birth control was "not a matter that the President wants to visibly [sic] touch at this time," Rockefeller was shunted off to McGeorge Bundy.[45]

Other officials urged full speed ahead. Noting that presidential statements had "produced little controversial commotion," Bill Moyers began to gather officials from interested agencies to plan population initiatives for the administration's 1966 legislative program. Moyers's efforts gained momentum from recommendations of the 1965 White House Conference on Health, which for the first time held a panel on family planning. Congress, too, entered the birth control debate, when in June 1965 Sen. Ernest Gruening (D.-Alaska) persuaded a Senate subcommittee to hold hearings on the subject. Testimony and public discussion surrounding the hearings portrayed birth control as a solution to poverty, illegitimacy, and racial unrest.[46]

Pressures at the grass-roots level came from community-action agencies seeking funds from the Office of Economic Opportunity to provide family planning services. Corpus Christi, Texas, secured the first Community Action Program (CAP) grant for family planning, and by the end of 1965 CAP had allocated $3 million to community-action agencies to promote birth control. In 1968, 151 family planning projects operated with CAP funding. More than any other factor, the potential of birth control as a weapon in the war against poverty created the about-face in federal policy.[47]

The administration worked carefully to defuse two particular sources of opposition. White House aides made sure that Catholic leaders participated in official gatherings on family planning and cultivated sympathetic Catholic leaders. Federally supported family programs operated under the mandate that no individual would receive contraceptive services "inconsistent with his or her moral, philosophical, or religious beliefs." Federal guidelines forbade "coercion or compulsion" and proscribed local agencies from requiring that individuals use contraceptive services as a condition for their participation in any other assistance programs.[48]

Such guarantees sought to disarm opposition from African Americans as well as from Catholics. Officials seized upon birth control as one of the solutions to black poverty and racial turmoil, but they were well aware that black nationalists and other African Americans equated birth control with genocide. Thus, family planning advocates pointed to research demonstrating black preferences for smaller families and, following the position of the National Urban League, characterized the failure to make contraceptive services available to poor black families as a form of discrimination that denied "welfare recipients one of the principle means of family health and progress utilized by more affluent couples."[49]

Johnson's advocacy of family planning was recognized in 1966 when he received the first Margaret Sanger Award in World Leadership, named for the nation's pioneer in birth control. By 1969 the federal government was distributing $30 million for birth control through Health, Education and Welfare (HEW), CAP, the Public Health Service, and Aid to Families with Dependent Children, which had a new congressional mandate to offer family planning services to welfare recipients. In 1968 Johnson created the Center for Population Studies and Human Reproduction in the National Institutes of Health. Later that year, responding to pleas from John D. Rockefeller III, Mary Lasker, and other advocates—and over the objections of some aides who predicted "potential political booby traps"—he appointed a President's Committee on Population and Family Planning.[50]

Johnson's appointments to the committee and its subsequent report maintained the separation of birth control from women's rights. Co-chaired by HEW secretary Wilbur J. Cohen and John D. Rockefeller III, the eighteen-member committee included just two women, and they were known as family planning experts, not as champions of women's interests. The committee's report, received by Johnson in a public ceremony in January 1969, noted that family planning services were now available to one million poor women but that an additional five million continued to lack access. Urging greater federal efforts, the report used language such as "freedom of choice" and "the full right to choose," phrases that were becoming bywords of the feminist movement. But the committee's rationale for this "basic human right" lay in population control and the elimination of poverty, not in the welfare of women as women.[51]

Feminists soon claimed reproductive freedom in their own terms and rapidly left the administration behind. In addition to promoting material gains for poor women, Johnson's initiatives placed the imprimatur of the federal government on birth control and helped to legitimize reproductive rights as an issue for the burgeoning feminist movement. In November 1967 the National Organization for Women adopted a "Bill of Rights for Women" demanding not only "widespread sex education and provision of birth control information and contraceptives" but also repeal of "all laws penalizing abortion."[52]

Soon those issues were taken up by the Citizens' Advisory Council on the Status of Women, the body that Johnson himself had nurtured and whose members he had appointed. In April 1968 two council task forces examined the abortion issue. Mirroring the administration's focus on birth control as a weapon against poverty but going beyond the administration in pointing to "archaic abortion laws" as a denial of "women's rights," the Task Force on Health and Welfare urged that family planning services and legal abortion be made available "under the same conditions to all women regardless of economic status." Similarly, the Task Force on Family Law and Policy insisted that "the right of a woman to determine her own reproductive life is a human right" and advocated repeal of laws declaring abortion a criminal offense.[53]

The council, composed of private citizens, endorsed these recommendations, but the cabinet and agency heads who constituted the Interdepartmental Committee on the Status of Women (ICSW) approached the proposals gingerly. The ICSW used the occasion of its 1968 report to highlight the Johnson administration's advances on behalf of women. The report appended the task force recommendations and noted their endorsement by the council but refrained from supporting decriminalization of abortion. Terming "controversial" some of the task force's recommendations, the ICSW instead suggested that these issues be given "widest possible visibility and serious consideration."[54]

Poverty and Welfare

The Johnson administration's dissociation of birth control with women's rights and expanding opportunities for women found a parallel in its approach to welfare policy even though women constituted a majority of recipients in the nation's major welfare program, Aid to Families with Dependent Children (AFDC). In fact, women were neglected throughout the administration's war on poverty, which was aimed primarily at alleviating poverty among men. When administration officials did include women in antipoverty programs, it was to enlist more privileged women as volunteers in the war on poverty, an approach compatible with middle-class women's historic involvement in helping the disadvantaged. Moreover, the major change in federal welfare policy, the social security amendments of 1967, represented an actual setback for poor women though one accepted only reluctantly by the administration.

Instead of viewing sex discrimination measures and other policies as efforts to improve women's opportunities as independent individuals operating in the public sphere, architects of the war on poverty persistently looked upon poor women as ''dependents,'' whose problems stemmed from the lack of a male breadwinner or from their male relatives' inadequate income-earning opportunities. Growing in part from concerns about crime, juvenile delinquency, and racial unrest, the war on poverty was conceived to enable the poor to achieve ''full responsibility and manhood.'' This male-orientation of the war on poverty was apparent in the administration's Economic Opportunity bill proposed in early 1964. One of its key features was the Job Corps, designed to help poor young men become ''primary breadearners'' through employment training programs in urban residential centers.[55]

The Job Corps proposal immediately ran into trouble with Edith Green, a member of the House Committee on Education and Labor whose support was critical to passage of the antipoverty program. Under questioning by Green, administration officials were hard-pressed to explain the contradiction between Johnson's efforts to expand women's opportunities in public life and the exclusively male focus of the Job Corps proposal. Thus Green was able to obtain an informal understanding that women would be included, and the administration quickly gathered a task force to plan a women's Job Corps. Nonetheless, Green, Women's Bureau Director Mary Keyserling, and other critics protested that the first-year budget allotted only one-sixth of the places for women, whose unemployment in the sixteen-to-twenty-one-year age group was higher than that of men in a comparable age group.[56]

At first, women did not achieve even that one-sixth allotment, and Green noted the disparity in 1966, when 1,518 women were enrolled in Job Corps centers in contrast to more than 18,000 men. The numbers of women gradually increased, but by 1968 women constituted less than 30 percent of enrollments, and only 18 of the 109 Job Corps centers were serving women.[57]

Although poor women continued to occupy the margins of new antipoverty programs, the president did not hesitate to exploit the potential for mobilizing support among nonpoor women for his war on poverty. As the Job Corps got under way, Lady Bird Johnson and Women's Bureau staff members encouraged the organization of Women in Community Service (WICS). Representing members of four traditional women's organizations—the National Council of Catholic Women, the National Council of Jewish Women, the National Council of Negro Women, and United Church Women—WICS took on the task of recruitment for the women's Job Corps.[58]

In 1967 the administration expanded its network of female volunteers by organizing a conference on Women in the War on Poverty and then by creating a Women's Advisory Council on Poverty. Composed of leaders of more than twenty women's organizations, including the League of Women Voters, the YWCA, the National Federation of Business and Professional Women's Clubs, and the AFL-CIO Women's National Auxiliaries, the Advisory Council provided means for the administration to influence public opinion and to marshal support for antipoverty programs. When Johnson pointed out in his remarks to the conference on Women in the War on Poverty that "long before the New Deal, the Fair Deal, and the New Frontier—the women's groups were fighting poverty in the neighborhoods and in the legislative halls," he recognized the entirely traditional nature of these activities for middle- and upper-class women.[59]

Poor women themselves fell victims to newer conceptions of gender roles when Congress altered welfare policy in the social security amendments of 1967. Reflecting hostility to rapidly rising welfare rolls, spiraling federal spending, and a resulting budget deficit and manifesting a growing backlash against antipoverty programs, legislators approved a freeze on welfare payments for dependent children as well as a work requirement for mothers and fathers receiving public assistance through Aid to Families with Dependent Children. In stipulating that welfare mothers seek employment or enroll in training programs, the social security amendments imposed requirements on poor women that were increasingly seen as a right of choice for nonpoor women.[60]

The key sponsor of the welfare restrictions was Congressman Wilbur D. Mills (D.-Ark.), who chaired the House Ways and Means Committee. Before reporting the social security bill out of his committee, Mills had attached two changes affecting poor women, neither of which was aired at the committee hearings. One placed a freeze on federal AFDC funding by restricting federal payments for children under twenty-one with absent fathers to the proportion of children in each state being supported in 1967. The punitive aspect of the freeze with an implicit distinction between "deserving" and "undeserving" families was evident in that it applied in cases of illegitimacy or desertion but not in cases where the father was dead or unemployed.[61]

The second change, referred to as the Work-Incentive Program

(WIN), was intended to get welfare recipients off the rolls and into jobs. It allowed recipients to retain a portion of wages without loss of public assistance but also provided for AFDC payments to be withheld if the head of the family refused work or training, regardless of that person's responsibility for the care of small children. Mitigating the work-or-training requirement were provisions of federal assistance for states to establish job-training programs and day-care centers. In addition, the bill required the states to offer birth control information to all welfare recipients who requested it.[62]

Mills's defense of his committee's work reflected popular hostility to the growing public investment in programs for the poor and a determination to balance the federal budget. "Our committee felt the time had come when the taxpayers want us to be rough and . . . we intend to be rough in a constructive manner but we are not inhuman about it," he asserted. Privately, Mills also indicated the extent to which racism influenced legislators' views and public attitudes about the government's responsibility for welfare. In response to Johnson's appeal to abandon the welfare-freeze proposal, Mills gave an example of why it was needed. Referring to an African-American woman in his hometown, the congressman complained, "That Negro woman's now got eleven children. My proposal will stop this."[63]

Mills was able to push his own version of the social security bill through the House by obtaining a ban on any amendments from the floor. In the Senate, however, the welfare restrictions succumbed to strong opposition from administration officials, social service professionals, civil rights and religious organizations, and other liberal groups. Thus the Senate version of the social security bill eliminated the welfare freeze and protected mothers with children at home from the work requirement.[64]

Debate over the welfare restrictions revolved around deciding on the best strategies to make welfare recipients self-sufficient, whether the nation was able to provide the jobs, training, and child care necessary for economic independence, and how best to promote the well-being of children. A minor strand of the debate, however, reflected a growing feminist consciousness as well as a division among women activists. Martha Griffiths, the most ardent feminist in Congress, supported the work requirement, arguing that no adult should have the choice to work or be supported by the state; she insisted that the woman on welfare "and her children . . . would be far better off if she were educated, given work training and a job and made self-reliant."[65]

Women who opposed the work requirement implicitly challenged Griffiths's middle-class-based conception of what would constitute actual equality for women. The opponents also defined the issue in terms of women's rights, but their arguments expressed an awareness of how class differences complicated defining an appropriate equal rights strategy, and they demanded that priority be given to women's values. Presenting the position of the YWCA, for example, Dorothy Ferebee defended the principle that all women should have the right to work but argued that mothers also should have the right "to be at home, and to be dependent during certain critical child rearing years if they so decide." To impose work requirements on welfare mothers, she asserted, would discriminate against poor women, depriving them of a basic right that privileged women enjoyed. In addition, Ferebee challenged the masculine value system that placed "a higher value on work outside the home than within it." NOW also protested the work-incentive proposal, charging that it would be "punitive, undemocratic and un-American to deny welfare mothers of [sic] the *option* of choosing whether to work or stay home with their children."[66]

The most dramatic opposition to the welfare restrictions came from welfare mothers themselves, members of the newly formed, predominantly black and female National Welfare Rights Organization (NWRO). Staging a demonstration at the Senate hearings, these welfare mothers insisted that the committee hear from those people most familiar with child-rearing under the welfare system. "We know best what we want for our children," NWRO's vice-chair Beulah Sanders declared, "because we had them." Welfare mothers indicated their outrage at the work-requirement provision, called WIN by its sponsors, by giving it their own acronym, "WIP."[67]

Opponents of the welfare restrictions were able to prevail in the Senate bill, but Mills and his House associates refused to yield in the conference committee that met to reconcile the two bills. The Senate reluctantly went along with the freeze and the work requirement for welfare parents, and so did Johnson, considering perhaps that welfare restrictions were not too high a price to pay for a bill that contained his primary objective, an increase in social security benefits for the elderly. Moreover, Johnson had tried to talk Mills out of the freeze, but his ability to influence the congressman was limited by his dependence on Mills's support for a proposed income tax surcharge deemed critical to the administration's economic program.

When Johnson signed the social security amendments, he stressed the improvements in aid to the elderly, widows, orphans, and the disabled. Noting that the welfare system "today pleases no one," he criticized the "severe restrictions" imposed by Congress and pledged to implement "compassionate safeguards . . . to protect deserving mothers and needy children." In practice, welfare mothers escaped the most punitive welfare restrictions. Johnson delayed imposition of the freeze, and Congress repealed it in 1969. Moreover, because the work-training programs were consistently underfunded and because men were favored in the programs that were available, the coercive aspects of the work requirement were not applied to welfare mothers.[68]

Nonetheless, Johnson's reluctant collaboration with Congress represented a sharp break in government policy. Even though it was widely understood among officials that welfare mothers often had to seek employment to make ends meet, the original welfare program of 1935 carried the assumption that public assistance should enable mothers with children to remain at home. In all the discussion over the social security amendments, women alone defined welfare policy as a women's issue. And they participated on the margins of debate, their position ultimately defeated. Johnson's continuing inability to see poverty as at least in part a women's issue was evident in his appointment of a special commission to examine the entire welfare system: The twelve-member commission included just one woman, Anna Rosenberg Hoffman.[69]

The marginalization of women in Johnson's war on poverty reflected both the brief duration of his leadership in expanding women's opportunities and his limited conception of women's needs and interests. After the fanfare over women's appointments in 1964, Johnson's role shifted to that of responding to pressures originating elsewhere. Although he acted affirmatively on a number of policy initiatives for women, his signing of the military service bill was the only instance in which he seized the opportunity to make a public case for women's rights. The 1966 meeting of the CACSW and state commissions on women was the gathering that launched NOW and the last of these meetings that he attended. When John Macy, chairman of the Civil Service Commission and member of the PCSW, suggested that the president mark the release of the committee's 1968 report with a public event, Johnson declined the opportunity to identify himself with women's aspirations.[70]

After 1965, of course, Johnson was increasingly preoccupied with the war in Vietnam and with political strife and racial turmoil at home. Although women's demands had grown appreciably since the early 1960s, feminism had not yet developed into a compelling political force. Nevertheless, the president's abandonment of the initiative on women's issues bespoke the nature and depth of his commitment in the first place.

Johnson's leadership on women's issues was based on the perspectives of privileged women and oriented to providing opportunities for them—women such as those who were in his circle of associates. Moreover, the nascent feminist movement itself, composed primarily of white, middle-class women, was slow to shape an agenda that accounted for the different circumstances of women across class and racial lines. Thus the women who began to benefit from the policy changes of the Johnson years were largely those women already situated to take advantage of new opportunities and rights, not poor women whose gender seemed virtually irrelevant to policymakers.

The invisibility of poor women as women in the administration's poverty policies was also evident in its family planning initiatives. The president articulated the need for birth control in order to minimize poverty, not to increase women's autonomy although in this case poor women benefited considerably. Circumstances unrelated to women's gender interests also drove other advances for women in the Johnson years. Many of the antidiscrimination measures, for example, would have been inconceivable absent the legislative precedents and moral climate established by the civil rights movement, which women activists turned to their own advantage. And expansion of women's opportunities in the military was promoted in part by necessities arising from the Vietnam War.

Nonetheless, Johnson's personal and political impulses were not inconsequential to the improving climate for women's aspirations. He went out of his way first to associate himself with the policy initiatives of the Kennedy Administration and the PCSW and Equal Pay law and then continued to make his own mark by appointing women to government positions. Moreover, his support for or acquiescence in policy advances for women in the areas of employment discrimination, military service, jury selection, and birth control established a foundation for subsequent reform.

Most important, the president's initial eagerness to exploit public opportunities to identify his administration with women's issues raised expectations among women themselves. To be sure, the demands of the emerging women's movement quickly outpaced the administration's intentions. Yet that in itself further mobilized feminist activism, preparing it in the ensuing years to build upon the foundations that Johnson had played a modest part in beginning.

Notes

1. Lyndon B. Johnson, *The Vantage Point: Perspectives of the Presidency, 1963–1969* (New York: Holt, Rinehart and Winston, 1971), pp. ix, 339–40.

2. The most important studies of the Johnson administration's policies concerning women are Carl M. Brauer, ''Women Activists, Southern Conservatives, and the Prohibition of Sex Discrimination in Title VII of the 1964 Civil Rights Act,'' *Journal of Southern History* 49 (February 1983): 37–56; Cynthia Harrison, *On Account of Sex: The Politics of Women's Issues, 1945–1968* (Berkeley: University of California Press, 1988); and Patricia G. Zelman, *Women, Work, and National Policy: The Kennedy-Johnson Years* (Ann Arbor, Mich.: UMI Research Press, 1982). Leila J. Rupp and Verta Taylor, in *Survival in the Doldrums: The American Women's Rights Movement, 1945 to the 1960s* (New York: Oxford University Press, 1987), explore feminist activism leading to the resurgence of the movement. See also Jo Freeman, *The Politics of Liberation: A Case Study of an Emerging Social Movement and Its Relation to the Policy Process* (New York: David McKay, 1975).

3. Transcript, Esther Peterson Oral History Interview, November 25, 1968, by Paige Mulhollan, pt. 1, p. 26, Lyndon B. Johnson Library (hereafter cited as LBJL); Liz Carpenter, *Ruffles and Flourishes* (Garden City, N.Y.: Doubleday, 1970), p. 170; transcript, Elizabeth Carpenter Oral History Interview, December 3, 1968, by Joe B. Frantz, tape 1, LBJL; Lewis L. Gould, *Lady Bird Johnson and the Environment* (Lawrence: University Press of Kansas, 1988), pp. 18–20, 32–33.

4. Carpenter, *Ruffles and Flourishes*, pp. 5–6, 30–31; Liz and Les [Carpenter] to Senator [Lyndon Johnson], n.d., Subject File, box 100, Lyndon Baines Johnson Archives (hereafter cited as LBJA), LBJL. The letter was most probably written after Johnson's heart attack in July 1955.

5. *Public Papers of the President: Lyndon B. Johnson, 1965* (Washington, D.C.: Government Printing Office, 1966), p. 809 (hereafter cited as *Public Papers*); Liz Carpenter to Jack [Valenti], November 19, 1964, EX PR 18, White House Central Files (WHCF), LBJL.

6. Carpenter, *Ruffles and Flourishes*, pp. 35–36. Liz Carpenter's voluminous papers at the Johnson Library indicate how frequently her duties ranged beyond managing public relations concerning the Johnson's family and social life to include women's issues and other policy areas. In 1967, for example, Sargent Shriver called upon Carpenter to work with the Women's Advisory Council on Poverty (Sargent Shriver to Elizabeth Carpenter, September 27, 1967, Carpenter's Alpha File, box 106, White House Social Files [WHSF], LBJL).

7. See, for example, Emily George, *Martha W. Griffiths* (Washington, D.C.: University Press of America, 1982); Patsy S. Mink to John Bailey, July 26, 1965, box 6, Martha Griffiths Papers, Bentley Historical Library (BHL), University of Michigan, Ann Arbor.

8. Memorandum from Henry H. Wilson, Jr., to John Macy, April 12, 1967, "Griffiths," box 25, Henry H. Wilson, Jr., Office Files, LBJL; memo from Robert E. Kintner to Henry Wilson, March 27, 1967, "9/13/66–5/10/67," FG 655, WHCF, LBJL. The tendency of some administration aides to dismiss women's concerns was also evident in their treatment of feminist organizations. See, for example, the comment of Harry McPherson, "These women are 'inconsolable'—nothing you can say will satisfy them," on a memo from Marvin Watson to Harry McPherson, September 25, 1967, box 58, HU 3, WHCF, LBJL.

9. Zelman, Women, Work, and National Policy, pp. 37, 41–43.

10. Gould, Lady Bird Johnson and the Environment, pp. 78–80; Clarence G. Lasby, "The War on Disease," in The Johnson Years, Volume Two: Vietnam, the Environment, and Science, ed. Robert A. Divine (Lawrence: University Press of Kansas, 1987), pp. 186–91, 197–210.

11. Transcript, Peterson Oral History Interview, November 25, 1968, pt. 1, p. 12.

12. Robert Dallek, Lone Star Rising: Lyndon Johnson and His Times (New York: Oxford University Press, 1991), p. 189.

13. Joseph A. Califano, Jr., The Triumph & Tragedy of Lyndon Johnson: The White House Years (New York: Simon and Schuster, 1991), pp. 169–70.

14. Ibid., p. 16.

15. Ibid., p. 17. Marguerite Rawalt attributed the quote to Johnson; see Judith Paterson, Be Somebody: A Biography of Marguerite Rawalt (Austin, Tex.: Eakin Press, 1986), p. 133. Johnson used a similar quote in making awards to female federal employees; see Public Papers, 1963–1964, p. 330.

16. Harrison, On Account of Sex, provides the most complete account of the President's Commission on the Status of Women (PCSW) and its relationship to the growing feminist movement.

17. Harrison, On Account of Sex, pp. 182–83.

18. Ibid., pp. 89–105; Zelman, Women, Work, and National Policy, pp. 23–38; Peterson Oral History Interview, pt. 1, pp. 16, 27; Esther Peterson to Jack Valenti, June 3, 1964, Horace Busby Office Files, box 43, LBJL.

19. Public Papers, 1963–1964, pp. 767–68; Harrison, On Account of Sex, pp. 173–74; Public Papers, 1965, pp. 807–9; Public Papers, 1966, pp. 657–60.

20. Harrison, On Account of Sex, pp. 174–75; Zelman, Women, Work, and National Policy, pp. 41–48; Public Papers, 1963–1964, pp. 150, 204, 208, 211, 242, 257, 289, 298, 305, 398, 619; New York Times, April 1, 1964, p. 25.

21. Public Papers, 1965, p. 562; press release on Task Force on Federal Programs for Career Advancement, May 11, 1966, "Task Force/Career Advancement," FG 600, WHCF, LBJL.

22. Zelman, Women, Work, and National Policy, pp. 52–53; Harrison, On Account of Sex, p. 174. Letter, NOW to the president, November 11, 1966, and October 27, 1967, box 58, HU 3, WHCF, LBJL. Esther Peterson noted the missed opportunities to appoint women to federal judgeships (transcript, Peterson Oral History Interview, November 25, 1968, p. 30).

23. Zelman, Women, Work, and National Policy, pp. 57–71; Harrison, On Account of Sex, pp 176–82. Brauer, in "Women Activists," pp. 37–56, provides the most complete account of Title VII.

24. Harrison, *On Account of Sex*, pp. 192–205; letter, Harry C. McPherson, Jr., to Sara Jane Cunningham, September 28, 1966, HU 2-1, box 45, WHCF, LBJL; letter, Betty Friedan et al. to the president, March 6, 1967, EX SP2, box 85, WHCF, LBJL.

25. Memo, Harry C. McPherson, Jr., to the president, October 12, 1967, EX HU 2-1, box 44, WHCF, LBJL. See letters from women's organizations to the president in HU 3 GEN, box 58, WHCF, LBJL.

26. *Public Papers, 1963–1964*, pp. 580–82; letter, Beatrice M. Truitt to Margaret Price, May 5, 1964, box 1, Margaret Price Papers, BHL.

27. "Status of Recommendations Made at October 1965 DACOWITS Meeting," n.d., box 16, Margaret Price Papers; Maj. Gen. Jeanne Holm, *Women in the Military: An Unfinished Revolution* (Novato, Calif.: Presidio Press, 1982), pp. 122–23, 192–98.

28. *American Women: The Report of the President's Commission on the Status of Women* (New York: Charles Scribner's Sons, 1965), p. 53; Holm, *Women in the Military*, pp. 205–43.

29. *Public Papers, 1967*, p. 20.

30. *In Pursuit of Equality: Who Serves When Not All Serve? Report of the National Advisory Commission on Selective Service* (Washington, D.C.: Government Printing Office, 1967), pp. 11, 16. Composed of military officials and civilians, the commission included three women among its twenty members: Oveta Culp Hobby, WAC commander during World War II; Anna Rosenberg Hoffman, former assistant secretary of defense and longtime Johnson associate; and Jeanne L. Noble, an African-American educator. The commission also recommended that women be permitted to serve on local draft boards.

31. "Project on the Utilization of Women in the Armed Services," n.d., box 16, Margaret Price Papers; Holm, *Women in the Military*, pp. 190–203; Congress, House, Subcommittee no. 1, Committee on Armed Services, *Hearings on H.R. 16000*, 89th Cong., 2d sess., September 21, 1966, 11029–69; Jack L. Stempler to Barefoot Sanders, October 31, 1967, LE/ND9, box 140, WHCF, LBJL. The army appointed its first woman brigadier general in 1970, the air force followed in 1971, and the navy appointed its first female rear admiral (lower half) in 1972. According to Jeanne Holm, who was WAF director at the time, the suggestion to DOD for removal of the 2-percent limit came from the air force, which customarily took the lead in the utilization of women. She also contended that none of the services believed that the former limit would ever be exceeded.

32. *Hearings on H.R. 16000*, pp. 11057–61, 11063–68, Congress, House, 90th Cong., 1st sess., *Congressional Record*, May 1, 1967, p. 11303.

33. Ibid., p. 11302; Congress, House, Subcommittee no. 1, Committee on Armed Services, *Hearings on H.R. 5894*, 90th Cong., 1st sess., April 20, 1967, 382–84; *Congressional Record* May 1, 1967, p. 11302.

34. *Hearings on H.R. 16000*, pp. 11039, 11042, 11046; *Congressional Record* May 1, 1967; 11302–3; Congress, Senate, 90th Cong., 1st sess., *Congressional Record* October 26, 1967, pp. 30134–35.

35. Jack L. Stempler to Barefoot Sanders, October 31, 1967, and Barefoot Sanders to Marvin Watson, November 1, 1967, LE ND9, box 140, WHCF, LBJL; invitation to signing of H.R. 5894, November 4, 1967, EX HU 3, box 58, WHCF, LBJL; press release, November 8, 1967, "Signing of

Women in Military Bill,'' box 44, Liz Carpenter's Subject Files, WHSF, LBJL; *Public Papers, 1967*, pp. 998–1000.

36. Julia Butler Hansen et al. to the president, June 14, 1966, EX LE/ HU, box 65, WHCF, LBJL.

37. Ernest Angell to the president, March 2, 1966, Milner Alexander to the president, March 18, 1966, LE/HU, box 67, WHCF, LBJL; Henry H. Wilson, Jr., to Catherine May, February 26, 1966, Barefoot Sanders to Margaret Chase Smith, April 23, 1966, EX LE/HU, box 65, WHCF, LBJL; Patterson, *Be Somebody*, pp. 161–63; Joyce Capps to Martha Griffiths, June 1, 1966, Emma C. McGall to Martha Griffiths, August 5, 1966, Griffiths Papers, box 79.

38. Congress, House, Subcommittee no. 5, Committee on the Judiciary, *Civil Rights: Hearings on H.R. 14765 and Related Bills*, 89th Cong., 2d sess., May 4–5, 10–12, 17–19, 24–25, 1966, 1078–79, 1317; Julia Butler Hansen et al. to the president, June 14, 1966, EX LE/HU, box 65, WHCF, LBJL.

39. Congress, House, 89th Cong., 2d sess., *Congressional Record* (July 26–28, and August 1, 1966), pp. 17125–26, 17241–42, 17527, 17768–72; Maurine B. Neuberger to Martha Griffiths, August 5, 1966, box 79, Griffiths Papers.

40. Patterson, *Be Somebody*, pp. 174–75; Congress, Senate, Committee on the Judiciary, *Civil Rights Act of 1967: Hearings before the Subcommittee on Constitutional Rights*, 90th Cong., 1st sess., August 1, 8, and 9, 1967, 74, 98.

41. Congress, Senate, 90th Cong., 1st sess., *Congressional Record* December 8, 1967, p. 35634; *New York Times*, September 18, 1968, pp. 1, 94.

42. *Public Papers of the Presidents: Dwight D. Eisenhower, 1959* (Washington, D.C.: Government Printing Office, 1960), pp. 288–89; *Public Papers, Lyndon B. Johnson, 1966*, p. 95. Eisenhower himself changed his mind in 1965. See *New York Times*, June 23, 1965, pp. 1, 21.

43. *Family Planning: A Guide for State and Local Agencies* (New York: American Public Health Association, 1968), p. viii; Congress, Senate, Subcommittee on Employment, Manpower, and Poverty, Committee on Labor and Public Welfare, *Family Planning Program: Hearings on S. 2993*, 89th Cong., 2d sess., May 10, 1966, 101; *American Women*, pp. 109–10.

44. *Public Papers, 1967*, p. 469; *Public Papers, 1968*, pp. 27, 138.

45. Memo from Horace Busby to Liz Carpenter, January 7, 1965, ''Memos for Liz Carpenter,'' box 18, Horace Busby, Jr., Office Files, LBJL; John D. Rockefeller III to the president, March 3, 1965, Jack Valenti to the president, March 9, 1965, McGeorge Bundy to John D. Rockefeller III, March 16, 1965, EX WE, box 1, WHCF, LBJL.

46. Bill Moyers to Harry McPherson, July 12, 1965, Bill Moyers to Joe Califano, August 3, 1965, EX WE, box 1, WHCF, LBJL; *New York Times*, November 5, 1965, June 23, 1965, pp. 1, 21; Rickie Solinger, *Wake Up Little Susie: Single Pregnancy and Race before Roe v. Wade* (New York: Routledge, 1992), pp. 206–11.

47. Harold L. Shappard, *Effects of Family Planning on Poverty in the United States* (Kalamazoo, Mich.: W. E. Upjohn Institute for Employment Research, 1967), pp. 25–26; Elinor Langer, ''Birth Control: U.S. Programs Off to Slow Start,'' *Science* 156 (May 1967): 765; Office of Economic Oppor-

tunity, *Conference Report on Family Planning* (Washington, D.C.: Government Printing Office, 1968), pp. 2, 4.

48. *Family Planning Program: Hearings on S. 2993*, pp. 3, 6, 18–19; Harry C. McPherson, Jr., to Bill Moyers, January 29, 1966; Joe Califano to the president, November 15, 1966; press release from the Office of Economic Opportunity, "Statement by Sargent Shriver on Family Planning Programs," November 15, 1966; Douglas Cater to the president, November 29, 1966, EX WE, box 1, WHCF, LBJL.

49. Frederick S. Jaffe to Harry McPherson, Jr., October 4, 1965, "Task Force/Population and Family Planning," box 366, FG 600, WHCF, LBJL; *Family Planning Program: Hearings on S. 2993*, pp. 100–103.

50. Califano, *Triumph & Tragedy*, pp. 154–56; Mary Lasker to the president, November 8, 1967, Charles L. Schultz to Mr. Califano, June 10, 1967, Joe Califano to the president, July 12, 1967, EX WE, box 2, WHCF, LBJL.

51. *Population and Family Planning: Report of the President's Committee on Population and Family Planning* (Washington, D.C.: U.S. Department of Health, Education and Welfare, November 1968), pp. 1, 2, 14, 43.

52. Press release, National Organization for Women, November 20, 1967, Griffiths Papers.

53. Report of the Task Force on Health and Welfare to the Citizens Advisory Council on the Status of Women, *Women and Their Families in Our Rapidly Changing Society* (Washington, D.C.: Government Printing Office, 1968), p. 38; *1968: Time for Action: Highlights of the Fourth National Conference of Commissions on the Status of Women* (Washington, D.C.: Government Printing Office, 1969), pp. 79–80.

54. *American Women, 1963–1968: Report of the Interdepartmental Committee on the Status of Women* (Washington, D.C.: Government Printing Office, 1968), p. 30.

55. Diana Pearce, "Welfare Is Not *for* Women: Why the War on Poverty Cannot Conquer the Feminization of Poverty," in *Women, the State, and Welfare*, ed. Linda Gordon (Madison: University of Wisconsin Press, 1990), pp. 265–79; Zelman, *Women, Work, and National Policy*, pp. 79–80.

56. Zelman, *Women, Work, and National Policy*, pp. 80–85; Ralph Dungan to Jack Valenti, May 14, 1964, EX WE, box 1, WHCF, LBJL.

57. Zelman, *Women, Work, and National Policy*, pp. 82–84; *New York Times*, March 1, 1966, p. 23; *American Women, 1963–1968*, p. 12.

58. Mrs. William Cooper to Mrs. Lyndon Johnson, January 4, 1966, Office of Economic Opportunity press release, January 23, 1966, Liz Carpenter's Alpha File, box 127, WHSF, LBJL.

59. Sargent Shriver to Elizabeth Carpenter, September 27, 1967, Carpenter's Alpha File, box 106, WHSF, LBJL; *Public Papers, 1967*, p. 514.

60. Jean Taft Douglas Bandler, "Family Issues in Social Policy: An Analysis of Social Security," (Ph.D. diss., Columbia University School of Social Work, 1975), pp. 380–98.

61. Congress, House, Committee on Ways and Means, *Social Security Amendments of 1967: Report on H.R. 12080*, 90th Cong., 2d sess., 1967.

62. Ibid.

63. Mills quoted in Califano, *Triumph & Tragedy*, pp. 245–46. See also Congress, House, 90th Cong., 1st sess., *Congressional Record* August 17, 1967, pp. 23052–54.

64. Congress, Senate, Committee on Finance, *Social Security Amendments of 1967: Hearings before the Committee on Finance on H.R. 12080,* 90th Cong., 1st sess., August 28–31 and September 11–12, 18–19, 1967, pp. 1010–14, 1236–37, 1262–63, 1374–76, 1385–86, 1500, 1794–97, 1916–18, 2027–31, 2038–45, A78–79.

65. Ibid., pp. 1811–15; Martha Griffiths to Dolores T. Owens, July 9, 1968, box 92, Griffiths Papers.

66. *Social Security Amendments of 1967: Hearings on Finance on H.R. 12080,* pp. 1502–3, 1633–34, A227–28; National Organization for Women, press release, November 20, 1967, box 92, Griffiths Papers. Other women's organizations opposing the welfare restrictions in the Senate hearings included the American Association of University Women, the American Nurses Association, the National Consumers' League, and the National Council of Negro Women. Later, the Citizens' Advisory Committee on the Status of Women also condemned the work requirement, insisting that "no aspect is more crucial than protection of the right to choice between employment and full-time homemaking by women with children in low-income families commensurate with the right to this choice by women in middle-income families." See *Women and Their Families in Our Rapidly Changing Society,* p. 2.

67. *Social Security Amendments of 1967: Hearings on H.R. 12080,* pp. 1463–73; Guida West, *The National Welfare Rights Movement: The Social Protest of Poor Women* (New York: Praeger, 1981), p. 291.

68. Daniel P. Moynihan, *The Politics of a Guaranteed Income: The Nixon Administration and the Family Assistance Plan* (New York: Vintage Books, 1973), pp. 132–33, 141–42, 357–59; Mimi Abramovitz, *Regulating the Lives of Women: Social Welfare Policy from Colonial Times to the Present* (Boston: South End Press, 1988), pp. 334–41.

69. *Public Papers, 1968,* p. 15.

70. John W. Macy, Jr., to the president, September 6, 1968, James R. Jones to Mrs. Ashton Gonella, October 7, 1968, FG 686, box 385, WHCF, LBJL.

4 | Mixing Moderation with Militancy: Lyndon Johnson and African-American Leadership

Steven F. Lawson

WHEN LYNDON JOHNSON LEFT the White House in 1969, America stood divided over his handling of affairs related to war and peace. Disturbed by the deteriorating quality of life in their cities and confounded by the intractability of combat in the swamps and jungles of Vietnam, they doubted the credibility of the president and the Great Society he had pledged to create. By the mid-1970s both the war against poverty and against the Vietnamese had ended, neither successfully, and the underlying problems of racism and foreign interventionism persisted. Over the two-and-one-half decades after Johnson stepped down from office, the racial policies of his successors ranged from "benign neglect" to outright hostility. Whatever his shortcomings, and they were many, LBJ was the last president to offer committed leadership that challenged racial injustice. The inferno of ghetto uprisings that ignited Miami and Los Angeles during the 1980s and early 1990s dramatically refocused national attention on the unfinished legacy bequeathed by the Johnson administration. Although Johnson's failures remain evident from the vantage point of today's hindsight, it is easier to see them as the result of a flawed vision of black emancipation rather than of a deliberate disengagement from civil rights concerns.

President Johnson exhibited leadership for social change that suited his background and ideology. A consummate legislator, he placed great faith in the passage of laws to obliterate racial discrimination. Having climbed his way up the electoral ladder from congressman to president, it is hardly surprising that LBJ conceived of reform in such a traditional manner. He summed up his fundamental political philosophy to the Mississippi civil rights leader Charles Evers: "If you want to change the system, get in it and make what you want to make out of it."[1] If legislation held the key to unlocking the door to racial justice, then success depended upon cultivating basic skills in lobbying and building alliances. To the pragmatic Johnson, the bottom line consisted of counting votes, for as he informed

Clarence Mitchell, the chief representative on Capitol Hill of the National Association for the Advancement of Colored People (NAACP): "Clarence, you can get anything that you have the votes to get. How many votes have you got?"[2] Johnson drew energy from the lawmaking process and never seemed to tire from participating in it. His presidential assistant Joseph Califano recalled him poring over projections of congressional roll calls after a hectic day and "devour[ing] these tally sheets like a baseball fanatic reviewing the box scores of his home team."[3]

Artful in the give-and-take of legislative horse trading, Johnson sought out black leaders who knew how to strike a bargain. His political upbringing had taught him to recruit allies who represented identifiable constituencies and could deliver votes. According to Joseph Rauh, the liberal lawyer who lined up with the president on civil rights but broke with him over the Vietnam War, "Johnson always had this idea, . . . if you deal with the right person and get him, then the issue will go away."[4] On racial matters this meant consulting the Big Six civil rights officials, A. Philip Randolph, the revered labor and protest leader, and the heads of the National Urban League, NAACP, Congress of Racial Equality (CORE), Southern Christian Leadership Conference (SCLC), and Student Nonviolent Coordinating Committee (SNCC).[5] Just as the president invited spokespersons of important interest groups to the White House to plot legislative strategy, so too did he consult the heads of national civil rights groups. "It was like bringing George Meany and Walter Reuther and four labor leaders in to talk for labor," presidential counselor Harry McPherson explained. "You had the six in to talk for the Negroes."[6]

Johnson felt comfortable negotiating with black leaders who often willingly joined him in playing by the rules of the legislative game. If the president believed that by summoning these designated representatives to the Oval Office he heard the opinions of African Americans who counted politically, the chief executive was carrying on the practice of his predecessors who listened to delegates from virtually the same groups. Johnson was astute enough to realize that he could not stage-manage the rapidly unfolding civil rights drama, however; he discerned that civil rights leaders would have to retain their independence or their credibility would be challenged by more militant blacks. Realizing that the black leaders with whom he conferred could be dismissed as "Johnson people" and thereby lose some of their effectiveness, the president encouraged those leaders he trusted to keep up the pressure on him. He reportedly told Roy

Wilkins, the executive secretary of the NAACP, "You can hit me a little bit. You can take a pot shot at me. I can understand that."[7] For the crafty Johnson, bargaining was a two-way street: Civil rights leaders would make demands on him, and he would "use them when he wanted support to push for something or 'raise a little hell.' "[8] Naturally there were limits to Johnson's tolerance of criticism, and his patience with individuals lasted as long as they shared his fundamental values and faith in working through the political system.

From the outset of his administration, the president welcomed civil rights leaders into the White House. Within two weeks after the Kennedy assassination, Johnson huddled with the NAACP's Wilkins, Whitney Young of the Urban League, Martin Luther King, Jr., of SCLC, James Farmer of CORE, and A. Philip Randolph. (There is no record of a SNCC representative meeting with Johnson during this same period.) The new chief executive was familiar to most of these leaders, having dealt with them as a senator and then as vice-president, when he directed Kennedy's program to promote equal employment opportunity. The Texan quieted any lingering doubts that African Americans had reason to worry about a southerner in the White House. Farmer remembered the president encouraging him "that whenever we had a problem in this movement or wanted to talk to him, call; the call would get through to him. . . . And it did."[9]

The NAACP's Roy Wilkins occupied the position of Johnson's number-one civil rights confidant.[10] McPherson recalled that the "president really loved Roy Wilkins," and apparently the feeling was mutual. After a particularly memorable address by Johnson in March 1965, the NAACP chief declared: "I had waited all my life to hear a President of the United States talk that way. And at that moment, I confess, I loved LBJ."[11]

Wilkins personified the kind of leader whom Johnson trusted. Like LBJ, he advocated legislative lobbying, litigation, and lining up new voters as the preferred means to achieve racial equality. Wilkins approached politics with the pragmatic toughness that Johnson appreciated. A moderate in a movement that was growing more militant throughout the 1960s, Wilkins steadfastly backed up the president in defending his domestic and foreign policy programs from attack by black dissidents. Presidential counselor George Reedy, who had been with Johnson since his Senate years, advised his boss early on to consider Wilkins as "*the* Negro leader." Reedy summed up the White House consensus in praising Wilkins for his "judgment and sense of fair play."[12]

Next to Wilkins, Johnson developed the closest ties with Whitney Young. As chair of President Kennedy's Committee on Equal Employment Opportunity, Vice-President Johnson had touched base regularly with the director of the Urban League, an organization devoted to opening up the job market to African Americans. Young, like Wilkins, regarded LBJ as a far more capable leader on civil rights than Kennedy, whom he believed was slow to exhibit the necessary "political conviction [and] guts" in confronting racial inequality.[13] The chief executive thought so highly of the Urban League official that he tried to persuade him to accept a position in his administration, an offer Young declined.[14]

Refusing a governmental appointment, Young successfully resisted the president's legendary arm-twisting by convincing Johnson that he could be of greater assistance to him from the outside. Young argued persuasively that he could better fulfill their common objectives if he remained in his "present spot, that it was a unique position and one from which I could exercise a maximum influence and control."[15] Moderate, responsible, and levelheaded, the Urban League director expressed "his total support" for LBJ and vowed to "do anything . . . to help him."[16] He meant it. When black and white liberals began abandoning the president over the Vietnam War, Young stuck by him. On a tour of Vietnam sponsored by the Urban League in mid-1966, Young took the opportunity to trumpet the administration's civil rights achievements during a period when most of the news that black GI's received from home stressed heightened racial tensions.[17]

A. Philip Randolph rounded out the triumvirate of black leaders among the Big Six whom the president most admired. The founder of the Brotherhood of Sleeping Car Porters, Randolph had merged his role as a labor leader with that of an independent champion of civil rights. A socialist and one-time radical, by 1963 the seventy-four-year-old Randolph had become the elder statesman of the movement. His "natural eloquence," advocacy of an interracial labor-liberal coalition, and sponsorship of the 1963 March on Washington gave him standing among all segments of the freedom movement. The White House respected him as a sensible and reliable leader and turned to him when it wanted to keep quarreling civil rights factions in check.[18] Having observed the national political scene since the Great Depression and organized protests against discrimination that grabbed the attention of several presidents, Randolph considered LBJ the most supportive. "President Roosevelt didn't have the contact with the Negro leaders that President Johnson has had," he recounted from firsthand experience and added: "President Truman was a man committed to civil rights, but he was not as accessible as President Johnson."[19] Together with Wilkins and Young, Randolph backed the president on such thorny issues as Vietnam, and in 1964 Johnson awarded him the Presidential Medal of Freedom.

One consequence for black leaders such as Wilkins, Young, and Randolph who identified so closely with Johnson was that the relationship narrowed the limits within which they might disagree with the White House. Those individuals who strayed too far from the acceptable boundaries risked falling out of presidential favor. The case of James Farmer is both instructive and somewhat puzzling.

The head of CORE, the interracial group that had pioneered nonviolent direct-action techniques in the postwar black freedom struggle, Farmer started out on excellent terms with Johnson. A native of Marshall, Texas, the hometown of the president's wife, he contrasted LBJ's cordiality to him with Kennedy's aloofness; in discussions with Johnson shortly after he became president, Farmer found him open, enthusiastic, and responsive. For the next year, Farmer received the flattering "Johnson treatment"—his phone calls got through and his "written communications reached him without languishing on the desks of aides."[20] Unlike Wilkins and Young, however, Farmer led a group that relied principally on confrontational demonstrations. This approach had brought CORE into conflict with the Kennedy administration over the Freedom Rides in 1961, and it eventually proved troublesome for the Johnson regime as well. With comprehensive civil rights legislation meandering its way through Congress in late 1963 and 1964, the administration emphatically wanted CORE to refrain from "staging street demonstrations which might get people's backs up." The White House wanted Farmer's organization to function instead like traditional interest groups, lobbying for legislation and trying "to coordinate its activities through the White House."[21]

Though CORE gladly joined the successful coalition behind passage of the Civil Rights Act, by late summer 1964, Farmer's congenial relationship with the president had begun to suffer. The precise reason is difficult to ascertain. Farmer attributed the rift to his unwillingness to agree to a call initiated by Wilkins in June for a civil rights moratorium on mass demonstrations until after the November presidential election. Wilkins, reflecting Johnson's thinking, feared that further agitation would fuel a white backlash and benefit the Republican nominee, Barry Goldwater, a foe of the 1964 Civil Rights Law. Farmer believed that the president was "furious" with his dissenting position and retaliated by reducing his access to the White House. "The president's political career had led him to equate disagreement with disloyalty," Farmer complained.[22]

Farmer's assessment may be correct, but it needs some qualification. Though the number of the CORE leader's recorded contacts with the president decreased after June 1964, it did not fall off significantly.[23] Of course the quality rather than the quantity of these interactions may have declined, as Farmer asserted, yet documentary evidence in the Johnson Library suggests that the situation was more complicated. Farmer refused to toe the administration's line on the moratorium, but he continued to cooperate with the White House to defuse potentially troubling confrontations. On July 30, a day after Farmer joined civil rights leaders in discussing Wilkins's suggestion for a halt to demonstrations, presidential assistant Lee White spoke with the CORE director about "how frustrating it is that those who apparently want to defeat Senator Goldwater take action that can only result in aiding him." Farmer reportedly agreed and "expressed the view that it was mighty tough to combat, but he would do his best."[24] Apparently, the CORE chief kept his word. In early August White inquired about whether the group would picket the president on his trip to Syracuse, New York, in protest of the failure of the federal government to solve the murders of three civil rights workers in Mississippi, two of whom were CORE staff members. Farmer replied that the local chapter would not embarrass Johnson and instead would quietly turn over a petition to the president's staff.[25] In late October, several weeks before the election, Farmer again assisted the administration. White House aides heard a rumor that 400 CORE members from New York City were traveling to Maryland to participate in a protest that might cause a serious disturbance. On October 22 White informed the president that "our relations with Farmer are good enough to ask him for his cooperation in seeing to it that this not be done at this time." Several days later, Farmer assured White that "the top leadership of CORE squelched the plan."[26]

The moratorium controversy by itself did not produce an irreparable breach between Johnson and Farmer, but it accentuated the widening gap between them. Given CORE's increasing militancy, Johnson never felt comfortable with Farmer again, who, in contrast to Wilkins, Young, and Randolph, did not show the kind of loyalty the president demanded. The CORE leader had been helpful, but LBJ probably did not consider him totally reliable. Farmer subsequently campaigned with the other civil rights leaders for the president's suffrage legislation in 1965 and was invited to the signing ceremony in August. Yet Johnson, who could be as petty as he was generous, tried to snub Farmer by refusing to give him one of the souvenir pens.[27]

Farmer did not fall from presidential grace by himself; the Reverend Martin Luther King, Jr., experienced an even more volatile relationship with the president. From the beginning King and Johnson never felt entirely at ease with each other, nor did they develop the personal rapport LBJ shared with Wilkins and Young. Part of the difficulty stemmed from a clash of two dominant personalities. King's close assistant, Andrew Young, believed that the chief executive and the minister had trouble communicating because the president liked to do all the talking. "Of course Dr. King was a talker himself," Young recounted, so they had trouble in establishing "a give and take kind of relationship."[28]

Yet the uneasiness between King and Johnson involved more than conflicting personalities; they differed fundamentally in their attitudes toward social reform. Johnson favored measured change produced through lawsuits and legislation. King found these methods useful, but he chose to wage his struggle through mass demonstrations and civil disobedience, tactics designed to spotlight white racism, make liberal officials in Washington uncomfortable, and force them to heed black demands. Johnson's desire to undertake reform while preserving social order collided with King's readiness for disruption through provocative nonviolent protests.[29]

Nevertheless, these tensions did not keep Johnson and King from cooperating on common objectives. They needed each other. The civil rights activist required the power of the federal government to shatter entrenched white opposition to equality, and the president used King's demonstrations to rally support for his legislative plans. In 1964 the Atlanta minister, unlike Farmer, did not attack Wilkins's suggestion for a moratorium during the presidential campaign, and he supported the Johnson-orchestrated compromise at the Democratic nominating convention that left civil rights forces from Mississippi angry with the administration.[30] The 1965 protests in Selma, Alabama, climaxed friendly relations between the two as King took a respite from conducting voting-rights demonstrations to confer twice with the president and otherwise kept in touch by telephone.[31] Johnson's performance in securing passage of the Voting Rights Act deeply pleased King, and one of his associates told presidential assistant Richard Goodwin that the minister "now felt the Negro cause was actually going to succeed."[32]

During this period conflicts arose, but generally they were settled easily. Louis Martin recalled that there were "protocol" problems in scheduling appointments with the president because King wanted to see him alone, without Wilkins and Young, whom he believed took advantage of his international prestige.[33] After King won the Nobel Peace Prize in 1964, the president had to decide whether to attend a November banquet in his honor; LBJ chose against it because, as Attorney General Nicholas Katzenbach pointed out, King and Wilkins were "locked in a power struggle" and Johnson's attendance would "elevate King over" his close NAACP friend.[34] Instead the president met alone with the Nobel laureate the following month. By mid-1965 the scheduling problems Martin referred to had been resolved. Lee White reported to Johnson with some satisfaction that King had learned not to announce unilaterally "that he is coming to meet the President," behavior that in the past had disturbed the publicity-conscious and secrecy-minded White House.[35]

The uneasy alliance fractured as Dr. King increasingly shifted his attention from traditional civil rights matters and voiced opposition to the president's escalation of the war in Vietnam and the consequent weakening of his domestic Great Society programs. In August 1965 he urged President Johnson to halt the bombing of North Vietnam and negotiate with the Viet Cong. He also began to focus on the economic misery in northern urban ghettos inflamed by rioting, a concern that led him to link American militarism abroad with materialism and racism at home. Privately Johnson cautioned the minister, but according to King he "never asked me not to speak out on Vietnam."[36] Over the next year King continued to criticize the president's Southeast Asian policy, but he refrained from becoming an active leader in the antiwar movement until 1967; by then the two leaders had ceased meeting with each other. They had not spoken face-to-face for about a year, and Andrew Young remembered that the last time they talked over the phone had been around Thanksgiving 1966 when King called LBJ to denounce the war. Actually the initiative for curtailing the relationship came from King, not Johnson; the disgruntled civil rights leader declined several invitations to come to the White House.[37]

Although the president appeared willing to keep open the lines of communication, he grew increasingly furious with King. Throughout the 1960s the FBI had been investigating King's possible connections with Communists, and the bureau's director, J. Edgar

Hoover, eagerly furnished the president with reports reinforcing his belief that "King might be subject to communist manipulation."[38] In April 1967, after King delivered a blistering attack against the United States as "the greatest purveyor of violence in the world today," the administration became hysterical: John P. Roche, the Brandeis University professor and White House intellectual-in-residence, privately informed Johnson that King "has thrown in with the commies" and characterized him as "inordinately ambitious and quite stupid."[39] Yet Johnson was less concerned about King's alleged role as a subversive or a sexual pervert (Hoover's eavesdroppers had picked up "evidence" of King's extramarital affairs) than about traditional political considerations. The president fretted, Joseph Califano has explained, that the minister's impassioned antiwar broadsides "would provoke a conservative backlash, not just against King but against the Great Society."[40]

To reduce the negative fallout from King's assaults, LBJ looked to the black leaders he trusted. The White House delighted in the efforts Wilkins and Whitney Young made, albeit unsuccessfully, to convince King to put aside the antiwar issue for the greater good of the civil rights movement. The president dispatched Young to South Vietnam as part of a team of observers to monitor national elections, and his glowing reports served to counter King's criticism and to drive a wedge between the minister and the other moderate civil rights leaders.[41]

Relations deteriorated sharply over the Vietnam War, and King's growing radicalism on domestic issues added to the cleavage. As David Garrow and Adam Fairclough have shown, after the ghetto uprisings in 1965 the civil rights leader increasingly moved to the Left in analyzing the connection between capitalism and racism. A putative democratic socialist, Dr. King condemned the Johnson administration for retreating on the battlefields of the war on poverty and urged the chief executive to establish a massive jobs program providing employment for everyone, black and white, who needed it. On this issue, unlike Vietnam, the White House could not argue that King had no business meddling. LBJ's response was not to take any new departures but to try to line up King behind the administration's programs, believing "that King should work harder to get Congress to pass his legislation already on Capitol Hill."[42] In this instance as in others, the president preferred to deal with King on the terrain he knew best—the legislative arena. Growing more radical and disillusioned with the political mainstream, however, the Atlanta minister found little common ground to occupy with his former presidential ally.

Moving in the opposite trajectory from King and Farmer, Bayard Rustin saw his welcome improve at the White House. A former Communist and a pacifist who had served a prison term for failing to comply with the draft during World War II, Rustin helped pioneer CORE-initiated freedom bus rides in 1947. During the 1950s he acted as an adviser to King and helped him organize the SCLC. His radical background alone would have made him suspect to the federal government, but his homosexuality compounded the distrust. Nevertheless, by 1963 Rustin has become a close associate of A. Philip Randolph, some of whose esteem rubbed off on him. He ran a labor institute bearing Randolph's name, and Rustin served as a useful liaison between King, with whom he maintained good relations, and the administration. Over Johnson's five-year tenure, Rustin received an increasingly more favorable reception from White House officials as he shared their positions on important matters concerning civil rights strategies and especially the Vietnam War. Although he faulted the administration for limiting spending on its poverty program, the value of Rustin's political stock with the president generally rose as King's dropped.[43]

Least acceptable of the Big Six were the leaders of SNCC, who reflected precisely the kind of style that differed most from Johnson's. Showing an antielitist bent, they expected leadership to emerge from local communities and decisions to grow out of group-centered deliberations. Given SNCC's orientation, neither John Lewis, its chairman, nor James Forman, its executive secretary, could have developed the same relationship with Johnson as did Wilkins, Young, or even King.

More than any other organization in the early 1960s, SNCC mobilized young people to challenge racial discrimination in innovative and exciting ways. Its militancy was well known, but as long as the group adhered to a nonviolent, interracial vision of achieving equality the Johnson administration tolerated its iconoclasm. The president, however, remained skeptical of SNCC's moralistic and generally uncompromising posture, which did not conform to his brand of pragmatic politics. The 1964 bargain related to the seating of Mississippi Freedom Democratic Party (MFDP) delegates, which had been hammered out in the time-honored manner of national conventions, satisfied Johnson's election agenda but left SNCC convinced of the duplicity of white liberals and the federal government.[44]

The shaky peaceful coexistence broke down by mid-1966.

SNCC took an early lead in denouncing United States involvement in Vietnam, questioning whether young men should cooperate with the draft. Encouraging civil rights work as an alternative to military service, in January 1966 the organization berated the United States for murdering the Vietnamese people by "pursuing an aggressive policy in violation of international law."[45] Privately, Vice-President Hubert Humphrey spoke for the administration in condemning SNCC's statements as "the most outrageous attacks on the President." He also echoed the dismay expressed by Wilkins and Young, Johnson's staunchest defenders, that the White House treated SNCC "with a sort of benevolent equality on a par with the NAACP and Urban League."[46] The tenuous link between SNCC and the administration finally severed in May when the group withdrew from the planned White House Conference on Civil Rights, indicating that it considered white liberals as no better than southern white racists.[47]

SNCC's position of noncooperation reflected significant internal changes within the organization. Stokely Carmichael replaced John Lewis, and his election signaled the transformation of SNCC from an interracial group supporting the tactic of nonviolence into one dedicated to black nationalism and retaliatory self-defense. Lewis, an admirer of Dr. King, had cooperated in planning the White House Conference scheduled for June; and though Johnson administration officials viewed him as a radical, he was the type of "restrained" leader they could deal with. Under Lewis, McPherson remarked, "SNCC was still an organization that you could invite to the White House without getting a hand grenade thrown through the window before they came."[48] In contrast, Carmichael led SNCC along an all-black course and delivered incendiary speeches with menacing antiwhite overtones. He also offended the White House in a personal way: SNCC prepared to lead antiwar demonstrations in Washington on August 6, which coincided with the wedding of the president's daughter Luci. Johnson's civil rights allies rushed to denounce SNCC's plan as "in poor taste" and "politically untenable." In turn, SNCC dismissed their complaint and called them "messengers . . . for the Boss Man."[49] Subsequently, in a September 1966 recommendation concerning a meeting between civil rights leaders and the president, McPherson advised: "There is no longer any need to have SNCC . . . represented."[50]

Over the next few years, the administration entered into an adversarial relationship with SNCC. As the group shifted its sights from the rural South to the urban battlefields of the North, Carmichael and his successor, Hubert "Rap" Brown, became targets of government surveillance, especially through the FBI's provocative counterintelligence program (COINTELPRO).[51] Carmichael's black-power rhetoric appeared to federal officials to fuel violent uprisings in black ghettos, and his unauthorized travels to Cuba, North Vietnam, and China in 1967 aroused their anticommunist suspicions.[52]

Johnson and his White House advisers strongly encouraged the Justice Department to prosecute Carmichael for inciting riots. The usually sensible McPherson did not much care whether the SNCC leader constituted a "clear and present danger" or that his inflammatory statements might have been protected under the First Amendment; civil liberties aside, he wanted Carmichael behind bars "because he was helping to destroy the consensus on which progress depended."[53] As violence rocked black ghettos in summer 1967, concern with agitators such as Carmichael surfaced within Johnson's cabinet. Secretary of State Dean Rusk asked, "Don't we have any remedy for these people?" and Secretary of Health, Education and Welfare John Gardner queried, "Surely there must be a limit to what a man can say?"[54]

Despite these views, which Johnson shared, the federal government did not indict Carmichael; the president reluctantly accepted the counterarguments presented by Attorney General Ramsey Clark. A fellow Texan whose father had sat on the United States Supreme Court, Clark resisted the intense political pressure to make an example of Carmichael and display the administration's toughness in fighting crime. After a thorough investigation of Carmichael's statements, Clark concluded that the government lacked the necessary evidence to "support the prosecution under an interpretation of the law that was constitutionally valid." Nor could the Justice Department dig up any other statute that might produce a conviction of Carmichael based on his trips to Communist countries that were off limits to American citizens.[55] Johnson abided by the attorney general's decision despite the conservative political attacks it generated. Nevertheless, privately he took a dim view of Clark's constitutional caution; the president confided to Califano that if he "had ever known that [Clark] didn't measure up to his daddy, I'd never have made him Attorney General."[56]

Even if Carmichael had been less outspoken in his criticism of administration policies, the White House would have clashed with SNCC over its efforts to develop grass-roots leadership that challenged the political establishment. The controversy over the Child Development Group of Mississippi (CDGM) provides a case in point. An outgrowth of the movement to organize disfranchised and impoverished blacks in the Delta State, the CDGM became a Head Start program funded through Johnson's War on Poverty agency, the Office of Economic Opportunity (OEO). Veterans of SNCC and the MFDP saw in the preschool education project a means of building upon the political organizing drives that years of voter registration had begun. They hoped to expand the notion of political participation to include control over decisions affecting the daily lives of poor people customarily neglected by the electoral system. Following intensive recruitment, by the end of summer 1965 CDGM operated over eighty centers serving nearly 6,000 children in forty towns throughout the state.[57]

Recognized for its innovative approaches to education, the CDGM nonetheless ran afoul of powerful Mississippi politicos. United States senator John Stennis, the chair of the Appropriations Committee and a Johnson supporter on Vietnam, frowned upon the close involvement in the Head Start program of civil rights activists, particularly those militants associated with SNCC. He prevailed upon Sargent Shriver, the OEO director, to launch an investigation into charges that CDGM had managed its projects in a fiscally irresponsible manner and had failed to include a sufficient number of whites in its ranks. In effect, Stennis claimed that CDGM was masquerading as a black nationalist front. White House staff member McPherson became convinced that CDGM consisted of "dedicated and sensible people" who clearly performed good deeds, but he was concerned about the unfavorable political repercussions that would occur if the administration did not assuage Stennis.[58]

As it had done at the 1964 Democratic National Convention with respect to seating the MFDP, the administration fashioned a compromise that preserved the CDGM but in weakened form. After first cutting off its funds for violating OEO management procedures, in late 1966 Shriver relented and agreed to funnel poverty money to a reformed CDGM, which would share supervision over Head Start programs with a rival group of moderate whites and blacks.[59] Rather than endanger the rest of the War on Poverty from budget slashing by Stennis's Appropriations Committee, the White House chose to reach an accommodation that safeguarded measured economic and political change in Mississippi. While keeping the radically inclined CDGM alive, the administration endorsed a more conventional brand of interracial leadership, one more in tune with its version of political pragmatism.

This entire episode has received too little notice from historians. By examining the administration's handling of the problem, scholars can open up new vistas on approaches the federal government used to influence the shape of the black freedom struggle in the South. Decisions reached in Washington had a profound effect upon which groups of blacks and whites would obtain vital resources, thereby influencing the course of racial advancement. The resolution of the CDGM conflict suggests that the issue involved not only considerations of race but also of class, a pattern that John Dittmer has sketched concerning the MFDP convention settlement.[60]

The CDGM resolution illustrates the Johnson administration's inclination to handle civil rights issues through regular political channels and according to traditional methods of negotiation. In contrast to seemingly unpredictable protest leaders who spelled trouble for the president, Johnson leaned more frequently on black elected officials. Shortly after the crushing defeat of Goldwater in 1964, Hobart Taylor, Jr., a black presidential adviser, pointed out a theme that would become constant during LBJ's term: the need to increase the number of minority elected officials. Taylor wanted Johnson to deemphasize his reliance on established civil rights leaders who, he asserted, were "no substitute in the long run for the development of effective political leadership in the traditional sense."[61] LBJ declined to abandon his loyal civil rights allies, but at the same time his advisers sought to achieve closer contact with elected black officials at the local level. Following passage of the 1965 Voting Rights Act the number of black officials began to swell both in the South and the North. Johnson confidant and deputy director of the Democratic National Committee, Louis Martin, urged the chief executive to "find ways and means to tie these newly elected legislators and other Negro officeholders to the President and the national party."[62]

It did not take any arm-twisting to convince Johnson to cultivate these officials. He appeared at gatherings arranged by Martin and Clifford Alexander, swapping stories with members of the audience as one elected politician to another. McPherson remembered that the president never had a better time than at these receptions; they spilled over into the White House Rose Garden and were like "a love feast every time."[63] The chief executive felt a special bond with these officials because they too had campaigned for office and exercised the skills it took to win. Moreover, they met Johnson's definition of responsibility. "Here were people," Alexander explained, "elected by other people who had to go back . . . [and] would be held accountable in a few years."[64]

We know about Johnson's feeling for black political officials in general, but the record reveals much less about his relations with specific elected leaders. In fact, much more evidence exists about the administration's interaction with national civil rights leaders than with black politicians. Part of the discrepancy stems from the circumstances: Relatively few black elected officials were serving in Washington.[65] Furthermore, it was not until late in his term that African Americans began winning important posts at the local level, most notably Carl Stokes as mayor of Cleveland, Ohio, and Richard Hatcher as mayor of Gary, Indiana. The administration took special delight in the victory of Stokes, whom one Johnson aide described as ''a great guy and an extremely valuable political property [who] represents the kind of 'black power' we need in the Democratic Party.''[66] Those observers interested in studying the complex relationship between the White House and the most influential black elected leader during this period, Adam Clayton Powell, should consult Charles V. Hamilton's judicious biography on the controversial Harlem congressman.[67] From examining this and other such relationships one can evaluate how the administration and African-American elected officials each balanced their civil rights concerns with other political interests.

One elected official who after 1966 gained increased notice from the White House was Barbara Jordan. The president took a keen interest in the Texas state senator from Houston, who later became a U.S. congresswoman, and ''was peacock proud'' of this ''role model he often claimed to have discovered.'' The archives, however, do not yield much data on Jordan that illuminate her budding leadership role; it would be helpful to investigate and identify the political qualities that brought Jordan to her fellow Texan's attention.[68]

Little information exists on the administration's dealings with female civil rights leaders. Except for Dorothy Height, the head of the National Council of Negro Women, an organization founded by Mary McLeod Bethune, a close associate of Franklin and Eleanor Roosevelt, the representatives of national civil rights organizations consulted by the White House were men. This situation clearly reflected the president's conception of the civil rights struggle as a form of interest-group politics. For him, social change came from the top down, with the president expected to provide the necessary political and moral leadership; thus conceived, the chief executive's contact with black women would be limited. Women played crucial roles within the freedom movement, but they tended to exert their greatest influence at the grass-roots level and in a manner that often did not garner extensive publicity or media attention.[69] When black women such as Barbara Jordan came up the political ladder in conventional ways, then Johnson might recognize them as leaders.

Despite an affinity with black male leaders who acted moderately and responsibly, White House officials realistically understood that they could not call the shots and control a dynamic, independent African-American freedom movement. As Bruce Miroff, a scholarly critic of the president's style of leadership acknowledged, the Johnson administration did not engage in a "conspiracy to manipulate black activists" but at most "attempted to keep on top of [constantly] changing issues."[70] This was especially true starting in summer 1964 when violent racial uprisings swept through black ghettos of the urban North. Although the administration tried to defuse potential trouble spots before they exploded and to keep the lines of communication open, presidential advisers admitted that "a lot of this is essentially uncontrollable. It will happen no matter what the federal government does."[71]

The president derived scant assistance from his chosen black leaders, who themselves had no effective control over these racial outbursts. As the black liberation struggle rejected integration and nonviolence, leaders such as Wilkins, Young, Farmer, and King became less relevant as peacekeepers. A resident of Detroit, whose streets erupted in violent fury in summer 1967, exhorted African Americans to cease being "house niggers and slaves like Whitney Young and Roy Wilkins—and to stand up and fight like Stokely Carmichael and [heavyweight boxing champ] Cassius Clay [Muhammed Ali]."[72] Recognizing this leadership vacuum, presidential aides sought to figure out how to recruit young leaders whose voices meant something to the new rebels; they failed ultimately to discover an acceptable alternative to Carmichael. Indeed the quest was impossible, and McPherson finally had to admit that the administration could not anoint any leader who would be respected by disillusioned blacks. Anyone whom the White House touched was "poison" to them, he asserted, because the "hand of the Man's authority on their shoulder was damning . . . to the real militants."[73]

The administration held few options. During the years of urban insurrections from 1964 to 1968, federal officials struggled to decipher the meaning of the turmoil in communities about which they knew almost nothing. The rage manifested in ghetto revolts came predominantly from a younger and poorer element whose experiences remained foreign both to white liberals and their older, middle-class black allies. Desiring to expand its network of informed black sources, the administration nevertheless wanted nothing to do with Carmichael or other black nationalists; White House officials refused even to consider black power advocates as legitimate leaders. Although Rap Brown and Carmichael "are trying to stir rebellion," McPherson advised the president, "they have few troops to call their own; they represent bitterness not people."[74] Along with Louis Martin, he believed that black power advocates were "not interested in dialogue," and even those who were not terrorists "seemed to be visionaries who have no real appreciation of the realities of American life save for the suffering that Negroes experience."[75]

Johnson's assistants did not think the president could talk with militants spouting black power slogans, and they hatched a plan to find out for themselves what was happening in the nation's racial battlefields. McPherson confessed that it was a "desultory way" of gathering information; however, neither the president nor his civil rights loyalists "had maintained a political apparatus in each city, through which intelligence flowed continuously to" the White House.[76] Without publicity, in 1967 presidential assistants fanned out through inner-city streets in Baltimore, Chicago, Cleveland, Detroit, Los Angeles, New York City, Oakland, Philadelphia, and other cities, spending several days in each location talking to people who reflected all shades of opinion. Much of what they heard inspired pessimism. After touring Chicago, Sherwin J. Markman reported that it "was almost like visiting a foreign country—and the ghetto Negro tends to look on us and our government as foreign."[77] Accompanied by Clifford Alexander and Louis Martin, McPherson visited Brooklyn's Bedford-Stuyvesant section and discovered just how out of touch the established leadership was; listening to an angry woman whip up an enthusiastic crowd in defense of retaliatory violence, McPherson remarked, "I would bet she knows her neighborhood better than any organization politician in it."[78]

Nevertheless, the president's emissaries detected some hope. Despite encountering palpable hostility, they found the president still popular among ghetto residents, at least among those people who believed in taking constructive measures to relieve bleak conditions. Men such as the Reverend Louis Sullivan of Philadelphia, who ran a successful job-training program out of his church, furnished the kind of leadership that appealed to the White House; he was "the essence of the best of the new Negro middle-class . . . [who] are responsible, articulate, and deeply involved in the problems of their race," according to Markman. Moreover, Sullivan and others like him had particular appeal for the president because he "is solely concerned with civil rights and does not become involved in Vietnam debates."[79] Johnson's observers were heartened that if the administration cooperated with leaders such as Sullivan and stayed the course in waging the War on Poverty (as well as that in Vietnam), then progress would continue to be made.[80]

What did these impromptu forays accomplish? Probably not very much besides proving what the administration already knew—that its leadership ties to the ghetto were thin. The visit to Detroit in May 1967 did not turn up a clue that a disastrous riot would break out only two months later, nor did the travelers to Oakland in March mention the Black Panther party, a gun-toting cadre of youths whose efforts to combat excessive force by the police resulted in several deadly encounters with law officers.[81] Yet some good came out of these eyewitness accounts. Alexander thought that the president used them in support of legislation to improve living conditions in the ghetto. Johnson insisted that although measures to exterminate disease-carrying rodents or to subsidize apartment rents would not immediately forestall violence, they would show his determination to forge ahead for the long haul. "If men of good will kept their eyes on the main thing," McPherson explained the president's thinking, "we would pass the laws that would speed the process."[82] Ultimately, however, the Great Society never lived up to its promises, and more effective programs would have done a great deal toward reducing the administration's credibility gap among disgruntled African Americans.

Better communication still might have narrowed some of the divide between the federal government and militant blacks, but the administration proved incapable of closing the split that had grown into a huge gulf. Political considerations played a large part as the White House tempered its concern for the plight of blacks with the calculation that it would alienate disaffected white voters who were showing signs of defecting from the Democratic party. Yet the rift was fundamentally irreconcilable. The president and the new black activists inhabiting the ghetto spoke a different language, one distinct from that which Johnson customarily heard from Wilkins and Young. The chief executive could enter into a dialogue with middle-class black leaders whose notion of civility and decorum conformed to his own, yet he had no way of speaking to young, impoverished African Americans who rejected his standards of behavior and rhetoric. Johnson could not possibly communicate with angry black rebels, as Farmer persuasively noted, "who would tell it like it is and call him an MF [motherfucker]."[83] As Sherwin Markman pointed out after visiting Chicago: "There is even a language of the ghetto. . . . As one man put it to me, 'Why should we have to speak the white man's language?' "[84] When Johnson heard these unfamiliar and dissonant voices, Clifford Alexander declared, it did not "hit his ear too well."[85]

The Johnson who might encourage criticism from Wilkins and Young could not abide it from outsiders who did not share his values and faith in the system. Though he once remarked to Richard Goodwin that he did not "expect gratitude" from African Americans, the president's bruised feelings belied these words. Those aides and civil rights allies who knew him best agreed that Johnson took the ghetto rebellions as a personal insult. According to Young, "he seemed to feel . . . what man has done more and why doesn't everybody know this and why aren't they appreciative?"[86] Needing to explain why ungrateful blacks tarnished his Great Society, the president believed despite considerable evidence to the contrary that the riots were instigated by an unspecified conspiracy. "Even though some of you will not agree with me," he lectured the cabinet in summer 1967, "I have a very deep feeling that there is more to that than we see at the moment."[87] Without conjuring up the possibility of sinister outside forces lurking behind the riots, how else could Johnson explain to himself why blacks did not give him sufficient thanks?

The work of the Kerner Commission illustrates the limits of Johnson's understanding. In the wake of a round of destructive riots in summer 1967, the president created the National Advisory Commission on Civil Disorders to study conditions in the ghetto that bred despair and violence. Headed by Democratic governor Otto Kerner of Illinois, the bipartisan membership included two African Americans, Roy Wilkins and Republican senator Edward Brooke of Massachusetts. The appointment of Wilkins and Brooke to the panel of eleven reflected Johnson's continued faith in moderate black leaders, a faith not shared by ghetto dwellers. A distressed McPherson reported to his boss after a visit to Harlem that residents there considered the two appointees as " 'office' leaders—they have no following on the streets; they neither understand nor are understood by people on the streets."[88]

Given the moderate composition of the body, the president received a jolt when the commission issued its report the following March. Attributing the blame for the riots to white racism, the group recommended a massive federal spending program to deal with the manifold problems. As he had responded to the outbreak of the riots, Johnson bristled at what he perceived to be the commission's failure to recognize his many accomplishments in fighting racial discrimination. Feeling personally aggrieved, he confided to Califano that the report was "destroying his interest in things like this."[89] Neither his reliable friend Wilkins nor his devoted assistant McPherson could convince the hurt chief executive that the commission's handiwork showed him no disrespect, and the stubborn Johnson basically ignored the panel's findings.[90]

Events occurring shortly after the release of the Kerner Commission's report further tested the administration's relations with black leaders. The assassination of Dr. King on April 4, 1968, unleashed a spontaneous wave of rioting throughout the country, including within the nation's capital. Califano and McPherson persuaded the president to convene a White House meeting the next day with African-American and congressional leaders. Johnson, who had not seen the slain minister for two years and whose estrangement from him was virtually complete, decided to set aside his personal pique and use King's death to help heal the nation's racial wounds. He turned "instinctively" to those leaders who, unlike Dr. King, had stuck with him throughout the years. Led by Wilkins and Young, the list included Bayard Rustin, Dorothy Height, Clarence Mitchell, Leon Sullivan, and two city officials who exhibited the political leadership he admired, Walter Washington, appointed by Johnson as mayor of the District of Columbia, and Mayor Richard Hatcher of Gary, Indiana. Walter Fauntroy represented the SCLC, and King's grieving father regretfully declined an invitation to attend but wanted the president to know that "his prayers are with [him]."[91]

The White House also invited Floyd McKissick, the director of CORE. Following Farmer's departure as head of the group in March 1966, McKissick had guided the organization on a black power and antiwar path. For nearly two years the administration had excluded him from the White House but in this instance relented, perhaps because it wanted to include one representative from a group at the forefront of the new black activism yet whose ties went back to the old civil rights coalition. And McKissick, for all his expressed militancy, was no Stokely Carmichael or Rap Brown. Whatever the intention, McKissick never made it to the meeting. When he arrived at the White House gate with two assistants who had not received invitations, the guard cleared McKissick but not his companions. The CORE director refused to participate without the unauthorized pair, and Johnson aides, hearing about the brouhaha during the meeting, apparently decided that to allow all three in would disrupt the affair.[92]

Had McKissick attended, the president quite likely would not have satisfied him. Johnson greeted his guests by asking their support "as responsible Negro leaders." After listening to them reaffirm their commitment to nonviolence and urging "concrete and meaningful action to counter dialogue in the streets," the chief executive reminded them of all that he had achieved. Still upset with the Kerner Commission, he reiterated his long list of accomplishments in reversing racial discrimination. He realized that more remained to be completed, and he pledged to pursue what he did best—to obtain legislation for fair housing and to press Congress to appropriate additional funds to wipe out poverty. His most telling remarks came at the end of the forty-seven-minute session because they indicated that he expected the moderate black leaders he had relied upon to share the responsibility for his failures as well as successes. "I have taken every opportunity to get through to the young people. How well I have gotten through remains to be seen," LBJ declared and then pointedly asked those leaders assembled: "But also—how well have you gotten through?"[93]

"Not very well," was the answer shouted back from the riot-torn streets of the cities. Following King's assassination, a week of violence plagued more than 100 communities, leaving 46 people dead, over 3,000 injured, and 27,000 incarcerated and costing in excess of $45 million in property damages; it required 21,000 federal troops and 34,000 National Guardsmen to restore peace.[94] The violence did not cause Johnson to retreat, however. Facing the white backlash whipping through Congress, he managed to secure additional civil rights and housing legislation already in the congressional hopper. Even with Johnson's political world collapsing around him under the weight of Vietnam and urban rebellions, he continued to pull the legislative strings that he had mastered during his thirty-odd years in Washington.[95]

Holding the line also meant that Johnson did not intend to entertain new legislative initiatives while under siege, especially those proposals from black activists outside his recognized leadership circle. The Poor People's Campaign, originated by Dr. King, underscored this point. Mobilized as a nonviolent, interracial army of several thousand poor people to descend upon Washington, D.C., and to expose the inadequacy of the nation's skirmish against poverty, the protest began on May 12, a little over a month after King's death. The SCLC chief had not drawn up a long list of specific demands; instead he wanted poor people to gain pride from forming their own collective movement that would publicize their plight and prod the nation to action. King's successor, the Reverend Ralph D. Abernathy, implemented the hazy plan whose centerpiece became the construction of "Resurrection City," where the poor from diverse racial and ethnic backgrounds "would live together in peace and mutual respect."[96]

The Johnson administration greeted the campaign with patient apprehension. Coming so soon after the April riots, the president thought the demonstration would prove both dangerous and futile. Yet the chief executive ordered his cabinet secretaries to prepare a review of their programs and when visited by delegations of the poor they should "listen very closely and sympathetically to their appeals."[97] The Justice Department carefully monitored the activities of the protesters, and Attorney General Clark together with other administration officials attempted to cooperate with Abernathy, whom they considered a moderate leader within the context of this potentially disruptive confrontation. Fearing that the campaign was attracting hard-to-control militants who "would be pleased to see this 'peaceful' approach fail," Clark sought to find "a constructive purpose . . . to make it work so that the country sees that nonviolence can achieve something."[98]

The administration generally achieved its goal of maintaining peace. Widespread bloodshed was avoided, Washington escaped massive dislocations, and the president did not go down in history as another Herbert Hoover who brutally ejected depression-era Bonus Marchers from the nation's capital.[99] The administration made some minor "changes and improvements" in federal programs to give Abernathy "something to report back to his people."[100] In effect, the White House waited the protesters out. Besieged by conflicts in internal leadership, drenched by rain, and mired in mud, Resurrection City mocked Abernathy's plan for creating a model city of racial brotherhood. Federal officials allowed the demonstrators to convene a "Solidarity Rally" on June 19, but by then the impoverished, makeshift community was about to collapse. A few days later, D.C. police arrested the small remaining band of diehard protesters, including Abernathy, which did spark a brief outbreak of violence in Washington's black neighborhoods.[101]

Although Johnson exhibited considerable forbearance, he could not bring himself to show forgiveness. He refused to agree to several advisers' requests that he meet personally with Abernathy; as he had with King, the president felt his successor failed to display the proper gratitude. Speaking to a gathering of 50,000 people on Solidarity Day, Abernathy criticized the administration's record over the past five years as a series of "broken promises," thereby guaranteeing that Johnson would shun him.[102] A comprehensive scholarly history of the Poor People's Campaign remains to be written; when it is, the chronicler must take into account the complex nature of the president, who abhorred the protest but tolerated it. Ramsey Clark's comments will serve as a useful touchstone:

> Resurrection City appalled Johnson. He loves Washington. It represents everything good that he believes in . . . physical beauty, grace in government, heroic monuments, human dignity. To see these pitiful poor people with . . . their ugliness and misery sprawled on the monument grounds—really hurt him— deeply hurt him. I think he was quite courageous in controlling himself and in letting us proceed as we did.[103]

To the end Johnson remained faithful to his vision of civil rights leadership. A moderate in militant times, he tried to keep the political center from crumbling. Amid a turbulent racial revolution, he steadfastly attempted to direct social change along conventional lines, and the black leaders most closely associated with him did little to shift him off course. No more than he did they control the new outrage and militancy that fueled the ghetto upheavals and the movement toward black nationalism. The issue of racial justice grew more complicated. No longer a southern problem with middle-class blacks at the forefront, as the battleground shifted northward it became marked by class and generational conflicts. The president and his black advisers did not speak or comprehend the language of the militants, either in a literal or a symbolic sense. To them, as with most other Americans, civil disorders meant wanton riots, not political rebellions, and black power signified "kill Whitey," not racial pride. Aware of the communication problem, the White House could still do little to improve the situation.

Johnson's definition of social reform compounded the problem. Tolerating mass demonstrations as a necessary evil, he believed that what really counted was the power of interest groups to apply concerted pressure on congressional lawmakers to swing votes in their favor. From this vantage point, the black revolt could be mediated in Washington by leaders who knew their way around the legislative chambers. Thus, the White House cut itself off from many grassroots activists directly responsible for providing direction and meaning to the black freedom struggle. Unlike most issues that appeared before Congress, the black revolt could not be handled simply through manipulation of the well-worn machinery of pluralistic politics.[104]

Johnson sided with moderate black leaders not only because they displayed their loyalty to him but also because of his historical experiences. Having cut his political teeth during the New Deal, he consumed certain lessons about the perils of waging reform. At the height of ghetto insurrections in 1967, when militants scorned traditional civil rights leaders, McPherson reminded the president of how the Left had hurled abuse at Franklin Roosevelt. "To the Communists," he noted, "Roosevelt was a fascist, because he wanted to preserve a voluntary life in America."[105] Picking up this theme, United Nations Ambassador Arthur Goldberg, a former secretary of labor and U.S. Supreme Court justice, warned the chief executive against dismissing the NAACP as "outdated." After all, the rising strength of organized labor in the 1930s reminded him that the "radical leadership of that movement has largely vanished with time, or become part of the social mainstream."[106]

Looking back over Johnson's career, one is struck by his remarkable growth on civil rights issues. The transformative power of the black freedom struggle converted him from a routine defender of African Americans into the most vigorous advocate of racial equality ever to occupy the Oval Office. This progression, however laudatory, did not prepare him for the bitterness and anger that accompanied the black revolution in its later stages. An intensely prideful man who felt no better than when he was fully in control of events, Johnson did not fathom that black leaders could have their own separate agendas; nor was it their style to pay him gratitude for actions they thought he should have been carrying out in the first place. Like most white leaders of his period and region, the Texan retained, as James Farmer commented, "an element of paternalism" in dealing with a generation of blacks who prized their autonomy and self-direction.[107]

Even had Johnson's personality and ideology not been an obstacle, the president faced formidable practical constraints in collaborating with black leaders. Independent of Johnson, the freedom struggle generated a white political backlash that turned increasingly hostile to the goals of black advancement. Legislative wizard that he was, the president still could not magically make disappear the mounting congressional opposition to extension of the Great Society. From the perspective of the 1990s it hardly seems possible that even by embracing leaders more militant than Wilkins and Young could Johnson have deflected the onrushing force of conservatism, which would propel Republicans into the White House for twenty of twenty-four years following Johnson's retirement from office.

President Johnson left an ambiguous legacy of racial reform. He aroused great passions in Americans who hailed him as a second great emancipator or derided him as "Lynchum B. Johnson."[108] That he was neither goes without saying. Indeed he was a committed centrist, a liberal reformer by the standards of his era, who responded to a mighty social revolution sometimes too cautiously and defensively but with much more compassion and enterprise than any president before and after him. The animosity he elicited should be tempered by a recognition of his great worth. Roger Wilkins, Roy's nephew and director of the Justice Department's Community Relations Service, poignantly expressed the ambivalence toward Johnson of many African Americans who saw their racial consciousness raised during the 1960s. Wilkins had grown more radical than his uncle and felt sorely disappointed that the moderate president had failed to come sufficiently to terms with the anger manifested in black militancy. When he stepped down in 1969 and thought about Johnson, the younger Wilkins had "hated him." Yet decades later he admitted that "if you ask most knowledgeable blacks who was the best President for blacks, most of them will answer Lyndon Johnson." And after years of painful soul-searching, he candidly acknowledged, "That is my answer."[109] This bittersweet feeling captures both the agony and the triumph accompanying President Johnson's troubled leadership.

Notes

1. Charles Evers Oral History Interview, April 3, 1974, by Joe B. Frantz, p. 13. All cited manuscripts and oral history interviews are in the Lyndon B. Johnson Library (hereafter cited as LBJL) unless otherwise noted.

2. Denton L. Watson, *Lion in the Lobby: Clarence Mitchell Jr.'s Struggle for the Passage of Civil Rights Laws* (New York: William Morrow and Company, 1990), p. 432.

3. Joseph A. Califano, Jr., *The Triumph & Tragedy of Lyndon Johnson: The White House Years* (New York: Simon and Schuster, 1991), p. 54.

4. Joseph L. Rauh Oral History Interview, August 8, 1969, by Paige Mulhollan, tape 3, p. 14.

5. As the legendary founder of the 1941 March on Washington movement, Randolph was sought out because of the personal respect he commanded, not because of his formal position as head of the Negro American Labor Council. Sometimes included under the heading of Big Six organizations was the National Council of Negro Women.

6. Harry McPherson Oral History Interview, March 24, 1969, by Thomas H. Baker, pt. 4, tape 2, p. 17; Carl T. Rowan, *Breaking Barriers: A Memoir* (Boston: Little Brown, 1991), p. 233.

7. Boy Wilkins with Tom Mathews, *Standing Fast: The Autobiography of Roy Wilkins* (New York: Viking Press, 1982), p. 311; Louis Martin Oral History Interview, May 14, 1969, by David G. McComb, p. 32; Nicholas deB. Katzenbach Oral History Interview, November 16, 1968, by Paige E. Mulhollan, tape 1, p. 29; Bayard Rustin Oral History Interview, June 30, 1969, by Thomas H. Baker, tape 2, p. 15; Robert Weaver Oral History Interview, November 19, 1968, by Joe B. Frantz, tape 3, p. 5.

8. Nancy J. Weiss quoting Robert Weaver, in *Whitney M. Young, Jr., and the Struggle for Civil Rights*, (Princeton, N.J.: Princeton University Press, 1989), p. 148.

9. James Farmer quoted in Bernard J. Firestone and Robert C. Vogt, eds., *Lyndon Baines Johnson and the Uses of Power* (New York: Greenwood, 1988), p. 177.

10. See Weiss, *Young*, p. 148. The resources of the Johnson Library can be used to document the close communication links the president maintained with civil rights leaders. The library has files of index cards containing notations of meetings and telephone conversations between Johnson and civil rights leaders as well as other prominent individuals. Arranged in alphabetical order and cross-filed by subject, this material allows a researcher to glimpse which people had access to the chief executive and from whom he sought advice. By themselves these cards, which were prepared by his secretaries during the White House years, serve mainly as a log containing no indication of the substance of the discussions. They must be consulted in conjunction with the Diary Backup Files, which provide memorandums related to scheduled and off-the-record meetings (the same does not hold true for telephone calls). Although every instance of contact was not logged, these records offer valuable clues to the pattern of presidential communication with various leaders and groups. Wilkins had fifty-nine note-card citations, followed by Young with forty-four.

11. Wilkins, *Standing Fast*, p. 307; McPherson Oral History Interview, April 9, 1969, by Thomas H. Baker, pt. 5, tape 1, p. 11. In this nationally televised speech to Congress at the height of the SCLC's voting rights campaign in Selma, Alabama, Johnson eloquently voiced the refrain of the civil rights movement, "We shall overcome."

12. George Reedy to president, November 29, 1963, Diary Backup Files, box 1 (original emphasis).

13. Weiss, *Young*, p. 145; Whitney M. Young, Jr., Oral History Interview, June 18, 1969, by Thomas H. Baker, p. 4: Wilkins, *Standing Fast*, p. 296.

14. Whitney Young Oral History, p. 9; [Lee White] Notes for Discussion with Martin Luther King, January 13, 1965, White House Central Files (WHCF), Whitney Young Name File, box 41. Young was offered the post of deputy director of the poverty program.

15. Whitney Young Oral History, p. 9; Weiss, *Young*, p. 105.

16. Joseph Califano to president, June 4, 1966, WHCF, Whitney Young Name File, box 41.

17. Joseph Califano to president, July 25, 1966, WHCF, EX HU 2, box

4. Just before leaving office in January 1969, Johnson bestowed on Young the Presidential Medal of Freedom, and in return Young gave the president a copy of his book, *Beyond Racism*, with the inscription: "To Lyndon B. Johnson who more than any President almost makes this book unnecessary" (Weiss, *Young*, p. 164).

18. Paula F. Pfeffer, *A. Philip Randolph, Pioneer of the Civil Rights Movement* (Baton Rouge: Louisiana State University Press, 1990), p. 272ff. For example, Randolph was selected as honorary chair of the 1966 White House Conference on Civil Rights, a contentious affair (see note 47).

19. A. Philip Randolph Oral History Interview, October 29, 1968, by Thomas H. Baker, p. 16; Lee White to president, December 5, 1963, Diary Backup Files, box 2; Hubert H. Humphrey to president, August 5, 1965, Richard Goodwin Files, box 2; Evers Oral History, p. 16; Clifford Alexander to Harry McPherson, October 3, 1966, McPherson Files, box 22.

20. James Farmer, *Lay Bare the Heart: An Autobiography of the Civil Rights Movement* (New York: Arbor House, 1985), pp. 296, 220–22.

21. First quote, George Reedy to president, December 4, 1963, Diary Backup Files, box 2; second quote, Lee White to president, December 4, 1963, Diary Backup Files, box 3.

22. James Farmer Oral History Interview, July 20, 1971, by Paige Mulhollan, tape 2, p. 4; Farmer, *Lay Bare the Heart*, p. 298; David Garrow, *Bearing the Cross: Martin Luther King, Jr., and the Southern Christian Leadership Conference* (New York: William Morrow and Company, 1986), p. 343. Johnson did not officially ask for a moratorium. See Roy Wilkins Oral History Interview, April 1, 1969, by Thomas H. Baker, p. 12; Lee White to president, August 19, 1964, WHCF EX HU 2, box 3.

23. A perusal of the dairy card files notes a drop from six to five contacts.

24. Lee White to president, July 30, 1964, WHCF, James Farmer Name File, box 23. Referring to CORE, White told Johnson, "Even in the case of those organizations that feel they must not join a moratorium, they can make every effort to encourage their followers to hold their demonstrations to specific objectives and make every effort to prevent them from becoming leaderless riots with attendant looting and violence" (Lee White to president, August 19, 1964, Diary Backup Files, box 8). Farmer himself distinguished between riots, which he condemned, and peaceful protests, which he would not suspend. David H. McClain, "The Politics of Freedom: Conflicts between Lyndon Johnson and James Farmer during the 1964 Presidential Campaign," p. 23, unpublished paper, HIS 350L, University of Texas, LBJL.

25. Lee White to president, July 30, 1964, White to Jack Valenti, August 4, 1964, both in WHCF, James Farmer Name File, box 23.

26. White told the president that "Farmer's people did their job effectively" (Lee White to president, October 22, 1964, WHCF, Farmer Name File, box 23). Farmer also helped rein in the Brooklyn chapter of CORE in its attempt to hold a disruptive "stall in" on the highways leading to the New York World's Fair in Queens. Farmer led more conventional protests against specific targets at the exposition site (McClain, "Politics of Freedom," p. 42).

27. Wilkins interceded with the president and secured a pen for

Farmer. Johnson's spite was fully in evidence when he worked behind the scenes to deny Farmer a federal grant to establish an adult literacy program. Farmer, *Lay Bare the Heart*, pp. 304–5; Charles Hamilton, *Adam Clayton Powell, Jr.: The Political Biography of an American Dilemma* (New York: Atheneum, 1991), p. 397.

28. Andrew Young Oral History Interview, June 18, 1970, by Thomas H. Baker, p. 13, adds that King had a warmer relationship with President Kennedy.

29. Califano, *Triumph & Tragedy*, p. 276; Andrew Young Oral History, p. 18. King's very first meeting with President Johnson set the pattern. When the chief executive met with him on December 3, 1963, LBJ delivered the same message as he did to the other black leaders that demonstrations would upset legislative deliberations on the pending civil rights bill. At a press conference following the meeting, however, King declared his intention of renewing protests that had been suspended in the mourning period since Kennedy's death. This response irked the White House because "Dr. King had a completely different story outside than he did in [Johnson's] office about the question of demonstrations." *New York Times*, December 4, 1963, p. 1; Lee White to president, December 4, 1963, Diary Backup Files, box 2.

30. Garrow, *Bearing the Cross*, pp. 343, 350. The White House and the FBI monitored King and kept tabs on his position concerning the seating of delegates from the Mississippi Freedom Democratic Party; note, August 19, 1964, WHCF EX PL ST 24, box 81.

31. Lee White to president, March 9, 1965, Diary Backup Files, box 15.

32. Richard N. Goodwin, *Remembering America: A Voice from the Sixties* (New York: Harper and Row, 1988), p. 310.

33. Martin Oral History Interview, p. 31; Andrew Young Oral History Interview, pp. 16–17.

34. Jack Valenti to president, November 13, 1964, WHCF, Roy Wilkins Name File, box 312; Lee White to president, December 18, 1964, WHCF, Martin Luther King, Jr., Name File, box 144.

35. Lee White to president, July 23, 1965, WHCF, Martin Luther King, Jr., Name File, box 147. King Met with LBJ on August 5, 1965, for what he called a "fruitful and meaningful" discussion as he relayed his concerns about racial problems in the North (Garrow, *Bearing the Cross*, p. 436).

36. Garrow, *Bearing the Cross*, p. 440.

37. Ibid., 548–49; Martin Oral History Interview, p. 31.

38. See David Garrow, *The FBI and Martin Luther King, Jr.: From "Solo" to Memphis* (New York: W. W. Norton, 1981); Califano, *Triumph & Tragedy*, p. 277; Ramsey Clark Oral History Interview, April 16, 1969, by Harry Baker, tape 4, p. 21.

39. John P. Roche, "Eyes Only," to president, April 5, 1967, WHCF, Martin Luther King, Jr., Confidential Name File, box 147.

40. Califano, *Triumph and Tragedy*, pp. 277, 218–19.

41. Weiss, *Young*, pp 160–62.

42. Califano, *Triumph & Tragedy*, p. 218; Clifford Alexander to president, January 11, 1967, WHCF, Louis Martin Name File, box 127; Martin Luther King, Jr., King to Lyndon B. Johnson, July 25, 1967, Willard Wirtz to president, July 28, 1967, Harry McPherson to president, July 28, 1967, all in

Mcpherson Files, box 32; David Garrow, "From Reformer to Revolutionary," in *Martin Luther King, Jr., and the Civil Rights Movement*, ed. David J. Garrow (Brooklyn: Carlson Publishing, 1989), pp. 427–36; Adam Fairclough, *To Redeem the Soul of America: The Southern Christian Leadership Conference and Martin Luther King, Jr.* (Athens: University of Georgia Press, 1987), p. 383.

43. Lee White to president, August 10, 1965, WHCF, EX HU 2, box 3; Lee White to president, November 2, 1965, WHCF, EX HU 2/MC, box 22, complimenting Rustin on his help in organizing the White House Conference on Civil Rights. See correspondence from Lee White to president, August 11, 12, 13, 19, 1964, WHCF, EX PL 1/St 24, box 81, on the controversy over seating the Mississippi Freedom Democratic Party; and on Vietnam, see Roche, "Eyes Only," to president, April 5, 1967, WHCF, Martin Luther King, Jr., Confidential Name File, box 147. Fairclough, *To Redeem the Soul*, pp. 23–24. Rustin did severely criticize the administration in 1966 for ignoring the $180-billion Freedom Budget proposal he devised with Randolph to promote full employment over ten years (Pfeffer, *Randolph*, pp. 287–90). Clifford Alexander to Harry McPherson, October 3, 1966, WHCF, Whitney Young Name File, box 41. John D'Emilio is currently at work on a much needed biography of Rustin.

44. John Dittmer, "The Politics of the Mississippi Movement, 1954–1964," in *The Civil Rights Movement in America*, ed. Charles Eagles (Jackson: University of Mississippi Press, 1986), pp. 65–93; Wilkins, *Standing Fast*, pp. 305–6.

45. Clayborne Carson, *In Struggle: SNCC and the Black Awakening of the 1960s* (Cambridge: Harvard University Press, 1981), p. 188.

46. Humphrey to Califano, January 22, 1966, WHCF EX HU 2, box 4; Carson, *In Struggle*, p. 189.

47. On the White House Conference and its relationship to black leadership, see Steven F. Lawson, "Civil Rights" in *Exploring the Johnson Years*, ed. Robert A. Divine (Austin, University of Texas Press, 1981), pp.110–11, and Lawson, *In Pursuit of Power: Southern Blacks and Electoral Politics, 1965–1982* (New York: Columbia University Press, 1985), pp. 43–49. The Johnson Library holds the records of this conference, and materials found in files designated WHCF EX HU 2/mc are also helpful. Oral histories with McPherson, Ben Heineman (April 16, 1970, by Joe B. Frantz), Clifford Alexander (February 17, 1972, by Joe B. Frantz), and Ramsey Clark (March 21, 1969, by Harri Baker) are also useful.

48. McPherson Oral History, pt. 4, tape 2, p. 7; John Lewis to A. Philip Randolph, December 14, 1965, White House Conference on Civil Rights, "To Fulfill These Rights" Files, box 66.

49. Dr. King joined his old civil rights comrades in criticizing SNCC. Martin Luther King, Jr., A. Philip Randolph, Roy Wilkins, and Whitney Young to Stokely Carmichael, August 3, 1966, and SNCC Central Committee to Roy Wilkins, August 4, 1966, Marvin Watson Files, box 18. I would like to thank Lewis Gould for directing me to this material.

50. Harry McPherson, *A Political Education: A Journal of Life with Senators, Generals, Cabinet Members and Presidents* (Boston: Little, Brown and Company, 1972), p. 357. He also included CORE, which was moving in the same antiwar, black nationalist direction as SNCC.

51. Kenneth O'Reilly, *"Racial Matters"*: The FBI's Secret File on Black America, 1960–1972 (New York: Free Press, 1989). This book and Garrow's on the FBI and Dr. King show that the Johnson administration had a clandestine relationship with black leaders that the papers of the Johnson Library do not generally reveal. Also of interest on a more visible level, the record of a White House meeting on March 12, 1965, notes the presence of Hubert "Rap" Brown, who would become SNCC's head and a White House nemesis ("President's Schedule, March 12, 1965, Washington Civil Rights Delegation," Diary Backup Files, box 15). At the time, Brown was representing the Non Violent Action Group, a SNCC affiliate at Howard University.

52. Carson, *In Struggle*, pp. 276–77.

53. McPherson Oral History, pt. 5, tape 2, p. 9; McPherson, *Political Education*, p. 363.

54. Cabinet Dossier no. 1, Report, August 2, 1967, Cabinet Meeting Files, box 9. Carmichael was out of the country at the time.

55. When the Logan Act, barring private citizens from attempting to influence relations between a foreign government and the United States, was suggested as a possible basis for prosecution, Clark sarcastically responded that he "could make a better case against George Romney [the Republican governor and presidential aspirant who had visited Vietnam] than they could against Stokely." Larry Temple to president, January 19, 1968, Stokely Carmichael Confidential Name File, box 144; Clark, Oral History, pt. 4, p. 28; see also Ralph A. Spritzer memo for Ramsey Clark, August 14, 1967, "Sedition and Inciting Rebellion: Re: Stokely Carmichael," box 75, Ramsey Clark Papers. The government did prosecute H. Rap Brown for crossing state lines with a gun when he was under a felony indictment in Cambridge, Maryland. Clark thought the five-year prison sentence was too "harsh" under this "peculiar and technical statute."

56. This remark came after the August 2, 1967, cabinet meeting cited in note 54. See also Roger Wilkins, *A Man's Life* (New York: Touchstone, 1982), p. 229. The administration's frustration with and animosity toward Carmichael reached silly proportions. Presidential counselor John Roche reported that he had "planted a rumor that Stokely is really *white*" (Roche to Marvin Watson, "Eyes Only," December 22, 1967, WHCF, Stokely Carmichael Confidential Name File, box 144).

57. Allen J. Matusow, *The Unraveling of America: A History of Liberalism in the 1960s* (New York: Harper and Row, 1984), p. 253; Polly Greenberg, *The Devil Has Slippery Shoes: A Biased Biography of the Child Development Group of Mississippi* (London: Macmillan, 1969). See also the Johnson Library's Administrative History of the Office of Economic Opportunity.

58. McPherson, *Political Education*, pp. 353–55. He speculated that the Democrats would have trouble carrying the state in the 1968 presidential election, which it had already failed to do in 1964.

59. Matusow, *Unraveling of America*, p. 254; Christopher Jencks, "Accommodating Whites: A New Look at Mississippi," *New Republic*, April 16, 1966, p. 22; Nicholas Lemann, *The Promised Land: The Great Black Migration and How It Changed America* (New York: Vintage, 1991), pp. 324–27. Critics charged that McPherson engineered the deal to create the moder-

ate Mississippi Action for Progress (MAP), a group of loyal Johnson whites and blacks. The organization included as co-chair Aaron Henry, the NAACP leader from Clarksdale who had led the MFDP contingent at the 1964 Democratic National Convention but had moved away from the black radicals in the state (Greenberg, *Devil Has Slippery Shoes*, p. 640). On efforts to back Henry and moderate whites in capturing the Democratic party, see Lawson, *In Pursuit of Power*, 114–15, 196–200, and Aaron Henry Oral History Interview, September 12, 1970, by Thomas H. Baker.

60. Dittmer, "Politics of the Mississippi Movement." Dittmer is currently completing a book on the movement in Mississippi, which contains a chapter on CDGM. For Johnson Library holdings on the CDGM, see War on Poverty Files, October 14, 1966, to November 1, 1966, and April 1, 1967, to April 20, 1967, WHCF GEN WE 9, boxes 41 and 42. Another related event that deserves further study concerns the takeover of the Greenville, Mississippi, Air Base by displaced black farm workers. See Nicholas Katzenbach to president, February 14, 1966, WHCF EX HU 2/St 24, box 27, and James C. Cobb, " 'Somebody Done Nailed Us on the Cross': Federal Farm and Welfare Policy and The Civil Rights Movement in the Mississippi Delta," *Journal of American History* 77 (December 1990): 928–33.

61. Hobart Taylor, Jr., to president, November 27, 1964, Adam Clayton Powell Name File, box 280.

62. Louis Martin to Harry McPherson, December 12, 1966, box 55; Louis Martin to Jim Jones, October 3, 1966, box 47; Harry McPherson to Marvin Watson, December 12, 1966, box 55, all in Diary Backup Files; Clifford Alexander to president, November 11, 1966, WHCF EX PL 2, box 86; Clifford Alexander to president, January 19, 1966, WHCF, Louis Martin Name File, box 127.

63. McPherson Oral History, pt. 5, tape 1, p. 17.

64. Alexander Oral History, tape 2, pp. 10–11; June 4, 1973, tape 3, p. 29. The quote is drawn from a composite of statements.

65. In 1968 there were five black members of the House of Representatives, all Democrats, and one Republican in the Senate. A sixth congressman, Adam Clayton Powell, had been barred from taking his seat.

66. John P. Roche to Marvin Watson, October 4, 1967, WHCF, Carl Stokes Name File, box 588.

67. Charles V. Hamilton, *Adam Clayton Powell*; see also Wil Haygood, *King of the Cats: The Life and Times of Adam Clayton Powell, Jr.* (Boston: Houghton Mifflin, 1993).

68. Califano, *Triumph & Tragedy*, p. 207; see also Barbara Jordan and Shelby Hearon, *Barbara Jordan: A Self Portrait* (Garden City, N.Y.: Doubleday, 1979); Barbara Jordan Oral History Interview, March 28, 1984, by Roland C. Hayes; and Memorandum for the Record, February 15, 1967, Diary Backup Files, box 55.

69. See Steven F. Lawson, "Freedom Then, Freedom Now: The Historiography of the Civil Rights Movement," *American Historical Review* 96 (April 1991): 467–69.

70. Bruce Miroff, "Presidential Leverage over Social Movements: The Johnson White House and Civil Rights," *Journal of Politics* 42 (February 1981): 17.

71. Richard Goodwin to president, May 4, 1964, WHCF EX HU 2, box

2; Douglass Cater to president, May 19, 1964, WHCF, EX HU 2, box 2; Hobart Taylor, Jr., to president, July 17, 1964, WHCF, EX HU 2, box 3; Hobart Taylor to president, October 13, 1964, WHCF, EX HU 2, box 3.

72. James C. Gaither to president, May 9, 1967, WHCF, EX WE 9; notes of president's meeting with Kenneth Crawford, *Newsweek*, July 19, 1967, Diary Backup Files, box 71; Farmer Oral History, tape 2, p. 18; Clark Oral History, March 21, 1969, tape 3, p. 16; Califano, *Triumph & Tragedy*, p. 211; claims that Wilkins blamed the riots on Communist instigation.

73. McPherson Oral History, pt. 5, tape 1, p. 12; Katzenbach Oral History, tape 1, p. 30; Burke Marshall Oral History Interview, October 28, 1968, by Thomas H. Baker, p. 27; McPherson, *Political Education*, pp. 356–58.

74. Harry McPherson to president, July 26, 1967, WHCF, EX HU 2, box 5.

75. Harry McPherson to president, September 7, 1966, McPherson Files, box 22; McPherson to George Christian, August 1, 1967, WHCF, EX HU 2, box 6. Though White House Press Aide Andrew Hatcher, who was black, recommended a presidential meeting with black militants other than Carmichael and Brown, he also suggested that the government should establish an "almost CIA type operation to keep watch over the ghettos." George Christian to president, July 31, 1967, WHCF, EX HU 2, box 6. McPherson still wanted to collaborate with traditional African-American leaders. Admitting that they "have not much more contact with, or power of persuasion over the terrorists than NAM [National Association of Manufacturers] does," he saw them representing "whatever Negro leadership there is in the country." Prominent in civil rights, business, labor, religious, educational, and political affairs, they might speak out in support of using "lawful means for gaining their legitimate ends." McPherson argued for this approach in terms the chief executive best understood: Just "as in a period of labor strife the White House talks with representatives of labor and industry," he counseled, "in a racial revolt we should talk to responsible representation of the Negro community." LBJ liked the idea, but the proposed meeting apparently never took place. McPherson to president, July 26, 1967, and Louis Martin memo for McPherson, July 25, 1967, both in WHCF, EX HU 2, box 5. See attached list containing the names of fifty-three people whom McPherson, Louis Martin, and probably the president viewed as legitimate black leaders. The plan called for these leaders to invite the president to meet with them.

76. McPherson, *Political Education*, p. 375. One inquiry for future research should concern the extent to which the White House used the Justice Department's Community Relations Service to establish communication with ghetto activists to head off potential explosions. Its director, Roger Wilkins, argued that the president refused to rely on this agency to build bridges to grass-roots leaders who articulated real grievances. The question remains why. See Wilkins, *A Man's Life*, pp. 185, 242.

77. Sherwin Markman to president, February 1, 1967, WHCF, EX WE 9, box 28.

78. Harry McPherson to president, August 14, 1967, WHCF, EX HU 2, box 6.

79. Sherwin Markman to president, May 9, 1967, WHCF, EX WE 9, box 28 or 29. For another report that commented on the lack of interest in

Vietnam within the ghetto, see Thomas E. Cronin to president, May 31, 1967, WHCF, EX WE 9, box 29.

80. James Gaither to president, May 9, 1967, WHCF, EX WE 9, box 29; Bill Graham to president, June 16, 1967, James C. Gaither Files, box 252.

81. James Gaither to president, May 9, 1967, WHCF, EX WE 9, box 29; Sherwin Markman to president, August 15, 1967, Gaither Files, box 352; Markman to president, March 14, 1967, WHCF, EX WE 9, box 28; McPherson Oral History, pt. 4, tape 2, p. 18.

82. McPherson, *Political Education*, p. 376; Alexander Oral History, tape 2, p. 14.

83. Farmer Oral History, tape 2, p. 27.

84. Sherwin Markman to president, February 1, 1967, WHCF, EX WE 9, box 28.

85. Alexander Oral History, tape 2, p. 22. In an otherwise revealing article, Kenneth O'Reilly writes that following the 1967 riots the FBI argued that moderates had paved the way for the radicals, and Johnson became "fully committed to smearing the civil rights movement." However, I have not found this to be the case with respect to Johnson's attitude toward Wilkins, Young, and their allies. See Kenneth O'Reilly, "The FBI and the Politics of Riots," *Journal of American History* 75 (June 1988): 104.

86. Whitney Young Oral History, p. 13; Wilkins, *Standing Fast*, p. 313. Alexander, in Oral History, tape 2, pp. 13, 15, 22, observed the same phenomenon but attributed some of the blame to Roy Wilkins for not doing more to keep Johnson from taking the riots as a personal affront. See also Roger Wilkins, *A Man's Life*, p. 231.

87. Minutes cabinet meeting, August 2, 1967, Cabinet Papers, box 9.

88. Harry McPherson to president, August 14, 1967, WHCF, EX HU 2, box 6. Califano, in *Triumph & Tragedy*, p. 219, maintains that the president created the commission to head off an independent congressional investigation that might produce a negative political fallout for the administration. In addition to Kerner, Wilkins, and Brooke, the members of the commission were I. W. Abel, James C. Corman, Fred R. Harris, Herbert Jenkins, John V. Lindsay, William M. McCulloch, Katherine Graham Peden, and Charles B. Thornton.

89. Califano, *Triumph & Tragedy*, pp. 261, 262.

90. Harry McPherson to Califano, March 1, 1968, McPherson Files, box 32; McPherson to president, March 18, 1968, McPherson Files, box 53; Wilkins Oral History, p. 21. The papers of the Kerner Commission are housed at the Johnson Library. It is questionable whether the chief executive would have responded to the commission more favorably even if the tone of the report had not offended him. He was in no mood to advocate sweeping increases in expenditures for domestic programs while the Vietnam War continued. In 1966 his White House Conference on Civil Rights recommended big public spending programs that the president chose to ignore; instead he concentrated on passing legislation that would not require great expenditures: protection of civil rights workers and fair housing.

91. McPherson Oral History, pt. 5, tape 1, p. 13; Califano, *Triumph & Tragedy*, p. 277; Lyndon B. Johnson, *The Vantage Point: Perspectives of the Presidency, 1963–1969* (New York: Holt, Rinehart and Winston, 1971), p. 175; Harry McPherson to Joseph Califano, April 5, 1968, 3:30 A.M., James

Gaither to president, April 5, 1968, 8:35 A.M., Diary Backup Files, box 95. Also attending the meeting were Judge Leon Higginbotham (see his Oral History Interview, October 7, 1976, by Joe B. Frantz), Clarence Mitchell III, and Bishop George Baber; from the administration: Warren Christopher, Thurgood Marshall, whom Johnson had appointed to the U.S. Supreme Court, Robert Weaver, and Steve Pollak; from Congress: Senators Mike Mansfield and Thomas Kuchel, Speaker John McCormack and Congressmen Carl Albert and William McCulloch. Mayor Carl Stokes of Cleveland, Charles Evers, and A. Philip Randolph could not attend. Tom Johnson to president, April 7, 1968, Tom Johnson's Notes of Meetings, box 2.

92. James Gaither to president, April 5, 1967, 4:50 A.M., Joseph Califano to president, April 5, 1967, 11:22 A.M., Diary Backup Files, box 95; "Handwritten Notes" (Joseph A. Califano's) folder, n.d., Diary Backup Files, box 96; McPherson, *Political Education*, p. 365; Martin Oral History, 34-37. The two men who accompanied McKissick were Roy Innis and Wilfred Ussery.

93. Tom Johnson to president, "Notes of the President's Meeting with Negro Leaders," with attachments, April 7, 1968, Tom Johnson's notes of meetings, box 2. For security reasons, Johnson did not attend King's funeral and sent Vice-President Humphrey in his place to head a delegation of administration officials; he also arranged for Roy Wilkins and Whitney Young to accompany them. Joseph Califano to president, April 8, 1968, Diary Backup Files, box 95. Roger Wilkins does not recall the White House cooperating in facilitating participation of federal officials at the funeral (Wilkins, *A Man's Life*, p. 214). For the president's public remarks on the assassination, see *Public Papers of the Presidents: Lyndon B. Johnson*, vol. 1 (Washington, D.C.: Government Printing Office, 1970), p. 493. After proclaiming a national day of mourning, Johnson canceled a planned address to Congress scheduled for April 8.

94. Harvard Sitkoff, *The Struggle for Black Equality, 1954-1980* (New York: Hill and Wang, 1981), p. 221.

95. Lawson, *In Pursuit of Power*, chapter 3.

96. Ralph David Abernathy, *And the Walls Came Tumbling Down* (New York: Harper and Row, 1989), p. 502; Fairclough, *To Redeem the Soul*, pp. 363-65.

97. Cabinet minutes, May 1, 1968, Cabinet Papers, box 13; Califano, *Triumph & Tragedy*, p. 287; McPherson Oral History, pt. 5, tape 2, p. 2.

98. Cabinet minutes, May 1, 1968, Cabinet Papers, box 13. See also minutes of April 3, 1968, in box 13; Matthew Nimetz to Califano, April 25, 1968, and Nimetz to Warren Christopher, April 18, 1968, James Gaither Presidential Task Force Files, box 36. For a harsh view of King and the SCLC, see Larry Temple to president, February 14, 1968, WHCF, EX HU 2, box 7.

99. Matthew Nimetz to Joseph Califano, May 16, 1968, Gaither Presidential Task Force Files, box 36, with enclosed pages 256-65 from Arthur Schlesinger's *Crisis of the Old Order* depicting the 1932 march.

100. Joseph Califano to president, May 21, 1968, Gaither Presidential Task Forces Files, box 36. Knowing the chief executive, Califano made it clear that the changes were based not on pressure but on their merits and had "been in the works for some time."

101. In early June, Bayard Rustin had taken over as organizer of the

June 19 rally, which pleased the administration as the best way to achieve a peaceful demonstration. Frustrated with SCLC officials, Rustin subsequently stepped down. Ramsey Clark to Larry Levenson, June 3, 1968, box 34, Clark Papers.

102. Califano, *Triumph & Tragedy*, p. 287; James Gaither to Harry McPherson, June 21, 1968, Gaither Presidential Task Force Files, box 36; McPherson to president, June 20, 1968, McPherson Files, box 53. Also in attendance at the peaceful rally were moderates such as Whitney Young and Roy Wilkins as well as several administration representatives.

103. Clark Oral History, tape 5, p. 17.

104. Clarence Mitchell, the NAACP's premier lobbyist, epitomized Johnson's model of leadership. Dubbed the "101st Senator," Mitchell thought protests could be helpful in publicizing grievances, but the real work of resolving them took place on Capitol Hill. As Johnson came under assault for not acting swiftly enough to combat long-standing racial and economic ills, Mitchell stood "militantly" with him and became "increasingly disillusioned with . . . [those] who urge new programs but are unwilling to concentrate on passage of proposed programs." Barefoot Sanders to president, April 29, 1968, Clarence Mitchell Name File; Watson, *Lion in the Lobby*, p. 592; McPherson, *Political Education*, p. 300; Johnson, *Vantage Point*, p. 177. See also Jack Valenti to president, January 26, 1965, WHCF, Clarence Mitchell Name File, box 480; Jim Jones to president, October 18, 1967, Diary Backup Files, box 76; Clarence Mitchell Oral History Interview, April 30, 1969, by Thomas H. Baker, p. 18.

105. Harry McPherson to president, July 26, 1967, EX HU 2, box 5.

106. Cabinet minutes, August 2, 1967, Cabinet Papers, box 9. For the influence of FDR on Johnson and other post–New Deal presidents, see William E. Leuchtenburg, *In the Shadow of FDR: From Harry Truman to Ronald Reagan* (Ithaca, N.Y.: Cornell University Press, 1983).

107. Farmer Oral History, p. 27. Despite his break with Johnson, Farmer was an insightful critic.

108. Quoted in Greenberg, *Devil Has Slippery Shoes*, p. 513.

109. Wilkins, *A Man's Life*, p. 229.

Part 2 | LBJ Abroad

5 | The U.S. and NATO in the Johnson Years

Lawrence S. Kaplan

SINCE WORLD WAR II EUROPE has been the focus of American foreign relations. And since 1949 the Atlantic alliance has been the front line of containment of Soviet communism. In the words of David Calleo, NATO was "the rather elaborate apparatus by which we have chosen to organize the American protectorate in Europe."[1] Until 1963 other parts of the world had been fringe areas despite intrusion of crises in Korea, Guatemala, Indochina, and the Suez Canal in the 1950s. The Soviets were considered to have created turmoil in those regions to divert America from its primary concern—the defense of Europe. In the course of fashioning an Atlantic community to whose fortunes it became attached, the nation had abandoned its tradition of nonentanglement with Europe, the hallmark of American foreign policy for the first century and a half of its history.

Through its involvement in the Vietnam War the Johnson administration appeared to turn the clock back, to return the United States to its earlier concerns with the Pacific rim. It was not that the administration intended to abandon the new links to Europe; the Soviet peril there remained virulent as the status of West Berlin remained unresolved, as the Soviet buildup of nuclear weapons after the Cuban missile crisis escalated, and as the Brezhnev doctrine was imposed on Czechoslovakia at the end of the Johnson administration. But the combination of the president's unfamiliarity with Europe and the dominance of the Vietnam War in America's consciousness seemed to push NATO into the background during the Johnson years. How much attention could U.S. policymakers devote to framing a coherent NATO policy when communism's new locus of East-West confrontation was in the enclosed jungles of Southeast Asia rather than in the open plains of northern Europe?

The coincidence of rising tensions in Asia at a time of lower tensions in Europe helped to facilitate a benign neglect of Europe during the Johnson years. The removal of Berlin and Cuba as crisis points after 1962 opened the way to the Harmel initiative in 1967, with its emphasis on détente as well as on defense.[2] The relative calm in Europe permitted observers to judge that the ability of the United States during the Kennedy administration to surmount Soviet challenges in the Caribbean and in central Europe had compelled the Soviets to surrender, at least in the short run, their aspiration to dissolve the Atlantic alliance.

There is nothing unreasonable about this evaluation. Certainly there can be no caviling about the dominance of Indochina in America's consciousness in the absence of clear and present danger in Europe. The Czech crisis of 1968 was carefully identified by the Soviet Union as a problem of the Warsaw bloc and not a reason for conflict between NATO and the Warsaw countries.

Under these circumstances challenges to the survival of NATO from both Americans and Europeans were inevitable, and they stemmed in large measure from the pall cast by the Vietnam War on American foreign affairs. From the American side there was a growing public anger against a Europe that did not rally to the United States defense of South Vietnam. Congressmen were prepared to act on this discontent by withdrawing U.S. troops from Europe unless the European partners changed their behavior. From the European side there was a rising fear, stoked by Gaullists, that American anticommunist fervor masked an essential weakness dangerous to Europeans. The issue was not simply that America would withdraw troops because of pique over its allies' behavior; Europeans were concerned that U.S. troops would be moved out of Europe to fill a need in Asia.

Another challenge to the alliance arose during the Johnson years from an apparent waning of the Cold War in Europe. Pundits in the mid-1960s speculated that the alliance had served its purposes and should disband.[3] Although Khrushchev's personality was volatile and his actions often unpredictable, his nation was not Stalin's Soviet Union. Western Europe in the mid-1960s believed that it could coexist with its eastern neighbors. Its push to détente that characterized the latter part of the Johnson administration would not have advanced as far as it did without a certain confidence that Soviet aggressiveness had abated.

Questions then may be raised: (1) In light of the nation's absorption with Vietnam, how important was the Atlantic alliance to the Johnson administration? (2) If the Soviet threat had receded, what centripetal forces were still at work to keep the alliance alive? (3) Since NATO did survive, what new relationships were fashioned between Americans and Europeans during the Johnson years? Superficial evidence points to potentially fatal divisions within NATO, divisions reflected in the failure of the multilateral force (MLF) to create a new nuclear partnership in Europe, in the expulsion of the United States and NATO from France in 1966 and the concurrent departure of France from NATO in that year, and in the recurrent Mansfield resolutions seeking American withdrawal of troops from Europe. Each of these issues created serious problems for U.S. policymakers; how they were resolved was a measure of the success or failure of Johnson's NATO policies.

I

The MLF, with its implications for an integrated European military entity sharing nuclear power with the United States, was a reflection of the European orientation of President Johnson's advisers. Despite the president's Texas provincialism and his discomfort with the Kennedy advisers he had inherited, Johnson's foreign policy was shaped by the same Ivy League advisers who had been associated with Kennedy—and with Eisenhower and Truman as well. Johnson may have been, as Philip Geyelin characterized him in 1966, "a caricature of an American Westerner, with an uncultivated accent and an often unintelligible turn of phrase," who resented the manners of the eastern intellectuals.[4] Still, Johnson retained most of them. McGeorge Bundy stayed on as special assistant for national security. When he left in 1966 his successor, Walt W. Rostow, was as much an Ivy League product and Kennedy administration veteran as Bundy had been. The two key figures in the cabinet, Dean Rusk and Robert McNamara, were both Kennedy appointees. For a variety of reasons the influence of these two men increased rather than decreased under Johnson; Rusk enjoyed a prominence as secretary of state he had not had under Kennedy, and McNamara's presence was increasingly felt as Johnson looked to the Pentagon for advice.

The concept of a genuinely integrated force excited and inspired a dedicated group of American diplomatists who saw in the MLF an opportunity to advance the cause of European unification. The MLF was conceived in the Eisenhower administration by former chairman of the Policy Planning Council Robert Bowie; it derived from a plan of the Supreme Allied Commander, Europe, Gen. Lauris Norstad, to fill a gap in medium-range ballistic missiles with a land-based multinational force under his authority. The concept became entangled in inter- and intradepartmental wrangling in Washington and in doubts among potential European participants during the Kennedy years. But if the MLF acolytes in the State Department, most of them followers of Jean Monnet, had failed to win the full support of the White House or the Defense Department, they did not give up their vision. For them a multilateral force represented an important step toward completing a United States of Europe; at the same time the MLF could thwart the efforts of Germany and other countries to achieve nuclear capabilities for themselves. If successful, these advocates expected even Britain and France, with their nuclear armory, to join the MLF.[5]

As of 1963 the force was to consist of twenty-five surface ships, each armed with eight POLARIS A-3 missiles and having mixed-manned crews to be drawn from member nations. The ships' weapons system would be owned and controlled by the participating allies; the crews would serve as individuals rather than as members of national groups. A key element in the plan was the collective management of weapons by the MLF, not by the United States. It was clear that the use of warheads would not be freed from U.S. control, but the advocates hoped ultimately that the MLF would be independent of a U.S. veto.[6]

A new task force, headed by Gerard Smith as special adviser to the secretary of state, lobbied both in Europe and in the United States for quick implementation of the president's presumed endorsement of the MLF. Although the adherents of the concept were better posed for success in 1964 than they had been at the end of 1963, they had trouble attracting the attention of NATO governments, including their own. The Congress had more important concerns on its agenda than the vague and slightly unsettling notions about a new entity. Richard Russell, chairman of the Senate Armed Services Committee, went along with his colleagues to push aside Smith's recommendations. The forthcoming 1964 presidential election was Johnson's first priority as well as the Senate's. Before the election campaign reached a climax the momentous Civil Rights bill took center stage in summer 1964, and the amorphous MLF almost disappeared from the president's sight at this time.[7]

The European allies, except for the Germans, were equally uninterested. Both the German and the British leaders were insecure in their positions, and France was increasingly alienated from all aspects of NATO. On the other side of Europe the Soviets raised the tone of their opposition, pointing to dangers of German control of nuclear weapons.[8]

When Johnson's attention was once again focused on Europe and the MLF, it was only after his reelection and after the accession of Harold Wilson as Britain's prime minister. Whatever hopes the

MLF supporters had entertained about the British Labour party maintaining its preelection position against an independent nuclear capability were quickly dashed. Wilson's Labour government had no intention of moving Britain into the MLF. The prime minister had too many negative elements to contend with, including anti-German sentiment in his own party and nationalist pride in ownership of nuclear weapons among Conservatives. Thus Wilson's need to satisfy both constituents and opponents pushed him to a search for alternatives to the MLF.[9]

Until December 1964 and Wilson's meeting with Johnson the only public supporter of the MLF in Europe was the Federal Republic. Given the fragility of the Erhard administration the MLF's friends in Washington had an incentive in Bonn to complete negotiations for an agreement by fall 1964. When Johnson met Erhard in June the Smith team tried to take advantage of Bonn's apparent support. The U.S. ambassador to NATO, Thomas Finletter, went to Bonn to follow up the Johnson-Erhard communique, which claimed that the MLF was making "a significant contribution to the military and political strength of NATO and that efforts should be continued to ready an agreement by the end of the year."[10] If this timetable could be met German Gaullists would be isolated, and Erhard's gamble in embracing the MLF would be justified. These expectations energized the MLF Working Group, established in October 1963 with permanent representatives from the United States, United Kingdom, Italy, West Germany, Greece, Turkey, and Belgium. The Working Group in turn had set up a military subgroup under the U.S. chairman, Adm. M. G. Ward, to examine and report on the military and technical aspects of the MLF.

Nothing much was to come of these preparations or of the putative German acceptance of the MLF, essentially because of the continued inattention of the Johnson administration. Partly the lack of action resulted from the wariness of the allies, who had joined the Working Group with the clear proviso, in the case of the British and the Belgians, that their attendance did not constitute any commitment. But the major obstacle in the way of the MLF's progress at this time was probably the intervention of Britain in the person of Prime Minister Harold Wilson.

To replace the MLF the British came up with the alternative of an Atlantic Nuclear Force (ANF). The idea did not originate with Wilson; British military leaders had aired it with the German defense minister Kai-Uwe von Hassel in June who in turn shared it with McNamara. But Wilson quickly seized on the ANF as a means of fulfilling the Labour pledge to renounce an independent nuclear deterrent while finding a home for the British force. And even if the ANF did not materialize, it would divert attention from the MLF. In his outline of the concept the prime minister noted that the House of Commons on December 16 would deposit the British POLARIS missiles, with the British V-bombers force, and with whatever the French might wish to supply, would join these national contributions to "some kind of mixed-manned and jointly owned element in which the nuclear powers could take part." Reference to mixed-manned elements was a fig leaf to cover abandonment of an integrated force. The virtue of this broader nuclear force was that it would keep nuclear forces under national control and enlarge the British presence at the same time.[11]

President Johnson might have accepted the ANF approach during his meeting with Wilson in Washington on December 7–9, 1964. To prepare for Wilson's visit, the president finally gave the MLF his full attention, and he learned of a variety of powerful pressures inhibiting further U.S. involvement: limited congressional support, hostility of the French, uneasiness in Bonn, and opposition by Moscow, which objected to a German finger on the nuclear trigger in any form. As for the ANF, at best it could become an Anglo-American force, which would alienate the Germans and confirm de Gaulle's thesis about the Anglo-Saxon conspiracy.

In this new context Johnson's closest advisers, Bundy and McNamara, who had always entertained reservations about the MLF, worked to minimize an American role. By the end of November Bundy told his colleagues that he was "reaching the conclusion that the U.S. should let the MLF sink out of sight."[12] The critical moment occurred at a meeting between the president and his advisers two days before Wilson arrived in Washington. Under-secretary of State George Ball, the leading MLF supporter, fought a losing battle, arguing that no negative action should be taken until a major effort with Congress had been made. The president was not convinced. Though he might share with the MLF enthusiasts a concern that inaction would be potentially dangerous if it fostered an independent German nuclear effort, he sensed that he could not overcome Senate opposition. He doubted if he could sell to the Senate a proposal about which the European partners were in doubt. "I don't want to be a Woodrow Wilson," he was reported to have noted, "right on a principle, and fighting for a principle, and unable to achieve it."[13]

Nor was it clear that he truly believed in the principle. If the Europeans really wanted such a force, let them work something out and then come to Washington. The United States would not inhibit Western Europe from seeking ways to integrate the nuclear force, but it would no longer take the initiative. To make sure that the world knew the White House position, the memorandum (NSAM 322) was leaked to the press. As Harlan Cleveland, Finletter's successor as U.S. permanent representative to the North Atlantic Council, observed, Johnson had come to the same ambivalent position President Kennedy had taken, namely, to "encourage the enthusiasts to see if they could bring it off, but not get committed to it personally. When it looked as if they weren't bringing it off and there was too much flak from the Hill, and so on, the President torpedoed it on the basis of a memoir from Mac Bundy."[14]

The MLF was effectively dead in December 1964. Its vital signs had disappeared, but its acolytes continued to keep the faith, at least until an obituary had been published. They seized on vague statements and casual references as proof that their vigil ultimately would be rewarded. At his new conference in January 1965 the president fed those hopes by noting that European governments were still discussing MLF proposals and that "we will continue to follow the progress of these talks with the greatest of interest." John Leddy, who joined the administration as assistant secretary of state for European affairs in May 1965, had a vague sense that the MLF was still alive at that time, but he believed, as did George Ball, that it was finally buried in December 1965.[15]

Although many of the MLF enthusiasts in the State Department had regarded McNamara and Bundy as fellow travelers, their kinship was always questionable. McNamara's abiding conviction was that Western security rested in centralized control of nuclear weaponry in American hands and the building of conventional forces as a major deterrent. The multilateral force in contrast involved the creation of a new nuclear entity and a concomitant downplaying of conventional forces. For both McNamara and Bundy the MLF also contained too many loose ends. Their memories of the Bay of Pigs in 1961 inclined them to be skeptical of programs that were not fully thought through. Given the additional factor of widespread opposition it was not surprising that the MLF failed to materialize. The surprise in retrospect is that the concept lingered as long as it did.

A cynical interpretation of the MLF would identify it as a means of the United States fostering an illusion of sharing control of nuclear weaponry while enjoying the reality of Europeans paying for it. A more benign view would identify America's support for the concept as a genuine effort to promote European integration and an equally genuine effort to restrain the Federal Republic from developing its own nuclear capability. No matter which interpretation is the more accurate, the MLF debate served to dissolve, if not solve, some critical problems of the alliance. It did deflate excessive German pressure for more nuclear involvement. The MLF, or at least its fate, satisfied the British partner as well. The British received the POLARIS missile without having to pay the penalty of assigning their nuclear force to NATO; the ANF served as the diversion its designers had hoped it would.

II

The MLF did not resolve the French connection, however. Few observers in Washington seriously expected France to join the MLF or de Gaulle to lessen his opposition to U.S. leadership. But there was a possibility that if the MLF had succeeded, an isolated de Gaulle would have been compelled to join it.

This outcome was doubtful at best. The MLF's rise and fall only confirmed de Gaulle's conviction that the Anglo-Americans would never grant France equality in the alliance, and after 1964 he accelerated France's steady pace of dissociation from NATO. De Gaulle's pronouncements often had a casual air, as if they were impromptu statements, but his moves in fact were carefully prepared and brilliantly staged. Timing was always of the essence. De Gaulle would not act until all his pieces were in place: A French nuclear capability had to be visible; the Algerian war had to be concluded; and a working relationship with both the Federal Republic and the Soviet Union had to be established.

Before Johnson entered the White House the French fleets in the Mediterranean and the Atlantic had already been removed from SHAPE and from SACLANT commands. The change was for the worse after Kennedy's death. In 1965 France ostentatiously refused to participate in FALLEX '66, a military exercise for allied general staffs, which had been proposed by Gen. Lyman L. Lemnitzer, Supreme Allied Commander (SACEUR), to test allied communications and alert systems. But because the exercise was intended to implement a new strategic concept that de Gaulle had rejected, the exercise was unacceptable to him. The only concession that Lemnitzer could achieve for the operation was an agreement with Gen. Charles Ailleret, the French chief-of-staff, to permit a few French officers to serve as token participants.[16]

It is hardly surprising, then, that Lemnitzer in letters written in spring 1965 should have characterized his relations with France as turbulent. He noted that when he took on the assignment as SACEUR he was already concerned about an "element of vindictiveness creeping into Franco-American relationships, particularly in the Political field."[17] Nevertheless, with all the problems posed by France's behavior Lemnitzer never sensed that de Gaulle's animosity was ad hominem. Conceivably, there was an element of condescension in the relationship but if so it reflected the French president's attitude toward any American.[18]

Although de Gaulle's personal treatment of Lemnitzer may have yielded some psychological balm for the wounds he inflicted, Lemnitzer's colleagues in Washington lacked even that palliative to sustain the shock caused by de Gaulle's letter to President Johnson of March 7, 1966. In four paragraphs, the French president made it clear that France intended to withdraw from the military organization of the alliance and expected as a consequence prompt removal of NATO forces from French soil.[19] As U.S. Permanent Representative Harlan Cleveland noted, if it was a shock, it may have been because de Gaulle had spoken so often about such an outcome but had taken only piecemeal steps until then. At his previous press conference on February 21, 1966, he had implied that no definitive action would take place until 1969, when, according to Article 13 of the North Atlantic Treaty, any party may withdraw one year after it has given notice to its fellow members.[20]

De Gaulle did not say that he was withdrawing from the alliance but only from the military side of the organization. He presented similar letters to heads of states or governments of Britain, West Germany, and Italy on March 9, yet even when those letters were delivered, ambiguities about France's position remained. In Foreign Minister Maurice Couve de Murville's explication of March 9, it was clear that France would not denounce the North Atlantic treaty itself and that its specific objective concerned French forces in Lemnitzer's Supreme Headquarters (SHAPE) and the stationing of allied forces on French territory.[21]

The action caused consternation in the administration. Walt W. Rostow, chairman of the State Department's Policy Planning Council, tried to find compensation for "a NATO without France." Use the occasion, he suggested, to tighten the alliance and to move forward on some form of nuclear sharing or a scheme of a multilateral foreign exchange offset that would lift the morale of the allies. He also urged the president to leave "an empty chair" for France to reclaim in the future.[22]

The president did not panic. He neither granted legitimacy to de Gaulle's actions nor threatened reprisals for them. Cleveland noted that while his "private references to General de Gaulle stretched his considerable talent for colorful language," he "imposed an icy correctness on those who had reason to discuss French policy in public."[23] Johnson softened the tone of a stiff letter of protest that Secretary of State Rusk had presented on the grounds that de Gaulle was not going to change his mind regardless of the arguments Americans might take up against him. Johnson noted in his memoirs that he told the secretary of defense that "when a man asks you to leave his house, you don't argue; you get your hat and go." John L. Leddy provided Johnson's variation of that image: "Well, when that old man talks I just tip my hat to him. When he comes rushing down like a locomotive on the track, why the Germans and ourselves, we just stand aside and let him go by, then we're back together again." This remarkable composure, in Gen. Andrew Goodpaster's judgment, was maintained because Johnson did not feel he was engaged in a personal confrontation with de Gaulle; rather, it was a confrontation between two nations.[24]

Some of Johnson's advisers thought that the president's reaction was too complacent. Undersecretary of State George Ball disagreed with a soft line on the ground that de Gaulle had repudiated a "solemn agreement." France's behavior called for a rebuke far stronger than the administration's authorized response.[25]

Francis C. Bator, special assistant to the president for national security affairs, strongly supported Johnson's attitude. But Bator objected to a draft of the president's letter that would have deleted "a place of honor" from a sentence that referred to France's resuming her role in the future. Bator's logic failed to persuade Johnson, however, and the final version simply referred to "her place." Bator's point was that a gracious ending, "with an offer of a golden bridge," not only would underscore America's restraint but would also expose the fact that it was de Gaulle, not the United States, who was isolating France.[26]

Many of the allies were sympathetic to at least some of de Gaulle's charges against the United States. Europeans could agree that America was sluggish in helping the organization adjust to new circumstances and that it had exploited NATO for its own imperial purposes. Portugal, increasingly upset with the allies' lack of sympathy for its colonial problems, used de Gaulle's attack on NATO to express its own frustrations with American leadership of the alliance. Canada's conspicuous silence owed much to its concern about Quebec's reactions. West Germany and Belgium hoped that some way would be found to placate their alienated neighbor.[27]

Despite the tensions NATO succeeded in maintaining its solidarity in the face of a traumatic situation. France went ahead with its schedule, with one ultimatum following another. On March 29 de Gaulle dispatched a memorandum specifying the timetable for the transfer of American and NATO commands from French territory as well as for the termination of all French personnel in NATO commands; the target date was April 1, 1967.[28]

This deadline inevitably posed daunting challenges to General Lemnitzer both in his capacity as SACEUR and as commander of U.S. forces in Europe. The expulsion order contained special problems inasmuch as the original bilateral accords had included, as de Gaulle's note of March 10 specifically pointed out, depots at warehouses at Deols-La-Martinerie, U.S. headquarters at Saint-Germaine, and pipelines, supply lines, and air bases.[29] Lemnitzer had to meet deadlines that his political superiors had accepted, and he did so quickly and effectively.

It was a minor miracle that he was able to locate a new headquarters in Belgium and then to complete the transfer before the deadline. Finding the new headquarters in Casteau, near Mons, was itself a problem; the SACEUR would have preferred to have been as close to the capital in Brussels as he had been in Paris. Any further distance, he felt, would damage the effectiveness of his mission.[30] And though the Belgian government had welcomed NATO, it was a qualified welcome; the civilian headquarters would be allowed to move to Brussels but not the military. Claiming that it was inadvisable to place SHAPE in an urban setting, the government offered sites in the southern part of the country where there was land available belonging to the state with some of the infrastructure already established. Belgian reasoning behind the offer of Casteau was probably based less on the fear of Brussels being a magnet for an enemy attack and more on the anticipation of the economic help some 1,700 SHAPE families might give to the depressed province of Hainaut.[31]

Lemnitzer managed as well as was possible in a difficult situation. Had he pressed too hard for a better site he would have given ammunition to Gaullist charges of American domination; he had no alternative but to accept a location 50 kilometers from the capital. As it was, the Belgian press sniped at the decision. One newspaper claimed that Lemnitzer's reluctance to move to suitable quarters in

Casteau was not because of the distance from the airport but because of the inconvenience it would cause families of SHAPE senior officers accustomed to the amenities of Paris.[32]

Once the question of location was settled the removal of SHAPE from Paris went quickly. As Lemnitzer recalled less than two years later, "It was an enormous undertaking and involved movement of over 100,000 U.S. personnel and over one million tons of supplies and equipment of all types. . . . We had less than six months to complete enough of the headquarters so we could shift our operations from France by 1 April 1967, thereby beating the deadline to everyone's surprise."[33]

Lemnitzer rightly took pride in his accomplishment. More than any other American leader he understood the damage that de Gaulle's actions had inflicted on the organization. McNamara seemed to regard the apparent ease with which the SACEUR effected the change as an augury of a reconstituted NATO. Yet some problems emerged from the gloss that the secretary of defense put on the meaning of the move to Belgium. The relocation, in his view, would be an opportunity to reshape the troop structure in Europe to make it more efficient and less costly.[34]

Two days after Lemnitzer opened his headquarters at Casteau, McNamara announced that the relocation would permit considerable financial savings for the United States, ranging from annual foreign exchange in excess of $100 million per year to almost 40,000 personnel and their dependents formerly stationed in France.[35] De Gaulle had accelerated the secretary's cost-cutting program, which might have required a much longer time to put into effect had France not imposed drastic changes on SHAPE.

McNamara's expectations were postulated on the assumption that the removal of France from SHAPE would be "in no way disabling" to the military posture of the alliance. French territory, he believed, was not necessary to the defense of the West: "Neither the United States nor its allies have ever contemplated a way in which falling back upon French soil through the battle field of Germany was an acceptable strategy for the alliance." Forward defense meant the West German frontier. So although French cooperation was desirable, according to the secretary of defense, it was not vital to military planning.[36]

This was not the picture of Europe seen from Lemnitzer's perspective. As he contemplated the significance of the secretary of defense's plans for streamlining American forces in Europe, he was quoted as saying that "one more benefit of this sort and we will be out of business."[37] The SACEUR was convinced that the defense of Europe, at the frontier in particular, required a commitment of manpower and equipment at a level that could not be replaced by European counterparts. Lemnitzer saw McNamara's position encouraging Senate critics to increase pressure to replace American forces with European in the central sector. McNamara had support from Secretary of the Treasury Henry Fowler, who informed the president that the financial drain in Europe "is our Achilles heel, which could destroy NATO."[38]

McNamara and his advisers failed to perceive, as did Lemnitzer, that troop levels were only part of the equation. NATO's communication system had suffered a wrenching upheaval. The east-west flow between France and Germany of the supply and communications lines had to be diverted to a north-south axis, as German ports replaced French ports for logistical materials shipped from the United States. This shift was forced on NATO only a few years after the Berlin crisis of the early 1960s had exposed the old north-south supply lines to be painfully vulnerable. Even if the dislocation were to be only a temporary problem, "the disrepair," as a Senate report observed, "of American military arrangement is apparent." This somber conclusion was reinforced by presidential adviser John J. McCloy's warnings that France's defections might be the first of many as the alliance unraveled. To restore NATO to a "strong and convincing status," he asserted, we "should be searching our minds to find a means of reestablishing the faith of our non-French allies in the NATO organization itself. It is no time to lead a procession of withdrawals."[39]

The status of NATO in 1967 was impressive not because the alliance was in a state of disarray, as Lemnitzer and McCloy saw it, but because it managed to gather new strength despite de Gaulle's action and McNamara's reaction. The alliance did not dissolve in 1967. In his own fashion de Gaulle shrewdly minimized the damage he had done without abandoning his independent stance. Even as Lemnitzer was preparing to pack up and leave France, the French leader arranged to allow continued operation of the oil pipeline from the west to Germany across French territory, and he subsequently granted permission for flights of allied aircraft from Britain to southern Europe in French airspace. Had de Gaulle continued his initial voiding of all bilateral overflight agreements, France would have joined Austria and Switzerland to form a neutral belt of nations—an Elysian Curtain, as Cyrus Sulzberger called it[40]—splitting NATO into two parts and further reducing flexibility in troop dispositions.

In exchange for this concession the French made sure that they would enjoy the benefits of the new sophisticated air alert system, NATO Air Defense Ground Environment (NADGE), which they deemed essential to France's security. Although NADGE would be an integrated as well as an improved air defense system, it was important enough to justify France's contributing a share of the costs, thus ensuring that a French company would be a member of the consortium constructing the system. A similar convergence of French national interest with the interests of the alliance permitted the French to keep a military presence in Germany, although not under NATO auspices.[41]

III

De Gaulle's careful concessions served to keep SHAPE alive in its new Belgian home, but other consequences of France's withdrawal energized the alliance in a more positive fashion. First, France's separation from the military organization meant separation as well from the Standing Group of the Military Committee, the Anglo-American-French inner circle at the Pentagon that excluded the other powers. The Standing Group disbanded in 1966. The North Atlantic Council then created an International Military Staff (IMS) to replace it, with headquarters in Brussels and with every nation that contributed forces to be represented in this new group.[42] Although the establishment of a broader military planning unit did not mean that each member had an equal voice in determining strategy, it responded to the long-standing demand for consultation by the smaller nations.

At the same time, by circumstance rather than by design, the enormous influence that had been exercised by the Supreme Allied Commander from Eisenhower to Norstad diminished under the new arrangements. Clearly, the loss was a product of Lemnitzer's personality, which did not lend itself to political leadership, but it was also the result of SHAPE being physically removed from the political headquarters and the International Military Staff in Brussels. The distance was psychological as well as physical; it enhanced the IMS at the expense of the SACEUR.

Arguably, the most concrete by-product of the NATO diaspora was the creation of the Nuclear Planning Group (NPG) in 1966.[43] What the MLF could not accomplish—to supply a NATO vehicle for sharing nuclear knowledge and nuclear decisions—the NPG did, up to a point. The new committee did not have the scope of the MLF, but its relatively modest aspirations offered a better chance for success. As the MLF moved away from the agendas of the Johnson administration, Secretary McNamara could claim that the "Nuclear Planning Group, which we are developing, meets the needs of our allies, especially Germany. It will more closely tie in Germany with the U.S. and U.K." How this would be done was left unsaid. McNamara's key point at the NSC meeting was that the NPG "will end talk of the Multilateral Force."[44]

The NPG's origins may be found in a formal proposal made at a meeting of NATO defense ministers in Paris on May 31, 1965, before France left the organization, to seek "ways in which consultation might be improved and participation by interested allied countries extended in the planning of nuclear forces, including strategic forces." It was McNamara who inspired the idea, according to John Leddy, and who pushed it past objections of State Department officials in May 1965 at a time when MLF adherents had not yet given up on their cause. McNamara years later noted that "if I could do things differently, I would have introduced the Nuclear Planning Group much earlier than I did as a means to draw the Europeans into nuclear affairs. The NPG only came to mind after it looked like the MLF would fail. I really didn't think of it earlier."[45]

Once the MLF was out of the way the North Atlantic Council acted with dispatch. A Special Committee of Defense Ministers collaborated in setting up three working groups that began operations in February 1966, the month that de Gaulle issued his expulsion orders. In December of that year the Defense Planning Committee agreed to establish within NATO two permanent bodies for nuclear planning—a Nuclear Defense Affairs Committee to make policy and a subordinate Nuclear Planning Group of seven members to manage the detailed work.[46] The NPG embodied McNamara's concerns for educating the allies to the realities of nuclear warfare and for sharing, at least to some degree, the nuclear planning process.

The president responded to McNamara's enthusiasm by showing a personal interest in the NPG, thereby according it a status it might not have had otherwise. Francis Bator wanted Johnson to emphasize to the allies that the establishment of the NPG was a major step forward in demonstrating "NATO's will to come to grips with the tough issues of organizing nuclear defense."[47]

As in the case of the MLF there was an element of deception in the American promotion of the NPG. The administration hoped to coax the allies into believing they were now fully involved in the planning process. Without the handicap of MLF's high visibility, where the gap between promise and fulfillment was easily exposed, the NPG meetings indulged in generalities that might become specific in the future. The administration could anticipate in April 1967 that "the main result of the meeting—apart from general education—will be agreement on a series of further joint studies . . . on such major issues as the use of tactical nuclear weapons." The ultimate acceptance of the strategy of "flexible response" (MC 14/3) had its way paved by America's openness to consultation in 1967 even though the assignment of studies for their own sake often seemed to be the main order of business.[48]

The absence of France from NATO defense councils also revived the older Defense Planning Committee (DPC). The DPC had been in existence since 1963, but as long as France remained as a member there was no consensus on advice to the SACEUR or to policymaking in any coherent form. With the French seat vacated the committee gained stature. The Council's communique of December 16, 1966, was uncharacteristically understated when it relegated to a footnote the DPC's mission to deal with all questions concerning an integrated defense system involving fourteen member nations.[49]

The new role of the DPC deserved more recognition. It was under DPC auspices that the new strategy of flexible response became NATO policy in 1967 after four years of seemingly fruitless American lobbying. Though the European allies had accepted the bankruptcy of "massive retaliation" as embodied in MC 14/2, formulated in 1957, they resisted the Kennedy and Johnson pressures to elevate conventional defense over nuclear, partly for reasons of cost, mostly for fear that raising the threshold of nuclear response could inhibit American use of the nuclear deterrent under any circumstance.

At the Athens meeting of the North Atlantic Council in 1962 McNamara had articulated his thesis about the viability of conventional warfare and the irrelevance of strategic nuclear weaponry to a cool if not hostile audience. The secretary of defense, however, did not give up his efforts to instruct the allies on the dangers of nuclear warfare. His Draft Presidential Memorandum (DPM) in 1964 spelled out the U.S. conception of the relationship between tactical nuclear weapons to nonnuclear forces; McNamara's subsequent DPMs challenged even the utility of tactical nuclear weaponry. As McNamara noted in 1967, "The danger of escalation, once the 'firebreak' between nonnuclear and nuclear war has been crossed, and the damage, if escalation occurs, cautions against our ability to limit nuclear war."[50]

The secretary of defense failed to convince the Europeans. Although they could accept a role for conventional forces, they rejected his sweeping judgment that these troops could substitute for nuclear capabilities in blocking a major Soviet nonnuclear assault. Moreover, the U.S. withdrawal of its own troops from the central sector as the demands of the Vietnam War grew increasingly damaged McNamara's credibility.

By the end of 1966 he had recognized that there would be no major increases in expenditures for conventional defense by the allies. Consequently, the United States was willing to accept a compromise in MC 14/3 that committed NATO to respond at whatever level of force—conventional or nuclear—was chosen by the aggressor. The apocalyptic level of a strategic nuclear response would be reached only in the event of a major nuclear attack. McNamara was still confident that NATO could manage with conventional means to cope with anything except a full-scale assault from the Warsaw bloc. Thus even though the nuclear option was built into NATO's new strategic concept, it was unlikely that it would be used.[51] In sum, it was apparent that a compromise, unacceptable had France kept its seat in the DPC, could be ratified after France withdrew.

IV

NATO's acceptance of MC 14/3 signaled a renewal of faith in the American connection with Europe. If the allies were still unwilling to spend the funds needed to support one part of the flexible-response doctrine, conventional forces, at least they recognized the value of a graduated rather than an automatic response to Soviet provocation. This breakthrough in December 1967 took place at the same meeting of the North Atlantic Council in which the Harmel report on "The Future Tasks of the Alliance" was accepted.[52]

The Harmel initiative, too, was a by-product of France's departure from the organization. When Belgian Foreign Minister Pierre Harmel proposed in December 1966 a broad examination of the future tasks facing the alliance, France was too distracted by the fallout from its disengagement to raise difficulties about a political reorientation of the alliance.[53]

But the meaning of the Harmel report involved more than the diminished role of France in the alliance; it represented, as did the NPG and the resuscitated DPC, the new authority of the smaller nations. In a sense the participants in the "Harmel exercise" were repeating the efforts that the Wise Men of 1956 had attempted in vain:

namely, to find some way to tell the larger powers that their voices should be heard. In 1956 the report of the Committee of Three on Non-Military Cooperation in NATO asked and received approval from the council for wider consultation among the member states in political matters, but the larger powers largely ignored its recommendations.[54] The Suez crisis, which occurred while the Wise Men were formulating their proposals, dramatized the exclusion of their countries from the agendas of the United States, the United Kingdom, and France.

In 1967 the smaller powers were able to make the larger pay attention to their concerns, not just with a vague promise of future consultation but through a specific program that won the support of the United States. In fact, Eugene Rostow, under-secretary of state for political affairs, noted that he devoted considerable time to the Harmel exercise and took pride in generating "wholly new political impulses" in the alliance. In accepting the Harmel report in December 1967 the North Atlantic Council elevated détente to the level of defense as a major function of the alliance. Its key statement was that "military security and a policy of detente are not contradictory but complementary."[55]

American planners were under no illusion about the difficulties in moving toward a new role for the alliance. As one report prepared for the National Security Council observed, important differences remained "between nations like Denmark and Canada that placed primary emphasis on *detente* and Greece and Turkey whose main preoccupation is with the Communist threat." Moreover, security arrangements would have to be made to take into account German sensitivities. And even as the United States welcomed the anticipated findings of the Harmel report, Europeans had to understand that the "special responsibilities" of the superpower required American "involvement in all phases of eventual negotiations on European security." If the allies still felt that they did not have a big enough role in NATO, "the ultimate answer to the lack of balance in the Alliance can only come from the Europeans themselves— through their unification."[56]

A feeling of satisfaction was expressed in the declaration on Mutual and Balanced Force Reductions, or the "Reykjavik signal," presented at the North Atlantic Council meeting of December 1967. This declaration followed from the recommendations of the Harmel report and seemed to portend a practical means of pursuing détente without risking the destabilization of Western Europe. The ministers were now ready for further "discussions on this subject with the

Soviet Union and other countries of Eastern Europe and they call on them to join in this search for progress toward peace."[57] The optimism implicit in this communique should have been tempered by concerns about the Soviets once again hampering Western access to Berlin. Though it did contain a warning that "progress toward general détente should not be over-rated," the tone of the communique belied this mild caveat.[58] Then the sudden and brutal Soviet intervention in Czechoslovakia two months later in August 1968 shocked the allies and disrupted the momentum for détente.

But the disruption was only temporary, and the reaction of the United States and NATO was carefully measured. It was not that the president and his advisers relegated the action against Czechoslovakia to the sidelines as an internal Warsaw Pact matter. They were distressed about the overthrow of the liberal Dubcek government and would not credit Soviet Ambassador Anatoly Dobrynin's statement that the Czechs had invited Warsaw forces into the country. Rusk was particularly chagrined at the timing of this action, just when strategic-missile talks, among other aspects of détente, appeared to show promise. Gen. Earle G. Wheeler, chairman of the Joint Chiefs of Staff, claimed that the "message is an insult to the United States" but that there was no military action that the United States could take. Clark Clifford, secretary of defense since McNamara's resignation in February 1968, agreed with Wheeler. The situation appeared to be more difficult than the failed Hungarian revolution of 1956 if only because there was a better relationship with the Soviet Union in 1968.[59]

The upshot of the agonizing in the National Security Council was a vigorous protest at the United Nations but little more. The administration offered a strong affirmation of Jefferson's belief in governments based on the consent of the governed and a weak compliance with the Warsaw Pact's coup de main on the grounds that U.S. interests were not affected. By September it was obvious that the Soviets were not going to invade Romania, let alone West Berlin. Former U.S. ambassador to the Soviet Union Llewellyn E. Thompson underscored this passive stance when he urged that the United States should not encourage Czech refugees to come to America "but only . . . welcome them" if they managed to escape. This "welcome" was compromised by his concern that the Soviets would regard any active encouragement as evidence of the West's interfering in the internal affairs of Czechoslovakia. Secretary Rusk disagreed: the United States should open its doors to refugees "because if we do not, the refugees might return to Czechoslovakia and oppose the existing government. This would not be in our interests." Neither adviser would allow the plight of refugees to jeopardize the fragile but peaceful relationship with the Soviet Union.[60]

V

It is understandable that domestic tensions over the war in Vietnam have been assigned responsibility for the caution the United States displayed when the Warsaw Pact forces ousted the Dubcek regime from Prague. A presidential campaign was in progress at the time, with President Johnson a self-declared lame duck and Vietnam the preoccupation of both political parties. Yet it is doubtful if Vietnam was responsible for the mild response to the Soviet-led invasion; rather, the response reflected NATO's hope to keep détente alive and its belief in the Soviet government's assurances about the limits of its actions. If the Czech crisis had a domestic impact, according to Clifford it was to inhibit for the short run the efforts of such congressional figures as Senator Mansfield to reduce the American presence in Europe.[61]

Still, the administration was clearly diluting the caliber of American troops in Europe by transferring units to Vietnam. This action reflected the long-standing objective of the secretary of defense, beginning in the Kennedy administration, to reduce the financial burden of NATO membership by basing U.S. troops in the United States and flying them over for regularly scheduled exercises. The operation to fly the combat-ready Second Armored Division from Texas to Germany, dubbed Exercise Big Lift, was conducted in October 1963, when Vietnam posed a troublesome but not an all-absorbing problem for the Kennedy administration. McNamara found proof that an entire armored division could be flown to Europe, draw its supplies and equipment from depots there, and be ready to participate in NATO maneuvers at any time. The Vietnam War combined with France's withdrawal from the organization to facilitate reforms made in the name of efficiency and of economy. If there was no massive cut in U.S. forces, it was due in good measure to the influence of such strong-willed presidential advisers as John J. McCloy who made a persuasive case for keeping force reductions to a minimum.[62]

Similarly, the burden of the Vietnam War accounted for the increasingly strident American cries for Europeans to assume a greater share of the costs in money and manpower. The Senate resolutions on troop reduction and burden sharing, introduced in 1966 and repeated over the next few years, reflected public resentment of Europe's indifference or hostility to America's problems in Southeast Asia. McNamara therefore had strong popular support for his demands for the allies to pay directly for American troops on their soil or to offset the costs by purchasing weapons or bonds from the United States. One of the more enduring sources of friction in the alliance after 1960 was over the effect of the cost of financing American forces abroad upon the balance of payments, particularly in Germany. Although a dominant subject of diplomatic conversations in the Johnson administration, these matters were essentially a legacy from the Kennedy era.

From 1961 to 1964 the United States and the Federal Republic, as well as France and Italy, had worked out bilateral offset agreements, which mandated purchase of American military equipment to offset the costs of the American military presence in those countries. By mid-1966 the financial difficulties of the three major allies—the United States, the United Kingdom, and the Federal Republic—reached a point at which the Americans and the British claimed that they would keep their forces intact in Germany only if new arrangements were made. The U.S. deficit in balance of payments was blamed directly on Europe.[63]

On August 31, 1966, Mike Mansfield, Senate majority leader, gathered forty-three sponsors to introduce the first of many subsequent resolutions calling for substantial reduction of the U.S. presence in Europe unless the allies increased their support. A potential deadlock was in the making. Britain had been suffering from a sterling crisis and was in much worse financial shape than the United States. Germany enjoyed a surplus in its balance of payments, but the country was experiencing an economic recession as well as a budget deficit, brought on by its purchase of U.S. military equipment under the offset agreements.[64]

To resolve the issue, the State Department proposed a trilateral approach in August 1966. John J. McCloy was appointed the U.S. chief representative on October 11 and spent the balance of that year and part of 1967 fending off domestic critics and contending with German and British opposition. His task was made even more difficult by the fall of the Erhard government and the worsening economic crisis in Britain. Erhard's coalition government fell in late October, but it was not until December 1 that his successor Kurt Georg Kiesinger took over. Three more months passed before the Germans were ready to resume the trilateral negotiations. Wilson's government managed to survive in part because of Johnson's offer to have the Department of Defense place some $35 million worth of orders for military equipment to help Britain's foreign-exchange squeeze. At home, the secretaries of state, defense, and treasury agreed that there should be no troop reductions that would seriously reduce U.S. capacity to deter a nonnuclear attack, but they could not agree on how deep any cuts should be.[65]

State Department officials understandably were more politically attuned to European sensibilities in the internal debate over troop reductions. Although both State and Defense agreed to dual-basing in the United States and West Germany, Secretary Rusk wanted to limit the withdrawals to two of three brigades of only one army division, and McNamara asked for four of six brigades from two divisions. McCloy strongly opposed both proposals in light of the military capabilities of the Warsaw Pact countries and the volatile political situation in Europe. He did recognize some merit in the principle of dual-basing of no more than one division and three air wings if the allies agreed and if U.S. capacity to rotate and reinforce rapidly showed that no substantial impairment of the military deterrent would occur.[66]

The president essentially accepted McCloy's advice to pursue a compromise that made clear that security, not financial considerations, would be the primary factor in determining U.S. force levels. This prejudgment determined the course of the trilateral negotiations. Monetary compensation, whether in the form of European procurement of U.S. equipment or of purchases of U.S. bonds, would be a matter of diplomatic bargaining, but the negotiations would not be conducted under the threat of U.S. withdrawal from Europe.[67]

By spring 1967 the administration managed to induce the British to cut back their demands for a complete offset of their costs of their Army of the Rhine and to accept something less than a complete closing of their gap in foreign exchange. U.S. purchases of $40 million worth of British equipment helped to convince the British to scale down their claims. The Germans offered to have the Bundesbank purchase $500 million in medium-term U.S. government bonds during fiscal year 1968 and promised not to convert their dollar holdings into gold.[68] The United States in turn scaled down its redeployment plan; 96 instead of 144 aircraft would be redeployed from Germany. The "Final Report on the Trilateral Talks" was signed on April 28, 1967, at the conclusion of the last trilateral meeting.[69]

McCloy deserved Johnson's congratulations for a successful negotiation, but the president himself played a vital role in the process.

He recognized the centrality of the Congress in whatever success was achieved, and he understood just how tenuous the victory might be. In 1967 there was a three-to-one majority in favor of substantial troop cuts. A few congressmen would hold out, he thought, but "the rest of them will run just like turkeys." If the administration prevails, he told McCloy after a breakfast meeting with congressional leaders, it is "not because that's the way the Congress really feels, but because it is the way I managed it; first of all they were my guests, eating my breakfast, then I laid out a very hard line, more arbitrary than I like, which made it difficult for them to disagree with the President of the United States." But tough as his stance was, Johnson understood the limits of his authority. As he pointed out, he had "dealt with those babies for thirty years."[70] Senator Mansfield's reaction to the final agreement showed the reason for his wariness; the arrangement for Germans to purchase special U.S. government securities earned his scorn. The Senate majority leader claimed that Germany would be winning new profits from their loans rather than bearing their fair share of the defense of Europe.[71]

VI

Despite formidable opposition in the Congress and in the country Johnson managed to surmount domestic challenges to the alliance. When he left the White House in 1969, he claimed that his "greatest single fear" was that the nation would relapse into isolationism, "whether out of boredom or frustration, out of lack of money, or out of simple foolishness." In his memoirs he took issue with critics who claimed that his preoccupation with Vietnam caused neglect of Europe and of opportunities to effect a détente with the Warsaw Pact countries.[72] He had reason to protest; indeed, he might have made a stronger case than he did. Not even the Soviet intervention in Czechoslovakia stopped his efforts on behalf of a nuclear proliferation treaty with the Soviet Union. Although his attention was rarely focused on Europe, when it was, his reasoning on NATO affairs was usually sound, particularly when he considered congressional implications. At these times he did not always follow the lead of even his most trusted advisers. Where his own experience could come into play, his expertise served him well. The Mansfield resolutions never became law.

But NATO policy was only fitfully at the head of his agenda; policy was made by the experts around him to whom he had given his trust. Logically, Secretary of State Rusk should have been primus inter pares, and to a degree he was. Rusk occupied a more important role than he had under Kennedy, but his personality and his focus on Vietnam stood in his way. Undersecretary of State Ball felt that it was hard to get Rusk's attention on anything except Vietnam; consequently, Ball claimed to have "sort of taken the lead on European policy."[73] Ball undoubtedly overstated his role. Although he did grant Bundy "some independent" views, Ball might have added that Bundy's close connections with the president in his two years as adviser on national security provided him with greater influence than the undersecretary of state ever carried: Witness their respective positions on the MLF.

Of the men around Johnson, McNamara's weight was most felt in almost every aspect of foreign military affairs, from the MLF to Vietnam. Replacement of the MLF with agencies that granted new authority to the smaller nations, a troop-reduction program following France's withdrawal from the organization, pressures for burden sharing and cost reduction, and movement away from nuclear defense were primarily the work of Secretary McNamara. Not all of these efforts were positive. There was an inherent contradiction in McNamara's vigorous espousal of costly conventional-force contributions by the European partners and his emphasis on reducing the American part of the equation. If a reformed and reorganized American military establishment in Europe could be substantially smaller and still effective, Europeans had little incentive to build up their own conventional forces. McNamara never exorcised European suspicion that a high nuclear threshold in the document of flexible response masked American willingness to use nuclear weapons under any circumstances. While American manpower in Europe declined from 416,000 in 1962 to 291,000 at the end of the Johnson years, Soviet conventional strength in Europe increased from 475,000 to over 500,000 personnel, figures that help to explain why Europe's image of security differed from McNamara's.[74]

Diversion of resources to Vietnam did affect the Atlantic alliance as it affected other aspects of Johnson's foreign and domestic policies. Congressional pressures would not have been as strong as they were without the debilitating effects of an escalating war in Southeast Asia. The American military presence in Europe was a logical target for critics, particularly when Europeans appeared either to oppose or to stand aloof from the American war in Asia.

Yet the course of NATO's history probably would have been much as it was without the destructive impact of the Vietnam War. The crisis with France, the failure of the MLF, the Harmel initiative, and détente occurred independently of other facets of American foreign military policies. The issue of force withdrawals and the tensions over balance of payments with allies were still by-products of Secretary McNamara's vision even if they were exacerbated by the Vietnam conflict. NATO's departure from France was an unexpected opportunity to accelerate reforms McNamara had regarded as necessary. Whether or not the realignment of force deployments was necessary, it was not the result of the war in Asia.

The Johnson administration of the alliance was not without flaws. Its dismissal of the MLF was graceless, and in general the manipulation of allies by the superpower too often was overbearing. Even the success of the trilateral negotiations inspired rebuke for its obvious slighting of the smaller allies. And while the administration was giving its blessing to the work of the Harmel committee in 1966, it had to fend off understandable complaints by Harmel, among others, that the three larger powers were reviving the idea of a "directorate."[75] If the administration managed to calm the Harmel group, it did less well in handling a potential Turkish invasion of Cyprus in 1966. Johnson's threat to cut off all military assistance if Turkey employed weapons designed for NATO use was a crude exercise of a superpower's weight even though its intentions were reasonable.[76]

The sins of commission and omission could be expanded. But in retrospect the Johnson years found NATO accepting, no matter how reluctantly, the American position on nuclear warfare and flexible response at the same time that the United States moved, with some reservations, toward a more genuine consultation on such vital issues as nuclear technology and nuclear proliferation. The elevation of détente to equality with defense reflected the increased visibility of the smaller members of the alliance. Above all, it was on Johnson's watch that NATO successfully met de Gaulle's challenge. Given the volatile history of the alliance, John Leddy may have understated the situation when he observed shortly before the North Atlantic Council met at Reykjavik in June 1968 that "NATO is in a better state of health than the pessimists predicted a few years ago."[77]

Notes

1. David Calleo, *The Atlantic Fantasy: The U.S., NATO, and Europe* (Baltimore: Johns Hopkins University Press, 1970), pp. 27–28.

2. See in particular Marc Trachtenberg, "The Berlin Crisis," in *His-*

tory and Strategy (Princeton, N.J.: Princeton University Press, 1991), pp. 223–24.

3. John Lewis Gaddis, "The Long Peace: Elements of Stability in the Postwar International System," in *The Long Peace: Inquiries into the History of the Cold War* (New York: Oxford University Press, 1987), pp. 215–45.

4. Philip Geyelin, *Lyndon Johnson and the World* (New York: Frederick A. Praeger, 1966), p. 7.

5. John D. Steinbruner, *The Cybernetic Theory of Decision: New Dimensions of Political Analysis* (Princeton, N.J.: Princeton University Press, 1974), pp. 220–23; Arthur Schlesinger, Jr., *A Thousand Days: John F. Kennedy in the White House* (Boston: Houghton Mifflin, 1965), pp. 854–55.

6. Paul H. Nitze, *From Hiroshima to Glasnost: At the Center of Decision, A Memoir* (New York: Grove Widenfield, 1989), pp. 211–12; Steinbruner, *Cybernetic Theory*, pp. 255–56; David N. Schwartz, *NATO's Nuclear Dilemmas* (Washington, D.C.: Brookings Institution, 1982), pp. 108–9.

7. Steinbruner, *Cybernetic Theory*, pp. 286–88.

8. Ibid., p. 287; Geyelin, *Johnson and the World*, pp. 166–67.

9. Geyelin, *Johnson and the World*, p. 166.

10. Joint communique issued at Washington by Johnson and the chancellor of the Federal Republic of Germany (Erhard), June 12, 1964, in *American Foreign Policy: Current Documents 1964* (Washington, D.C.: Government Printing Office, 1967), p. 537.

11. Andrew J. Pierre, *Nuclear Politics: The British Experience with an Independent Strategic Force, 1939–1970* (London: Oxford University Press, 1971), pp. 276–77.

12. David Klein memorandum to Bundy, October 10, 1964, White House/National Security Files (WH/NSF) MLF Gen, vol. 2, boxes 23–4, Lyndon B. Johnson Library (hereafter cited as LBJL); NATO Nuclear Policy, Bundy memorandum to Rusk, McNamara, and Ball, November 25, 1964, "The Future of NATO," National Security Archive, Washington, D.C. Unless otherwise indicated, all citations to documents and oral histories refer to material in the Johnson Library.

13. Geyelin, *Johnson and the World*, pp. 169, 171; LBJ memorandum for secretary of state and secretary of defense, November 14, 1964, "The Future of the Nuclear Defense of the Atlantic Alliance," MLF Gen, vol. 2, WH/NSF, box 23.

14. White House memorandum for the president, December 4, 1964, "The Wilson visit," WH/NSF memoranda to president, vol. 7, National Security Archives, Washington, D.C.; Harlan Cleveland Oral History Interview, August 13, 1969, by Paige E. Mulhollan, tape 1, pp. 37–38; the memorandum mentioned by Cleveland was probably Bundy's memorandum to the president, December 6, 1964, "MLF—An Alternative View," with a copy of his memorandum of June 15, 1963, to JFK, WH/NSF memorandum to president—Bundy, vol. 7.

15. President's news conference at the LBJ Ranch, January 16, 1965, *Public Papers of the Presidents of the United States*: 1: 57–58 (hereafter cited as *Public Papers*); Oral History Interview, March 12, 1969, by Paige Mulhollan, pp. 3–4, AC 75–5; Cleveland Oral History Interview, p. 20. George W. Ball Oral History Interview, July 9, 1971, by Mulhollan 2, pp. 20–21.

16. Lawrence S. Kaplan and Katherine A. Kellner, "Lemnitzer: Surviving the French Military Withdrawal," in *Generals in International Politics: NATO's Supreme Allied Commander, Europe*, ed. Robert S. Jordan, (Lexington: University Press of Kentucky), p. 104.

17. Lemnitzer to Adm. Harry W. Hill, June 22, 1965, box 42, 1–228–71, Lemnitzer Papers, National Defense University Library, Washington, D.C.

18. De Gaulle to Lemnitzer, February 7, 1967, box 48, L–355–71, Lemnitzer Papers; Lemnitzer to Lydia and Bill (Lemnitzer), March 20, 1967, box 66, Family, ibid.

19. Letter from de Gaulle to Johnson, March 7, 1966, *American Foreign Policy: Current Documents 1966* (Washington, D.C.: Government Printing Office, 1969), pp. 317–18; French memorandum to the fourteen representatives of the NATO governments, March 29 and 30, 1966, ibid., pp. 324–26.

20. Harlan Cleveland, *NATO: The Transatlantic Bargain* (New York: Harper and Row, 1970), p. 102; Charles E. Bohlen, *Witness to History* (New York: W. W. Norton, 1973). As U.S. ambassador to France, he admitted to being "fooled by de Gaulle," after being told in January that France would do nothing precipitate; reply made by the president of the French Republic to a question asked at a news conference, February 21, 1966, *American Foreign Policy: Current Documents 1966*, pp. 316–17.

21. March 29 memorandum, *NATO Letter* 14 (May 1966): 24; see also French memorandum to the fourteen representatives of the NATO governments, March 8 and 10, 1966, *American Foreign Policy: Current Documents 1966*, pp. 318–19.

22. Rostow memorandum to the president, March 7, 1966, IT 34 NATO, box 58.

23. Cleveland, *NATO: Transatlantic Bargain*, pp. 105–6.

24. Lyndon B. Johnson, *The Vantage Point: Perspectives of the Presidency, 1963–1969* (New York: Holt, Rinehart and Winston, 1971), p. 305; Leddy Oral History Interview, March 12, 1969, p. 12, AC 75-5; Gen. Andrew J. Goodpaster Oral History Interview, June 21, 1971, by Paige Mulhollan.

25. George Ball Oral History Interview, July 9, 1971, 2: 122.

26. Bator memorandum to the president, "Your Letter to de Gaulle," March 18, 1966, Papers of LBJ, IT 34 NATO, box 58. Letter from Johnson to de Gaulle; March 22, 1966, *American Foreign Policy: Current Documents 1966*, pp. 321–23.

27. *American Foreign Policy: Current Documents 1966*, pp. 321–23; *New York Times*, March 18, 1966.

28. French memorandum to the fourteen representatives of the NATO governments, March 29 and 30, 1966, *American Foreign Policy: Current Documents 1966*, pp. 324–26.

29. *American Foreign Policy: Current Documents 1966*, p. 320. For more detail, see Department of State *Bulletin* 54 (18 April 1966): 617–18.

30. These recommendations were largely the product of Working Group D on Relocation, undated memorandum to the secretary of defense, "Evaluations of Relocation Alternatives, Box 164, L–1502-7h; Lemnitzer letter to Secretary-General Brosio, May 3, 1966; Air Marshal MacBrien's

memorandum to Lord Coleridge, July 26, 1966, "Broad Outline of the Requirement When Relocated in Belgium," all in Lemnitzer Papers.

31. Count Charles De Kerchove letter to Lemnitzer, August 12, 1966, box 45, 1–1502, Lemnitzer Papers.

32. Lemnitzer letter to Norstad, July 8, 1966, box 44, L–316–7, ibid; *New York Times*, August 22, 1966; *Pourquoi Pas*'s comment was listed in a continental press summary, August 11, 1966, box 163, L–1495–71, Lemnitzer Papers.

33. Lemnitzer to Brig. Gen. Orwin C. Talbott, August 28, 1967, box 45, L–327–71, Lemnitzer Papers.

34. "The Crisis in NATO," *Hearings* before the Subcommittee on Europe of the Committee on Foreign Affairs, H.R., 89th Cong., 2d sess., March 17, 1966, p. 37. Testimony of Assistant Secretary of Defense John T. McNaughton, who noted that the Defense Department was looking for alternatives that would make efficient use of modern logistic knowledge and equipment and which "would bring the costs down."

35. News release, ODS (Public Affairs), statement by secretary of defense on relocation of U.S. forces from Europe, April 3, 1967.

36. "The North Atlantic Alliance," *Hearings* before the Subcommittee on National Security and International Operations of the Committee on Government Operations, U.S. Senate, 89th Cong., 2d sess., pt. 6, June 21, 1966, p. 187; McNamara's statement.

37. Quoted in Cyrus L. Sulzberger, *New York Times*, June 8, 1966.

38. Note Mansfield resolution on troop reduction, January 19, 1967, Sen. Res. 49, 90th Cong., 1st sess., in "United States Troops in Europe," *Hearings* before Subcommittee of Foreign Relations and Armed Services Committee, April 26, 1967, pp. 1–2; Henry H. Fowler, secretary of the treasury, memorandum to the president, May 25, 1967, "Problems ahead in Europe," NSC meetings, vol. 4, IAV51, box 2.

39. "The Atlantic Alliance: Unfinished Business," a study submitted by the Subcommittee on National Security and International Operations to the Committee on Government Operations, U.S. Senate, 90th Cong., 1st sess., March 1, 1967, pp. 2, 5, 7; McCloy to Walt W. Rostow, February 17, commenting on a paper by Assistant Secretary of Defense for International Security Affairs John McNaughton on proposed troop withdrawals from Europe, February 17, 1967, NATO Gen, vol. 4, box 38.

40. *New York Times*, July 31, 1966; Eliot R. Goodman, "De Gaulle's NATO Policy in Perspective," *Orbis* 10 (Fall 1966): 716–17; a background paper for an NSC meeting in December 1966 noted de Gaulle's willingness to permit NATO's use of facilities in peacetime "provided these are under French management." State Department paper, December 10, 1966, for NSC meeting, December 13, 1966, appended to summary notes of 566th NSC meeting, December 13, 1966, NSC meetings, vol. 4, box 2.

41. *Aviation Week and Space Technology*, May 29, 1967, p. 315; Michael Harrison, *The Reluctant Ally: France and Atlantic Security* (Baltimore: Johns Hopkins University Press, 1981), pp. 155–56.

42. NATO Facts and Figures (Brussels: NATO Information Service, 1976), pp. 219–20. Meeting of the North Atlantic Council (NAC) June 8, 1966, *Texts of Final Communiques, 1949–1974* (Brussels: NATO Information Service, n.d.), p. 171 (hereafter cited as *NATO Communiques*).

43. Meeting of NAC, Paris, December 15–16, 1966, *NATO Communiques*, p. 180.

44. Summary notes of 566th NSC meeting, December 13, 1966, NSC meetings, vol. 4, box 2.

45. *NATO Communiques*, p. 165; Leddy Oral History Interview, March 12, 1969, p. 6; quoted in Jane E. Stromseth, *The Origin of Flexible Response: NATO's Debate over Strategy in the 1960s* (New York: St. Martin's Press, 1988), p. 80.

46. Schwartz, *NATO's Nuclear Dilemmas*, pp. 182–85; meeting of NAC, Paris, December 15–16, 1966, *NATO Communiques*, p. 180.

47. Bator memorandum to president, ''Your Meeting with McNamara and the NATO Nuclear Planning Group (NPG)—12 Noon, April 7,'' April 6, 1967, NATO Gen 5, box 37.

48. Ibid., with enclosure on ''Background Material on the Nuclear Planning Group.''

49. Meeting of NAC, Paris, December 15–16, 1966, *NATO Communiques*, p. 177.

50. Remarks by McNamara, NATO ministerial meeting, Athens, National Security Archive, Washington, D.C.; McNamara draft memorandum to president, January 15, 1965, ''Role of Tactical Nuclear Forces in NATO Strategy,'' ibid.; McNamara draft memorandum to president, January 6, 1967, ''Thereafter Nuclear Forces,'' ibid., p. 6; Stromseth, *Origins of Flexible Response*, pp. 58–68.

51. Stromseth, *Origins of Flexible Response*, pp. 58–68; McNamara draft memorandum to president, September 21, 1966, ''NATO Strategy and Force Structure,'' National Security Archive, Washington, D.C., Freedom of Information Act.

52. Ministerial meeting of NAC, Brussels, December 13–14, 1967, *NATO Communiques*, p. 197.

53. Ministerial meeting of NAC, Paris, December 15–16, 1966, ibid., pp. 179–80; Cleveland, *NATO: Transatlantic Bargain*, p. 143.

54. Ministerial meeting of NAC, Paris, December 11–14, 1956, ''Resolution of the Report of the Committee of Three on Non-Military Cooperation in NATO,'' *NATO Communiques*, p. 104; ministerial meeting of NAC, Paris, May 4–5, 1957, ibid., p. 99.

55. Eugene V. Rostow Oral History Interview, December 1, 1968, by Paige Mulhollan, AC 74–72. Report of the council, ''The Future Tasks of the Alliance,'' ministerial meeting of NAC, December 13–14, 1967, *NATO Communiques*, p. 19.

56. State Department paper, undated, ''Problems Ahead in Europe,'' pp. 5–7, NSC meetings, vol. 4, box 2.

57. Ministerial meeting of the NAC, Reykjavik, June 24–25, 1968, *NATO Communiques*, pp. 206, 209–10.

58. Ibid., pp. 206–7.

59. Notes on emergency meeting of the National Security Council, August 20, 1968—President Johnson, Rusk, General Wheeler, CIA director Helms, vice-president, Ambassador Ball, Walt Rostow, Leonard Marks, George Christian, Tom Johnson, Notes of Meetings, box 2.

60. Summary notes, 590th NSC meeting, September 4, 1968, ''U.S.,

Europe, and the Czechoslovakian Crisis," p. 2, Tom Johnson's Notes of Meetings, box 2.

61. Tom Johnson memorandum to the president, August 22, 1968, with notes of cabinet meeting of August 22, Tom Johnson's Notes of Meetings, box 2.

62. Rostow Oral History Interview, AC 74-72.

63. Trilateral Negotiations and NATO, undated, NSC paper, Background to the Negotiations, p. 1; Trilateral Negotiations and NATO, Book 1, NSC History, box 50.

64. Ibid., p. 2.

65. Ibid., pp. 2-6; Analysis of Major Decisions in Trilateral Talks, undated, "The Decision to Offer the British $35 million in Purchases," Trilateral Negotiations and NATO, Book 2, NSC History, box 50.

66. Trilateral Negotiations and NATO, ibid., pp. 7-8; Eugene Rostow, Robert Bowie, John Leddy, and Jeffrey Kitchen, memorandum to secretary of state, and "OSD Proposal for Reducing U.S. Troops in Europe," Trilateral Negotiations and NATO, Book 4, NSC History box 51; Eugene Rostow, in a memorandum to the secretary, January 30, 1967, "Force Levels in Europe, ibid., believed that the risks of the plan "are out of proportion to the possible benefits." McCloy memorandum to the president, "Force Levels in Europe," Trilateral Negotiations and NATO, Book 2, NSC History, box 50; Bator claimed to prefer McNamara's position to McCloy's but "my bad dream is another *Skybolt*, with painful consequences at home" (Bator memorandum to the president, February 23, 1967, "U.S. Position in the Trilateral Negotiations," ibid).

67. Trilateral Negotiations and NATO, Book 2, NSC History, box 50, pp. 8-9.

68. Bator memorandum to the president, March 8, 1967, "Your 12:45 P.M. Meeting with John McCloy on the Trilaterals," ibid. Bator was convinced that the promise not to convert German dollar holdings into gold was the more valuable part of the Bundesbank offer. (In effect, this would have put them on a dollar standard.) Johnson, *Vantage Point*, pp. 309-11.

69. Trilateral Negotiations and NATO, Book 2, NSC History, box 50, pp. 9-16.

70. Bator memorandum for the record, March 2, 1967, "President's Conversation with John McCloy Concerning U.S. Position in Trilateral Negotiations, 10:45-11:40 A.M., Wednesday, March 1, 1967," ibid.

71. *Congressional Record*, June 19, 1968, reprinted in "United States Troops in Europe, *Report* of the Combined Subcommittees of Foreign Relations and Armed Services Committees on the Subject of United States Troops in Europe to the Committee on Foreign Relations and Committee on Armed Services," U.S. Senate, October 15, 1968, pp. 88-89.

72. Johnson, *Vantage Point*, pp. 491-92; 475.

73. Ball Oral History Interview, 2, p. 17.

74. Richard Hart Sinnreich, "NATO's Doctrinal Dilemma, *Orbis* 19 (Summer 1976): 466.

75. Secretary of state to American embassy in Ottawa, no. 65140, October 13, 1966, for Harmel via the Belgian embassy, Trilateral Negotiations and NATO, Book 3, NSC History, box 51; Bator memorandum to the presi-

dent, October 12, 1966, Bator memorandums, box 1—a voice for the Italian ambassador at Columbus Day parade.

76. The full text of President Johnson's letter of rebuke was published in the Turkish newspaper, *Hurriyet*, on January 14, 1966.

77. Memorandum for the record, summary of NSC meeting on NATO, June 19, 1968, NSC meetings, vol. 5, box 2.

6 | Choosing Sides: Lyndon Johnson and the Middle East

Douglas Little

ASK ANYONE ABOUT LYNDON JOHNSON'S foreign policy, and, as Dizzy Dean used to say to Pee Wee Reese, ninety-nine times out of ten the conversation turns to Vietnam. That is probably as it should be, for Vietnam was the long jagged scar across LBJ's presidency that David Levine captured so well in his memorable 1966 "gallbladder" cartoon. Our fascination with Lyndon Johnson's blunders in Vietnam, however, may have led us to underestimate the significance of critical decisions he made in another part of the world that is in the news far more today than Southeast Asia—the Middle East.

When LBJ moved into the Oval Office in November 1963, the Middle East was comparatively quiet, in no small measure because of the relatively even-handed policies that the Eisenhower and Kennedy administrations had pursued during the preceding five years. After forcing a diplomatic showdown with Israel over Gaza in 1957 and after sending U.S. Marines to Lebanon a year later to thwart Muslim radicals backed by Egypt's Gamal Abdel Nasser, Ike had moved quietly to improve relations with both Tel Aviv and Cairo. By January 1961 small arms and nonlethal American military equipment were on their way to Israel, small amounts of surplus American grain were arriving in Nasser's United Arab Republic (UAR), and small signs were surfacing that continued American support for Saudi Arabia, Iran, and other conservative states in the Muslim world hinged upon more rapid progress toward economic and political modernization.

Once JFK had settled into the White House, he accelerated Ike's initiatives in the Middle East. With Kennedy's blessing, the Pentagon agreed to sell Israel a score of HAWK surface-to-air missiles, the State Department nudged the Shah of Iran and the House of Saud toward long overdue social reforms, and the Agency for International Development (AID) shipped Egypt $2.5 billion worth of U.S. wheat under the auspices of Public Law 480 (PL-480), the Food for Peace Program. Despite some Arab-Israeli and inter-Arab flareups, through autumn 1963 the Kennedy administration managed to avoid playing favorites.[1]

By the time the Six Day War erupted in June 1967, however, such policies seemed but a weak antidote to the violent ethnic and ideological tensions that were polarizing the region. Convinced that Moscow's recent inroads in the Middle East made it necessary to choose sides, the Johnson administration moved to strengthen pro-Western regimes from Tel Aviv to Tehran and to isolate left-wing Arab nationalists in Cairo and elsewhere. For twenty-five years, most scholars have attributed this pronounced shift in America's Middle East policy to the idiosyncrasies of a president one historian had nicknamed "Big Daddy from the Pedernales." No one can deny that Lyndon Johnson's strong personality influenced his political decisions both at home and abroad. LBJ did, after all, hope to woo Jewish voters by cultivating close ties with pro-Israel organizations such as the American Israel Public Affairs Committee (AIPAC). He did welcome campaign contributions from his friends in the oil industry and he did appreciate their concerns about stable prices and stable sources of supply, whether in his native Lone Star State or halfway around the world in the Persian Gulf. And he did have a West Texas horse trader's scorn for visionaries like Nasser, whose commitment to dignity, sovereignty, and other abstract principles made back-room deals impossible.

Yet it would be a serious mistake to interpret LBJ's change of course in the Middle East as merely the product of partisan calculations, petropolitics, and personal whim. Rather, Lyndon Johnson's tilt toward Israel, Iran, and Saudi Arabia and his tilt away from Egypt were parts of a broader attempt to address three problems that have bedeviled U.S. diplomacy in the region since the mid-1960s. By cementing a special relationship with Tel Aviv, LBJ hoped to allay Israeli anxieties and thereby prevent nuclear proliferation in the Middle East. By supporting the Shah and the House of Saud, LBJ hoped to develop regional proxies who could fill the vacuum created in the oil-rich Persian Gulf by Britain's decision to abandon its empire east of Suez. And by isolating Nasser, LBJ hoped to check the tide of Soviet-backed revolutionary nationalism that seemed to be sweeping the Arab world. The outcome of these policies would determine whether American interests in the Middle East would be secure for a generation or whether the United States would face decades of political chaos, economic crisis, and war.

I

Few Americans can have expected such an ambitious Middle Eastern agenda from the sad-eyed former Senate majority leader who seemed at first so ill at ease in his unexpected role as leader of the Free World. Like most vice-presidents, LBJ had languished in the long shadow of the man in the Oval Office and was frequently left in the dark about JFK's diplomatic initiatives. Far more interested in and far more suited for domestic politics than foreign affairs, Johnson had served as Camelot's de facto ambassador to Congress while holding his international assignments to a minimum. Having spent most of his adult life on Capitol Hill, it is hardly surprising that during the grim days following the tragedy in Dallas, LBJ seemed more at home in the Senate cloak room than in the White House situation room.[2]

Yet the quarter-century Johnson spent in Congress and at Blair House had transformed him into something of an apprentice statesman in those areas such as the Middle East where politics and diplomacy intersected. LBJ's ties to the small Texas Jewish community and his horror at the Holocaust had helped make him a staunch friend of Israel long before he became president. As early as 1938 Congressman Johnson pressed immigration officials in Washington to lift restrictions on Jewish refugees seeking asylum in the United States. A decade later Senator Johnson worked behind the scenes to facilitate the clandestine flow of American arms to the Haganah, Israel's fledgling army.[3] Once LBJ emerged as Senate majority leader in 1954, he befriended Israeli ambassador Abba Eban, who recalled long afterward that "there was something about Israel that stirred [Johnson's] pious memories."[4] LBJ's outspoken opposition to United Nations sanctions against Israel in the wake of the 1956 Suez crisis and his vocal support for Israeli efforts to secure American military aid in 1958 did not go unnoticed among Jewish leaders either in Texas or nationwide.[5] According to AIPAC's I. L. "Si" Kenen, by the early 1960s the Israel lobby counted Vice-President Lyndon Johnson among its most loyal allies in Washington.[6]

LBJ's support for Israel, however, did not blind him to broader American interests in the Middle East. Deeply concerned about growing Soviet influence among the Arabs in early 1957, Johnson played a pivotal role in securing passage of the Eisenhower Doctrine, which gave Ike the authority to use American economic aid and military force to prevent the Kremlin from fishing in troubled waters from the Persian Gulf to the Eastern Mediterranean. Although LBJ declared publicly that the doctrine might be interpreted as pro-Arab and anti-Israel, privately he called it a "good bill" and worked hard to win bipartisan support on Capitol Hill so that "the Russians and Arabs will decide the country is united."[7]

The importance of supporting anti-Soviet regimes in the Middle East was brought home firsthand to Vice-President Johnson five years later when he visited Iran, Lebanon, Turkey, and Cyprus. "These rimland states stand a lonely and exposed guard against communist expansion to the oil of the Middle East [and] to contiguity with the chaotic Arab world," he pointed out in a September 1962 postmortem for JFK. Eager to dispel the widespread fear among pro-American conservatives that neutralists such as Nasser "are nearer our hearts than are . . . our friends," LBJ urged Kennedy to step up U.S. military and economic aid so that Iran and its neighbors could "maintain their armed forces along the underbelly of the Bloc."[8]

Johnson's worries about the Soviet threat, however, were overshadowed during summer 1962 by developments that JFK's inner circle regarded as real progress toward achieving long-term stability in the Middle East. First had come the news in June that Nasser would keep his dispute with Israel "in the ice box" in exchange for a generous multiyear PL-480 package. Shortly thereafter had come signs from Iran and Saudi Arabia that the pace of social and economic modernization would be accelerated. And then in August had come word that Tel Aviv would consider an American-backed proposal to resettle thousands of Palestinian refugees inside Israel in exchange for U.S. HAWK antiaircraft missiles.[9]

Yet before the year was out, JFK's ambitious initiatives in the Middle East had begun to crumble, and LBJ's worries seemed less farfetched. In late September pro-Nasser military officers seized power in Yemen, an archaic kingdom on the shores of the Red Sea. Fearful that Nasser might use the newly created Yemen Arab Republic (YAR) to stir up trouble next door in Saudi Arabia or in Britain's Aden Protectorate, Riyadh and London secretly began to funnel arms to Yemeni royalists determined to overthrow the military regime. When YAR president Abdullah al-Sallal appealed for help, Nasser dispatched 70,000 troops to Yemen, unleashed his air force against royalist base camps in Saudi Arabia, and beamed anti-British propaganda into Aden over Radio Cairo. Johnson must have murmured "I told you so" when reports began to arrive early in the new year that "the Soviets are landing new supplies in Cairo which are earmarked for the Yemen operation."[10] Determined to reassure Saudi Arabia's crown prince and soon-to-be-king Faisal, Kennedy stationed a squadron of U.S. Air Force jets at Dhahran in April 1963 as part of "Operation Hard Surface" and warned Nasser that America would stand by the House of Saud.[11]

While American pilots played cat and mouse with Egyptian MIGs high over Southwest Arabia, American diplomats in Tel Aviv warned that Nasser's meddling in Yemen and his calls for the overthrow of Jordan's King Hussein might play into the hands of Israeli hardliners such as Prime Minister David Ben Gurion. Riots among Palestinians on Jordan's West Bank in January 1963 had already led Ben Gurion to scuttle the refugee resettlement plan unveiled the previous August, and some observers in Washington worried that if the unrest spread, the Israelis might think the unthinkable. Ever since the Central Intelligence Agency had learned in late 1960 that Israel was constructing an atomic reactor at Dimona capable of producing weapons-grade plutonium, top U.S. officials feared that the Jewish state would seek a nuclear deterrent ''to intimidate the Arabs and to prevent them from making trouble on the frontiers.'' With shiploads of Soviet military hardware flowing into Egypt and with Palestinian radicals calling for a war to liberate their homeland, the Israelis hinted during spring 1963 that unless they received an iron-clad American security guarantee, they might ''go nuclear.'' By offering Ben Gurion and his successor, Levi Eshkol, informal U.S. commitments, Kennedy persuaded Israel grudgingly to permit American inspectors to visit Dimona to ensure that the reactor was being used only for peaceful purposes.[12] But when JFK left for Dallas in November, he was well aware that Nasser's calls for radical change from Jordan to Yemen continued to create high anxiety in Israel and in Saudi Arabia.

Although Vice-President Johnson seems to have known little about the Dimona reactor and even less about Operation Hard Surface, he could see from his perch as presiding officer of the Senate that Kennedy's even-handed policies in the Middle East were in deep trouble. In October AIPAC had joined forces with oil company lobbyists to support an amendment to the 1963 foreign aid bill proposed by Sen. Ernest Gruening of Alaska that would cut off all U.S. economic assistance to Egypt should Nasser attack Israel or Saudi Arabia.[13] With the Israelis poised to divert the waters of the Jordan River to irrigate the Negev desert despite Arab opposition and with the Saudis stepping up their aid to the Yemeni royalists, Nasser would be sorely tempted to strike in both directions. Having watched the Senate pass the Gruening amendment by a 65-to-13 margin on November 7, Johnson hardly could have been surprised to learn soon after entering the Oval Office that the Middle East would require urgent presidential attention. As early as December 3 the National Security Council (NSC) staff predicted ''real trouble'' in Yemen, where ''Nasser has the bear by the tail'' and where ''airing of UAR's record will of course make it all the harder for LBJ not to cut off aid under Gruening Amendment.'' As for the Arab-Israeli dispute, quick action was required on a ''whole complex of problems,'' including ''security guarantee, aid to UAR, arms requests, Dimona and missiles, Jordan waters, [and] refugees'' lest Nasser underestimate Washington's commitment to Tel Aviv.[14]

The new president moved quickly to reaffirm that commitment. ''We are close friends and will remain so,'' LBJ told Foreign Minister Golda Meir and Pres. Zalman Shazar at a reception following Kennedy's funeral on November 25. ''Israel can count on this.'' The many friends of Zion who moved into LBJ's inner circle during the following four years helped foster much closer ties with Israel. To be sure, two Kennedy holdovers at Foggy Bottom—Secretary of State Dean Rusk and Assistant Secretary for Near Eastern Affairs Phillips Talbot—continued to press for an even-handed approach to the region as did White House Middle East expert Robert Komer. Their views were offset, however, by those of such high-ranking pro-Israel figures as Vice-President Hubert Humphrey, Ambassador to the United Nations Arthur Goldberg, and Walt Rostow, who replaced McGeorge Bundy as national security adviser in 1966. White House counsel Myer Feldman and his successor, Harry McPherson, ensured that Johnson's door was always open to such prominent leaders of the American Jewish community as Abraham Feinberg and Arthur Krim, both of whom doubled as Democratic party notables. Brandeis University professor-turned-presidential-speechwriter John P. Roche made no secret about his own pro-Israel views. Nor was Israeli diplomat Ephraim Evron bashful about making Israel's case during his frequent visits to the LBJ Ranch outside Austin.[15]

Such pro-Israel sentiments notwithstanding, the Johnson administration worried that Tel Aviv's well-publicized plans to begin unilaterally diverting the Jordan River in early 1964 could spell real trouble for American interests in the Middle East. On January 13 Nasser convened a summit conference in Cairo; the first item of business was to develop a ''unified Arab response to imminent Israeli offtake of water from [the] Jordan River system.'' Rejecting calls from Syrian radicals for a military showdown with Tel Aviv, Nasser preferred to thwart the Israelis by having the Arab states upstream draw off large amounts of water for their own irrigation projects.[16] Lest he be charged with ''having gone soft on Israel as a result [of] US aid,'' however, Nasser also called for the establishment of a Unified Arab Command (UAC) to coordinate inter-Arab strategy against the Israelis and for the creation of a Palestine Liberation Organization (PLO) dedicated to the destruction of the Jewish state. Yet precisely because he wished to avoid an open breach with the United States, Nasser counseled moderation, "averted an imminent threat of Arab-Israeli hostilities," and opposed any "interference with Western access to Arab oil."[17]

Fresh signs of an American tilt toward Israel later that winter soon led Nasser to reconsider his relatively moderate course. After LBJ unveiled plans on February 6 for Israeli-American "cooperative research in using nuclear energy to turn salt water into fresh water," for example, Nasser angrily charged that "the Johnson administration is treating the Arabs unfairly" and that the United States "intends to help Israel develop atomic weapons."[18] Rumors that Johnson planned to slash economic aid earmarked for Cairo while stepping up military assistance for Tel Aviv "revived Arab fears that a Democratic administration in Washington is bound to favor Israel, especially in an election year" and prompted the CIA to issue "Storm Warnings . . . for US–Arab Relations."[19] Having become convinced by early March that "US policy was slanted in favor of the Israelis," Nasser unleashed a barrage of radical propaganda designed to undermine Western interests from Libya to Aden and resumed his efforts to acquire more sophisticated weapons from the Kremlin.[20]

With the approach of spring, top American officials began "taking a hard look at our current policy toward Nasser." Secretary of State Rusk complained during an NSC meeting on April 2 that despite millions of dollars worth of U.S. economic assistance, "the Egyptians have done many things harmful to our interests, such as sending more troops into Yemen rather than withdrawing them, exerting various types of pressure against the British," and refusing "to slow down the arms race" with Israel.[21] At a pair of meetings with LBJ the next day, Undersecretary of State Averell Harriman, who had just returned from a whirlwind tour of North Africa, confirmed that Radio Cairo was fanning the fires of "super Arabism and anti-Israeli sentiment in Libya." Because of "Nasser's influence," Harriman explained, King Idris "has asked us to negotiate the removal of our base at Wheelus [airfield]," something that might easily "jeopardize US oil investment in Libya," which claimed the region's largest petroleum reserves west of Suez. "Very much concerned about Libya," President Johnson asked Harriman to work with the U.S. Information Agency (USIA) to combat Nasser's propaganda.[22]

Throughout April and into May, American officials sought to

contain Nasserism without driving Egypt more fully into the Kremlin's orbit. The State Department's Policy Planning Council argued that an abrupt cutoff of U.S. economic aid "could make Egypt into a sort of Middle Eastern China in which either this or a successor government would turn to more radical policies or to the Soviet bloc."[23] Ambassador John Badeau, the chief architect of JFK's rapprochement with Nasser, urged the Johnson administration to continue "seeking to broaden areas of understanding and cooperation" with Egypt and cautioned Washington not to overreact to the propaganda broadcast by Radio Cairo.[24] The CIA likewise tried to downplay the significance of Soviet premier Nikita Khrushchev's mid-May visit to Egypt, where he was expected to pledge another $180 million for the second stage of the Aswan Dam.[25] As late as May 24, even Dean Rusk recommended that Johnson "reaffirm U.S. desire to cooperate with the U.A.R."[26] The next day, however, Nasser and Khrushchev issued a joint communique defending "the inalienable rights of the [Palestinian] Arabs," demanding the "liquidation of foreign military bases in Libya, Oman, Cyprus, [and] Aden," and confirming Washington's worst fears regarding a Soviet-Egyptian offensive against Western interests in the Middle East.[27]

Among those people most concerned about the deepening ties between Cairo and Moscow were the Israelis, who had been pressing the Johnson administration for six months to sell them 300 M-48 tanks. Despite the obvious political bonus that would come from such assistance to the Jewish state during an election year, top U.S. officials balked and sought "to link tanks to our concern over Israel's move toward a missile (and perhaps even nuclear) capability."[28] Nevertheless, Israel's friends in Washington attempted throughout the spring to use their contacts with Myer Feldman to pry loose a military aid package. "I have rarely been exposed to as much pressure," Feldman told LBJ on May 11, "as I have had recently on the question of tanks for Israel."[29] For their part, Israeli leaders made it clear in mid-May that unless the "US rapped Arab knuckles more sharply" and "embraced Israel even more closely," the Jewish state would seek its own "independent deterrent capability."[30] Despite such pressure, Johnson refused to become directly involved in supplying Israel with M-48s; instead, he sent Feldman to Tel Aviv on May 16 to urge the Israelis to "explore tank prospects with the [West] Germans and the UK" and to caution them against "going for a nuclear capability."[31]

Two weeks later Prime Minister Levi Eshkol arrived in Washington for two days of talks with LBJ. Troubled by "Khrushchev's all-out pandering to the Arabs in Cairo,'' Johnson's aides urged the president to remind Eshkol how important it was "to keep the Arabs from leaning too far toward the USSR," which meant telling Eshkol that "as to *tanks*, we can't provide them directly" and that as to the Dimona reactor, "*We're violently opposed to nuclear proliferation.*"[32] Johnson softened the blow by insisting "he was foursquare behind Israel on all matters that affected their vital security interests" and by offering "to help Israel in every way possible to get a sufficient quantity of tanks" from West Germany. But he was blunt with Eshkol regarding atomic weapons. "If Israel is not going to get into nuclear production," LBJ asked on June 1, "why not accept IAEA [International Atomic Energy Agency] controls and let us reassure Nasser about Dimona?"[33] Johnson hammered home the point in a second meeting the next day, promising to "work on [West German chancellor Ludwig] Erhard" to free up tanks for Israel but insisting on "*Dimona reassurances*" in return. Stressing "our common aim of keeping the Soviets out of the Middle East," he evidently told Eshkol, "Let's not give Khrushchev a free ride."[34] In any event, Johnson's "soft sell to Eshkol" seems to have worked. Before leaving town on June 3, the Israeli leader "agreed to let us reassure Nasser on Dimona" and sent word that he was "highly pleased" with the West German tank scheme.[35]

Like their Israeli counterparts, British officials had spent spring 1964 seeking U.S. support in combating Nasser's efforts to stir up trouble among Arab radicals. For months Whitehall had claimed that Egypt and the YAR were secretly funneling aid to Marxist guerrillas who opposed Britain's plan to transform its Aden Protectorate into an autonomous pro-Western South Arabian Federation.[36] When Foreign Secretary R. A. Butler asked for American help during a visit to Washington in late April, Johnson and Rusk were "sympathetic" but noncommittal.[37] Six weeks later Minister of Defence Duncan Sandys complained to Undersecretary of State George Ball about America's "detached attitude" toward South Arabia. Could not U.S. support for Britain's campaign to "stop UAR subversive activities" in Aden, Sandys asked, be just "a little more robust?" Although Ball "understood Sandys' point," he insisted that "if there were marked change in US policy toward Nasser, he would feel he had nowhere to go but the USSR."[38]

Ball's line of reasoning offered little comfort for Britain or for such other friends in the region as Saudi Arabia, which had been calling for a marked change in America's policy toward Egypt for six months. When the proxy war in Yemen between Nasser and the

House of Saud began to heat up in late 1963, the Johnson administration let it be known in both Cairo and Riyadh that the "USG
would not stand idly by if UAR should attack Saudi Arabia." But
LBJ's decision to pull Operation Hard Surface out of Dhahran on
schedule in January 1964 led some Saudis to charge that America
was selling out to Nasser.[39] Before the month was out, however, Johnson commissioned an interagency study of Saudi defense needs. For
its part, the State Department tended to minimize the Egyptian
threat to Saudi Arabia and to insist that "sustaining progress of development and reform program is doubtless best investment for security of country against subversive attacks." A Pentagon survey, on
the other hand, recommended a multimillion dollar military package, including 150 HAWK antiaircraft missiles, 36 F-5 jets, and 3
early warning radar stations. In late June Johnson sent word to Faisal,
who had become king three months earlier following a palace coup,
that America would "play a positive role in assuring delivery on the
best possible terms of the material suggested in the air defense survey report for Saudi Arabia."[40]

Saudi, British, and Israeli second-guessing of America's rapprochement with Nasser merely accelerated a reassessment that was
already well under way in Washington by summer 1964. Although
pressure was mounting on Capitol Hill for LBJ to invoke the Gruening amendment and cancel all U.S. economic aid for Egypt, the
White House succeeded in bottling that proposal up in committee.[41]
But by late August Robert Komer worried that Nasser's increasingly
radical rhetoric might trigger an "Arab-Israeli flap" or a "Yemen
flare-up," in which case "Goldwater latches on to UK/Israeli/oil
company line" to begin "beating [the] anti-Nasser drum" just before
election day.[42] During a White House briefing session with Lucius
Battle, who had just been tapped to succeed Ambassador Badeau in
Cairo, top U.S. officials brought out a long list of complaints that
Nasser needed to address soon. Unless Egypt ceased its "export of
revolution" to the Arabian Peninsula, halted its "campaign against
UK positions in the Near East," and reined in the anti-Israel zealots
inside the Unified Arab Command, there was little hope for preserving amicable relations with the United States.[43]

The gloom in Washington deepened in September after Nasser
convened a second Arab summit in Alexandria, where he promised
to drive Zionism and Western imperialism from the Middle East.
Some U.S. officials took heart that by attending the summit, King
Faisal had managed to open a Saudi-Egyptian dialogue that promised
to stabilize the chaotic situation in Yemen. But Nasser remained

more determined than ever to drive the British out of South Arabia. And to make matters worse, he vowed to provide the PLO with approximately $30 million for a "Palestine Army to be trained and financed through the Unified Arab Command" in order to "prevent Israel from consolidating the status quo."[44] Although Nasser did prove unexpectedly receptive when John J. McCloy, LBJ's coordinator for disarmament, arrived in Cairo on September 28 with an American proposal to keep nuclear weapons out of the Middle East, he remained "sensitive to charges by other Arabs that he was soft on Israel" and hinted that Egypt would continue to seek guided missiles from the Soviet Union.[45] More and more, Komer remarked ruefully on October 6, America's principal problem in the Middle East was becoming "how to avoid the gathering storm against a tolerable relationship with Nasser, which would leave him in Nikita's hands."[46]

Khrushchev's sudden resignation nine days later did not help matters. Rumors flew that the Soviet leader had been forced out because "he promised the Egyptians a credit of $180 million . . . without bothering to let his colleagues know he was doing it."[47] Long afterward, Ambassador Battle recalled that Nasser and his aides "had a fairly deep concern about reestablishing the relationship that they feared had been ruptured by the fall of Khrushchev, particularly when relations with the UAR were one factor in that demise."[48] Battle accordingly warned Washington in mid-November to expect a fresh round of anti-Western rhetoric designed to "allay fears that post-Khrushchev Sov[iet] leadership would turn away from UAR."[49]

But even Battle did not anticipate the events that followed. After listening to Nasser criticize American intervention in the Congo, an angry mob of African students stormed the USIA library in Cairo on November 26 and burned it to the ground. When Nasser offered neither compensation nor an apology, Lyndon Johnson summoned Egyptian ambassador Mustafa Kamel to the White House. "How can I ask Congress for wheat," he exploded, "when you burn down our library?" After Egyptian MIGs downed a cargo plane owned by Texas oilman and longtime LBJ crony John Mecom three weeks later near Alexandria, killing its two-man crew, Ambassador Battle hinted that there would be no further U.S. aid until Egypt made amends. Outraged by what he regarded as American blackmail, Nasser journeyed to Port Said, where on December 23, with Soviet deputy prime minister Alexander Shelepin at his side, he told a huge crowd "that those who do not accept our behavior can go and drink from the sea." Lest LBJ miss the point, Nasser added, "We are not going to accept gangsterism from cowboys."[50]

II

Disappointed but hardly surprised by Nasser's response, Lyndon Johnson and his top aides moved swiftly toward a major reorientation of American policy in the Middle East early in the new year. Noting that "no one is particularly interested in ostentatious feeding of the hand that bites," National Security Adviser McGeorge Bundy urged LBJ "simply [to] stop talking with [Nasser] about aid for a while, but not to engage in a public row."[51] This meant, as Robert Komer put it on January 4, 1965, "continuing existing aid to Nasser, while holding off any new commitments."[52] The president evidently agreed, for when Ambassador Kamel called at the State Department four days later, Dean Rusk explained that any extension of America's Food for Peace program in Egypt beyond June 1965 would require careful White House scrutiny. "If USG did not continue PL-480 program," Kamel retorted, he "could not conceive how we could keep the US and the West in the Near East."[53]

The Johnson administration was well aware that the abrupt cancellation of PL-480 wheat shipments to Egypt could jeopardize broader American interests in the Muslim world, especially among the pro-Western regimes that rimmed the Persian Gulf, where U.S. oil firms had invested several billion dollars. By 1965 Saudi Arabia, Iran, and their smaller neighbors exported 3.5 million barrels of petroleum annually, one-third of the Free World's output. Although America imported less than 10 percent of its oil from the Middle East, nearly three-quarters of Western Europe's petroleum imports originated in the Persian Gulf.[54]

On January 13 Averell Harriman and Phillips Talbot reviewed the delicate situation with eight multinational oil executives including Thomas Barger, president of the Arabian American Oil Company (ARAMCO). Barger wanted to crack down on Nasser, whose anti-Western propaganda was undermining U.S. influence from Libya to Iran. Because ARAMCO and other companies already faced a serious financial challenge from the profit-hungry Organization of Petroleum Exporting Countries (OPEC), Barger feared that once Nasserism spread to the Persian Gulf, nothing could prevent the "unthinking use of oil as a political weapon by radical Arabs." Talbot conceded that something must be done to refute "the notion that the Near Eastern oil producing countries can dominate and thereby control the international energy market," but he preferred employing U.S. economic aid as a carrot rather than as a stick. Harriman agreed. Pointing out that "nothing would please the Russians more than for the US to break with Nasser," he urged the oil executives to think twice before supporting congressional efforts to "end American aid to the UAR."[55]

By late January angry congressmen on both sides of the aisle were trying to prevent Nasser from receiving the final installment of the three-year PL-480 package he had negotiated with JFK. Although Johnson and Rusk warned congressional leaders that "only the Soviets will benefit from such a situation," the House approved legislation freezing all food shipments to Egypt on January 26.[56] The next day Rusk appeared before a closed-door session of the Senate Foreign Relations Committee in an effort to prevent similar action by the upper chamber. An abrupt end to PL-480 aid might lead Nasser to react "irrationally and with vindictiveness," at which point, Rusk warned, "we [are] going to need some troops . . . to support very important American interests," including "billions [of dollars] in investments in the Arab world." Was it not "far better to permit us to send the remaining bushels of wheat than to face a choice of perhaps having to send soldiers?" The Senate replied on February 3 by amending the House bill to permit LBJ to resume the PL-480 program if he deemed it "in the national interest" to do so.[57]

Before the month was out, however, the Johnson administration would decide to send neither wheat nor soldiers to the Middle East but arms. For almost a year, U.S. policymakers had been struggling to preserve the delicate military balance between Israel and Jordan, where King Hussein see-sawed between pleasing his longtime friends in the West and pandering to the half-million pro-Nasser Palestinian refugees camped on the West Bank. Hussein had visited Washington in April 1964 to remind LBJ of Arab opposition to Israel's diversion of the Jordan River and to ask him for American aid. Before leaving Amman, the king told reporters that "Jordan may start shopping in Moscow for military hardware" if it could not acquire arms from the United States.[58] When Johnson refused to provide the tanks and planes Hussein requested, Nasser urged the king to turn to the Kremlin. By mid-summer, Komer feared that "we may have to say some mighty tough words to Hussein if we want to turn him aside from accepting Soviet arms."[59] Indeed, later that autumn one State Department official actually drafted a proposal entitled "Some Unthinkable Thoughts: A Jordan without Hussein."[60]

Yet a moment's reflection persuaded most Americans that the

alternatives to Hussein—a pro-Nasser military regime with ties to Moscow or, worse still, a PLO dictatorship—made the twenty-nine-year-old monarch the lesser of many evils. "Extended discussions" with Jordanian officials during winter 1964–1965 made it clear that without a sizable American military aid package, King Hussein would have no choice but "to accept Soviet/U.A.R. arms, which in his view and ours would compromise his independence and increase the threat to Israel."[61] Although Hussein's threats put LBJ "in a lather over Jordan," by late February 1965 the White House was willing to approve an arms package that included 250 M-48 tanks and the promise of American help in securing supersonic aircraft in Western Europe.[62] In return, Hussein must confirm that he did "not plan to station tanks on the West Bank" and that he would not seek jet planes from the Soviet Union. The Johnson administration's rationale was simple: "If we deny arms to Jordan, we will multiply the risks of losing it."[63]

Arms sales to Jordan, however, seemed certain to complicate American relations with the Israelis, whose own quest for M-48 tanks from West Germany had fallen through at the last moment. According to Komer, "LBJ had to twist [Ludwig] Erhard's arm" during a White House visit in June 1964 in order to win the chancellor's reluctant agreement to provide tanks for Israel.[64] Later that summer the Pentagon quietly cleared the way for a triangular arrangement whereby the United States would provide 200 new M-48s to West Germany, which in turn would deliver 200 older M-48s from its own inventory to Israel.[65] But the Israelis had received only ninety tanks before the story leaked to the West German press in early 1965. After critics charged that Bonn's relations with the Arabs would be poisoned, Erhard backed out of the deal in mid-February. Coming as it did at precisely the moment that Washington was considering military aid for Amman, Bonn's decision to renege on its commitment to Tel Aviv led the Johnson administration "to conclude that the wisest course would be to sell arms to Jordan and to Israel too" although in the latter case there would be strings attached.[66]

When Averell Harriman and Robert Komer flew to Tel Aviv to break the news to the Israelis in late February, Levi Eshkol, Golda Meir, and Deputy Minister of Defense Shimon Peres questioned the wisdom of selling U.S. tanks to Jordan and regarded any conditions on American aid to Israel as extraordinarily unwise. Harriman sought to allay Israeli anxieties by offering "to consider the direct sale of military equipment Israel needed, at the appropriate time, and with appropriate coordination of the publicity problem."[67] In return, however, the Israelis must pledge that they "would not undertake preemptive action" against their Arab neighbors and that "they would not develop a nuclear weapons capability."[68] The Israelis saw too many risks and too many conditions in the American proposal. "As long as Jordan remained at war with Israel, Israel could not agree to Jordan's being armed," Eshkol explained. "However, if in the global view of the United States arms to Jordan seemed the best course, . . . this should not be done before agreement was reached on direct U.S. supply of arms to Israel." In short, Israel was making early and open delivery of American tanks and jets its price for going along with U.S. policy in Jordan; and, Shimon Peres added, "There could be no strings on arms."[69]

Harriman left for Washington empty-handed on March 1 while Komer remained in Tel Aviv seeking a last-minute compromise. Well aware that time was not on their side, White House and State Department officials worried that the Israeli-American arms impasse would "reinforce Israel's tendency to go nuclear, as its best means of maintaining a deterrent edge."[70] After all, rumors had been circulating since November 1964 that the Dimona reactor had "gone critical," and Israel had recently decided to develop a medium-range surface-to-surface missile.[71] Few officials at the Pentagon can have been surprised, then, when Harriman passed along an Israeli shopping list in early March that included seventy-five B-66 bombers, "an aircraft capable of carrying an Israeli developed nuclear weapon."[72]

Ultimately, Tel Aviv found the lure of American military hardware too strong and Washington found the danger that Israel would achieve nuclear capability too grave. As a result, Komer and Shimon Peres were able to reach a gentleman's agreement on March 10. Although the text of this accord remains classified, available documents provide a relatively good idea of the terms it entailed. In exchange for Israel's "tacit acquiescence in Jordan arms sale" and its acceptance of "full IAEA safeguards on all their nuclear facilities," the United States agreed to provide the Jewish state with 210 M-48 tanks and to consider providing up to 24 jet fighters if Tel Aviv was unable to obtain comparable aircraft in Western Europe. The Israeli arms deal was to be financed by a revolving credit and was to remain secret for several months.[73]

Meanwhile, the Johnson administration hoped to minimize the diplomatic fallout in the Arab world by highlighting U.S. arms sales to Jordan and by treating military aid for Israel as a necessary part of America's delicately balanced approach to the Middle East. Well aware that Egypt's reaction to the arms sales would be crucial, LBJ sent Nasser a message on March 18 stressing his personal desire to continue "to cooperate in any way we can in mutual Arab-US interest" and warning that any anti-American outburst in Cairo could "jeopardize USG's restrained and even-handed approach to [the] Arab-Israel problem." Nasser retorted that Johnson's claims of impartiality actually cloaked an American decision to isolate Egypt and its radical allies by arming both Israel and Muslim conservatives.[74]

The Egyptian leader was not far off the mark. The next day the State Department informed American diplomats from Khartoum to Kuwait City that the Johnson administration was "reexamining its relationship with the UAR" in light of its deepening conviction that "moderate Arab leaders are important asset to US."[75] Two weeks later the CIA predicted that Nasser would "strike out against Western interests" by "heating up" the Arab-Israeli dispute, by "continuing to organize and support guerrilla and terrorist operations in Aden and Oman," and perhaps even by "try[ing] to persuade the oil-producing Arab states to bring pressure on the West."[76]

Nasser wasted little time fulfilling this prophecy. In early April he began to supply guns to left-wing rebels attempting to overthrow the pro-Western regime in the mineral-rich Congo, prompting a vigorous American protest delivered "in words of one syllable."[77] Later that spring he told PLO leaders gathered in Cairo that "the only force capable of liberating Palestine is Arab revolutionary action."[78] And he cultivated closer ties with the Kremlin by denouncing U.S. military intervention in Indochina and by backing such pro-Soviet organizations as the Front for the Liberation of South Yemen (FLOSY) and the Popular Front for the Liberation of the Occupied Arab Gulf (PFLOAG). "The Near East is not yet at the Viet-Nam stage of anti-Western insurgency," the State Department concluded grimly as autumn approached, "but Soviet advisors have already infiltrated the inner circles of the Arab military in Egypt, Syria, and Yemen."[79]

Nevertheless, some U.S. policymakers still hoped that Nasser's desire for American economic assistance would lead him to moderate his radical activities. Thus when Cairo pressed repeatedly for the renewal of the PL-480 agreement that had expired on June 30, Washington replied that the resumption of food shipments was contingent upon some demonstration of Egyptian good faith.[80] American officials thought they detected just such a signal in Yemen, where in late August Nasser began "talking peace, not war" with Saudi Arabia's King Faisal.[81] Six weeks later Dean Rusk appeared before the

Senate Foreign Relations Committee to propose a six-month PL-480 package that would enable America to regain "some leverage on Nasser."[82] For his part, Nasser seemed grateful to learn just before Thanksgiving that Washington was willing to resume food shipments. "We have nothing to gain from bad relations [with] your country," he told Ambassador Battle on November 24, "and we will do everything possible to improve them." Despite protests from Nasser's foes on Capitol Hill, the Johnson administration announced a short-term $55 million Food for Peace agreement with Egypt on January 3, 1966.[83]

The new year, however, saw the Middle East rocked by sudden changes that short-circuited Egyptian-American relations and galvanized U.S. ties with Israel and Muslim conservatives. First came the news in late February that Britain would abandon its huge military base at Aden within two years. The Johnson administration had first become aware in December 1964 that Harold Wilson's new Labour government desired to curtail defense spending by scaling back Britain's commitments in the Middle East.[84] Convinced that "any precipitate British withdrawal from the Aden area . . . would result in a chaotic situation in South Arabia harmful to general Western interests," the State Department in October 1965 began to prepare plans for America "to react quickly with small forces in local crises in the oil-rich Persian Gulf and elsewhere in the region."[85] During the months that followed, U.S. officials warned Wilson, Foreign Secretary Michael Stewart, and Minister of Defence Denis Healey that Britain's departure from Aden would leave a dangerous vacuum and play into the hands of radical groups such as FLOSY and PFLOAG.[86] "The United States," Healey recalled long afterward, "after trying for thirty years to get Britain out of Asia, the Middle East, and Africa, was now trying desperately to keep us in." With the release of Healey's Defence White Paper on February 22, 1966, the Johnson administration realized that it might be forced to assume commitments that until the last moment it had hoped the Wilson government would continue to honor.[87]

America's problems in the Middle East mounted the next day when Syria was rocked by a coup d'etat that brought to power the most extreme wing of the Ba'ath party, an organization committed to socialism, Arab unity, and the destruction of Israel. Because the Ba'athist takeover had "coincided with a Soviet decision to increase its interest in the Middle East," Moscow moved swiftly to enhance its influence in Damascus, offering the new regime a $133 million credit to construct a dam on the Euphrates River and stepping up deliveries of Russian arms. By late may the CIA prophesied that ''Syria will almost certainly maintain its vitriolic anti-Western posture and close ties with the Communist bloc.''[88] Worse still, Ba'athist leaders such as Col. Hafez al-Assad were encouraging Fatah, a shadowy group of Palestinian guerrillas led by Yasir Arafat, to step up its raids against Israeli villages from base camps in the Golan Heights ''in flagrant violation of international law.''[89]

The emergence of Fatah sanctuaries inside Syria merely strengthened the case that Tel Aviv had been making in Washington since mid-1965 that swift Israeli reprisals inflicted with American military hardware were the only antidote to Palestinian radicalism. Israeli retaliatory raids against PLO base camps on the West Bank had prompted the Johnson administration to hold up delivery of U.S. tanks until Eshkol offered fresh assurances in August that Israel ''has no aggressive intentions toward Jordan.''[90] Two months later, just as the first M-48s were beginning to arrive in Haifa, Israeli air force chief of staff Ezer Weizman flew to Washington to report that his attempt to buy jet aircraft in Western Europe had been unsuccessful. Israel, Weizman told Robert Komer on October 18, needed over 200 U.S. jets, including several dozen F-4 Phantom fighter-bombers capable of carrying nuclear weapons. Stunned by the scope of Weizman's shopping list, Komer insisted that Israel try again to secure French Mirages and added that ''what Eshkol did about Dimona and IAEA controls will have a tremendous influence'' on Washington's deliberations over Tel Aviv's request for jet aircraft.[91] But because 1966 was an election year, the White House began to feel ''very heavy pressure'' from Congress to do more for the Israelis. ''There's no doubt whatsoever in my mind,'' Komer told McGeorge Bundy on February 8, ''that Hill and Zionist pressure will sooner or later force us to sell planes to Israel.''[92]

The threat of Israeli nuclear capability, however, seems to have been at least as important as off-year elections in ensuring that the decision to ship American jets to Tel Aviv was made sooner rather than later. After a month of bargaining, U.S. policymakers persuaded the Israelis drastically to scale down the number of aircraft requested and to table plans to acquire the supersonic F-4. On March 23 LBJ approved the sale of forty-eight slower A-4 Skyhawks to be financed by a $72 million credit.[93] Although the text of the agreement remains classified, the subsequent arrival of a four-man American inspection team at Dimona on April 2 suggests that U.S. officials insisted on some sort of quid pro quo regarding Israel's nuclear capability.[94] Predictably, the Skyhawk deal evoked ''heavy criticism from the Arabs'' and "left a residue of distrust and suspicion" from North Africa to the Persian Gulf. But as a State Department briefing paper declared on the eve of Johnson's meeting with Israeli president Zalman Shazar in early August, "if Israel is unable to obtain its valid conventional arms requirements, those in Israel who advocate acquisition of nuclear weapons will find a much more fertile environment for their views."[95]

The Johnson administration hoped to counteract Arab indignation over the latest round of arms sales to Israel by cultivating closer ties with pro-Western Muslim conservatives. The first step in this direction came in early April 1966 when the United States reaffirmed its "special relationship" with Jordan by selling a squadron of A-4 Skyhawks to King Hussein, whom LBJ now regarded as a "firm and reliable friend."[96] Later that month American engineers completed work on a microwave communications system that snaked across 1,000 miles of mountains from Turkey to Pakistan to provide early warning against possible Soviet aggression along the Northern Tier.[97] Less obvious but more significant were U.S. efforts to strengthen Saudi Arabia and Iran, two regional proxies that might be capable of filling the vacuum created once Britain began to liquidate its string of protectorates that stretched from Aden to Bahrain.

King Faisal, who ruled the largest and most thinly populated of the Arab oil states, was increasingly eager to cooperate with the United States in stabilizing the situation in the Arabian Peninsula and the Persian Gulf. Although the Johnson administration had committed itself to meeting Saudi Arabia's air defense needs in mid-1964, the deal was not consummated for almost eighteen months. Some Americans worried that the $300 million price tag for the proposed military package would prevent Faisal from "moving forward in the area of economic development and social reform." Others evidently feared that U.S. military support might tempt the Saudis "to press the cause of the more extreme royalists" in Yemen more vigorously.[98] But according to Frank Brenchley, who headed Whitehall's Arabian Department during the mid-1960s, the biggest obstacle U.S. policymakers encountered was "the powerful Jewish lobby which automatically objected to all arms supplies to Arab countries." Unwilling to risk another bitter fight on Capitol Hill, the State Department advised the Saudis "to split the package" between Britain and the United States. In December 1965 Faisal signed a joint air defense agreement calling for "10 batteries of U.S. HAWK missiles and 3 squadrons of U.K. Lightning interceptor aircraft."[99]

Shortly thereafter, King Faisal arrived in Tehran to seek Iranian support for an "Islamic Conference" of Middle East conservatives he was organizing as a counterweight to the Arab radicals and their Soviet backers.[100] The CIA reported in February 1966 that Radio Cairo had "already expressed some criticism of Saudi purchases of Western arms" and that Nasser was outraged that "Faisal is working for the formation of a conservative Islamic bloc hostile to the UAR."[101] Eager to encourage the fledgling Islamic Conference, LBJ invited Faisal to the White House in June 1966 to reaffirm America's commitment to the House of Saud. Troubled at "how Moscow exploits local nationalists like Nasser," Johnson stressed that "we will not let Saudi Arabia get swallowed up." Indeed, he wanted to work with Faisal "to fill the gap the British will leave in South Arabia and the Persian Gulf."[102] Delighted by this show of support, the king evidently hinted that he would like additional American arms. Although Faisal did not come away from the White House with the tanks he apparently sought, three months later LBJ did approve the sale of $100 million worth of nonlethal military equipment—mostly trucks and jeeps—to signal America's budding partnership with Saudi Arabia.[103]

By all accounts, the strongest and most ambitious candidate to succeed Britain as guardian of the Persian Gulf and guarantor of stability in the Muslim world was the Shah of Iran, who hoped to combine his nation's enormous oil wealth with American weaponry to recapture the ancient grandeur of Cyrus the Great. Iranian-American relations had been somewhat strained during the early 1960s when JFK pressed for fundamental social and political reforms that the Shah feared would undermine Pahlavi rule.[104] Indeed, judging from his successful vice-presidential visit to Tehran in mid-1962, Lyndon Johnson seems to have been one of the few New Frontiersmen who got along with the ruler ensconced upon the Peacock Throne. As instructed, LBJ did gently remind the Shah that only by reducing Iran's "relatively heavy and inflexible military expenses" could "progress [be] made in the fields of economic well being of the population and in social justice." But Johnson also told Kennedy afterward that "we must accept the Shah, with his shortcomings, as a valuable asset" because "we have no acceptable alternative."[105]

Once LBJ entered the Oval Office, he became more convinced than ever that Iran could serve as a strategic asset for America in the Middle East. For his part, the Shah moved quickly to improve relations with Washington by edging forward with land reform and by granting U.S. military personnel in Tehran full diplomatic immunity. "What is going on in Iran," President Johnson remarked as early as June 1964, "is about the best thing going on anywhere in the world."[106] Although the Shah came under increasing fire during 1965 from Islamic fundamentalists such as the Ayatollah Ruhallah Khomeini and from left-wing nationalists such as the Mujahadeen i-Khalq, he remained a key figure in U.S. plans for Middle East security.[107] Like his friend in the White House, the Shah was increasingly "worried that the British may eventually withdraw from the Persian Gulf and that Nasser may move in." According to the CIA, this concern explained Iran's "interest in Faisal's efforts to create an Islamic movement of Arab and non-Arab Muslim countries" during early 1966.[108]

Yet as the year wore on, America's relationship with Iran began to show serious signs of strain. Unhappy over the slow growth of his oil revenues, the Shah sought OPEC's help in securing better terms from the American-controlled consortium that ran Iran's petroleum industry. He was unhappier still over Washington's reluctance to approve a four-year $200 million credit to provide Iran with military hardware similar to equipment that was already arriving in Jordan and Saudi Arabia. Because of the perceived "papa knows best" attitude about the need to hold down Iranian defense spending, Ambassador Armin Meyer warned the White House on May 23, "We are about to alienate the Shah." Unless the United States opened wide the doors to its arsenal, Iran would most likely seek arms from the Soviets.[109] After carefully reviewing Iranian security needs, President Johnson approved the $200 million arms credit in early July. Then at the last minute, the Shah insisted that the package be upgraded to include F-4 Phantom jets comparable to the MIG-21s Moscow had just promised to Cairo and Baghdad. "He genuinely fears that the UAR and Iraq have designs on his oil producing southern provinces," National Security Adviser Walt Rostow told LBJ on July 19; and "with the British pulling out of South Arabia and retrenching in the Persian Gulf, I'm not sure he isn't right." Two weeks later, the president agreed to provide the Shah with two squadrons of Phantoms, a decision that finally cemented America's relationship with its Iranian proxy.[110]

By summer 1966, then, the broad outlines of LBJ's new policy in the Middle East had begun to emerge. To provide stability in the Persian Gulf in the wake of Britain's withdrawal east of Suez, the United States had agreed to sell Iran and Saudi Arabia nearly half a billion dollars worth of military hardware. To promote Israeli security and to prevent Tel Aviv from pursuing nuclear capability, Washington had for the first time agreed to provide the Jewish state with offensive weapons. And to control the rising tide of radicalism that threatened to erode Western influence throughout the Arab world, the Johnson administration had scaled back economic aid for Egypt and had scrambled to isolate the pro-Soviet regime in Syria. According to Harold Saunders, who succeeded Robert Komer as White House Middle East expert in June 1966, these "constructive developments" suggested that America was "doing pretty well." Israel was "clearly here to stay," America could count on the "cooperation of like-minded Arabs" in Riyadh and Amman, and "Soviet gains have been far less impressive than we feared." Saunders emphasized, however, that Washington must still work hard to "buy time for an Arab-Israeli accommodation." As the Arab world became more polarized, Nasser might "feel forced to talk a more radical game in order to stay in line with his radical company." And this possibility, Saunders warned, "encourages groups like the Fatah and PLO," which meant that "chances of a flareup [would] increase" during the months ahead.[111]

III

The countdown for the ultimate flareup—the Six Day War—began during autumn 1966. In September LBJ himself requested "a special study of Soviet penetration in the Middle East"; it "revealed a pattern of serious Soviet advances," particularly in Egypt, Syria, and Iraq, "sparked by emotions generated by the Arab-Israeli confrontation."[112] For months the CIA had been warning that "Nasser's troubles with the West" and his desire for "greater Soviet support" would lead him to escalate his anti-Israel rhetoric and to step up his efforts "to undermine the British and Saudi positions in the Arabian Peninsula."[113] By early October Radio Cairo had resumed its fiery calls for the liberation of Palestine and Aden and for the overthrow of the House of Saud. Meanwhile, the Ba'athist regime in Syria sought to "improve its already close relations with Moscow, on which it depends for all its military supplies," by adopting "strident anti-Western positions."[114] And in Baghdad, where the Kremlin had earlier signed its "largest deal ever with Iraq," dozens of "advanced fighters and bombers" were on display. "There is no indication," Walt Rostow remarked on November 8, "that the Soviet Union is prepared to forego the leverage—and the power of disruption—it now enjoys through its Middle East sales of conventional arms," which by late 1966 totaled some $2.3 billion.[115]

Nor was there any indication that Moscow or Damascus intended to discourage Fatah's attacks on Israeli villages from hideouts in the Golan Heights and from the West Bank. For the better part of a year, Washington had cautioned Tel Aviv not to overreact to the PLO threat and had worked "to break down the 'fortress Israel' idea and to build bridges to the Arabs."[116] But as the November elections drew nearer and as Fatah's raids grew bolder, AIPAC and its friends in Washington wanted the Johnson administration to offer Tel Aviv more economic aid and to show greater understanding for Israel's predicament. The White House did release a $6 million Export-Import Bank credit on the eve of the balloting.[117] When an Israeli reprisal raid against the West Bank Palestinian village of Samu left more than thirty civilians dead on November 13, however, the United States "reacted sharply."[118] First, LBJ rebuked Prime Minister Levi Eshkol for this "unwise Israeli action" and sent word to King Hussein that America remained committed to the territorial integrity of Jordan."[119] Then on November 25, Washington refused to use its veto to stop the UN Security Council from censuring Tel Aviv. America's opposition to Israel's "retaliatory adventures" evidently had the desired effect, for Eshkol reacted with surprising restraint after yet another Fatah raid in January 1967. But according to Ambassador Walworth Barbour, the prime minister would need "much hand holding" in order to withstand the "considerable pressures for direct action" against the PLO and its friends in Syria.[120]

Israel was not alone in favoring direct action to curb Arab radicalism. Indeed, Saudi Arabia made no secret of its own desire for "early repressive action" against Arab radicals like those in Damascus, who in late 1966 were threatening to shut down the pipelines carrying Persian Gulf oil across Syria to the Eastern Mediterranean. The simplest way to thwart this new "Syrian-UAR strategy, supported by [the] Soviets, . . . to obtain control [of] NE oil," a high-ranking Saudi official told Ambassador Hermann Eilts on December 29, was "to conduct [a] successful coup d'etat" that would result in the "mass assassination" of Syria's Ba'athist leaders.[121] Although Washington rejected Riyadh's scheme and evidently steered clear of covert action elsewhere in the Arab world, the White House did send Harold Saunders to the Middle East early in the new year for a closer look at "Saudi and Persian Gulf affairs."[122]

For Saunders and other top U.S. policymakers, the most obvious way to reassure the Saudis and avoid further "polarization in the Arab world" during spring 1967 was to reverse recent Soviet gains in Egypt and Syria.[123] One possibility for improving Washington's relations with Cairo was to offer another short-term PL-480 wheat agreement like the one that had expired in July 1966. Diplomatic troubleshooter Robert Anderson and former World Bank president Eugene Black, both of whom had known Nasser for more than a decade, urged LBJ on February 9 "to find a way to get some wheat to Egypt."[124] No sooner had White House officials broached the subject on Capitol Hill, however, than Nasser delivered another "vitriolic attack" against America for supporting his conservative Arab rivals. This outburst prompted Iowa's Bourke Hickenlooper, the most senior Republican on the Senate Foreign Relations Committee, to inform Dean Rusk on March 6 that, in light of Nasser's "apparent plans for the conquest of South Arabia after the British pull out" and in light of the "ominous inroads which the Russians are making in the Red Sea area," he personally would do all that he could "to oppose additional aid to Egypt." Before the month was out, the Johnson administration had withdrawn the PL-480 proposal.[125]

The prospects for rebuilding Western influence in Damascus were even slimmer than in Cairo. In March 1967 the CIA called Syria "A Center of Instability" whose Ba'athist leaders were trying to "out-Nasir Nasir" by stepping up "Syrian support of the Fatah terrorist organization in its commando raids into Israeli territory." Although the Soviets had apparently "attempted quietly to discourage moves which could lead to hostilities in the area," the CIA believed that ties between Moscow and Damascus were still close enough to guarantee that "the Syrians will continue [to be] a thorn in the side of the US" and a dagger pointed at the heart of Israel.[126] With Middle East tensions rising and with Southeast Asian frustrations growing, it is hardly surprising that LBJ seems to have drawn a parallel between North Vietnam and an increasingly pro-Soviet regime in Damascus that was "sending Arab guerrillas across the borders of Syria, Jordan and Lebanon" to wreak havoc inside the Jewish state.[127]

Tel Aviv had been drawing just such a parallel for weeks in its latest bid to secure more military hardware from Washington. On February 1, 1967, the Israelis had requested 200 M-113 armored personnel carriers "to increase border surveillance" and "to prevent infiltration into Israel." The State Department was reluctant to provide the equipment, in part because Tel Aviv seemed to view relations with Washington as "a One-Way Street" but also because "Israel is not entirely leveling with us" about its Dimona reactor. In light of growing concern at Foggy Bottom "over the possibility of nuclear proliferation," the State Department evidently desired a "more tangible quid pro quo" before selling Israel the M-113s.[128]

While Tel Aviv pressed for a decision, ties between Syria and Fatah deepened, bringing "a sharp increase in the sophistication of attacks" against Israel later that spring.[129] After a Palestinian skirmish with Israeli farmers triggered a Syrian artillery barrage on April 7, Israel's air force bombed Fatah base camps in the Golan Heights and downed six MIGs in a dogfight just twenty miles from Damascus. Seeking to avert a full-blown regional conflagration, by mid-April the State Department favored providing Israel with 100 armored personnel carriers to bolster its counterinsurgency capability. The Pentagon, however, regarded such a move as "a serious mistake" that would likely "sharpen East-West polarization in the Middle East" and provide "further opportunity for the Soviets to gain influence."[130]

To help clarify the situation, in early May the White House dispatched Harold Saunders on his second fact-finding mission to the Middle East in four months. A short stop in Tel Aviv confirmed that the Israelis regarded "Arab terrorism as the greatest threat to their security today." Unless America stood firm against Nasser and the Arab radicals, Saunders predicted, Israel would never accept the Nuclear Nonproliferation Treaty (NPT) Washington was peddling in Tel Aviv. "Before signing an NPT," Levi Eshkol would insist that the United States persuade Russia to "keep the lid on the Arab arms inventory while the conventional balance is still in Israel's favor," terms the Kremlin would never consider. Once Saunders crossed to the West Bank, he learned that Israel's fears were not unfounded. "Don't make the mistake of thinking time will solve the refugee problem," angry Palestinian radicals told him as they swelled Fatah's ranks. From the banks of the Jordan to the shores of the Red Sea, Saunders could see that "the 'war of national liberation' as a technique has come to the Middle East," prompting America's friends to ask, "How can we stand against terrorist attackers in Vietnam and not in Israel or South Arabia?" In short, it would be difficult for the United States to avoid being drawn into the vortex of Middle East politics. "What this adds up to," Saunders reported gloomily on May 16, "is great pressure on us . . . to conclude with our friends that Nasser is a lost cause and throw in the sponge on trying to deal with him."[131]

Before the week was out, Nasser had taken steps that would ultimately lead LBJ to do just that. Ever since Tel Aviv's devastating air strikes against Syrian targets in early April, Damascus had been noisily insisting that only Cairo could prevent an all-out Israeli assault on the Golan Heights. Convinced that Syria was exaggerating the threat, Nasser made no move until mid-May, when the Kremlin confirmed that "the Israelis were massing their forces on the Syrian frontier" for an invasion. This news prompted Nasser to signal his support for Syria by sending UAR troops into the Sinai on May 17 to replace the UN Emergency Force (UNEF) that had patrolled the Egyptian-Israeli frontier for more than a decade.[132] Because of "some pretty militant public threats from Israel by Eshkol and others," Johnson's NSC staff privately acknowledged that "the Soviet advice to the Syrians that the Israelis were planning an attack was not far off."[133] Convinced that Israel must bear at least some responsibility for this "UAR brinksmanship" and that Tel Aviv must not "put a match to this fuse," LBJ warned Eshkol on May 18 that America would not be bound by Israeli actions "on which we are not consulted."[134] A few hours later Ambassador Barbour sent word from Tel Aviv that the Israelis did "not intend any military action" and that they were leaving "no 'automatic switches open.'"[135]

Heartened by Israel's show of restraint, Johnson took fresh steps to avoid a military conflagration. On May 19 he moved "to make sure [the] Arabs know what our declarations are" regarding territorial integrity in the Middle East. Later that same day, he pressed Soviet premier Alexei Kosygin to use his influence "in the cause of moderation" and urged UN Secretary General U Thant not to abdicate his responsibility for preserving peace in the Middle East. So long as Israel continued "to display steady nerves," LBJ told Eshkol on May 21, it should be possible to avert hostilities.[136] But the crisis deepened dramatically the next day when Nasser announced that he was closing the Straits of Tiran at the mouth of the Gulf of Aqaba to all Israeli shopping, a move that Tel Aviv regarded as an act of war. LBJ pleaded with the Egyptian leader to rescind his decision and to demonstrate the statesmanship necessary to "rescue the Middle East . . . from a war I believe no one wants."[137] Far from seeing Nasser as a statesman, however, Johnson and most of his White House aides probably agreed with the view that speechwriter John P. Roche offered in the vernacular of the Lone Star State: "I confess that I look on the Israelis as Texans," he told LBJ late on May 22, "and Nasser as Santa Ana."[138]

By the morning of May 23, there was little doubt that Israel preferred the role of Sam Houston at San Jacinto to that of Davey Crockett at the Alamo. A frantic Walworth Barbour telephoned Foggy Bottom from Tel Aviv to confirm that the Israelis were perilously close to launching a "preemptive strike" against Egypt to keep the straits open.[139] "There was tremendous pressure brought on Johnson to get him to come out for Israel," John Roche recalled years later; "Jewish pressure groups in this country were lined up all the way from Washington to California." As the day wore on, the White House mailroom was swamped by the first wave of 100,000 telegrams urging LBJ to stand by the Jewish state. "Israel," Abe Feinberg remembers telling his friend in the Oval Office, "would be economically castrated" if Nasser closed the straits.[140] Determined to prevent Tel Aviv from firing the first shot, Johnson moved swiftly to signal his continued support for Israel. First, he approved a $72 million American arms package that included the M-113 armored personnel carriers the Israelis coveted. Then he went on national television to condemn Egypt's actions in the Gulf of Aqaba as "illegal and potentially disastrous to the cause of peace." And finally, he indicated that the United States was exploring the possibility of a multinational naval flotilla to escort Israeli vessels through the Straits of Tiran. This response permitted Ambassador Barbour "to hold the Israelis off," but no one in Washington could be certain for how long.[141]

Lyndon Johnson convened an NSC meeting the next day to review America's options in the deepening crisis. The background materials Walt Rostow passed along made it clear that "the main issue in the Middle East today is whether Nasser, the radical states and their Soviet backers are going to dominate the area." He reminded LBJ that "two weeks ago, we expected South Arabia to provide the test" as to whether America would "back down as a major power" in the Middle East. "The current Arab-Israeli crisis," Rostow concluded, had merely "brought the test sooner than we expected." With Britain scaling back its presence east of Suez and with the Kremlin already sponsoring liberation movements such as FLOSY and the PLO, State Department experts favored isolating the Arab radicals by providing "strong support to Saudi Arabia" and quiet encouragement to Israel and to Iran.[142]

The most pressing question on the NSC's agenda for May 24, however, was how to prevent an Israeli attack on Egypt that seemed certain to spark a much broader conflagration. Secretary of State Rusk doubted whether U Thant and the UN Security Council could move swiftly enough to restrain Israel. Treasury secretary Henry Fowler wondered whether "economic sanctions" against Egypt might "hold the Israelis off," but few people around the table were optimistic. Fewer still held out much hope that the American-led multinational "Red Sea Regatta" LBJ had proposed the previous day would ever materialize. Egyptian submarines were prowling the Straits of Tiran and American antisubmarine units were "two weeks away." Unless Nasser relented, Israel seemed certain to launch pre-emptive air strikes against Egypt soon. Although key sections of the minutes remain classified, some U.S. officials evidently worried that Tel Aviv might resort to "unconventional weapons." Yet the NSC concluded that even without atomic bombs, "the Israelis can hold their own." The real problem, CIA director Richard Helms grumbled, was that America would "end up fully blackballed in the Arab world as Israel's supporter."[143]

For the next week and a half, the Johnson administration mounted a desperate holding action designed to buy time for a compromise that grew less likely with each passing day. When Israeli foreign minister Abba Eban arrived at the White House on May 26, LBJ counseled patience and remarked cryptically that "Israel would not be alone unless it acted alone."[144] The next day U.S. diplomats in New York City conferred with U Thant on how best to arrange an Arab-Israeli "breathing spell" under UN auspices.[145] Dean Rusk cabled Soviet foreign minister Andrei Gromyko on May 29 to urge the Kremlin to use its influence in Cairo to reopen the Straits of Tiran.[146] After King Hussein unexpectedly announced a Jordanian military alliance with Egypt on May 30, however, most Americans apparently believed that war was only a few days away.[147] In a last-ditch move, the White House sent Robert Anderson to Cairo, where he pleaded with his old Egyptian friend on June 2 to defuse the crisis. Eager for a compromise Nasser pledged not to strike first against Israel and agreed to send Egyptian vice-president Zacharia Mohieddin to Washington on June 7 for secret peace talks.[148]

But this was not nearly enough for Tel Aviv. Two days before Mohieddin's scheduled arrival at the White House, Skyhawk jets marked with the Star of David swooped across the Nile delta and destroyed Nasser's MIGs before they could get off the ground, enabling Israeli paratroopers to wrest Gaza and the Sinai from Egyptian control in short order. When King Hussein made good on his recent pledge to assist Egypt by unleashing his jets against the Jewish state just after midday on June 5, Israel retaliated swiftly, decimating the Jordanian air force, overrunning the West Bank, and seizing Arab East Jerusalem. Neither the Israeli attack nor its outcome came as a surprise to Washington. The Johnson administration had been "confident Israel could stand off its enemies and win," Richard Helms told *New York Times* columnist Cyrus Sulzberger shortly afterward; "it was also certain that at a convenient moment Israel would strike first."[149]

Indeed, from the very start of the war, U.S. officials worried less

about the danger of an Israeli defeat than about the potential consequences of an Israeli victory. Fearful that the Kremlin might feel
compelled to intervene on behalf of its Arab clients, an "astonished
and dismayed" Dean Rusk had flashed word to Gromyko moments
after the shooting started that "we had assurances from the Israelis
that they would not initiate hostilities." America, he added, would
work through the United Nations to secure the earliest possible
cease-fire.[150] No more eager than Washington to see events spiral out
of control, on June 6 Moscow introduced its own UN cease-fire resolution stipulating that both sides must withdraw to the prewar armi-
stice lines, a condition Israel was not prepared to accept. As the
fighting dragged into its third day, LBJ asked McGeorge Bundy to set
aside his work at the Ford Foundation in order to chair an NSC "Special Committee" modeled on the crisis-management team JFK had
used during his showdown with Khrushchev over Cuba five years
earlier.[151] By the time that Bundy, Clark Clifford, and the other
members of the Special Committee held their first meeting on June
8, the Kremlin had begun to feel some trepidation about resupplying
its Arab allies and favored a simple cease-fire instead.[152]

Once a UN cease-fire was finally in sight, it was Israel's turn to
drag its feet in order to settle one last score. When war erupted on
June 5, the Syrians had taken Nasser's advice and remained largely
on the sidelines. Well aware that Moshe Dayan and other Israeli military leaders coveted the Golan Heights, the Pentagon evidently instructed the USS *Liberty*, an unarmed electronic surveillance vessel
stationed in the Eastern Mediterranean, to listen for any signs of an
impending attack on Syria. Just after 2:00 P.M. on June 8, three waves
of Israeli jets and warships attacked the *Liberty* with rockets and
torpedoes, killing 34 sailors and wounding 171. As the *Liberty*
limped back to port, the Israelis claimed to have mistaken it for a
much smaller Egyptian freighter, an explanation few people in Washington seem to have believed.[153] It was "inconceivable it was [an] accident," Clark Clifford told the NSC Special Committee the next
day. "I still do not know at what level in the Israel government the
attacks were launched," Dean Rusk confessed years later," but I am
convinced it was not trigger-happy local commanders."[154] In any
case, fifteen hours after the first rockets knocked out the *Liberty*'s
surveillance gear and eight hours after Syria accepted the UN cease-
fire, the Israelis stormed the Golan Heights and nearly triggered the
superpower confrontation that the White House had been seeking to
avoid.

Despite frantic appeals from Washington urging Tel Aviv to halt the offensive, by the afternoon of June 9 the Israelis were only forty miles from Damascus. According to the CIA, the attack was "aimed at overthrowing the left-wing Baathist party which the Israelis blame for starting the entire Middle East crisis."[155] No one inside the Johnson administration expected the Kremlin to stand idly by while Israel moved in for the kill. "The Soviets [had] hinted," Dean Rusk recalled long afterward, "that if the Israelis attacked Syria, they would intervene with their own forces."[156] Disturbed by Tel Aviv's willingness to maneuver in such "hair-raising proximity to [the] brink," top U.S. officials told Israeli diplomats on June 10 that Congress "had had its fill of the failure to stop the fighting" and that the White House wanted an effective cease-fire "without delay."[157]

Meanwhile, the Washington-to-Moscow Hot Line lighted up three times that morning with calls from Soviet premier Kosygin, who evidently warned that Russian military action was imminent. LBJ responded by deciding to "turn the Sixth Fleet around to sail toward the eastern Mediterranean," a move that "Soviet submarines monitoring the Fleet's operations would report immediately to Moscow." Ultimately, the Kremlin backed down, Israel accepted the cease-fire, and "everyone relaxed a bit as it became clear that the fighting was petering out." Lest the Israelis draw the wrong lesson about the fruits of their stubbornness, however, a testy Lyndon Johnson intended to remind them that "it wasn't Dayan that kept Kosygin out."[158]

Having kept Moscow out, Washington turned next to a problem of even greater significance in the wake of the Six Day War: how to keep the West in the Middle East oil business. Walt Rostow had warned LBJ a week before the fighting started that war would probably mean "we shall have to face issues like the cancelling of oil contracts."[159] The Arabs activated their oil weapon on June 6, when Iraq and Kuwait cut off all petroleum shipments to Britain and America. Algeria, Libya, and Bahrain followed suit the next day as did Saudi Arabia, which warned that ARAMCO would "be gravely responsible if any drop of our oil" found its way to U.S. or British consumers.[160] By mid-June, Arab oil exports had been reduced by 60 percent, most of the pipelines running from the Persian Gulf to the Eastern Mediterranean had been sabotaged, and striking petroleum workers had ransacked pumping stations and refineries from Libya to Kuwait.[161]

British and American policymakers worked closely with oil industry executives to break the Arab embargo. Freezing Arab assets in New York and London was ruled out because it seemed certain to "provoke takeover of oil and other interests" and to "cause a run on

Sterling." But U.S. and British officials did convene an Emergency Oil Supply Committee to help the multinational giants circumvent the embargo by diverting petroleum from the Western Hemisphere to Western Europe.[162] While supertankers laden with East Texas and Venezuelan crude changed course for Antwerp and Liverpool, tensions between Arab conservatives, who controlled the oil fields, and Arab radicals, who wielded the oil weapon, rose dramatically. By June 18 the CIA was reporting a serious rift between Egypt and Syria, both of which favored a complete cutoff of petroleum exports, and Saudi Arabia and Kuwait, neither of which was willing to forgo its oil revenues. Two weeks later the Kuwaitis were hinting that they might lift the ban on shipments to Britain and America and the Saudis were complaining that "restrictions on oil export are harming the Arab producers more than the boycotted nations." Before the summer was out the embargo had fizzled, Arab oil output was 8 percent higher than before the Six Day War, and relations between Cairo and Riyadh had cooled somewhat.[163]

Driving a wedge between radicals and conservatives in the Muslim world of course had been a central feature of the Johnson administration's strategy in the Middle East for nearly three years. The key to postwar stability in the region, McGeorge Bundy told LBJ as early as June 9, was to show "sympathy for good Arabs as against bad Arabs." Pointing out that Egypt and its left-wing allies had severed relations with the United States but that moderate regimes in Lebanon and Jordan had not, Bundy thought the time had come to "stop talking about 'the Arab world'" and to "start sorting these people out a bit."[164] Walt Rostow agreed that "we [must] . . . keep our lines open to those moderate Arab leaders who have resisted Nasser's pressure to break with us" and urged Johnson on June 14 to do some "handholding" by sending personal letters to Jordan's King Hussein and the Emir of Kuwait.[165] The president did much more than that for King Faisal, who held the key to lifting the Arab oil embargo. On June 30 LBJ approved a $25 million package of nonlethal military hardware for Saudi Arabia, including four C-130 aircraft. In mid-July, Bundy proposed similar "limited actions for the moderate Arabs" in "Jordan, Lebanon, Morocco and Libya."[166]

Yet even such limited American actions could not succeed without the help of Israel, which had always viewed the future of the Arab moderates as "a great question mark." The CIA believed that the Israelis would "favor the U.S. Government attempting to preserve [Saudi King] Faysal as a moderate leader around which the Arab world could be rebuilt." But Foreign Minister Abba Eban vowed on June 13 that Israel would not humor the Saudis by returning the West Bank or East Jerusalem to King Hussein.[167] To make matters worse, some U.S. officials believed that a postwar territorial stalemate would "probably increase pressure favoring going nuclear in both Israel and the Arab states." The NSC Special Committee discussed "nukes" and the importance of "guarantees for non-nuclears" at least twice during its deliberations.[168] Yet few people in Washington seem to have found Israel's position on nonproliferation reassuring. "Don't you be the first power to introduce nuclear weapons into the Middle East," Dean Rusk warned Abba Eban in mid-June. "No," the Israeli diplomat replied with a smile, "but we won't be the second."[169]

If ambiguity shrouded Israel's nuclear aspirations, there was growing clarity about both the nature and the consequences of its postwar territorial ambitions. As early as June 14 the NSC Special Committee concluded that the Israelis were almost certain to insist on retaining East Jerusalem, the West Bank, and the Golan Heights, a stance that Dean Rusk believed "wld create a revanchism for the rest of the 20th c." LBJ reaffirmed America's commitment to "justice for the refugees" and to "political independence and territorial integrity for all" in a well-publicized speech five days later, but his words rang increasingly hollow as Israel expelled thousands of Palestinians from the West Bank and annexed East Jerusalem.[170] After a summer of "Arab disenchantment" with Israel and its American patron, autumn brought an element of realism and a greater willingness, at least among the moderate regimes from Rabat to Riyadh, to consider the "peace for land" formula that Britain and America pushed through the United Nations on November 22.[171]

But the passage of UN Security Council Resolution 242 would mean little if Israel chose to sit tight. With the Israeli prime minister scheduled to visit the LBJ Ranch in early 1968, Johnson's top aides believed the time had arrived to ask what Eshkol's intentions for peace were. Washington should continue to provide Tel Aviv with "political support and the equipment it needs to defend itself," Harold Saunders told Walt Rostow on December 29, "but we can't tie ourselves to a 'Fortress Israel,'" especially "if Israel gets SSM's or decides to build nuclear weapons." Although many of the materials surrounding Eshkol's January 7 visit to the Texas White House remain classified, the talking points Rostow passed along to LBJ suggest that the president pressed hard not only for "Israeli concessions—on refugees, Jerusalem, . . . [and] avoiding permanent moves in occupied lands" but also for assurances on "Nuclear Weapons and

Missiles.'' Evidently Eshkol was not entirely convincing on either front, for LBJ refused to approve Israel's request for fifty F-4 Phantom jets. Israel would receive 30 A-4 Skyhawks to offset recent Soviet aircraft shipments to the Arabs, but there would be no Phantoms until Tel Aviv adopted less ambiguous positions on UN Resolution 242 and nuclear proliferation.[172]

Washington's hard bargaining with Tel Aviv reflected a growing American anxiety that Israeli intransigence on nuclear and territorial matters would alienate pro-Western Muslim leaders crucial to America's plans to retain access to Middle East oil. Eight days after Eshkol returned to Israel, Prime Minister Harold Wilson announced that Britain would phase out all of its military outposts in the Persian Gulf within three years. Coming as it did just six weeks after pro-Soviet guerrillas had forced Whitehall to abandon Aden far earlier than anticipated, Wilson's announcement meant that U.S. policymakers had to scramble to "fill the gap left by the British" in the Middle East. The simplest way to shore up sagging Western influence in the Persian Gulf and the Arabian Peninsula, Walt Rostow told LBJ on January 16, was to work more closely with Iran and Saudi Arabia, both of which were "rich and increasingly confident"; the United States ought to "give them both encouragement and sell them arms."[173]

Lyndon Johnson could not have agreed more. In short order, Washington approved King Faisal's request for an arms package including F-86 jets equipped with Sidewinder missiles, agreed to expedite the Shah's latest appeal for American military hardware, and mediated a complex dispute over drilling rights for offshore oil in the Persian Gulf that threatened to poison relations between Saudi Arabia and Iran.[174] Later that spring LBJ invited both the Shah and Saudi Crown Prince Khalid, Faisal's heir apparent, to the White House to review Persian Gulf security issues.[175] "Close cooperation between Shah and Faisal [is] of greatest importance," State Department officials pointed out on June 18, not only "in assuring stability in Gulf after British withdrawal" but also in "preventing opportunity for radical Arab exploitation or successful communist lodgment."[176]

By autumn 1968 Foggy Bottom's worse-case scenario did not seem farfetched. For months the CIA had been monitoring the growth of the Arab Nationalist Movement, a Palestinian extremist group headed by George Habbash that claimed thousands of members in underground cells from Libya to Kuwait. Reports from Cairo in June confirmed that the "Russians now have military and intelligence facilities in UAR greater than they even dreamed of two years ago.''[177] A month later a bloodless coup masterminded by Saddam Hussein and other Ba'athist radicals rocked Baghdad, opening the door to greater Soviet influence in Iraq.[178] By late October the CIA was frankly worried about the ''extremely critical'' situation next door in Syria, where the pro-Soviet minister of defense Hafez al-Assad seemed about to gain the upper hand.[179] Perhaps most ominous of all as 1968 drew to a close were the rumblings coming out of Jordan, where King Hussein's failure to halt the flow of Soviet weapons to Palestinian guerrillas had enabled the PLO to unleash increasingly bloody raids against both Israeli military installations on the West Bank and civilian targets inside Israel.[180]

The upsurge of Soviet-backed Arab radicalism during LBJ's last year in office played into the hands of Israel, which was positioning itself to join Iran and Saudi Arabia as America's ''third pillar'' in the Middle East. Throughout winter 1968 U.S. officials had ''leaned quite hard'' on the Israelis to cooperate with Gunnar Jarring, the UN emissary charged with brokering the peace-for-land settlement outlined in Security Council Resolution 242.[181] Nor did the Johnson administration seem any less determined to prevent Israel from using its nuclear arms; alarmed by reports that researchers at Dimona had actually begun to assemble atomic warheads, at least one top White House aide recommended that LBJ obtain an Israeli ''commitment to sign the NPT'' before providing Eshkol with the fifty Phantom jets he had requested in January.[182] Yet domestic pressures were mounting for America to embrace Israel as a strategic asset. Although in March LBJ has scrapped his own plans for a second term, political insiders such as Abe Feinberg insisted that the speedy sale of F-4 Phantoms to Israel could provide just enough votes in New York and California on election day to put Vice-President Hubert Humphrey in the White House. By early October AIPAC had managed to persuade seventy senators to sign an open letter urging the president to approve the Phantom deal.[183]

Nevertheless, geopolitical considerations seem to have been as important as election-year politics in LBJ's decision on October 9 to open arms negotiations with Israel. Middle East tensions had been rising for weeks, due as much to ''Arab aggressiveness'' and ''a more militant attitude in the Soviet leadership'' as to ''Israel's territorial ambitions.''[184] More and more convinced that the Arabs were mainly responsible for the ''increasing terrorism and violence in the area,'' in late October the White House tentatively agreed to sell Israel F-4 jets, provided the ''NPT-Phantom problem'' could be resolved.[185] Sparks flew when Pentagon officials tried to link this latest arms deal with nonproliferation. "Concerned with Israel's missile and nuclear plans and intentions," Assistant Secretary of Defense Paul Warnke told Yitzhak Rabin on November 4 that Tel Aviv must "update" its assurances on these matters.[186] Rabin was outraged and refused to sign what he later called "an unprecedented document" that would have permitted the United States to inspect "every Israeli arms-manufacturing installation," evidently including Dimona.[187]

U.S. policymakers were well aware that an Israeli-American rift would only embolden Nasser and the Arab radicals, whose deepening ties with the Kremlin were making them more intransigent and less willing to cooperate with UN mediator Gunnar Jarring. A peace-for-land settlement in the Middle East based on Resolution 242, Dean Rusk concluded gloomily on November 22, could never be achieved until Nasser told Jarring "what he had been up to now unwilling to tell him clearly: 'that the UAR is ready to work out and enter into a binding agreement with Israel.'"[188] Having effectively written Nasser off, the Johnson administration approved the sale of fifty Phantoms three days later, ultimately settling for Israel's reiteration of its ambiguous pledge not to be the first nation to introduce atomic weapons into the Middle East rather than insisting on formal ratification of the nonproliferation treaty.[189]

The fallout in the Arab world from the latest Israeli-American arms deal was lighter than expected. To be sure, Egypt, Syria, and Iraq denounced the Phantom sale and redoubled their efforts to secure comparable hardware from the Kremlin. But the reaction among conservative Arabs such as the Emir of Kuwait, who arrived in Washington on December 12 for long-scheduled talks with LBJ, was more measured. Some observers in Washington expected the Emir to blast America for its "pro-Israel policy" symbolized by the pending Phantom deal. After getting a "perfunctory" protest "off his chest," however, he proved far more interested in discussing American plans for the defense of the Persian Gulf once Britain withdrew in 1971.[190] Like the Shah of Iran and King Faisal, the Emir of Kuwait seemed to regard Arab radicalism as a more dangerous threat than Israeli expansionism; inside the Johnson administration, heads doubtless nodded in agreement.

As Lyndon Johnson prepared to depart the White House for the friendlier confines of the LBJ Ranch in January 1969, he bequeathed to his successor a "three pillars" approach toward the Middle East that placed a far higher priority on friendly relations with Israel, Iran, and Saudi Arabia than with Nasser and the Arab radicals. LBJ had quickly grown frustrated with the set of even-handed Middle

East policies he himself had inherited from Kennedy in November 1963. As early as spring 1964, Nasser's intense quest for Arab self-determination had collided with Johnson's accelerating drive to strengthen Western interests, generating considerable friction between Cairo and Washington. In contrast, the friendly personal relations LBJ developed with Levi Eshkol, King Faisal, and the Shah of Iran over the next three years helped make their nations strong candidates to succeed Britain as guarantors of regional stability. Not surprisingly, Egypt saw its multimillion dollar U.S. aid package reduced to a mere trickle by spring 1967. In the meantime, the Saudi and Iranian arsenals bristled with American military hardware while Israel emerged as a strategic asset armed with U.S. tanks and jets, courtesy of Lyndon Johnson.

Clearly, LBJ's pro-Israel policies resulted partly from pressure from friends of Zion on the White House staff, in Congress, and among the American Jewish community. But domestic politics was only one aspect of the story. By offering Israel conventional weapons, Johnson hoped to prevent Tel Aviv from opting for a nuclear deterrent that would touch off a dangerous new regional arms race. And by acquiescing in Israel's preemptive strike against Egypt and its radical allies in June 1967, he hoped to thwart an Arab war of national liberation not unlike the one America was losing in Vietnam. In short, preventing nuclear proliferation and combating revolutionary nationalism were at least as important for LBJ as winning elections.

Although loath to admit it publicly, Muslim conservatives apparently shared LBJ's pleasure over Israel's humiliation of Nasser, whose fiery calls for radical change during the mid-1960s had helped spark political unrest from Tripoli to Tehran. Since neither Libya's King Idris nor the Shah of Iran was eager to see his oil wealth swept away by a wave of Nasserism, each ruler gravitated toward the United States as did the Saudis and Kuwaitis. Once the Kremlin moved to rearm Nasser and the Arab radicals after the Six Day War, a full-blown U.S. partnership with Iran and Saudi Arabia paralleling America's special relationship with Israel was only a matter of time.

Yet success in the short run does not always ensure a similar outcome over the long haul. Ultimately, LBJ's policies could not stop Israel from retaining the occupied territories or from achieving nuclear capability. Nor could those policies check the rising tide of Islamic fundamentalism in Iran or prevent Saddam Hussein from cementing his own special relationship with Moscow. Ironically, however, Johnson's policies did help shape the coalition that enabled George Bush to win the war in the desert a quarter-century later.

Notes

1. On Eisenhower's and Kennedy's policies, see William Burns, *Economic Aid & American Policy toward Egypt, 1955-1981* (Albany: State University of New York Press, 1985), pp. 108-48, Steven Spiegel, *The Other Arab-Israeli Conflict: Making America's Middle East Policy from Truman to Reagan* (Chicago: University of Chicago Press, 1985), pp. 83-117, and Douglas Little, "From Even-Handed to Empty-Handed: Seeking Order in the Middle East," in *Kennedy's Quest for Victory: American Foreign Policy 1961-1963*, ed. Thomas G. Paterson (New York: Oxford University Press, 1989).

2. Philip Geyelin, *Lyndon B. Johnson and the World* (New York: Praeger, 1966), pp. 35-45; Doris Kearns, *Lyndon Johnson and the American Dream* (New York: Harper and Row, 1976), pp. 160-69.

3. Louis Gomolak, "Prologue: LBJ's Foreign Affairs Background, 1908-1948," (Ph.D. diss., University of Texas at Austin, 1989), pp. 30-35, 44-51, 94-96.

4. Abba Eban, *An Autobiography* (New York: Random House, 1977), p. 187.

5. LBJ to John Foster Dulles, February 11, 1957, and Arthur Minnich memcon, February 20, 1957, both in U.S. Department of State, *Foreign Relations of the United States, 1955-1957*, 22 vols. (Washington, D.C.: U.S. Government Printing Office, 1986-1992), 17: 139-40, 215-16; I. L. Kenen, *Israel's Defense Line: Her Friends and Foes in Washington* (Buffalo, N.Y.: Prometheus Books, 1981), pp. 148-53; Spiegel, *Other Arab-Israeli Conflict*, p. 120.

6. Kenen, *Israel's Defense Line*, p. 173.

7. Merle Miller, *Lyndon: An Oral Biography* (New York: G. P. Putnam, 1980), p. 478; Thomas M. Gaskin, "Senate Majority Leader Lyndon B. Johnson: The Formosa and Middle East Resolutions," in *Lyndon Baines Johnson and the Uses of Power*, ed. Bernard J. Firestone and Robert C. Vogt (New York: Greenwood Press, 1988), pp. 250-53; Robert Dallek, *Lone Star Rising: Lyndon Johnson and His Times, 1908-1960* (New York: Oxford University Press, 1991), pp. 511-13; John Foster Dulles phone call to LBJ, February 14, 1957, Memoranda of Telephone Conversations, John Foster Dulles Papers (Fredrick, Md.: University Publications of America, 1986), microfilm edition, reel 6.

8. LBJ to JFK, September 10, 1962, Vice-Presidential Security File, box 10, "Middle East Memos," Lyndon B. Johnson Presidential Library, Austin, Texas (hereafter cited as LBJL).

9. Little, "From Even-Handed to Empty-Handed," pp. 162-69; Mordechai Gazit, *President Kennedy's Policy toward the Arab States and Israel* (Syracuse, N.Y.: Syracuse University Press, 1983), pp. 41-44.

10. Howard Burris to LBJ, March 14, 1963, Vice-Presidential Security Files, box 6, "Memos to the Vice President from Colonel Burris, 7/62-4/63," LBJL.

11. Douglas Little, "The New Frontier on the Nile: JFK, Nasser, and

Arab Nationalism," *Journal of American History* 75 (September 1968): 510–22.

12. Gazit, *Kennedy, the Arab States and Israel*, pp. 49–55, 116–20; Seymour Hersh, *The Samson Option: Israel's Nuclear Arsenal and American Foreign Policy* (New York: Random House, 1991), pp. 124–26.

13. On the Gruening amendment, see Burns, *Economic Aid & American Policy toward Egypt*, pp. 144–46; Ernest Gruening, *Many Battles: The Autobiography of Ernest Gruening* (New York: Liveright, 1973), pp. 456–58; Kenen, *Israel's Defense Line*, pp. 170–72; and Dean Rusk, cirtel. November 8, 1963, President's Office File: Countries, box 127, "UAR—Security 1963," John F. Kennedy Presidential Library, Boston.

14. Komer to McGeorge Bundy, December 3, 1963, National Security File (NSF), Name File, box 6, "Komer Memos, Vol. 1," LBJL.

15. On pro-Israel sentiment among LBJ's advisers and friends, see Spiegel, *Other Arab-Israeli Conflict*, pp. 128–29; Kenen, *Israel's Defense Line*, pp. 148–53; and Edward Tivnan, *The Lobby: Jewish Political Power and American Foreign Policy* (New York: Simon and Schuster, 1987), pp. 59–60.

16. Ambassador John Badeau (Cairo) to Rusk, tels. December 13, 1963, and January 15, 1964; and Rusk to Goldberg, tel. January 17, 1964, NSF, Country File, box 158, "UAR Cables, Vol. 1," LBJL.

17. Benjamin Read to Bundy, February 12, 1964, NSF, Country File, box 159, "UAR Cables, Vol. 1," LBJL.

18. LBJ, "Remarks in New York City at the Dinner of the Weizmann Institute of Science," February 6, 1964, *Public Papers of the Presidents: Lyndon B. Johnson, 1963–64*, 2 vols. (Washington, D.C.: U.S. Government Printing Office, 1965), 1: 279–81 (hereafter cited as *Public Papers*); CIA cable 3/572910, February 9, 1964, NSF, Country File, box 159, "UAR Cables, Vol. 1," LBJL.

19. CIA, Special Memorandum 6-64, February 25, 1964, NSF, Memos to the President File, box 1, "Bundy, Vol. 2," LBJL.

20. CIA cable 3/574978, March 3, 1964, and Badeau of Rusk, tel. March 4, 1964, NSF, Country File, box 159, "UAR Cables, Vol. 1," LBJL.

21. "Minutes of the 525th NSC Meeting," April 2, 1964, NSF, National Security Council (NSC) Meetings File, box 1, LBJL.

22. "Meeting with President re Harriman's Report," April 3, 1964, NSF, Files of McGeorge Bundy, box 19, "Memos of Meetings with the President, Vol 1.," LBJL; "Minutes of the 526th NSC Meeting," April 3, 1964, NSF, NSC Meetings File, box 1, LBJL.

23. William Polk to Walt Rostow, April 7, 1964, and Rostow to LBJ, April 14, 1964, NSF, Country File, box 159, "UAR Memos, Vol. 1," LBJL.

24. Badeau to Rusk, tels. April 11 and May 2, 1964, "UAR Cables, Vol. 1," NSF, Country File, box 159, LBJL.

25. CIA Special Report, "The Soviet Union and Egypt," May 8, 1964, NSF, Country File, box 159, "UAR Memos, Vol. 1," LBJL.

26. Rusk to LBJ, May 24, 1964, NSF, Country File, box 159, "UAR Cables, Vol. 1," LBJL.

27. Badeau to Rusk, tel. May 25, 1964, and Komer to Valenti, May 25, 1964, NSF, Country File, box 159, "UAR Memos, Vol. 1," LBJL.

28. Komer to Bundy, December 3, 1963, and Komer to LBJ, February 18, 1964, NSF, Name File, box 6, "Komer Memos, Vol. 1," LBJL; Rear Adm. J. W. Davis, (deputy director of the Joint Chiefs of Staff) to Robert McNamara, January 18, 1964, NSF, Country File, box 145, "Israel—Tanks, Vol. 1," LBJL; Komer to LBJ, January 29, 1964, NSF, Country File, box 139, "Israel, Vol. 1," LBJL.

29. Feldman to LBJ, March 4 and 14, 1964, NSF, Memos to the President File, box 1, "Bundy, Vol. 2," LBJL; Feldman to LBJ, May 11, 1964, NSF, Country File, box 139, "Israel, Vol. 1," LBJL.

30. Barbour to Rusk, tel. May 15, 1964, NSF, Country File, Box 139, "Israel, Vol. 1," LBJL.

31. Komer memcon, May 18, 1964, NSF, McGeorge Bundy Files, box 19, "Meetings with the President, vol. 1," LBJL.

32. Komer to LBJ, May 28 and June 1, 1964, NSF, Country File, box 143, "Israel—Eshkol Visit," LBJL (emphasis in the original).

33. Feldman memcon, June 1, 1964, ibid.

34. Komer to LBJ, June 2, 1964, ibid. (emphasis in the original).

35. Komer to LBJ, June 3, 1964, ibid.

36. Rusk to Wheelock (Aden), tel. March 27, 1964, NSF, Country File, box 161, "Yemen, Vol. 1," LBJL; Badeau to Rusk, tel. May 10, 1964, NSF, Country File, box 159, "UAR Cables, Vol. 1," LBJL.

37. R. A. Butler, *The Art of the Possible: The Memoirs of Lord Butler* (London: Hamish Hamilton, 1971), pp. 256–57.

38. Ambassador David Bruce (London) to Rusk, tel. June 9, 1964, NSF, Country File, box 161, "Yemen, Vol. 1," LBJL.

39. State Department cirtels. December 9 and 23, 1963, NSF, Country File, box 161, "Yeman, Vol. 1," LBJL; State Department background paper, "US Commitment to Saudi Arabia," February 20–25, 1966, NSF, Country File, box 155, "Saudi Arabia, Vol. 1," LBJL.

40. "Summary of Recommendations of the U.S. Air Defense Survey Team on Saudi Arabia," n.d. (probably April 1965); General Adams to LBJ, tel. June 20, 1964, NSF, Country File, box 155, "Saudi Arabia, Vol. 1," LBJL; Rusk to Parker Hart (Riyadh), tel. May 7, 1964, NSF, Country File, box 161, "Yemen, Vol. 1," LBJL.

41. Burns, *Economic Aid & American Policy toward Egypt*, pp. 155–57.

42. Komer to Bundy, August 24, 1964, NSF, Name File, box 6, "Komer Memos, Vol. 1," LBJL.

43. "Major Issues in U.S.–U.A.R. Relations," n.d., attached to Komer to LBJ, August 24, 1964, NSF, Country File, box 159, "UAR Cables, Vol. 2," LBJL.

44. Boswell (Cairo) to Rusk, tel. September 12, 1964, and Rusk to Boswell, tel. September 18, 1964, NSF, Country File, box 159, "UAR Cables, Vol. 2," LBJL.

45. State Department memcon, October 6, 1964, NSF, Country File, box 159, "UAR Cables, Vol. 2," LBJL.

46. Komer to Bundy, October 6, 1964, NSF, Name File, box 6, "Komer Memos, Vol. 1," LBJL.

47. Ambassador Llewellyn Thompson testimony, January 14, 1965, U.S.

Senate, Historical Office, *Executive Sessions of the Senate Committee on Foreign Relations*, 17 vols. (Washington, D.C.: U.S. Government Printing Office, 1973–1991), 17: 184.

48. Lucius Battle Oral History, LBJL, pp. 14–15.

49. Battle to Talbot, November 19, 1964, NSF, Country File, box 159, "UAR Cables, Vol. 2," LBJL.

50. Burns, *Economic Aid & American Policy toward Egypt*, pp. 158–60; Mohamed Heikal, *The Cairo Documents* (Garden City, N.Y.: Doubleday, 1973), pp. 227–30.

51. Bundy to LBJ, December 24, 1964, NSF, Country File, box 159, "UAR Memos, Vol. 3," LBJL. White House aide Horace Busby told Bundy that "the President read this at the ranch" (Busby to Bundy, January 2, 1965, ibid.).

52. Komer to Bundy, January 4, 1965, NSF, Country File, box 159, "UAR Memos, Vol. 3," LBJL.

53. State Department cirtel, January 12, 1965, NSF, Country File, box 159, "UAR Cables, Vol. 3," LBJL.

54. On Persian Gulf oil output, see CIA, NIE 36–66, "The Eastern Arab World," February 17, 1966, NSF, National Intelligence Estimates (NIE) File, box 6, LBJL.

55. "Discussion of Near East Developments," January 13, 1965, NSF, Country File, box 116, "Near East, Vol. 1," LBJL.

56. Rusk to LBJ, January 22, 1965, NSF, Country File, box 159, "UAR Memos, Vol. 3," LBJL; Bromley K. Smith, memcon, January 22, 1965, NSF, Bundy Files, box 18, "Miscellaneous Meetings, Vol. 1," LBJL; Burns, *Economic Aid & American Policy toward Egypt*, p. 160.

57. Rusk testimony, January 27, 1965, *Executive Sessions of the Senate Committee on Foreign Relations*, 17: 245; Burns, *Economic Aid & American Policy toward Egypt*, pp. 160–63.

58. Hussein quoted in *Newsweek*, April 20, 1964, pp. 56–57.

59. CIA, "Nasir's Arab Policy: The Latest Phase," August 28, 1964, NSF, Country File, box 159, "UAR Cables, Vol. 2," LBJL; Komer to Bundy, July 24, 1964, NSF, Name File, box 6, "Komer Memos, Vol. 1," LBJL.

60. Harrison Symmes Oral History, Lauinger Library, Georgetown University, Washington, D.C.

61. "Recommendations on Near East Arms," n.d., attached to Ball to LBJ, n.d. (probably late February 1965), NSF, Country File, box 116, "Near East, Vol. 1," LBJL.

62. Ball phone call to Bundy, February 2, 1965, and Ball phone call to Rusk, February 5, 1965, Box 4, "Jordan," George W. Ball Papers, LBJL.

63. Minutes of the 544th NSC Meeting, February 1, 1965, NSF, NSC Meetings File, box 1, LBJL; Bundy to LBJ, February 19, 1965, NSF, Country File, box 145, "Israel—Tanks, Vol. 2," LBJL; "Recommendations on Near East Arms," n.d., attached to Ball to LBJ, n.d. (probably late February 1965), NSF, Country File, box 116, "Near East, Vol. 1," LBJL.

64. John Reilly phone call to Komer, June 2, 1965, Vice-Presidential Files: Foreign Affairs, "Visits and Meetings 1965," box 918, Hubert H. Humphrey Papers, Minnesota Historical Society, St. Paul, Minnesota; Bundy to LBJ, June 12, 1964, NSF, Memos to the President File, box 2, "Bundy, Vol. 5," LBJL.

65. Assistant Secretary of Defense John McNaughton to Komer, July 15, 1964, *Declassified Documents Reference System 1988* (New Carrollton, Md.: Research Publications Inc., 1988), microfiche, item 3237 (hereafter cited as *DDRS* for the appropriate year and item).

66. "Recommendations on Near East Arms," n.d., attached to Ball to LBJ, n.d. (probably late February 1965), NSF, Country File, box 116, "Near East, Vol. 1," LBJL; Spiegel, *Other Arab-Israeli Conflict*, p. 132.

67. State Department memcon, February 25, 1965, NSF, Country File, box 145, "Israel—Harriman Mission," LBJL.

68. "Recommendations on Near East Arms," n.d., attached to Ball to LBJ, n.d. (probably late February 1965), NSF, Country File, box 116, "Near East, Vol. 1," LBJL.

69. State Department memcon, February 26, 1965, NSF, Country File, box 145, "Israel—Harriman Mission," LBJL.

70. "Recommendations on Near East Arms," n.d., attached to Ball to LBJ, n.d. (probably late February 1965), NSF, Country File, box 116, "Near East, Vol. 1," LBJL.

71. State Department cirtel. no. 887, November 10, 1964, NSF, Country File, box 139, "Israel, Vol. 3," LBJL; Hersh, *Samson Option*, pp. 125, 143.

72. Deputy Assistant Secretary of Defense for International Security Affairs Peter Solbert to McGeorge Bundy, March 8, 1965, NSF, Country File, box 145, "Israel—Harriman Mission," LBJL.

73. "Recommendations on Near East Arms," n.d., attached to Ball to LBJ, n.d. (probably late February 1965), NSF, Country File, box 116, "Near East, Vol. 1," LBJL; "Draft Memorandum of Understanding," February 26, 1965, NSF, Country File, box 145, "Israel—Harriman Mission," LBJL; Komer to Rusk and Bundy, tel. March 10, 1965; Rusk to Barbour, tel. June 5, 1965; and Read to Bundy, June 14, 1965, all in NSF, Country File, box 139, "Israel, Vol. 4," LBJL.

74. "Recommendations on Near East Arms," n.d., attached to Ball to LBJ, n.d. (probably late February 1965), NSF, Country File, box 116, "Near East, Vol. 1," LBJL; Rusk to Battle, tel. March 18, 1965, NSF, Country File, box 161, "UAR—Nasser Discussions on Mid-East Arms," LBJL; Heikal, *Cairo Documents*, pp. 233–36.

75. State Department cirtel. no. 1750, March 19, 1965, NSF, Country File, box 116, "Near East, Vol. 1," LBJL.

76. CIA, NIE 36.1-65, "Problems & Prospects for the United Arab Republic," March 31, 1965, NSF, NIE File, box 6, LBJL.

77. Talbot (Tel Aviv) to Rusk, April 22, 1965, NSF, Country File, box 139, "Israel, Vol. 4," LBJL.

78. Read to Bundy, June 5, 1965, NSF, Country File, box 159, "UAR Memos, Vol. 4," LBJL.

79. On FLOSY and PFLOAG, see J. B. Kelly, *Arabia, the Gulf, and the West* (New York: Basic Books, 1980), pp. 26–41, 136–50. On Soviet influence, see "Protection of American Interests in the Near East," n.d., attached to Rusk to LBJ, September 23, 1965, NSF, Country File, box 159, "UAR Memos, Vol. 4," LBJL.

80. Komer to Bundy, June 21, June 22, and July 6, 1965, NSF, Name File, box 6, "Komer Memos, Vol. 1," LBJL; Battle to Rusk, tel. August 18, 1965, NSF, Name File, box 7, "Saunders Memos," LBJL.

81. Komer to LBJ, August 20, 1965, NSF, Name File, box 6, "Komer Memos, Vol. 1," LBJL; Bundy to LBJ, August 28, 1965, *DDRS 1986*, item 942.

92. Rusk testimony, October 13, 1965, *Executive Sessions of the Senate Committee on Foreign Relations*, 17: 1228-29.

83. Read to Bromley K. Smith, November 11, 1965, and Battle to Rusk, tel. November 24, 1965, NSF, Country File, box 159, "UAR Cables, Vol. 4," LBJL; Burns, *Economic Aid & American Policy toward Egypt*, pp. 165-66.

84. Glen Balfour-Paul, *The End of Empire in the Middle East: Britain's Relinquishment of Power in Her Last Three Arab Dependencies* (New York: Cambridge University Press, 1991), p. 84.

85. W. W. Rostow, "Alternatives for the US in the Persian Gulf–Arabian Sea Area Stemming from UK Defense Review," October 4, 1965, and State Department cirtel, October 15, 1965, both quoted in Karl Pieragostini, *Britain, Aden and South Arabia* (New York: St. Martin's Press, 1991), pp. 108, 167.

86. CIA, "Outlook for Aden & the Federation of South Arabia," November 5, 1965, NSF, Country File, box 155, "Saudi Arabia, Vol. 1," LBJL; *New York Times*, January 28, 1966, p. 10; Stewart comments, February 21, 1966, *Hansard, Commons, 1965-66* (London: Her Majesty's Stationery Office, 1966), vol. 725; Pieragostini, *Britain, Aden, and South Arabia*, pp. 105-7, 166-67; Frank Brenchley, *Britain and the Middle East: An Economic History 1945-1987* (London: Lester Crook, 1989), pp. 165-67.

87. Denis Healey, *The Time of My Life* (New York: Norton, 1990), pp. 278-81.

88. CIA, "Euphrates River Development," May 13, 1966, and CIA, "Syria under the Baath," May 20, 1966, NSF, Country File, box 156, "Syria, Vol. 1," LBJL.

89. Lyndon B. Johnson, *The Vantage Point: Perspectives on the Presidency 1963-1969* (New York: Holt Rinehart and Winston, 1971), p. 289.

90. John J. Jernegan memcon, June 3, 1965; Barbour to Rusk, tel. August 16, 1965, and Rusk to Barbour, tel. September 13, 1965, NSF, Country File, box 139, "Israel, Vol. 4," LBJL.

91. Komer memcon, October 18, 1965, NSF, Name File, box 6, "Komer Memos, Vol. 2," LBJL.

92. Komer to LBJ, January 18, 1966, and Rusk to Barbour, February 3, 1966, NSF, Country File, box 139, "Israel, Vol. 5," LBJL; Komer to Bundy, February 8, 1966, NSF, Name File, box 6, "Komer Memos, Vol. 2," LBJL.

93. Rusk to Barbour, tels. February 26 and March 26, 1966, and Barbour to Rusk, tel. March 29, 1966, NSF, Country File, box 139, "Israel, Vol. 5," LBJL.

94. Rusk to Barbour, tels. March 21 and 23, 1966, and Barbour to Rusk, tel. March 24, 1966, NSF, Country File, box 139, "Israel, Vol. 5," LBJL.

95. Benjamin Read to Walt Rostow, April 30, 1966, NSF, Country File, box 139, "Israel, Vol. 5," LBJL; "U.S. Arms Sale to Israel," n.d., attached to Rusk to LBJ, July 29, 1966, NSF, Country File, box 144, "Israel—Shazar Briefing Book," LBJL.

96. LBJ to Hussein, n.d. (probably late March 1966), NSF, Country File, box 139, "Israel, Vol. 5," LBJL; LBJ to Hussein, May 4, 1966, *DDRS 1991*, item 468.

97. Komer to LBJ, March 29, 1966, NSF, Robert Komer Files, box 1,

LBJL. Komer recommended that Dean Rusk attend the dedication ceremony on April 20.

98. McNaughton to Komer, 7 April 1965, and State Department background papers, "Future Prospects for Yemen" and "U.S. Involvement in the Yemen Problem," February 20–25, 1966, NSF, Country File, box 155, "Saudi Arabia, Vol. 1," LBJL.

99. Brenchley, *Britain and the Middle East*, pp. 140–41; State Department background paper, "U.S. Involvement in Yemen Problem," February 20–25, 1966, NSF, Country File, box 155, "Saudi Arabia, Vol. 1," LBJL.

100. Uriel Dann, *King Hussein and the Challenge of Arab Radicalism: Jordan, 1955–1967* (New York: Oxford University Press, 1989), pp. 144–45, 149–50; Nadav Safran, *Saudi Arabia: The Ceaseless Quest for Security* (Cambridge: Harvard University Press, 1985), pp. 119–20.

101. CIA, NIE 36.66, "The Eastern Arab World," February 17, 1966, NSF, NIE File, box 6, LBJL.

102. Rostow to LBJ, June 20 and 22, 1966, NSF, Country File, box 155, "Saudi Arabia—Faisal Trip," LBJL.

103. Safran, *Saudi Arabia*, pp. 119, 121–22, 198, 200–201.

104. James Bill, *The Eagle and the Lion: The Tragedy of American-Iranian Relations* (New Haven, Conn.: Yale University Press, 1988), pp. 131–53; James Goode, "Reforming Iran during the Kennedy Years," *Diplomatic History* 15 (Winter 1991): 13–29.

105. Ambassador Julius Holmes (Tehran) to Rusk, tel. August 25, 1962; and LBJ to JFK, September 10, 1962, Vice-Presidential Security File, box 2, "Trip to Middle East, 1962," LBJL.

106. LBJ quoted in Bill, *Eagle and Lion*, p. 178.

107. On LBJ and the Shah, see Barry Rubin, *Paved with Good Intentions: The American Experience and Iran* (New York: Oxford University Press, 1980), pp. 115–23, and Bill, *Eagle and Lion*, pp. 154–82.

108. CIA, NIE 34–66, "Iran," March 24, 1966, NSF, NIE File, box 6, LBJL.

109. CIA, NIE 34–66, "Iran," NSF, NIE File, box 6, LBJL; Rostow to LBJ, May 5, 12, and 23, 1966, *DDRS 1991*, items 452–54; Meyer to LBJ, tel. May 23, 1966, NSF, Country File, box 136, "Iran, Vol. 2," LBJL.

110. Rostow to LBJ, July 19, 1966, and LBJ to Shad, July 20, 1966, *DDRS 1991*, items 457–58; Howard Wriggins to Rostow, July 26 and August 2, 1966; and Rostow, "Tuesday Lunch Agenda," August 2, 1966, all in NSF, Walt Rostow Files, box 1, "Meetings with the President," LBJL.

111. Saunders to Rostow, June 24, 1966, *DDRS 1991*, item 1089.

112. Johnson, *Vantage Point*, p. 288.

113. CIA, NIE 36.1–66, "The Outlook for the United Arab Republic," May 19, 1966, NSF, NIE File, box 6, LBJL.

114. CIA, "Syria's Radical Future," October 10, 1966, NSF, Country File, box 156, "Syria, Vol. 1," LBJL.

115. Rostow to LBJ, November 8, 1966, and Rostow to J. William Fulbright, draft letter, November 8, 1966, *DDRS 1991*, item 152.

116. Arthur Goldberg to LBJ, May 19, 1966; Rusk to LBJ, May 30, 1966; Rostow to LBJ, May 31 and June 3, 1966, NSF, Country File, box 159, "UAR Memos, Vol. 4," LBJL.

117. Kenen, *Israel's Defense Line*, pp. 190–92; "U.S. Help for Israel,"

November 2, 1966; LBJ to Feinberg, n.d., attached to Rostow to LBJ, November 3, 1966, NSF, Country File, box 140, "Israel, Vol. 6," LBJL.

118. Rostow to LBJ, November 14, 1966, *DDRS 1991*, item 497.

119. Barbour to Rusk, tel. November 14, 1966, NSF, Country File, box 140, "Israel, Vol. 6," LBJL; LBJ to Hussein, November 23, 1966, cited in Dann, *Hussein and Arab Radicalism*, pp. 155, 198 n.4.

120. Kenen, *Israel's Defense Line*, p. 192; Barbour to Rusk, tel. January 17, 1967, NSF, Country File, box 140, "Israel, Vol. 6," LBJL.

121. Eilts to Rusk, tel. December 29, 1966, NSF, Country File, box 161, "Yemen, Vol. 2," LBJL.

122. Walt Rostow to Eilts, February 4, 1967, NSF, Name File, box 7, "Saunders Memos," LBJL.

123. "Minutes of NSC Meeting," February 8, 1967, NSF, NSC Meetings File, box 2, LBJL.

124. Rostow to LBJ, February 9, 1967, NSF, Name File, box 7, "Rostow Memos, Vol. 2," LBJL.

125. Lucius Battle Oral History; Hickenlooper to Rusk, March 6, 1967, "Countries—Egypt," Foreign Relations Committee Files, Box 133, Bourke Hickenlooper Papers, Herbert Hoover Presidential Library, West Branch, Iowa.

126. CIA, "Syria: A Center of Instability," March 24, 1967, NSF, Country File, box 156, "Syria, Vol. 1," LBJL.

127. Johnson, *Vantage Point*, p. 289.

128. Barbour to Rusk, tel. February 1, 1967; State Department background paper, "U.S.–Israel Relations, February 8, 1967, NSF, Country File, box 140, "Israel, Vol. 6," LBJL.

129. Saunders, "'Terrorist Origins of the Present Crisis," n.d. (mid-June 1967), NSF, NSC History File, box 17, "Middle East Crisis, Vol 1.," LBJL.

130. Undersecretary of State Nicholas Katzenbach to LBJ, April 17 and May 5, 1967, *DDRS 1988*, items 3317–18; McNamara to LBJ, April 17, 1967, and Assistant Secretary of Defense Townsend Hoopes to Rostow, May 1, 1967, *DDRS 1987*, items 1328–29.

131. Saunders to Rostow, May 16, 1967, attached to Rostow to LBJ, May 17, 1967, NSF, Name File, box 7, "Saunders Memos," LBJL.

132. Mohamed Heikal, *The Sphinx and the Commissar: The Rise and Fall of Soviet Influence in the Arab World* (London: Collins, 1978), pp. 174–75.

133. Saunders, "'Terrorist Origins of the Present Crisis," n.d. (early June 1967), NSF, NSC History Files, box 17, "Middle East Crisis, Vol. 1," LBJL; Walt Rostow to LBJ, May 17, 1967, NSF, Memos to the President File, box 16, "Rostow, Vol. 28," LBJL.

134. Rostow to LBJ, May 17, 1967, and LBJ to Eshkol, May 1[8], 1967, NSF, Memos to the President File, box 16, "Rostow Vol. 28," LBJL.

135. Barbour to State Department, May 18, 1967, quoted in Donald Neff, *Warriors for Jerusalem: The Six Days That Changed the Middle East* (New York: Simon and Schuster, 1984), p. 172.

136. Rostow memcon, May 19, 1967, NSF, Rostow Files, box 1, "Meetings with the President Jan/June 1967," LBJL; LBJ to Kosygin, n.d., enclosed in Rusk to AmEmbassy Moscow, tel. May 19, 1967, NSF, NSC History Files, box 17, "Middle East Crisis, Vol. 1," LBJL; Johnson, *Vantage Point*, p. 290; LBJ to Eshkol, May 21, 1967, NSF, Memos to the President File, box 16, "Rostow, Vol. 22," LBJL.

137. LBJ to Nasser, May 22, 1967, NSF, Memos to the President File, box 16, "Rostow Vol. 22," LBJL.

138. Roche to LBJ, May 22, 1967, NSF, NSC History Files, box 17, "Middle East Crisis, Vol. 1," LBJL.

139. Rusk to LBJ, May 26, 1967, NSF, NSC Country File, box 143, "Israel, Vol. 12," LBJL; Eugene Rostow Oral History, LBJL.

140. Roche and Feinberg quoted in Miller, *Lyndon*, pp. 478–79. On the influx of pro-Israel telegrams and letters, see Walt Rostow to Marvin Watson, May 24, 1967, Rostow memo, June 5, 1967, and Wilbur Jenkins to William Hopkins, June 15, 1967, all in NSF, NSC History Files, box 19, "Middle East Crisis, Vol. 6," LBJL.

141. "Israeli Aid Package," n.d., attached to Saunders to Lois, May 23, 1967, NSF, Country File, box 145, "Israel—Aid," LBJL; LBJ statement, May 23, 1967, *Public Papers, 1967*, 1: 561–63; Eugene Rostow Oral History.

142. Rostow to LBJ, May 23, 1967, and State Department, "Future of South Arabia," n.d. (mid-May 1967), Meeting Notes File, box 1, "Briefing Papers NSC Meeting," LBJL.

143. Minutes of the NSC Meeting, May 24, 1967, NSF, NSC Meetings File, box 2, LBJL.

144. Rusk to LBJ, May 26, 1967, NSF, Country File, box 143, "Israel, Vol. 12," LBJL; State Department Historical Office, "US Policy and Diplomacy in the Middle East Crisis, May 15–June 10, 1967," January 10, 1969, NSF, NSC History Files, box 20, "Middle East Crisis, Vol. 9," LBJL.

145. Nathaniel Davis (USUN) to Rostow, May 27, 1967, NSF, NSC History Files, box 20, "Middle East Crisis, Vol. 8," LBJL.

146. Rusk to Gromyko, May 29, 1967, enclosed in Rostow in LBJ, May 29, 1967, NSF, Memos to the President File, box 16, "Rostow, Vol. 29," LBJL.

147. Hussein's move seems to have been crucial in leading the Johnson administration to switch the "warning light" it had been flashing at Tel Aviv from "red" to "yellow." See William Quandt, "Lyndon Johnson and the June 1967 War: What Color Was the Light?" *Middle East Journal* 46 (Spring 1992): 216–22.

148. Rostow to LBJ, May 23, 1967, NSF, Memos to the President File, box 16, "Rostow, Vol. 28," LBJL; Anderson to LBJ, tel. June 2, 1967, NSF, NSC History Files, box 18, "Middle East Crisis, Vol. 3," LBJL.

149. Cyrus L. Sulzberger, *An Age of Mediocrity: Memoirs and Diaries 1963–1972* (New York: Macmillan, 1973), pp. 346–47.

150. Rusk to Gromyko, tel. June 5, 1967, Lot File 72D 192, box 927, Dean Rusk Papers, U.S. Department of State.

151. Davis to Rostow, June 6, 1967, NSF, Country File, Near East, box 116, "Middle East Crisis, Vol. 4," LBJL; Bundy to Tom Johnson, June 9, 1967, NSF, NSC History Files, box 19, "Middle East Crisis, vol. 7," LBJL. For more on the Special Committee, see John Prados, *Keepers of the Keys: A History of the National Security Council from Truman to Bush* (New York: William Morrow, 1991), pp. 180–83.

152. Saunders, minutes of the NSC Special Committee meeting, June 8, 1967, NSF, NSC History File, box 19, "Middle East Crisis, Vol. 7," LBJL.

153. Neff, *Warriors for Jerusalem*, pp. 246–63; James Ennes, *Assault on the Liberty* (New York: Random House, 1979), passim; Carl Marcy to Bourke

Hickenlooper, August 2 and 25, 1967, "Countries—Near East," Foreign Relations Committee Files, box 152, Hickenlooper Papers.

154. Clifford quoted in Saunders, minutes of the NSC Special Committee, June 9, 1967, NSF, NSC History Files, box 19, "Middle East Crisis, Vol. 7," LBJL; Rusk quoted in Neff, *Warriors for Jerusalem*, p. 356.

155. CIA, "Arab-Israeli Situation Report," June 9, 1967, NSF, NSC History Files, box 21, "Middle East Crisis, Vol. 11," LBJL.

156. Dean Rusk, *As I Saw It* (New York: Norton, 1990), p. 386.

157. State Department Historical Office, "U.S. Policy & Diplomacy in the Middle East Crisis, May 15–June 10, 1967," January 10, 1969, NSF, NSC History Files, box 20, "Middle East Crisis, Vol. 9," LBJL.

158. Saunders, "Hot Line Meeting June 10, 1967," October 22, 1968, and Saunders, minutes of the NSC Special Committee meeting, June 12, 1967, NSF, NSC History Files, box 19, "Middle East Crisis, Vol. 7," LBJL.

159. Rostow to LBJ, May 29, 1967, NSF, Memos to the President File, box 16, "Rostow, Vol. 28," LBJL.

160. Howard Cottam (Kuwait) to Rusk, tel. June 6, 1967, Enoch Duncan (Baghdad) to Rusk, tel. June 6, 1967, and Ahmed Zaki Yamani to ARAMCO, June 7, 1967, all in NSF, Country File, box 107, "Middle East Crisis, Vol. 4," LBJL. See also Brenchley, *Britain and the Middle East*, p. 150.

161. Daniel Yergin, *The Prize: The Epic Quest for Oil, Money and Power* (New York: Simon and Schuster, 1991), p. 155; CIA, "Arab-Israeli Situation Reports," June 11, 12, and 13, 1967, NSF, NSC History Files, box 21, "Middle East Crisis, Vol. 11," LBJL.

162. State Department Activities Report, June 6, 1967, President's Appointment File, box 66, "Diary Backup, May–June 1967," LBJL; Davis to Rostow, June 6, 1967, NSF, Country File, Near East, box 116, "Middle East Crisis, Vol. 4," LBJL; Yergin, *Prize*, pp. 556–57.

163. CIA to White House Situation Room, tel. June 8, 1967, NSF, Country File, Near East, box 116, "Middle East Crisis, Vol. 4," LBJL; CIA, "Arab-Israeli Situation Reports," June 18 and July 3, 1967, NSF, NSC History Files, box 21, "Middle East Crisis, vol. 11," LBJL; Yergin, *Prize*, p. 558.

164. Bundy to LBJ, June 9, 1967, and Saunders, minutes of the NSC Special Committee, June 9, 1967, NSF, NSC History Files, box 21, "Middle East Crisis, Vol. 7," LBJL.

165. Rostow to LBJ, June 14, 1967, NSF, Memos to the President File, box 17, "Rostow, Vol. 31," LBJL.

166. Bundy memo, July 11, 1967, and Bundy to LBJ, July 11, 1967, Harry McPherson Office Files, box 42, "Middle East," LBJL.

167. CIA, "Israeli Objectives in the Current Crisis," June 6, 1967, NSF, Country File, Near East, box 116, "Middle East Crisis, Vol. 4," LBJL; Barbour to Rusk, tel. June 13, 1967, NSF, NSC History Files, box 18, "Middle East Crisis, Vol. 5," LBJL.

168. Wriggins to Rostow, June 6, 1967, NSF, Country File, Near East, box 116, "Middle East Crisis, Vol. 4," LBJL; Saunders, minutes of NSC Special Committee, June 8 and 13, 1967, NSF, NSC History Files, box 19, "Middle East Crisis, Vol. 7," LBJL.

169. Rusk and Eban are quoted in Thomas J. Schoenbaum, *Waging Peace and War: Dean Rusk in the Truman, Kennedy, and Johnson Years* (New York:

Simon and Schuster, 1988), p. 463. Schoenbaum based his account on extensive interviews with Dean Rusk.

170. Saunders, minutes of the NSC Special Committee, June 14, 1967, NSF, NSC History Files, box 19, "Middle East Crisis, Vol. 7," LBJL; LBJ speech, June 19, 1967, *Public Papers, 1967*, 1: 630–34. On Israel's actions, see Neff, *Warriors for Jerusalem*, pp. 289–94, 318–24.

171. Wriggins to Bundy, July 13, 1967, McPherson Office Files, box 42, "Middle East," LBJL; Rostow to LBJ, October 3, 1967, *DDRS, 1991*, item 499.

172. Saunders to Rostow, December 29, 1967, Rostow to LBJ, "The Issues for Eshkol," January 5, 1968, Rostow to LBJ, "Talking Points for Prime Minister Eshkol," January 5, 1968, and "Notes of Johnson-Eshkol Meeting," January 7/8, 1968, all in NSF, Country File, box 144, "Israel—Eshkol Visit 1968," LBJL.

173. On the situation in Aden, see State Department cirtel., December 12, 1967, NSF, Country File, box 136, "Iran, Vol. 2," LBJL. On the pullout from the Persian Gulf, see Rusk to Eilts, tel. January 12, 1968, NSF, Country File, box 155, "Saudi Arabia, Vol. 2," LBJL, and Rostow to LBJ, January 16, 1968, NSF, Name File, box 7, "Rostow Memos," LBJL.

174. Rusk to LBJ, "Release of Arms for Saudi Arabia," January 19, 1968, and Consul Dhahran to Rusk, tel. January 31, 1968, NSF, Country File, box 155, "Saudi Arabia, Vol. 2," LBJL; Meyer to Rusk, tel. February 9, 1968, and Eugene Rostow to Meyer, tel. March 8, 1968, NSF, Country File, box 136, "Iran, Vol. 2," LBJL.

175. Rusk to Meyer, June 12, 1968, NSF, Country File, box 136, "Iran, vol. 2," LBJL; "Briefing Paper," n.d., attached to Read to Rostow, June 22, 1968, NSF, Country File, box 155, "Saudi Arabia, Vol. 2," LBJL.

176. State Department cirtel., June 18, 1968, NSF, Country File, box 155, "Saudi Arabia, Vol. 2," LBJL.

177. CIA, "The Arab Nationalists Movement," January 19, 1968, and Donald Bergus to Rusk, tel. June 15, 1968, NSF, Country File, box 160, "UAR, Vol. 6," LBJL.

178. For a discussion of the July 1968 Ba'athist coup in Iraq, see Marion Farouk-Sluglett and Peter Sluglett, *Iraq since 1958: From Revolution to Dictatorship* (London: Routledge Kegan Paul, 1987), pp. 107–26.

179. CIA cable no. 20818, October 25, 1968, NSF, Country File, box 156, "Syria, Vol. 1," LBJL.

180. Harrison Symmes Oral History.

181. Minutes of the NSC meeting, February 26, 1968, NSF, NSC meetings, box 2, LBJL.

182. Hersh, *Samson Option*, pp. 178–80, 186–88; Saunders to Rostow, June 19, 1968, NSF, Name File, box 7, "Saunders Memos," LBJL.

183. Reilly to Humphrey, May 10, 1968, Vice-Presidential Files: Foreign Affairs, "Coded Files—Miscellaneous Countries—Israel 1968," box 960, Humphrey Papers; Etta Zablocki Bick, "Ethnic Linkages and American Foreign Policy: A Study of the Linkage Role of American Jews in Relations between the United States and Israel, 1956-1968," (Ph.D. diss., City University of New York, 1983), pp. 166–67; Hersh, *Samson Option*, pp. 188–90; Spiegel, *Other Arab-Israeli Conflict*, pp. 161–63; Rostow to LBJ, October 8, 1968, NSF, Country File, box 142, "Israel, Vol. 10," LBJL.

184. Hilton to Wheeler and McPherson, September 12, 1968, and Rusk

to Hart, September 19, 1968, NSF, Country File, box 142, "Israel, Vol. 10," LBJL.

185. NSC paper, "23rd U.N. General Assembly, n.d. (September 25, 1968), Meeting Notes File, box 3, LBJL; Saunders to Rostow, October 25, 1968, and Robert J. Murray memcon, "Negotiations with Israel—F-4 & Advanced Weapons," November 4, 1968, NSF, Country File, box 142, "Israel, Vol. 10," LBJL.

186. Murray memcon, "Negotiations with Israel—F-4 & Advanced Weapons," November 4, 1968, NSF, Country File, box 142, "Israel, Vol. 10," LBJL.

187. Yitzhak Rabin, *The Rabin Memoirs* (Boston: Little and Brown, 1979), pp. 141–42.

188. Rusk to Robert Anderson (Tehran), tel. November 22, 1968, NSF, Country File, box 136, "Iran, Vol. 2," LBJL.

189. Warnke to Rabin, November 25, 1968, NSF, Country File, box 142, "Israel, Vol. 10," LBJL; Warnke to author, September 12, 1989.

190. State Department background paper, "Kuwait's Foreign Relations," December 3, 1968, Hart to Rusk, December 4, 1968, and Rusk to Cottam, tel. December 13, 1968, NSF, Country File, box 149, "Kuwait, Visit of the Amir," LBJL.

7 | Lyndon Johnson and Vietnam: The Final Months

Lloyd Gardner

"TONIGHT I WANT TO SPEAK to you of peace in Vietnam and Southeast Asia." These opening words of President Johnson's address to the nation on March 31, 1968, represented a symbolic triumph of sorts for those people around the president who wanted a change in the nation's policy toward the war.[1] Even the speech Johnson delivered that evening, however, was only a partial victory, and there would still be a series of painful struggles to gain Johnson's approval for alternatives to sending more troops and dropping more bombs.

The speech is usually remembered for its two dramatic announcements: the order to halt all aircraft and naval bombardment of North Vietnam, "except in the area north of the demilitarized zone," and the surprise ending that he would neither seek nor accept "the nomination of my party for another term as your President." Elsewhere, the speech revealed the continuing tension among the president's advisers and Johnson's own deep ambiguity. In one passage it even echoed Lincoln's warning about the coming of the Civil War:

> In these times as in times before, it is true that a house divided against itself by the spirit of faction, of party, of region, of religion, of race, is a house that cannot stand. There is division in the American house now. There is divisiveness among us all tonight.

Yet near the end Johnson reasserted the very assumptions that had produced Vietnam. In a gloss on John Kennedy's Cold War–inspired inaugural address, the speech read as if nothing had happened to shatter faith in either the ability of America to "win" such a war or the soundness of basic assumptions:

> But let men everywhere know, however, that a strong, a confident, and a vigilant America stands ready tonight to seek an honorable peace—and stands ready tonight to defend an honor-

able cause—whatever the price, whatever the burden, whatever the sacrifice that duty may require.

A few days before the speech, Johnson had appealed to his new secretary of defense, Clark Clifford, to help him find a way out of the dilemma. "I've got to get me a peace proposal," he told Clifford on the telephone. Johnson wanted to be the peace candidate—but he wanted a Churchill peace, not a Chamberlain peace.[2] Twenty years earlier, Clifford had devised a successful anticommunist election strategy for Harry Truman that enabled that president to overcome defections on the Right and the Left and to win an upset victory. Ever since, Clifford had been called upon by Democratic presidents as a major problem solver.

But circumstances were vastly different now, and Clifford would surprise many people in the Johnson inner circle with his proposals—though perhaps not the president himself. When disinterested histories come to be written fifty years in the future, said the *Washington Post* on January 3, 1969, some of the "most fascinating passages will have to do with the drama of the last few months, the civilized collision of Defense Secretary Clifford and Secretary of State Rusk."[3] Fifty years have not yet passed, but the documentation is now available, and perhaps emotions have cooled enough to permit a fruitful discussion of that "civilized collision" and "the drama" of that period. It would be inaccurate to see either Rusk or Clifford as catalysts rallying the president's advisers; instead, as the drama unfolded, both principals and background players wandered back and forth, sometimes actually switching sides. It would be wrong, also, to assume that Johnson was simply buffeted along, heeding whatever advice appeared at the moment to offer him some quick fix without actually thinking about the cumulative effect of his decisions. Given the conundrum American policymakers had made for themselves in Vietnam, the hesitations and reversals of the final months of the Johnson administration are not at all surprising.

Nevertheless, it can be argued that Johnson and his negotiators at the Paris Peace Conference did in fact manage to lay a basis for disengagement from the actual war; but neither Johnson nor his successor, Richard Nixon, could find a way to disengage successfully from the images of reality they had constructed, and worked from, since early in the Cold War. As a consequence, the Vietnam War would go on for seven more years.

It was not that policymakers were unaware of the situation. Even before the Tet Offensive in 1968, the concept of "limited war" had long since become a cruel irony. "We simply have to end this thing," Secretary of Defense Robert McNamara blurted out at a meeting chaired by Clifford; "I just hope you can get hold of it. It is out of control."[4] Vietnam threatened to undo everything the Cold War generation had accomplished: It had already undermined America's moral and economic leadership abroad and divided its citizenry into blocs of angry protestors that neither political party could reassemble into a cohesive force—except by exploiting the divisions through the negative politics of fear. The ruling New Deal coalition that had dominated national politics since 1932 and whose true heir was indeed Lyndon Johnson suffered the most from Vietnam. Whether the coalition could have survived the social upheavals and racial politics of the 1960s in any event is of course an imponderable; but Vietnam enervated its leadership, fatefully weakening its intellectual and political resiliency when it was needed the most.[5]

Tet simply snapped the cords. For months before the North Vietnamese/National Liberation Front (NLF)* offensive began at the end of January 1968, the administration had been promising the beginning of "a new phase" in the war. Accused of creating a "credibility gap," Johnson finally called upon his commander in Vietnam, Gen. William Westmoreland, to argue the case before an increasingly skeptical audience. "We have reached an important point when the end begins to come into view," Westmoreland assured the National Press Club on November 21, 1967. The enemy had failed, he went on, "in his desperate effort to take the world's headlines . . . by a military victory."[6]

Tet was not a military victory for the enemy, but the widespread attack across South Vietnam did capture world headlines, and it shattered the hopes for any "new phase" in the war—certainly any that would occur within a reasonable length of time. Even after the immediate shock of seeing the American embassy compound invaded by suicide guerrilla cadres had passed, the nation faced an interminable struggle that cast a dark shadow over its future.

Prompted by the Joint Chiefs of Staff, Westmoreland asked for 206,000 more troops to pursue the Tet "victory," thereby triggering the series of events that would lead to Johnson's March 31 speech. On February 27 Clifford met with Rusk, National Security Adviser

---

*Viet Cong (VC) was the derogatory name for Communists given to the insurgents by the South Vietnamese and used by Americans as well; the insurgents called themselves the National Liberation Front. I use both names here according to the context of the discussion.

Walt Rostow, outgoing defense secretary Robert McNamara, and key second-level advisers to consider ideas for a formal presidential response to Tet. Rusk and Rostow expressed their firm belief that the enemy had taken a real beating. The secretary of state apparently thought that the beating was severe enough that a proposal combining troop escalation with an offer to end the bombing north of the Twentieth Parallel, premised as before on North Vietnam's willingness to abandon efforts to overturn the Saigon regime by force, might now succeed. Rusk even suggested that troops be brought home from Europe to fill out the ranks if necessary.

If Westmoreland could get the reinforcements he requested, added Rostow, then he should be able to handle the situation until good weather returned. "What then?" snapped McNamara, nearly overwhelmed with conflicting emotions. "Let's not delude ourselves into thinking he cannot maintain pressure *after* good weather comes." Rostow apparently assumed that good weather would permit increased air attacks, but McNamara would not let that go unchallenged: "We are dropping ordnance at a higher rate than in [the] last year of WWII in Europe. It has not stopped him."

His face lined and eyelids darkened with strain, McNamara called the request "madness": "I've repeatedly honored the requests from the Wheelers of the world, but we have no assurance that an additional 205,000 men will make any difference. It still may not be enough to win the war. There is no [military] plan to win the war." Clifford then intervened to ask that they look at the situation from a different angle. After giving the nation optimistic reports from the beginning, how could the administration now get support for the economic controls and the other measures they acknowledged would have to be part of a further escalation: "How do we avoid creating [the] feeling that we are pounding troops down [a] rathole? What is our purpose? What is achievable?" It was time to reevaluate the entire posture in Vietnam, Clifford concluded.

"We are at a point of crisis," McPherson wrote in his notes. "McNamara expressed grave doubts over military, economic, political, diplomatic and moral consequences of a larger force buildup in SVN." The overarching question was whether anyone would present these profound doubts to the president, who had been closeted with Vietnam hawks at the LBJ Ranch.[7]

Johnson returned to Washington at 2 A.M. the next day in order to have breakfast with the chairman of the Joint Chiefs, Gen. Earle Wheeler, who had just returned from Saigon; most of those advisers who had attended the previous day's session were also present.

Wheeler did not minimize the situation he had found in Vietnam: "This offensive has by no means run its course," he warned. Although the South Vietnamese army had performed "remarkably well" in most areas, the initial attacks had nearly succeeded in a dozen places. Only the timely reaction of U.S. forces had averted a catastrophe. "In short," he reported, "it was a very near thing."[8]

While the Army of the Republic of Vietnam (ARVN) forces had retreated to defensive positions in the cities, the enemy was operating with relative freedom in the countryside, Wheeler continued, probably recruiting heavily and infiltrating entire North Vietnamese army units. No one could say what the enemy's reinforcement capacity was, but the recovery period was likely to be short, and control in those areas would be determined by which forces got there first. If General Westmoreland's request was not honored, he might be forced to surrender the two northernmost provinces of South Vietnam. "This, of course, would be a political hazard. It also would give the North Vietnamese a strong position for negotiating. It would, I believe, cause the collapse of the ARVN," Wheeler concluded.[9]

It was a somber meeting.[10] Wheeler had actually instigated the troop request from his office in Washington, prodding Westmoreland before his own trip to Saigon to issue such a call in the hope of forcing a decision that the JCS had long desired to mobilize the nation for an all-out effort to win a military victory.[11] His plan backfired. The only answer Wheeler could give one of the staunchest supporters of the war, Gen. Maxwell Taylor, who asked if Westmoreland could "hold" with the additional, 200,000, was less than reassuring: "Yes . . . unless the enemy ups the ante."

When Wheeler finished his report, the president expressed some concern about "trying to find out what the situation really is"[12] McNamara said that the troops could be found and outlined the costs, but he was now more than willing to express his profound doubts directly to the president. Adding another 200,000 men to Westmoreland's army would probably not produce any result other than a similar increase from the enemy; the key lay in how well the South Vietnamese could meet the crisis. He could recommend only the small increment of 15,000 already agreed upon. Some territory might be lost, but at least his suggested course would limit costs in lives and dollars and "help ease the growing dissension within our country."[13]

Wheeler agreed nothing could be decided that day but hoped a decision in principle would be forthcoming. Johnson was not ready to commit himself. As the meeting broke up, he turned to Clifford;

take a fresh look at things, he said—take a look at the balance of payments, the complications of a reserve call-up, alternative military strategies, peace moves—all of it: "Give me the lesser of evils. Give me your recommendations."[14]

Wheeler's reports at this meeting and later the same day at a cabinet meeting presented contradictory positions: On the one hand, Tet had been a great defeat for the enemy; on the other, ARVN was confined to a defensive strategy. The enemy had suffered huge losses but was successfully operating "out in the hinterland" to find new recruits. Americans had turned the tide of battle, but unless Westmoreland got his reinforcements the cities would be strangled. Wheeler argued that "it is imperative that we now go out after the Viet Cong forces that are trying to strangle the cities. A static defense will not do the job. It invites further attack."[15]

At the cabinet session Johnson indicated he had other doubts. The "big problem," he now cautioned, "was the impression we make with the public. . . . We have to be careful about statements like Westmoreland's when he came back and said that he saw 'light at the end of the tunnel.' "[16] Yet that was precisely what the president had wanted Westmoreland to say at that point. Now Johnson was waiting not for what his military advisers had to say but for what Clark Clifford would recommend, and that was a big change if not a new direction.

Clifford had a public reputation as a solid hawk, an opponent of bombing pauses and of negotiating concessions, and it was widely believed that the president had brought him in because McNamara had gone soft. But Johnson no doubt remembered Clifford's dissent from the decision to send 100,000 troops to Vietnam in July 1965 and his gloomy predictions that the enemy would match man for man in escalating the war. Despite these warnings, the president had followed that path anyway; now he was asking Clifford to find the way out.[17]

By the time the new secretary of defense reported to Johnson on March 4, 1968, the chairman of the Joint Chiefs was retreating from the recommendations in his report. Wheeler had been unable to supply a satisfactory answer to Taylor's question as well as to Clifford's lawyerly series of questions about whether the request for more troops was part of a "plan for victory."[18] Rostow, also taking part in these sessions, advised Johnson that the Clifford team was going to argue for a complete review of national strategy before responding to Westmoreland's troop request. "We don't know whether we are being asked to send forces to prevent a radical deterioration in our side's position," said the national security adviser, "or to permit [Westmoreland] to conduct in the second half of the year a vigorous offensive."[19]

In both the State and Defense Departments there were deep reservations, added Rostow, and a growing feeling that additional forces would constitute a "gross over-commitment" without bringing a resolution of the war any closer. "Behind that judgment, in turn, is a feeling that we can only attain our objectives in Viet Nam by a negotiation which brings the Viet Cong into the political process, and this negotiation, in turn, may not be much advanced by putting additional U.S. forces into the country."[20]

Clifford's oral presentation later that day did not refer to bringing the Viet Cong into the political process, but it did alternate between discussing specifics of the team's assignment and general questions about future policy—a strategy designed to draw out the president. "At this stage," he said, " it is clear that this new request by General Westmoreland brings the President to a clearly defined watershed."

The new secretary of defense raised the specter of future requests for more men, yet another 200,000 or even 300,000 "with no end in sight." It might be that such increases would actually thwart South Vietnam's ability to take over their own country; perhaps the search-and-destroy strategy was not the right one. Then he delivered a powerful courtroom-like summation:

> We can no longer rely just on the field commander. He can want troops and want troops and want troops. He must look [at] the overall impact on us, including the situation here in the United States. We must look at our economic stability, our other problems in the world, our other problems at home; we must consider whether or not this thing is tieing us down so that we cannot do some of the other things we should be doing; and finally, we must consider the effects of our actions on the rest of the world—are we setting an example in Vietnam through which other nations would rather not go if they are faced with a similar threat? . . .
> *Now the time has come to decide where do we go from here.*[21]

Clifford said later that Johnson was irritated with him, did not like seeing the growing disagreement with Rusk, and referred to the "Clifford approach" as a term of opprobrium, discounting what could be achieved through it.[22] At one point in the discussion on

March 4 the president did say, "Westmoreland is asking for 200,000 men, and you are recommending 20,000 or so?" Otherwise, his comments were subdued. Rusk, moreover, raised most of the same issues Clifford has posed. "Mr. President, without a doubt," said the secretary of state, "this will be one of the most serious decisions you will have made since becoming President. This has implications for all of our society."[23]

Starting from the same point did not mean, of course, that the two secretaries would end up in the same place. But they had agreed that Westmoreland's troop request could not be met without wreaking havoc with NATO commitments and without creating major disturbances in an already shaky "economic picture," both fundamental considerations. So many elements were involved in meeting Westmoreland's request, they also agreed, that the administration would need a general grant of congressional authority. And Rusk knew he could not get it—not, at least, without a debilitating fight. He would not go to Congress for something like the Tonkin Gulf Resolution, said the secretary of state, a veteran of Senator Fulbright's grillings on Capitol Hill, arguing, "We do not want a general declaration." "In the Senate," Johnson agreed, "we face a real problem. Anything that requires any authority may result in a filibuster."

The situation looked equally bleak on the negotiating front in Vietnam, said Rusk; "I wish we had a formula to bring about a peaceful settlement soon. We do not." He could suggest only that the administration's recent peace efforts be made public. Assistant Secretary of Defense Paul Nitze interrupted to say what Clifford had not quite dared, what Rusk doubted was possible: "We must get into negotiations some time soon. . . . We must make up our own minds when we want to cease the bombings and see what happens."[24]

At this point, Rusk offered a halt to the bombing "during the rainy period in the North." Johnson leaped at that idea: "Really, 'Get on your horses' on that." It is impossible to tell from the notes of this meeting whether the president believed he was asking Rusk for a public relations gesture or responding to Nitze's call for serious negotiations. But the meeting ended with Johnson's order to Wheeler to advise Westmoreland that he could expect only 22,000 new troops for the moment; "tell him to forget the 100,000."[25]

At another meeting the next day, Johnson told the same group of advisers, "It appears we are about to make a rather basic change in the strategy of this war." He then recited the elements of the change:

- We tell the ARVN to do more fighting.
- We tell them we will give 20,00[0] men; no more.
- We tell them we will do no more until they do more.
- We tell them we will be *prepared* to make additional troop contributions but not unless "they get with it."[26]

Throughout the month of March, Johnson operated on two levels; the decision not to authorize more than one-tenth of the troops Westmoreland had requested was coupled with other decisions to speed up the sending of newer, better equipment to the ARVN. Johnson had appeared somewhat surprised that the South Vietnamese had not been scheduled to receive such aid before. "If the ARVN are not equipped as well as the Vietcong, isn't that a sad commentary on us?" he asked.[27]

His public rhetoric certainly indicated no retreat from previous hard-line positions. Even as reports of the debates inside the administration were made public in the *New York Times* and as the results of Sen. Eugene McCarthy's strong showing in the New Hampshire Democratic primary and the news of Robert Kennedy's entrance into the race for the nomination made headlines, the president gave no outward sign that any basic changes would be made in the war policy. In private, however, he was also taking counsel with former secretary of state Dean Acheson.

Acheson had done an abrupt about-face on Vietnam. Although he had never considered Asian affairs as important as Europe's fate and had never accorded China equal status with Russia as a threat, he had offered his support on Vietnam as an administration cheerleader—in part, no doubt, because he was appalled at the behavior of dissenters, who, as Congress had done when he was secretary, insisted that their views be taken seriously. After Tet, however, he decided he needed to be much more thoroughly informed about events in that part of the world so far from East Coast America and Europe. He did not at all like what he learned.[28]

Johnson had facilitated Acheson's learning process, opening the doors to all top-secret information so that he could carry out his own investigations. The two met alone for lunch on March 14. The president was delayed in greeting his guest by a discussion of the gold crisis—a concern that was in the back of both their minds as they talked about Vietnam that afternoon.[29] Johnson began their conversation by repeating essentially the judgment that Wheeler and other observers had reported about Tet: It had been a "serious knock" but not a disaster. The VC and their allies had not succeeded in setting off a general uprising, but they would no doubt continue their efforts.

The president then said he was being pressed from various quarters to set up a "committee" to reconsider the entire Vietnam situation from start to projected finish. Acheson thought that most unwise; it would not provide Johnson with the advice he needed, and it would give the impression that he had lost confidence in himself. Instead, a review inside the government could produce projections about possibilities for using the present forces in Vietnam, with the objective of enabling the South Vietnamese to stand alone "at least for a period of time, with only a fraction of the military support it had now." Acheson continued:

> If this could not be accomplished at all or only after a very protracted period with the best that present numbers could do, it seemed to me that the operation was hopeless and that a method of disengagement should be considered. If, however, some measure of success could be expected, strategy should be redirected to obtaining that, even though it was far less than we had originally hoped. Therefore, he should not for the present commit himself to absolute positions.[30]

Johnson did not rail at Acheson for this "unwelcome" advice; he merely said that he had not committed himself to any absolute position and would not. Acheson certainly hoped that was so, for he believed that the JCS were leading the president "down a garden path."[31] When Johnson left to continue his discussions about the gold crisis, he sent Walt Rostow to hear Acheson repeat his views. "Walt listened to me with the bored patience of a visitor listening to a ten-year-old playing the piano" Acheson recalled.[32]

The gold crisis had an immediate impact on both current and former policymakers, especially on the "Atlanticists" who had long had doubts about Vietnam but who had otherwise ignored the dissenters.[33] After his luncheon with Johnson, Acheson wrote to a friend, "The gold crisis has dampened expansionist ideas. The town is in an atmosphere of crisis."[34] Indeed, on the day Acheson and Johnson lunched, the United States lost $400 million in gold. At the discussion before lunch, the president had refused to order the gold markets closed; after lunch he did so order. The next day he appealed to European leaders to help him hold the price at $35 an ounce "to avert a return to the world of the '30s' and . . . damage to U.S.–European political relations."[35]

The immediate crisis was ended through strenuous interventions by the central bank, but Westmoreland's request had put the gold card in the hands of those advisers advocating change. In hearings before the Senate Foreign Relations Committee in 1966, Secretary Rusk had brushed aside references to the peril threatening America's reserve stocks of gold; that attitude now was simply no longer possible.[36] The balance-of-payments difficulties that had begun appearing on accountants' ledgers as early as the last years of the Eisenhower administration had increased dramatically in recent years, largely, but not entirely, as a result of decisions not to raise taxes to pay for the Vietnam War. Tired of holding the bag jammed full to overflowing of overvalued paper dollars, European dissenters to America's profligate economic policies posed more of a threat, it now became apparent, than either antiwar liberals or prowar conservatives. The determination of these dissenters, led by France's Charles de Gaulle, to cash in the paper for gold had brought on the crisis.[37]

Thus, although Rostow's reaction to Acheson's proposals might have appeared condescending, the former secretary's opinion still carried great weight; along with the other pressures that Johnson had described at lunch, Acheson's words convinced him to summon the so-called Council of Wise Men a few days later.[38] Rostow and the other remaining hawks in the administration geared up, meanwhile, to make the case against changing policy. Their influence was still evident and could be seen in Johnson's "stand-up-and-be-counted" speeches in Minneapolis and Washington on March 18 and 19, which came close to calling dissenters traitors. It was very dangerous, the president said, for the enemy to believe they could "attack the moral fiber of our own country to the point where our people will not support the policy of their own Government, of their own men whom they have committed to battle." But Johnson's truculence could not hide his own growing doubts; "We have spent the weekend," he said in Minneapolis, "in an attempt to deal with the very troublesome gold problem."[39]

Meanwhile, other advisers weighed in with suggestions about the president's proposed speech to the nation. McGeorge Bundy wrote that it was a "miracle, in a way, that our people have stayed with the war as long as they have, but I do not see how we can carry them with us for very much longer if all we seem to offer is more of the same, with stalemate at a higher cost as the only prospect."[40]

Perhaps the most important letter, however, came from someone outside the administration, and not from one of the Wise Men.

James Rowe, a partner in a famous Washington law firm along with another Democrat from New Deal days, Thomas Corcoran, had known Lyndon Johnson from those early times. Rowe had advised Johnson on political matters over the years and never failed to speak his mind. Rowe had encouraged Johnson to believe that he was uniquely qualified to reinvigorate and modernize the old New Deal coalitions and to overcome the challenge that civil rights and racial matters posed to the nation but especially to believe that he was essential to the unity of the Democratic party. Rowe now sat at the head of an informal reelection committee.

The Minneapolis speeches, he wrote President Johnson, far from rallying support, "hurt us badly"; they had created a dire effect—they were dividing the party. By implying that all dissenters were unpatriotic, Johnson had caused much resentment and had even left war supporters disappointed.[41] Marvin Watson, the White House aide who met with Rowe's group, "was somewhat startled by the unanimity and strength of the views expressed by everyone there on the subject of Vietnam." The polls might show that there were more hawks than doves, but the middle group, in which Rowe counted the president, had dwindled alarmingly. Everyone at Democratic headquarters, he went on, had been calling around the country; they could turn up only "one or two isolated hawks. . . . Everyone has turned into a dove." He had gone to Clark Clifford, Rowe told Johnson, to ask him to "crank into the computer of decision" Rowe's census. It was only one of the many factors a president and a secretary of defense should consider, he had told Clifford, but it "had to be expressed very strongly because it could affect the power of the President to act on the other factors."[42]

Johnson had Rowe's letter at hand when he telephoned Clifford, asking the defense secretary to craft a peace proposal.[43] The president later expressed something like astonishment at the recommendations of the Wise Men who assembled in Washington for two days near the end of March; someone had poisoned the well, he was heard to say. It is difficult to credit these feelings at full value, given the opinions Johnson had heard from Acheson and Bundy—and especially from James Rowe. Everything they said had been said before—and in stronger terms.

George Ball had been a minority of one urging deescalation at the last meeting of the Wise Men in November 1967, but now the vote was six to three for deescalation with one undecided. McGeorge Bundy recorded:

There is a very significant shift in our position. When we last met we saw reasons for hope.

We hoped then there would be slow but steady progress. Last night and today the picture is not so hopeful particularly in the country side.

Dean Acheson summed up the majority feeling when he said that we can no longer do the job we set out to do in the time we have left and we must begin steps to disengage.[44]

Johnson later wrote that the comments of the Wise Men had surprised him because their outlook was so different from the information he had received in detailed military reports from Vietnam—yet they were "intelligent, experienced men." "If they had been so deeply influenced by the reports of the Tet offensive," he told Vice-President Hubert Humphrey, "what must the average citizen in the country be thinking?" He remained convinced, however, that the blow to morale was more from "our own doing" than from anything the enemy had accomplished: "We were defeating ourselves," he wrote in his memoirs.[45]

Johnson then demanded that he be given the same briefings as the Wise Men. The State Department's representative, Philip Habib, had left town and did not return, but JCS representative Gen. William DePuy and the CIA's "old Vietnam hand," George Carver, duly repeated what they had told the Wise Men. Johnson did not grill them as had the others, and the president was obviously more attuned as well to their insistence that the American "attitude" could be decisive during the critical period of the next two to four months.[46] Carver had added, however, that the United States could still "play with negotiations. Always can make some gesture."[47] In a sense, then, the president had obtained what he wanted from both the hawks and the doves and manipulated the situation to gain more freedom of action. What he could not do was to stand still.

Johnson had announced that he was replacing Gen. William Westmoreland, causing speculation about new beginnings on the eve of the Wise Men's gathering.[48] In the midst of their deliberations, the president met privately with Wheeler and Gen. Creighton Abrams—the putative successor to Westmoreland. Johnson told them about the depressing picture the Wise Men had been presented with the first night, so he could hardly have been surprised at the conclusions Bundy reported. Because the president knew about the tone of the briefings and the discussion, he wanted Abrams and Wheeler to counter those impressions, he said, at lunch later with the Wise Men: "Give them your plan, hope and belief"; it was the "civilians . . . [who are] cutting our guts out." Rusk interjected that unless some "reasonable date" could be put before the Wise Men, it would be impossible: "This country can't support a bottomless pit."[49]

It is not beyond argument that Johnson was compromising Wheeler and Abrams, given the questions that continue to swirl around the events of those crucial days. He had led Wheeler through an almost ritualistic recounting of Westmoreland's freedom to run the war as he saw fit, save for restrictions on the Demilitarized Zone (DMZ) and Laos and Cambodia, apparently in an effort to display to Abrams that it had not been the restrictions on Westmoreland that had brought matters to this pass. But he also delivered a lecture on the "panic in the last three weeks" that displayed a reality to Abrams far removed from the streets of Saigon.

"Our fiscal situation is abominable," the president began. A recitation of real and fancied dangers to national stability followed. How was he to hold the dollar steady, meet the military requirements in Vietnam, obtain a tax bill from Congress, and face the results of cutting back for domestic programs? "I will go down the drain. I don't want the whole alliance and military pulled in with it." There had to be a plan for some new peace initiative, he continued; "we must have something." He would not be surprised, absent some concrete plan, "if they repealed the Tonkin Gulf Resolution."[50]

National Security Adviser Walt Rostow was not surprised by the Wise Men's recommendations, but he was quite discouraged by this evidence that the establishment had lost heart. At the first briefing, he passed CIA director Richard Helms a note: "Dick: About the only hope we've got, I conclude, is that:—the North Vietnamese *do* mount a big offensive . . . —the 101, Airmobile, & the marines clobber them between now & May 15. Just like Lincoln in 1864."[51]

Perhaps only a North Vietnamese offensive would shake the Wise Men from their post-Tet, trance-like state and awaken them to the real situation. Throughout the war, Rostow had sought to convince Johnson (and himself) that there were parallels between the Vietnam conflict and the American Civil War; they could be seen, he felt, in the current travail over divided opinion and the near-despair many Americans had felt about the Union cause even as victory became inevitable. After the Wise Men finished their deliberations, Rostow mulled over another historical analogy: "I thought to myself," he would recall, "that what began in the spring of 1940 when Henry Stimson came to Washington ended tonight. The American Establishment is dead."[52]

The speech Johnson was to give on March 31, 1968, was rewritten; Vietnam had claimed its first president. Yet the State Department cable that went out to American diplomats in Asia, along with portions of the speech, explained that it was believed Hanoi would denounce the partial suspension "and thus free our hand after a short period." Besides, weather conditions over the next four weeks were likely to limit opportunities north of the Twentieth Parallel: "Hence, we are not giving up anything really serious in this time frame. Moreover, air power now used north of 20th can probably be used in Laos (where no policy change planned) and in SVN [South Vietnam]."[53]

It was Clifford's turn to feel discouraged. The cable demonstrated that there was a "large disagreement, only temporarily suppressed," between him and the president's other advisers.[54] Phrased in the most negative way in order not to alarm South Vietnam's president Nguyen Van Thieu, the cable nevertheless contained other hints that the suspension might be expanded to a "full bombing stoppage at a later point" should Hanoi respond in some positive way.[55] To be sure, even Clifford thought the chances of such a response were about 100 to 1, but he was mounting his own private Vietnamization campaign with South Vietnam's ambassador Bui Diem.[56]

Calling Bui Diem "an old friend," the secretary of defense had presented the situation with "complete candor" during an interview in his office on March 20, 1968. After reviewing the disillusionment that had set in since Tet, Clifford warned the ambassador that support for the war was lessening every day. That being so, "the challenge is to find some solution to the war within the period while our public is still prepared to support it." He regretted, finally, that he did not have "one optimistic comment to make to Ambassador Diem . . . in his view the American public was not simply prepared to go around the next corner. . . . Everybody was going to have to give up a lot. . . . the US public no longer believes in the possibility of a military solution to the war and that when the President talks of winning, he means winning an honorable peace, not a military victory."[57]

It was hardly to be expected, then, given Clifford's "candor," that Saigon would rejoice when Hanoi on April 3—contrary to all expectations—expressed a willingness to meet with American negotiators, albeit only in the first instance to discuss a complete halt in the bombing. What appeared to critics of the war as hardly any change in Vietnam policy struck President Thieu and his cohorts as a complete reversal of American policy since July 1965. Bui Diem had flown home to Saigon soon after his talk with Clifford, pondering what the secretary had meant by an "honorable peace." Diem's notes of the conversation conveyed the impression of an emotional secretary of defense declaring, "When Americans decide to do something, they do it. We have no choice. Now we have to win not a military victory but an honorable peace."[58]

But the element that struck Diem even more forcefully was the similarity in tone between Clifford's remarks and the "note of despair" he had heard in President Johnson's comments from the White House. The president seemed to him a changed man since their last interview, drawn and exhausted by the ordeal of a war that had become too heavy a burden. "If we don't win," Johnson said slowly and deliberately, "we are in deep trouble. I've tried my best, but I can't hold alone."[59]

Though he disagreed with the doves about many things, Walt Rostow had also been arguing for some time that a key element in bringing about what Clifford and others called an "honorable peace" depended upon South Vietnam's willingness to make an offer "to the VC to let them run as a political party under the Constitution." Rostow wrote to Johnson; "I believe you can persuade him [Thieu] to do it if he is assured on one point; namely, that if he does take the lead in this way, we shall not negotiate over his head a political settlement in the South."[60]

Vague talk about an honorable peace, as Bui Diem suggested, only fanned South Vietnamese fears, which began when Clifford first brought forth the idea and continued through Henry Kissinger's comments more than four years later.[61] It was unlikely (perhaps even unimaginable) that Thieu would ever make the offer Rostow thought necessary, but the point is that talk of an honorable peace may have prevented any other forces from arising to oppose Thieu's positions at critical junctures later.

Nevertheless, Johnson was evidently impressed with Rostow's point—backed up strongly by Ambassador Ellsworth Bunker—that substantive negotiations between the United States and North Vietnam risked destroying the South Vietnamese government altogether. Bunker argued that the South Vietnamese, having successfully overcome the effects of Tet, could not now be pressed into negotiations with the NLF without disastrous results. Ironically, then, the presi-

dent was put in the position of having his options limited, not by defeat—but because South Vietnam had come back strongly. Clifford
tried to turn the point, asking Bunker why, if the South Vietnamese
were gaining strength, they feared the NLF. Bunker replied, "They
are not afraid of them militarily, but politically. They are fearful if
they take [them] to their bosom, they'll end up running the show."[62]
Clifford failed not because Bunker was right in his estimates, neces-
sarily, but because of long-held assumptions about the Cold War and
about the Communists' methods of waging that struggle.

The upshot of these discussions was that the American delegation, headed by Averell Harriman, was put on a tight leash. In a variety of ways, Johnson's attitude toward Harriman displayed the president's concern not to allow himself to be pressured into
"concessions" that might cause the South Vietnamese government
to fall while he was still in the White House. As Harriman prepared
to leave for Paris, the site decided upon after much haggling, Secretary Rusk warned him that the talks were not to be used to pressure
Washington; on that basis, of course, there was likely to be little
progress.[63]

Thus, although the hawks had failed to convince the Wise Men
at the end of March to stay the course, they were now gaining back
some ground on the terms for negotiations.[64] Their growing strength
depended in turn upon South Vietnam's continuing ability to consol-
idate its recovery following Tet. The political arguments used by
Rowe, moreover, obviously had less weight now than before the
March 31 speech. Johnson's concern for a Democratic election victory had been lessened finally by his sense that the dominant elite in
the party, having encouraged him to become involved in Vietnam,
had now betrayed him to the Kennedys and their supporters.[65]

The long delay in choosing a site for the talks had added to Johnson's sense that he had received nothing in return for the March 31
speech. It was almost as if he still expected Hanoi to melt before his
blandishments like a recalcitrant senator. "I do not want Ho to get
[the] impression he can take this country away from us," the president declared at the end of April. "We are not reeling under the
Dove's attack. I have talked with a number of people."[66] Clifford was
gloomy about prospects for peace; infiltration rates were increasing,
he reported on the last day of April, 1968: "Captured documents do
not indicate an enemy moving toward peace."[67]

The next day, May 1, 1968, Clifford talked with David Lilienthal about his troubles with the Joint Chiefs. There had been a
"drumfire" from the military about infiltration before the bombing

limitations went into effect, he said, and the increase had in fact taken place. Lilienthal noted that Clifford "looked in real distress," but the defense secretary was "*sure* that now this country had a *policy* about Vietnam, for the first time." Clifford continued, "They've been put on notice that all of them, all the Asians that have been depending on Uncle Sam to fight for them have to get off their big fat Asian ass and defend themselves. . . . This country just can't stand this drain much longer and the Vietnamese had better know it. Last month for the first time in a long time this country imported more than it exported; our balance of payments is shaky; we have a fiscal crisis."[68] When Lilienthal saw Dean Rusk on May 3, however, the secretary of state assured him that Johnson "isn't going to let them go down the drain. And any new President won't either. . . . After all we have lost 20,000 Americans, dead. No one, whoever he is, can be President and just toss that away."[69]

Agreement on Paris as the negotiating site eased the pressure on Johnson and Clifford to resume bombing, but the Joint Chiefs of Staff argued hard against any further concessions in the instructions to American negotiators. They insisted that "in support of our national objective, the US negotiating objective must be to ensure the sovereignty of the Government of Vietnam." The JCS put forward under the rubric "terms" that could be imposed only as a victor's peace, which would have required the North Vietnamese simply to fold up their tents and go home. And military planners interpreted Johnson's 1966 pledge to withdraw American forces six months after a truce agreement, moreover, to mean that the withdrawal would begin six months after an agreement and if "violence thus subsides." They also planned for a residual force to remain in South Vietnam for up to five years.[70]

"The Joint Chiefs of Staff," Gen. Harold K. Johnson wrote Clifford on May 8, 1968, "are of the view that the United States is bargaining from a position of strength."[71] Certainly they believed that they were bargaining with Clifford from a position of strength. President Thieu had announced a goal of enlarging the South Vietnamese army to a strength of over 800,000 and a plan to draft eighteen-year-olds. Given the time they hoped they would have—if the United States did not agree to a coalition government, or a cease-fire in place, or a premature withdrawal under some other interpretation of the 1966 pledge—the war could still be won.[72]

The Joint Chiefs managed to place Gen. Andrew Goodpaster on the American delegation as a watchdog to keep Harriman and his co-chief, Cyrus Vance, from further concessions. Indeed, on the plane trip to Paris Goodpaster and Harriman began to argue about what the instructions required them to do. "Now it's our job to end this war," Harriman said soon after take-off, "to get the best terms we can, but to end the war." Goodpaster shook his head; those were not the instructions, he insisted.

What were the instructions? Harriman had been directed to find out how Hanoi would respond to a total bombing halt. But the predeparture discussion with President Johnson had left many issues open: Johnson talked about starting with a maximum position, which, as the discussion made clear, was essentially the JCS stance. But he had also said, "It is easier to retreat than move forward." During the meeting, Clifford and Rusk had begun a side argument over bombing between the Nineteenth and Twentieth parallels, and Johnson had intervened on the side of the defense secretary. Discussion of every subsidiary issue was tense because Rusk knew Clifford's interpretation of the president's "San Antonio formula" (see p. 219) for starting serious peace negotiations posited that the North Vietnamese would have to agree only not "to take advantage" of a bombing halt, an interpretation that would allow Johnson to back away gracefully from his maximum terms. Yet if Harriman was required to stay with the maximum demands as preconditions, Rusk's interpretation of the San Antonio formula would prevail.[73]

The debate over bombing limitations between the Nineteenth and Twentieth parallels continued at subsequent meetings of the president's advisers. Rusk made it quite plain that he believed pressure for concessions at Paris would come from inside the United States, and that was the issue that the argument over bombing in that narrow region was all about—regardless of the military value of the targets suggested by the JCS:

> I also am concerned that Hanoi thinks it can mobilize public opinion such that they can do anything and we must stop all our efforts. They must learn you did not withdraw in order to bend to their wishes. I would not oppose strikes between the 19th and 20th.[74]

Rusk believed then and later that Vietnam resembled earlier struggles in the Cold War. When—and only when—the Communists finally realized they could not win militarily or politically (as in the cases of the 1948 Berlin Blockage or the Korean War) would the war end. "I believed the time would come when the North Vietnamese would find the job ahead of them too tough, come to the table, negotiate at least a cease-fire, and call off their aggression," he wrote.[75]

Until that time, it was his job to hold the line at Paris—and in Washington. The Paris talks consisted at this stage of formal public presentations during which each side vented its spleen at the other's perfidious behavior. Harriman had always believed that the road to peace in Vietnam went through Moscow. Thus he met with Soviet ambassador Valerian Zorin on May 19, 1968, in the hopes of initiating a private discourse with the North Vietnamese under Russian auspices. Although he began with a hint to Zorin that President Johnson's "program" for South Vietnam and the NLF program offered some possibilities for a "rapprochement," the Russian diplomat gave him no encouragement to believe that any progress could be made without an unconditional halt to all bombing. Harriman's efforts to elicit some "informal" indication of what might be done also got absolutely nowhere. The conversation ended with Harriman's warning that Johnson was under great pressure to resume bombing. If that happened, then the president might not even be able to hold the line on a much wider air campaign against the North.[76]

Harriman's report of this conversation added weight to the arguments of those negotiators contending for bombing closer to the Twentieth Parallel. Clifford found himself defending his position virtually alone against Rusk, Rostow, and General Wheeler. When Johnson began to berate him as well, saying, "Haven't we let more men and ammunition get through because of this?" Clifford was forced to respond that that was entirely possible. But then he confronted the president with the inescapable facts of the Vietnamese dilemma. With the limitations that Johnson had put on the military, there were no real plans to win the war. If there could be no invasion of the north, no mining of the harbors, no invasion of sanctuaries, there could be no plan. Clifford concluded, "Then I do not believe you can win militarily. Our hopes must go with Paris."

It was a stalemate, said Clifford. "They can't win [the] war militarily. We can't win the war militarily." Johnson snapped, "I disagree." General Wheeler, who had his own dilemma to deal with since the JCS had used (and would use ever after) the argument that political limitations had caused American defeat in Vietnam, said uncertainly, "I disagree to some extent." When Johnson then asked how expenditures were running in the Defense Department, Rusk seized on the question in sarcastic fashion to challenge Clifford's appreciation of the stakes of the war: "Are you saving any money by not bombing North Vietnam?'' ''Now, now,'' Clifford came back, imitating Rusk's favorite response to critics worried about the costs of war, ''you can't put it on a cost basis.''[77]

Despite his bluster, Johnson again delayed a decision on reescalating the bombing. A week later, moreover, he was far more skeptical about the military necessity of bombing above the Nineteenth Parallel even though former secretary of defense Robert McNamara suggested that he would favor it if it would improve the bargaining position in Paris. Johnson professed to be worried about world opinion. North Vietnam's ridiculous denials about its forces engaged in South Vietnam notwithstanding, the president was not optimistic about ''our position in the world opinion. . . . Look at what Ho is doing. Hitler in his prime day didn't do this.''[78]

In *The Vantage Point*, Johnson reproduced portions of private memorandums from Dean Rusk supplementing his arguments against Clifford: ''It boils down to a question of will,'' Rusk insisted. Yet though he believed Rusk had gotten to the heart of the matter and though General Wheeler continued to argue that the increased casualties—the highest of the war in mid-May—could be blamed in part on the restraints, Johnson never did order bombing to be resumed above the Nineteenth Parallel. ''We put it off again, and again. . . . I still question whether we made the right decision,'' he wrote.[79]

On June 4, 1968, a letter from Soviet leader Aleksei Kosygin arrived in Washington. Harriman and Vance were present as the president listened to his advisers discuss its meaning; also attending this meeting were two famous experts on Russia, Charles Bohlen and Llewellyn Thompson, the past and present ambassadors to the Soviet Union. Kosygin's message promised that if the United States stopped the bombing the cessation could lead to a breakthrough and a peaceful settlement. It was known that North Vietnam's senior negotiator, Le Duc Tho, had stopped off in Moscow before taking up his assignment in Paris. Rusk insisted, nevertheless, that the message lacked ''clarity''; it was necessary, he said, to know beforehand what the North Vietnamese would do. Johnson agreed.

Rusk had uncharacteristically taken the lead in what others at the meeting felt was a ''preemptive strike'' against the doves.[80] His strategy worked, for the rest of the discussion became an attempt to answer the secretary of state. Clifford tried arguing that only by taking Kosygin's letter to mean what the administration wanted it to mean could progress be made. References were also made to the Zorin-Harriman conversation and to the possibility that this letter was in fact a response to the queries that Harriman had put to the Soviet ambassador in Paris. Zorin had appeared brusque and inflexibly committed to North Vietnam's positions. But it could be maintained that here was a more reasonable answer to American demands for some "informal" assurance that a total bombing cessation would be reciprocated by Hanoi. Clifford also pushed the argument that bombing had not lessened Soviet support for North Vietnam but had increased it, and, conversely, instead of increasing Soviet influence over Hanoi, had had the effect of lessening it. Thus Clifford maintained, "What will stop it [the war] is an arrangement with the Soviets so they can use their leverage—which we don't have—to bring the Soviets to force Hanoi to stop it."[81]

It was the sort of subtle political argument that Lyndon Johnson usually grasped instantly. But Clifford's efforts in this instance proved unavailing, even with the support of ambassadors Bohlen and Thompson. Johnson simply did not want to hear, for instance, that increased casualties had been caused by more intense fighting in the South, not by the bombing restraints. "We have softened," he complained; "they have done nothing." Clifford was being unrealistic, he added, which led to a bitter exchange:

Clifford: You called my position unrealistic. I believe it is realistic. We are not ending the War, even though we have massive firepower, huge B-52 flights, largest number of troops ever in Vietnam. We can't bring war to a conclusion militarily.
The President: I don't think being soft will get us peace.[82]

The reply to Kosygin followed Rusk's prescription for requiring a "clarification" of the action the North Vietnamese would take in exchange for an end to the bombing although Clifford and the others agreed that the draft of the reply was "all right."[83] In fact, these stipulations, the "Rusk formula," constituted a stiffening of earlier American positions, such as Johnson's San Antonio formula of September 1967; the president then had told an audience in that city that he was willing to stop all bombardment "when this will lead promptly to productive discussions. . . . We, of course, assume that while discussions proceed, North Vietnam would not take advantage of the bombing cessation."[84] Clifford had insisted that Kosygin's assurance in his June 4 letter that American security would not be damaged by a bombing halt constituted acceptance of the San Antonio formula, but again to no avail. After the discussion ended, Rusk told Harriman as they rode back to the State Department that Clifford had lost his nerve over Vietnam.[85]

It was harder, or at least as hard, for Harriman and Vance to negotiate in Washington as it had been in Paris. From outside the inner circle of high-level policy experts came a memorandum based on McGeorge Bundy's files, written by John P. Roche, a Johnson loyalist, who had been brought into the White House to fill the role of intellectual in residence that Kennedy had initiated with Arthur Schlesinger, Jr. Roche argued that there had been "two massive miscalculations" from the outset about Hanoi's eventual willingness to accept a Korean "solution." First, there had been a "mystical belief in the *strategic* value of airpower in a limited war"; second, there was virtually a "total" failure to appreciate the determination and military capacity of North Vietnam. Put together, these miscalculations overloaded McNamara's computer:

And when the computer was asked "Why haven't they negotiated?" it always came up with the same answer: "Because they haven't been punished *enough*." So everybody went scurrying around looking for new targets.[86]

Roche's preference for "men with rifles" was no solution, at least not by that point, but it highlighted from a different angle the arguments Clifford had been making. In Paris, meanwhile, Harriman and Vance had another session with Ambassador Zorin. The Russian said that he had been in close contact with Le Duc Tho, who had in effect confirmed the message Kosygin had sent to Washington. The North Vietnamese respected Harriman's "seriousness" and would be prepared to talk about "all the outstanding questions once the bombing question was settled." Efforts to go beyond that assurance into the "Rusk formula" yielded no results.[87]

In their first conversation, Harriman had suggested that a rapprochement between the NLF program and President Johnson's program might be possible; now he added a second hint, that a solution to the problem of full-scale negotiations might be found by having representatives from the United States and Saigon on one side of the table and North Vietnamese and NLF negotiators on the other, without any designations of status. Zorin showed "considerable interest" in this point, as well he should have; for when combined with the hints dropped earlier, it was the first offer suggestive of direct negotiations with the National Liberation Front. The American position had always been that the NLF was merely a puppet of the North and could not be allowed to shoot its way into power or even into a coalition.

Although Zorin's reaction to these hints hardly justified any optimism, Clifford and Harriman collaborated in an effort to suggest to the public that there were straws in the wind indicating movement in the negotiations. As Clifford put it in a telephone conversation, their problem was to prevent some "militarist gentleman" (Wheeler, or possibly even Rusk?) from saying that the talks were useless and that the bombing should be resumed. "What I think we must do," Clifford concluded, "is if there is ever any occasion in the most guarded manner to indicate that something is happening."[88]

Secret contacts between the American negotiators and the North Vietnamese had commenced by the end of June, and the former had put on the table a slightly different proposal. If Hanoi would give an indication of the reciprocal steps it would take beforehand, the United States would pretend that it had stopped the bombing as a unilateral measure. Even Dean Rusk believed that something was "stirring on the other side. . . . Still we must know what they would do if we stop bombing."[89]

Both those advisers who wanted to stop the bombing as an acceptable risk in order to begin serious peace negotiations and those who demanded with Secretary Rusk categorical assurances of reciprocal action beforehand feared most that time would run out. At a briefing for Republican candidate Richard Nixon, Rusk was able to reassert his belief that Vietnam was just like other Cold War crises. Asked by Nixon what would make the North negotiate seriously, the secretary answered half facetiously (but only half) that it would take 100,000 casualties between January and July and circumstances in which only women were left to put in the field. Rusk continued, "There was no reason why guerrillas had stopped sending men into Greece. There is no obj.[ective] reason why Berlin blockade was lifted." And in answer to Nixon's further query about where the war was lost, Rusk snapped, "In the editorial rooms of this country."[90]

As the Democratic National Convention approached, Johnson's resistance to appeals that he end the bombing of North Vietnam increased. Whether he feared being accused of playing politics with American lives or felt all the years of resentment against the eastern elite in the party welling up inside him, he demanded the final say on the party platform despite the pleas of supporters of Vice-President Humphrey, the man Johnson, however half-heartedly, had anointed to be his successor.[91]

Those advisers who pushed the president to continue the bombing returned to the argument that any sign that the United States was lessening its all-out pressure on the North would cause an internal collapse in the South. National Security Adviser Walt Rostow had been arguing for some time that President Thieu, at some future date, would have to agree to allow the NLF to participate in the political life of South Vietnam—as individuals. But when McGeorge Bundy made yet another appeal to end the bombing in mid-August, Rostow's draft reply backed off from asserting that view. It was hopeful, Rostow had originally written, that Thieu was trying hard to build a "big" non-Communist coalition to run "against the Communist popular front" he expected to face one day at the polls, but Johnson deleted that paragraph.[92]

Both the proponents of ending the bombing and those opposed agreed, however, that the United States should hold out in the negotiations for three objectives: the right of the government of South Vietnam to sit at the negotiating table, the reestablishment of the Demilitarized Zone, and an end to North Vietnamese rocket attacks on cities. At a crucial National Security Council meeting on September 25, the ambassador to the United Nations, George Ball, argued unsuccessfully that the administration should accept the minimal risk of ending the bombing to get talks started on that basis. Both sides, he insisted, were dug into doctrinal positions; an element of face was involved. Secretary Rusk shot back, "What about 'face' of other Orientals in the area—Koreans, Thais, and others?"

Besides, continued the secretary of state, what about the votes that would go for Nixon if a bombing halt produced no response? They would get them, anyway, said Ball. Then Johnson made a comment that confirmed Ball's decision to resign his position and to campaign for Hubert Humphrey: "I am not hell-bent on agreement. We have done things before on assumptions. We have been disappointed. When I make an assumption, I want a reason to make it. I doubt if all three things are sufficient to get us to stop it—shelling, DMZ, South Vietnam."[93]

Ball's sense of futility and his fear that Nixon would be elected (he was leading Humphrey by nearly twenty points in the polls) had led him to believe that not only must he resign, but he also must persuade the vice-president to announce that he would take the risk of ending the bombing. To convince Humphrey, Ball contacted Harriman and Vance in Paris to clear a proposed statement that the vice-president would halt the bombing without preconditions as an acceptable risk for peace. Humphrey also said that the United States would expect reciprocity from North Vietnam. Much of this was semantics. As Ball explained in a background press conference, "It is a token of good faith which enables the negotiations to move on without confronting the communists with the problem of an explicit oral promise which would be represented as a consideration, something for which they are not prepared to give anything explicitly as a consideration."[94]

When Ball called Johnson to read him a draft of the statement, the president had said that he was sure that Ball would try to persuade the press that it did not mark any departure from the line of policy the administration had been following. "I'm sorry Mr. President," Ball had replied, "but that's not quite the name of the game."[95] Humphrey's standings in the polls began to rise. Moreover, as for the negotiations, whether it was because the North Vietnamese feared that Nixon might resort to atomic weapons, as Ball had suggested at the National Security Council meeting, or a general belief by the North that the time had come for serious negotiations on the terms set forth without "oral promises," as Ball had put it to the press, the long-awaited break came in mid-October.

The American negotiators did not demand public statements about North Vietnam's response in exchange for a bombing halt, but it was understood that the three American "nonconditions" would be met. "We do not look on them as a condition for stopping the bombing but as a description of the situation which would permit serious negotiations and thus the cessation to continue," Cyrus Vance told Le Duc Tho. The chief North Vietnamese delegate responded that Hanoi know how to look at the problem realistically "and so should we."[96]

Whether an agreement could have been reached in June—Kosygin's letter to Johnson had said much the same thing—and whether continuing the bombing had produced more explicit understandings, especially about the participation of the government of South Vietnam in the peace talks, remain arguable propositions. Did George Ball's initiative in the Humphrey campaign and his contacts with Paris constitute a subtle signal to the North Vietnamese? Or, on the other hand, did fear of Richard Nixon force the shift in North Vietnamese positions?

From the American record, however, it is clear that even the staunchest hawks now agreed that American conditions for ending the bombing had in fact been met. At a meeting on October 14, 1968, Johnson's advisers agreed to a cessation of the bombing, including General Wheeler and Dean Rusk. "We'll try it," said the president; "we'll be scared, but let's try it."[97] Johnson was anxious to move ahead as soon as possible, but a series of technical problems developed around the timing of the bombing cessation and the actual commencement of substantive talks.

The United States had made it a sine qua non that the government of Vietnam (GVN) be represented as a full participant. For years, however, the United States had not been willing to recognize the NLF as a separate entity. Yet now, whatever maneuvers were employed lessened the standing of the GVN as it could not claim to be the sole legitimate representative of South Vietnam. North Vietnamese insistence that they could not produce the NLF at a day's notice, for example, was yet another subtle way of turning the talks into a four-party affair. Thus, even though Hanoi claimed the GVN was a puppet regime of the United States, it gained more by having the NLF present from the outset—a point not lost on Saigon. At stake, after all, was the governance of South Vietnam and the legitimacy of competing forces there, not the regime in the North; any negotiations on that basis weakened the Thieu government.

A week went by after the fundamental decision to end the bombing, and the timing had still to be straightened out. The South Vietnamese leader, President Thieu, now fully alerted to what was happening, had protested against any joint statement announcing the talks that included mention of the NLF as a full participant. "They want to treat the NLF as non-existent," Rusk pointed out, as the United States, he might have added, had once attempted to do. "He has worse problems at home," quipped Johnson, "than I do with Fulbright." But Walt Rostow saw precisely what was happening, partly as a result of the North Vietnamese claim that NLF delegates could not be produced for at least three days after the bombing ceased, and argued, "We cannot treat the NLF as an entity. The delay cannot be too long."[98]

Somewhat later, in another meeting, the president acknowledged Rostow's judgment and pointed out the implications of the direction in which the Paris negotiations were leading: "We do, in effect, recognize them by letting them sit down with us." For the next several minutes it was as if Johnson had said something that surprised them all:

Secretary Rusk: It's about like letting Stokely Carmichael sit at Cabinet meeting.
Secretary Clifford: It still seems like greater benefit than detriment.
The President: Factually, that's correct.

Secretary Rusk: Emotionally, that's not correct.
Walt Rostow: The South Vietnamese are afraid of how we play them in Conference—push them toward accepting a slippery slope—jam into coalition government.[99]

At that point, the conversation abruptly shifted to other topics; nevertheless, it had already cut close to the bone. In March Johnson had accepted the advice of the Wise Men to look for another way to end the war in Vietnam. He had held out throughout the summer against ending the bombing until American conditions had been met. South Vietnam's recovery after Tet had encouraged the hope that if actual negotiations took place, the military questions could be separated from issues having to do with the political future of South Vietnam; but the structure of the negotiations themselves, a structure insisted upon by Washington as an absolute condition for ending the bombing, had already undermined Saigon's position.

The Saigon regime protested vehemently to Ambassador Ellsworth Bunker, demanding that the language announcing the bombing halt should say that North Vietnam had agreed to discuss peace with the GVN. Bunker pointed out that Washington could not say that a three-power conference had been convened when it would be plain to the world that the NLF was there, but he assured Vice-President Nguyen Cao Ky that Johnson would reiterate Washington's position that the NLF presence did not constitute recognition by the United States. If that were so, of course, Hanoi could say that the GVN presence did not constitute recognition by North Vietnam.

Bunker professed to be offended by Ky's lack of trust in American assurances. "We have merited that trust," he insisted, "and they should not act as if they doubted our repeatedly stated position, which would be reiterated yet another time, that we do not recognize the NLF but regard it as a tool of Hanoi." But it was not a matter of trust, replied Ky: "If we sit down with the NLF as equals, the whole *raison d'etre* of this regime is finished."[100]

Although General Wheeler had agreed with the decision to halt the bombing, Johnson was anxious to get his field commander's approval as well as to preempt any Pentagon uprising or end runs to Congressional hawks. It was also necessary to have General Abrams's support to disabuse Thieu and Ky of any notion that they could manipulate divisions among American policymakers. Thus the general was called back to Washington. Johnson prepared a letter to Abrams, comparing him to Ulysses S. Grant and urging him to "keep the enemy on the run." Johnson's administration had three months left, and he wanted Abrams to "lean on the enemy with all the manpower and equipment we have accumulated. . . . Your President and your country are counting on you to follow the enemy in relentless pursuit," Johnson wrote, as if the peace negotiations were really simply a window display. "Don't give them a minute's rest. Keep pouring it on. Let the enemy feel the weight of everything you've got."[101]

It is hard to explain this letter except as a confusing maneuver to outwit Pentagon hard-liners. Throughout the summer months, Johnson had refused to end the bombing as a risk for peace out of concern for American lives—even one life he said at one point. Yet what he wanted Abrams to do would risk huge casualty lists that could be blamed on the decision to stop bombing. Moreover, he had told the Air Force commander in Vietnam, Gen. William Mommyer, that he hoped to beat the negotiating record of 1954, when peace was achieved in thirty days.[102]

When Abrams arrived in Washington, Johnson pressed him to agree that ending the bombing would not cause increased casualties. The general gave his approval to a cessation and even said that conditions had progressed to the extent in the past two months that an approach that had been militarily unwise a short time before was now fully acceptable. Abrams's optimism was reminiscent of earlier years: "We have now come to the stage of war we have always wanted to get. . . . we can hit infrastructure." The only danger was that a cease-fire on the ground would leave the GVN in a position in which they did not control their territory. Secretary Rusk was heartened by this news, which, he apparently believed, offered a way to finesse the NLF presence in the Paris talks. "I do not expect this to be wound up in a month," he said; "this may go on while you men wrap it up in South Vietnam."[103]

Abrams had really pepped up the meeting. Wheeler declared, "I think this [North Vietnamese agreement] is as much a symbol of defeat as erection of Berlin Wall. They have been clobbered. If they don't act in good faith, I would urge resumption and really let them have it. I would use fire hose rather than eye-dropper." If Abrams and Wheeler were right, then apparently the North Vietnamese were really at the talks to negotiate a face-saving surrender; they were suing for peace. The meeting ended on this note.

As Johnson prepared to brief the presidential candidates on his decision to end the bombing, word came that the South Vietnamese were delaying acceptance of the invitation to come to Paris to take part in the talks. When he put down the telephone, the president

turned to his aides: "That's the old Nixon." The fact of political fi-
nagling has now been established; Richard Nixon's agents worked
with intermediaries in an attempt to ensure that South Vietnam did
not accept an invitation to the Paris talks before the election.[104]

But to focus on that aspect of the situation in late October 1968
overemphasizes the immediate political situation in the United
States. South Vietnam's determination not to be maneuvered into
the Paris talks reflected a more realistic assessment of the situation
in Vietnam than General Abram's optimistic appraisal. Johnson was
not surprised by this turn of events; Abrams was, however: "They
talked about flags, name-plates"; then Abrams realized what had
happened—Saigon had been "overcome by logic." The president
mused, "If I were Thieu I wouldn't feel very kindly about it."[105]

Johnson felt trapped. If he proceeded with the plan without
Thieu's agreement to attend the talks, he would be accused of sell-
ing out South Vietnam. It would give the lie to the notion that the
United States had been fighting to ensure the principle of South
Vietnam and send a signal to America's allies in Asia and elsewhere.
He would be accused of giving in to the dissenters and sacrificing
foreign policy to politics. There was no end to the harm that would
be done by going ahead without Saigon.

On the other hand, the country had lost patience with the war
in Vietnam. General Abram's optimism might be grounded in the
evidence of South Vietnamese recovery and progress since Tet, but
American generals had too often proclaimed that victory was just
around the corner. Johnson could not afford to back away now from
the Paris talks. Neither Humphrey nor Nixon would have any
chance to end the war on decent terms if, at this crucial moment after North Vietnam had in effect agreed to American conditions for
the talks, Johnson allowed Thieu to veto the talks. Throughout the
war Johnson had feared the power of the conservative forces in the
United States, but if he tried to reverse the momentum for the peace
talks, no president would have the support of the nation. He would
wait a day or so. "If he [Thieu] keeps us from moving," Johnson declared to his advisers, "God help South Vietnam—because I can't
help him anymore, neither can anyone else who has my job."[106]

Thieu's declared reason for not agreeing to a joint statement announcing the bombing cessation and the opening of talks in Paris
was in reaction to Ambassador Harriman's statement to a South
Vietnamese representative that he could not force the North Vietnamese into direct talks with Saigon, an apparent retreat from
American assurances that such talks would take place. More threat-

ening messages were sent to Saigon. "If he breaks with us," Rusk cabled, "we are finished. The American people will not take this."[107]

Bunker tried to convince Thieu that Harriman's statement was not a retreat from the American position. It was precisely because the United States could not guarantee what the North Vietnamese would say about the NLF or direct negotiations that it was necessary to have a joint South Vietnam/U.S. statement defining their understanding of the purpose of the talks and whom the participants represented. Nothing could be done about what Hanoi said except to counteract it with such a joint declaration. But Thieu would not be calmed by diplomacy. He reacted "emotionally and disjointedly," Bunker reported, describing Thieu's response: "You are powerful. You can say to small nations what you want. We understand America's sacrifice for Vietnam. All Vietnamese know our life depends on US support. But you cannot force us to do anything against our interest. This negotiation is not a life or death matter for the US, but it is for Vietnam."[108]

Later reports of what Harriman had actually said, moreover, were at considerable variance with official versions of the conversation. According to press reports, the head of the American delegation had told Pham Dang Lam that South Vietnamese "pretensions" were "out of this world. . . . Your government does not represent all of South Vietnam, Mr. Ambassador, and you would do well to remember that."[109] Harriman's attitude, regardless of his exact language, was that the GVN would be coming to Paris to negotiate with the NLF about the future of South Vietnam. This intention was somewhat disguised under the formula that North Vietnam and the United States would discuss military conditions for an eventual cease-fire and mutual withdrawal while political discussions should ensue among the other participants. Actually, the hawks in the administration did not really object to that formula, provided that the North Vietnamese abided by the conditions set forth for ending the bombing. The Pentagon plan for withdrawal, it will be remembered, assumed not that all U.S. forces would be out six months after an agreement but six months after "violence subsided."

Their position, as stated by Abrams and others, was that the North Vietnamese had sued for peace because of the military situation in Vietnam; hence it would be possible to insist upon such conditions once the talks began. And Secretary Rusk had never abandoned his conviction that Vietnam was a variant on other crises in the Cold War. The proposed negotiations were some sort of hybrid between what had happened in Greece and in Korea. Don't go to

Paris to cover the peace talks, Rusk told a reporter, he would be wasting his time. Compromise was impossible. If the reporter wanted to know what was "really happening" he should watch the military reports.[110]

Meanwhile on October 31 Johnson, despite the developments in Paris and in Vietnam, announced an end to the bombing and the inauguration of substantive peace talks. He had waited as long as he could for South Vietnamese concurrence; even those advisers who had cautioned against risking a break with Saigon admitted that he had no alternative but to proceed. By prior agreement with the North Vietnamese there were no stated conditions for ending the bombing, but the president believed he had iron-clad assurances not only from the Vietnamese but from the Soviets as well on the three issues concerning the demilitarized zone, the shelling of South Vietnamese cities, and the participation of the GVN in the talks.

When Nixon won the election, the doves faced a new problem. The hawks were not unhappy with the idea of dual negotiations, but Saigon's refusal to join in the talks did not displease Secretary of Defense Clifford. It gave him an opportunity to press the point that the South Vietnamese and the Americans had separate goals. We want to finish fighting, achieve peace, and get out, he argued before Johnson and his colleagues. Thieu and Ky wanted to go on fighting because it kept their government afloat with American aid and prevented their thinking about tough negotiating problems.[111] A few days later Clifford took a dramatic step at a news conference. He had prepared his comments carefully, and when the question arose as to whether Johnson knew that South Vietnam would not go along when he announced the bombing halt, Clifford was ready with his answer. (Clifford later told Averell Harriman that Johnson had suggested that he have a press conference, and the secretary had spent some time thinking about what the president had wanted him to say. It would also emerge that Clifford believed it was up to him to offer a way out.[112])

Throughout the months of preliminary negotiations, Clifford began, Saigon had demanded representation at the talks; throughout that time it was known that the NLF would accompany the Hanoi delegation. Thieu's single objection—at first—was the timing. But then a new set of concerns and objections had developed, delays that amounted to an attempted veto. The president was absolutely right in not allowing this to happen. Clifford then put a clever spin on the military/political formula that was sure to infuriate his hawkish colleagues:

There are a great many subjects that can be covered between the United States and Hanoi of a military nature and that's our real function. We have been there as a military shield for South Vietnam. I have not anticipated that we would get into the political settlement of South Vietnam. That is up to South Vietnam and Hanoi.[113]

Saigon had demanded direct negotiations with Hanoi but not over questions having to do with the political future of South Vietnam. It had perhaps made that demand unwisely and simply as a way of holding off demands for talks with the NLF, but Clifford had seized on that error to separate the American mission in Vietnam from the ultimate political settlement. Rostow in fact had done some thinking about South Vietnam's political future and about what would have to be done to reintegrate the NLF into the political life of the South on an "individual" basis. There is less evidence that Rusk, convinced as he was of the way the war would end, had gone that far in his thinking. Thus Clifford was provided with his opening. Johnson, perturbed but unsure of how to respond, asked Rostow to provide him with a close analysis of Clifford's news conference.[114]

Saigon responded to Clifford immediately. At a press conference, the minister for information denied that President Thieu had ever gone back on his word. Asked what South Vietnam would do if Washington negotiated a withdrawal and left the country, the minister said that of course the United States was independent and could do as it liked: "Some say we can't win the war without the US, but it is also true that the US cannot win the war without us." This reasoning also applied, he concluded, to the peace.[115]

The information minister's statements confirmed Clifford's arguments inside the administration: Saigon had no intention of negotiating a peace. Instead, it would continue to hold over Washington's head the statements that had been made not only since the beginning of American involvement in Vietnam but also since the beginning of the Cold War. It would also hold Washington hostage with the 27,000 American lives that had been spent in an effort to construct an entity built on the American principle underlying the determination of free men everywhere to resist Communist expansion.

Johnson had announced the forthcoming talks, but he had not instigated further procedures. Clifford was anxious to start withdrawing American troops as a symbolic gesture. Rusk was predictably against the idea; that was the wrong way to achieve peace, he said; "we agreed to pour it on in South Vietnam after the bombing was halted." He would not have a token withdrawal; he would work instead toward "clearing out the DMZ." Still, Johnson would not take Clifford's side. He simply could not make the final leap into the opening Clifford had revealed at his news conference. In a confused statement that leveled a blast at the South Vietnamese and at the same time indicated that he would be justified in resuming the bombing, the president rambled on to a discouraging conclusion:

> I would like to leave office de-escalating—not escalating—but I do not want to make a phony gesture. I do not want to run. We have listened to dovish advisers. We have tested them. We don't want a sellout.[116]

Nevertheless, in private Johnson told Harriman that he could talk to the Hanoi delegation about anything, including troop withdrawals, if it could be kept absolutely quiet and out of the press.[117] A month later Thieu had still not agreed to attend the peace talks, and Johnson sent his last important message to Saigon. It explained that President-elect Nixon and he were agreed on the need for Saigon to send its delegation to Paris. The key section of the message, however, was President Johnson's declaration that the situation in Congress and with the American public was as volatile and dangerous as he had seen it in forty years of public service. He then warned against a "real avalanche of criticism directed in part at the American Government, but far more acutely damaging to the image of your Government."[118]

Johnson remained ambiguous to the end. He had urged Clifford and others to provide him with options at key points, from Tet to the very end of his administration; yet he would not take the openings offered, he would not act, and thus he was finally unable to escape the Cold War definition of the world that he had helped to construct for so many years. The Vietnamese, who had been incidental to the construction of that worldview, now held power over him and his successor as well. The South Vietnamese minister for information was right: America might leave Vietnam, but it could not win either the war or the peace without their participation—or without risking the Cold War.

In his memoirs Johnson second-guessed himself: Should he have sent so many troops in 1965? Should he have sent more—and faster? Did he make mistakes in limiting the bombing on March 31 and then completely stopping it seven months later? Did he do enough to make clear the "vital interests" that were at stake in Vietnam? He treats the questions as if he, personally, could have made all the difference. But Lyndon Johnson's courage and will were not at issue, whatever his hawkish advisers or he himself thought. Johnson's struggle to bring the Vietnam War to an end ultimately failed, it can be argued, because Clifford's responses to the president's pleas for help led to questions about the Cold War that could not yet be entertained. Richard Nixon came to office believing that he could deal with Vietnam quickly, as Eisenhower had with Korea, and then move on to a more acceptable Disraeli-like conservative alternative to the Great Society and the Cold War. Like Johnson, however, he found that he could not explain 27,000 American lives as some kind of ghastly mistake. Those deaths held him in thrall—as they had Lyndon Johnson—to a refracted vision of reality. There was indeed "No Exit from Vietnam." And so the war went on for four more years.

Notes

1. For accounts of the writing of the March 31 speech, see Harry McPherson, *A Political Education: A Washington Memoir* (Boston: Houghton Mifflin, 1988), pp. 424–42, and Clark Clifford with Richard Holbrooke, *Counsel to the President: A Memoir* (New York: Random House, 1991), pp. 522–24.

2. Don Oberdorfer, *Tet!* (New York: Doubleday, 1971), pp. 301–2.

3. "Clifford and Rusk," editorial, *Washington Post*, January 3, 1969, p. A12.

4. Clifford, *Counsel to the President*, p. 485.

5. For an excellent survey of the issues and events of the New Deal coalition years, see Steve Fraser and Gary Gerstle, *The Rise and Fall of the New Deal Order, 1930–1980* (Princeton, N.J.: Princeton University Press, 1989).

6. Extracts from Westmoreland's address, November 21, 1967, in Gareth Porter, ed., *Vietnam: A History in Documents* (New York: New American Library, 1979), pp. 352–54.

7. "Notes of Meeting," Feb. 17 [,1968], Meeting Notes File, box 2, Lyndon Baines Johnson Library (hereafter cited as LBJL), Austin, Texas, and additional notes taken by Joseph Califano, *The Triumph & Tragedy of Lyndon Johnson: The White House Years* (New York: Simon and Schuster, 1991), pp. 263–64.

8. Various accounts of Wheeler's oral and written report have become available. This quotation is taken from Lyndon B. Johnson, *The Vantage Point: Perspectives of the Presidency, 1963–1969* (New York: Popular Library, 1971), p. 391. This paragraph is also reconstructed from several additional sources; see Wheeler's memorandum to President Johnson, February 27, 1968, in National Security Files (NSF), Country File, Vietnam, box 127, LBJL; a summary of the memorandum in the Senator Gravel edition of *The*

Pentagon Papers: The Defense Department History of United States Decisionmaking on Vietnam, 4 vols. (Boston: Beacon Press, 1971), 4: 547; a summary of the discussion in one secondary account has Wheeler dramatically pausing to look up at Johnson and saying, "It was a very near thing" (Neil Sheehan, ed., *The Pentagon Papers* [New York: Bantam Books, 1971], pp. 596-97). But it is not at all clear that these words were in his oral presentation. See Mark Perry, *Four Stars: The Inside Story of the Forty-Year Battle between the Joint Chiefs of Staff and America's Civilian Leaders* (Boston: Houghton Mifflin, 1989), p. 189.

9. In addition to other sources cited for this report, see also "Notes of the President's Meeting to Discuss General Wheeler's Trip to Vietnam," February 28, 1968, Tom Johnson's Notes of Meetings, box 2, LBJL. Unfortunately, the complete notes of this meeting are not currently available although the full version is apparently the source for the account in President Johnson's memoirs, *Vantage Point*, pp. 391-92. An interesting difference appears in the written memorandum Wheeler gave the president from the Tom Johnson notes. In the former, Wheeler writes that the pacification program had been brought to a halt in many places and the "VC [Vietcong] are prowling the countryside." In Tom Johnson's notes, Wheeler is quoted as saying that pacification "is at a halt," but the Viet Cong "cannot roam at will in the countryside."

10. Johnson, *Vantage Point*, p. 391; Clifford, *Counsel to the President*, p. 486; Walt W. Rostow and David Ginsberg, "The March 31st Speech, Preface," November 8, 1968, NSF, National Security Council (NSC) History, box 47, LBJL.

11. Perry, *Four Stars*, pp. 184-91.

12. "Notes of the President's Meeting to Discuss General Wheeler's Trip to Vietnam," February 28, 1968, Tom Johnson's Notes, box 2, LBJL. The available version of the notes ends with a discussion of the ways the request could be implemented, before McNamara issued his strong dissent.

13. Johnson, *Vantage Point*, p. 392.

14. Ibid., p. 393.

15. "Cabinet Meeting of February 28, 1968," Cabinet Papers, box 12, LBJL.

16. Ibid.

17. For Clifford's 1965 position and George Ball's influence on Clifford, see Larry Berman, *Planning a Tragedy: The Americanization of the War in Vietnam* (New York: W. W. Norton and Company, 1982), pp. 120-21, and David L. DiLeo, *George Ball, Vietnam, and the Rethinking of Containment* (Chapel Hill: University of North Carolina Press, 1991), pp. 117-19.

18. Clark M. Clifford, "A Viet Nam Reappraisal: The Personal History of One Man's View and How it Evolved," *Foreign Affairs* 47 (July 1969): 601-22.

19. Rostow to LBJ, March 4, 1968, "The Clifford Committee," Documents Sanitized and Declassified from Unprocessed Files (DSDUF), box 4, LBJL.

20. Rostow to LBJ, March 4, 1968, DSDUF, box 4, LBJL.

21. "Notes of the President's Meeting with Senior Foreign Policy Advisers," March 4, 1968, Tom Johnson's Notes, box 2, LBJL (emphasis in original).

22. Interviews with Herbert Schandler, November 28, 1972, and February 15, 1973. See Herbert Y. Schandler, *Lyndon Johnson and Vietnam: The Unmaking of a President* (Princeton, N.J.: Princeton University Press, 1977), p. 245.

23. "Notes of the President's Meeting," March 4, 1968, Tom Johnson's Notes, box 2, LBJL.

24. Ibid. For a review of Paul Nitze's role in the 1968 Vietnam debates, see David Callahan, *Dangerous Capabilities: Paul Nitze and the Cold War* (New York: Harper Collins, 1990), pp. 288–316. Although Nitze was bold at this particular meeting, Clark Clifford's rapidly developing views soon sped past Nitze's lingering concerns about credibility. His principal tutors in the Department of Defense became Townsend Hoopes and Paul Warnke.

25. "Notes of the President's Meeting," March 4, 1968, Tom Johnson's Notes, box 2, LBJL.

26. "Memorandum for the President," March 6, 1968, enclosed notes of previous day's meeting, ibid.

27. "Notes of the President's Meeting," March 4, 1968, ibid.

28. Douglas C. Brinkley, *Dean Acheson: The Cold War Years* (New Haven, Conn.: Yale University Press, 1992), chap. 8.

29. Ibid., and Dean Acheson, "Meeting with the President," March 14, 1968, box 88, Papers of Dean Acheson, Harry S. Truman Library, Independence, Missouri.

30. Acheson, "Meeting with the President," March 14, 1968, Acheson Papers.

31. Townsend Hoopes, *The Limits of Intervention* (New York: W. W. Norton, 1987), pp. 204–5.

32. Acheson, "Meeting With the President," March 14, 1968, Acheson Papers.

33. Edwin Dale, the national economics reporter for the *New York Times*, had expressed his concern about "something really grave on your hands in the gold markets" at a Washington party attended by Pentagon figures. To his surprise, he thus learned about the administration debate over Westmoreland's troop request, and his information became the basis for the investigative report that the *Times* published on March 10, 1968, under a three-column headline, "Westmoreland Requests 206,000 More Men, Stirring Debate in Administration." See Oberdorfer, *Tet!* pp. 266–70.

34. Acheson to John Cowles, March 14, 1968, box 88, Acheson Papers.

35. Undated memo, "The Gold Crisis, November 1967–March 1968," NSF, NSC History, box 53, LBJL.

36. When Rusk appeared before the Senate Foreign Relations Committee on January 28, 1966, Sen. Stuart Symington asked, "How long do you think the United States can be almost the only financier of freedom and at the same time the defender of freedom, as it is, if our balance-of-payments problems continue to worsen?" Rusk's response was typical of the times: "I think we have to do what is required—and what is required turns primarily on our own interests as a nation, and on our commitments—and then try to get as much help as we can from others." U.S. Senate, Foreign Relations Committee, *Hearings: Supplemental Foreign Assistance Fiscal Year 1966—Vietnam*, 89th Cong., 2d sess. pp. 23–24.

37. For an excellent summary of the gold Achilles' heel of the Pax

Americana, see David P. Calleo, *The Imperious Economy* (Cambridge: Harvard University Press, 1982).

38. "Memorandum for Record: Summary of Dean Acheson's Proposal," March 14, 1968, NSF Country File, Vietnam, box 127, and Rostow to Johnson, March 16, 1968, NSC History, box 48, LBJL.

39. Hoopes, *Limits of Intervention*, pp. 205–6; *Public Papers of the Presidents: Lyndon B. Johnson, 1968–69* (Washington, D.C.: Government Printing Office, 1970), pp. 410–11 (hereafter cited as *Public Papers*).

40. Bundy to Johnson, March 21, 1968, President's Office Files, box 1; Bundy to Johnson, March 22, 1968, Reference File, Miscellaneous Vietnam Documents; see also Larry O'Brien to Johnson, March 21, 1968, NSF, Walt Rostow Office Files, box 5, LBJL.

41. Rowe to Johnson, March 19, 1968, Marvin Watson Office Files, box 32, LBJL.

42. Ibid.

43. Oberdorfer, *Tet!* pp. 311–12. From the discussion in Oberdorfer, it is clear he had access to Rowe's letter in writing his book.

44. "Summary of Notes," March 26, 1968, Tom Johnson's Notes, box 2, LBJL.

45. *Johnson, Vantage Point*, p. 418.

46. "CIA-DOD Briefing by General Depuy and George Carver, March 27[28], 1968," Tom Johnson's Notes, box 2, LBJL.

47. Ibid.

48. Perry, *Four Stars*, pp. 194–95.

49. "Notes of the President's Meeting with General Earle Wheeler, JCS, and General Creighton Abrams," March 26, 1968, Tom Johnson's Notes, box 2, LBJL. A somewhat different account of this meeting is in Clifford, *Counsel to the President*, pp. 515–16, where the source is not named.

50. "Notes of the President's Meeting," March 26, 1968, Tom Johnson's Notes, box 2, LBJL.

51. Untitled handwritten notes, March 25, 1968, Walt Rostow Office Files, box 6, LBJL.

52. Walter Isaacson and Evan Thomas, *The Wise Men: Six Friends and the World They Made* (New York: Simon and Schuster, 1986), p. 700.

53. Neil Sheehan et al., *The Pentagon Papers: As Published by the New York Times*, (New York: Bantam Books, 1971), pp. 622–23.

54. Clifford, *Counsel to the President*, p. 521.

55. Sheehan, *Pentagon Papers*, pp. 622–23.

56. Untitled notes, April 2, 1968, Tom Johnson's Notes, box 3, LBJL.

57. "Memorandum of Conversation," March 20, 1968, box 7, Papers of Clark Clifford, LBJL.

58. Bui Diem, with David Chanoff, *In the Jaws of History* (Boston: Houghton Mifflin, 1987), pp. 224–25.

59. Ibid., pp. 223–25.

60. Rostow to Johnson, April 2, 1968, Walt Rostow NSF Office Files, box 6, LBJL. In April 1966 the new national security adviser, Walt W. Rostow, was already recommending a slight variation on military and diplomatic measures, not a coalition government but somehow a legitimizing of the NLF opposition under other names. Hanoi still had to be convinced that the jig was up by military force before diplomacy could work. If the shaky

situation in Saigon could be improved, it was the time to escalate to see if it were possible to force a resolution of the conflict. Diplomatically, however, he believed word should be gotten to the VC that their destiny was to sit in with the Hanoi delegation at the peace conference and to seek to return to political life in South Vietnam as individuals. "The strain on our political and economic life and the strain on the South Vietnamese is all but intolerable" (Memorandum for the President, April 5, 1966, box 7, ibid.).

61. Diem, *In the Jaws of History*, p. 225.

62. See Bunker, "Viet-Nam Negotiations: Dangers and Opportunities," April 8, 1968, NSF, Country File, Vietnam, boxes 95–96, and "Notes of the President's meeting at Camp David," April 9, 1968, Meeting Notes File, box 2, LBJL.

63. Rudy Abramson, *Spanning the Century: The Life of Averell Harriman, 1891–1986* (New York: William Morrow, 1992), pp. 654–59, but see also, "Memorandum for Personal Files," April 9, 1968, and "Memorandum for Personal Files: Meeting and Lunch at Camp David," April 9, 1968, box 571, W. Averell Harriman Papers, Library of Congress, Washington, D.C., for important details of the Bunker/Clifford debates over Harriman's instructions. These memorandums also give a better feel for the tension than the minutes cited in note 62.

64. As an example of the steady stream of memos from Bunker and others, see Henry Cabot Lodge to Johnson, April 18, 1968, NSF, Country File, Vietnam, boxes 95–96, LBJL.

65. For one of many accounts of Johnson's long-standing feelings about intellectuals and their influence in the party going back to New Deal days and of the sense he had that they would inevitably be opposed to him and seek to betray him because of his regional and educational background, see James Rowe Oral History Interview, LBJL, especially p. 9.

66. "Notes of the Tuesday Luncheon," April 30, 1968, Tom Johnson's Notes, box 3, LBJL.

67. Ibid.

68. Lilienthal diary, May 1, 1968, box 213, Papers of David Lilienthal, Seely Mudd Library, Princeton University, Princeton, New Jersey.

69. Lilienthal diary, May 3, 1968, box 213.

70. Memorandum, "Negotiating Objectives for Vietnam," May 8, 1968, box 26, Clifford Papers; Johnson, *Vantage Point*, p. 248; and for military planning in 1968, see Jeffrey J. Clarke, *Advice and Support: The Final Years* (Washington, D.C.: Center for Military History, 1988), pp. 303–5.

71. Memorandum, "Negotiating Objectives for Vietnam," May 8, 1968, box 26, Clifford Papers.

72. Clarke, *Advice and Support*, pp. 303–5.

73. "Notes on the President's Meeting with Negotiating Team," May 8, 1968, Tom Johnson's Notes, box 3, LBJL; Clifford, *Counsel to the President*, p. 538.

74. "Notes of Tuesday Luncheon," May 14, 1968, and "Notes on the Meeting in the Cabinet Room," May 15, 1968, Tom Johnson's Notes, box 3, LBJL.

75. Dean Rusk, as told to Richard Rusk, *As I Saw It*, ed. Daniel S. Papp (New York: W. W. Norton, 1990), pp. 472–73. Rusk's memoir is far less de-

tailed than those of other participants and reflects the unflinching certainty he felt about his positions.

76. "Memorandum of Conversation," May 19, 1968, box 553, Harriman Papers.

77. "Notes of the Tuesday Lunch Meeting," May 21, 1968, Tom Johnson's Notes, box 3, LBJL.

78. "Notes of the President's Meeting with Foreign Policy Advisers," May 28, 1968, ibid.

79. Johnson, *Vantage Point*, pp. 508–9.

80. Abramson, *Spanning the Century*, p. 664.

81. "Notes of the President's Meeting with Foreign Policy Advisers," June 9, 1968, Tom Johnson's Notes, box 3, LBJL. Kosygin's letter itself remains classified.

82. Ibid.

83. Ibid.

84. For a discussion of the events surrounding the San Antonio formula speech, see Marilyn Young, *The Vietnam Wars, 1945–1990* (New York: Harper, Collins, 1991), chap. 11, especially pp. 210–12.

85. Abramson, *Spanning the Century*, p. 665.

86. Roche to Johnson, June 14, 1968, President's Office Files, Roche Memos, box 11, LBJL.

87. "Memorandum of Conversation," June 13, 1968, box 553, Harriman Papers.

88. See transcript of Clifford's news conference of June 20, 1968, and "Notes on Telephone Call," June 21, 1968, both in box 447, Harriman Papers.

89. "Notes of the President's Meeting with the Tuesday Luncheon Group," July 2, 1968, Tom Johnson's Notes, box 3, LBJL.

90. "Nixon," July 26, 1968, Tom Johnson's Notes, box 3, LBJL.

91. See, for example, Harry McPherson to Johnson, July 29, 1968, Reference File, Vietnam, box 1, LBJL.

92. McPherson to Clifford, August 13, 1968, Harry McPherson Office Files, box 53; Bundy to Johnson, August 15, 1968, and drafts of reply, August 22, 1968, both in NSF, Country, File, Vietnam, boxes 91–95, LBJL.

93. "Notes on the National Security Council Meeting," September 25, 1968, Tom Johnson's Notes, box 2, LBJL.

94. "Notes of the President's Weekly Luncheon Meeting," September 25, 1968, Tom Johnson's Notes, box 3, LBJL; transcript, "Deep Background," September 30, 1968, box 152, Papers of James Rowe, Franklin D. Roosevelt Library, Hyde Park, New York; Di Leo, *George Ball*, p. 174.

95. DiLeo, *George Ball*, p. 174.

96. "Notes of the President's Meeting," October 14, 1968, Tom Johnson's Notes, box 4, LBJL.

97. Ibid.

98. "Notes of the President's Meeting," October 22, 1968, ibid.

99. "Notes on President's Tuesday Luncheon," October 22, 1968, ibid.

100. Bunker to Rusk, October 25, 1968, box 6, Clifford Papers.

101. Johnson to Abrams, October 29, 1968, NSF, Country File, Vietnam, boxes 137–38, LBJL.

102. "Memorandum for the Record," October 23, 1968, ibid.

103. "Notes of the President's Meeting," October 29, 1968, Tom Johnson's Notes, box 3, LBJL.

104. Ibid.; for a concise account of the political maneuvering, see Stephen E. Ambrose, *Nixon: The Triumph of a Politician, 1962–1972* (New York: Simon and Schuster, 1989), pp. 201–22.

105. "Notes on Tuesday Luncheon," October 29, 1968, Tom Johnson's Notes, box 4, LBJL.

106. "Notes on Foreign Policy Meeting," October 29, 1968, ibid.

107. Rusk to Bunker, October 30, 1968, box 554, Harriman Papers.

108. Bunker to Rusk, October 29, 1968, and Bunker to Rusk, October 30, 1968, box 6, Clifford Papers.

109. Drew Pearson and Jack Anderson, "Washington-Saigon Feud," *Washington Post*, November 17, 1968, p. B7.

110. "Memorandum of Conversation," December 5, 1968, box 571, Harriman Papers.

111. "Notes on Foreign Policy Meeting," November 7, 1968, Tom Johnson's Notes, box 4, LBJL.

112. "Notes on Trip to Washington, December 6–10, 1968," December 10, 1968, box 556, Harriman Papers.

113. Transcript of news conference, November 12, 1968, enclosed in Rostow to Johnson, same date, DSDUF, box 2, LBJL.

114. Johnson memo, ibid.

115. American embassy, Saigon, to State Department, November 13, 1968, box 6, Clifford Papers.

116. "Notes on the Tuesday Luncheon Meeting," December 3, 1968, Tom Johnson's Notes, box 4, LBJL.

117. "Notes on Trip to Washington, December 6–10, 1968," December 10, 1968, box 556, Harriman Papers.

118. Bunker to Rusk, January 13, 1969, NSF, Country File, Vietnam, boxes 259–60, LBJL.

8 | Lyndon Johnson and Strategic Arms Limitation

Robert A. Divine

JUST BEFORE NINE O'CLOCK on Saturday morning, December 6, 1966, aides informed Lyndon Johnson that a plane carrying Secretary of Defense Robert McNamara and the members of the Joint Chiefs of Staff (JCS) would land within twenty minutes at Bergstrom Air Force Base, just outside Austin. The president dressed hurriedly and then flew by helicopter from his Texas ranch to the Federal Building in downtown Austin, arriving just before ten o'clock. Scheduled to award the Medal of Honor to a marine for heroism in Vietnam at 11:00 A.M., he devoted the next hour to making a critical decision regarding the nuclear arms race.

Robert McNamara had requested the meeting to present his dissent from the unanimous recommendation of the Joint Chiefs of Staff in favor of deploying a full-blown American antimissile defense system (ABM). The Soviets had already begun to build their own ABM around Moscow; Republicans as well as Democrats in Congress were calling for the United States to respond in kind. Convinced that the ABM would serve only to escalate the nuclear arms race, McNamara had flown to Texas twice in November in an effort to convince the president to defer any deployment decision. His emotions already at the breaking point over Vietnam, McNamara had startled those people on board the plane on December 6 when he ripped charts making the case for the ABM from the hands of Army Chief of Staff Harold K. Johnson.

McNamara had regained his composure by the time the meeting began in a conference room on the ninth floor of the Federal Building. The president took a seat opposite McNamara at one end of the long table; between them on either side sat the individual members of the JCS as well as National Security Adviser Walt Rostow and McNamara's deputy, Cyrus Vance. For the next hour, JCS Chairman Earle "Bus" Wheeler and Harold Johnson (who had a duplicate set of charts for the occasion) presented the case for deploying an ABM, while McNamara offered his dissenting opinion.[1]

For Lyndon Johnson, it was a difficult moment. Unlike the Great Society and Vietnam, arms control was not an issue close to his heart. With his Vietnam policy under relentless attack, he desperately needed the continued support of both Republican and Democratic hawks in Congress who favored the ABM. Aware of the way his own party had exploited the missile gap issue against the Republicans in the 1960 election, he did not want to give the GOP the same kind of opening in 1968. Yet he respected the intelligence and judgment of McNamara, his point man on Vietnam, and did not want to commit billions for an ABM when the war in Southeast Asia was already forcing him to cut back on his beloved Great Society programs.[2]

The meeting ended with a compromise that marked the beginning of a two-year attempt by Lyndon Johnson to limit the escalating nuclear arms race with the Soviet Union. In the course of those two final years of his administration, Johnson became a firm advocate of strategic arms control, seeing it ultimately as the finest legacy of his fatally flawed presidency. Even though he and his associates laid the basis for the Strategic Arms Limitation Talks (SALT I) agreements signed by Richard Nixon in 1972, LBJ failed to prevent the nuclear arms race from spiraling upward in the late 1960s.

I

The ABM issue arose at a time when the Soviet Union was beginning a determined effort to overcome a substantial American advantage in the strategic balance of power. Overreacting to the possibility of a missile gap in the early 1960s, the Kennedy administration had approved a massive deployment of both land-based Minuteman Missiles (ICBMs) and submarine-launched Polaris missiles (SLBMs). Without counting the fleet of 500 B-52 bombers, by 1967 the United States could deliver more than 1,700 warheads against Soviet targets—1,054 from ICBMs and 656 from 41 Polaris submarines. This enormous striking force was enough to destroy an estimated 50 percent of the Soviet population and to wipe out 80 percent of its industrial capacity, nearly double the goals set in 1963.

In response, the Soviets had begun a rapid buildup of their land-based ICBMs in the mid-1960s and a much slower increase in their small fleet of missile-launching submarines. By 1967 they had more than tripled the number of ICBMs, from 200 in 1964 to over 700; their SLBM capacity rose only slightly to 27. These figures indicated that the United States still enjoyed a comfortable strategic lead by the end of 1966, but there clearly was cause for future concern. The

CIA had badly underestimated the Soviets' ICBM buildup, predicting they would not reach the 700 level until 1969; it now appeared that they would achieve parity with the United States in land-based ICBMs by the end of the decade. More alarming was the Soviet decision to deploy the huge SS-9 ICBM, a missile capable of carrying a 25-megaton warhead—one large enough to threaten to wipe out American Minuteman silos in a first strike, thus limiting American retaliatory power to B-52 bombers and to the fleet of forty-one Polaris submarines.[3]

There were two possible responses to this Soviet missile buildup. The first would be to deploy an American ABM system designed to protect the American people from a devastating Soviet ICBM attack. McNamara, heeding the advice of the President's Scientific Advisory Committee, had opposed the original army system, Nike-Zeus, on grounds that the Soviets could fire more missiles than the system was capable of shooting down in space; also its radar was subject to jamming. But in 1963 the army began developing a more sophisticated system, Nike-X. Relying on a new phased-array radar less vulnerable to enemy attack, Nike-X used both long-range Spartan missiles to intercept Soviet ICBMs in space and short-range Sprint rockets to destroy any enemy warheads that entered the atmosphere. Defense Secretary McNamara still opposed an ABM system, claiming the Soviets could simply overwhelm it by building more ICBMs, but he allowed the army to spend $500 million a year on continued research and development. By 1966 the Pentagon had invested more than $2 billion in Nike-X, and Congress had infuriated McNamara in spring of that year by voting $167 million for its deployment. The defense secretary impounded the funds, but he faced increasing pressure from the Joint Chiefs, led by the army, to take the first steps toward an operational ABM system.[4]

Soviet moves toward their own ABM increased the pressure on McNamara. As early as 1963 American reconnaissance satellites had detected a network of missile installations and primitive radars stretching in an arc across the northwestern approaches to the Soviet Union from Tallinn in Estonia to Archangel. The CIA believed that what the Pentagon called the Tallinn network was only an air defense system limited to halting a bomber attack, but air force and army intelligence claimed it was capable of being upgraded into an ABM system effective against American missiles.

While debate raged over the possible danger from the Tallinn network, which had grown to 22 complexes with 396 missiles in place by 1966, American intelligence discovered that the Soviets had begun building an ABM system around Moscow. By early 1967 six sites were under construction around the Soviet capital, each holding sixteen Galosh missiles along with an advanced radar installation. Unquestionably, the Galosh system, as it was known in the Pentagon, had ABM capability; experts believed that with the addition of two more complexes the Soviets would be able to defend Moscow against an American ICBM attack by 1971. This development led the Joint Chiefs to make the recommendation for deploying Nike-X that McNamara opposed at the December 6 meeting in Austin with President Johnson.[5]

In his efforts to persuade LBJ to resist the pressure for an American ABM, McNamara expressed a strong preference for a second possible response to the Soviet initiative, the product of a technological breakthrough. A multiple-independently-targeted reentry vehicle— MIRV—offered a way to increase American nuclear striking power by delivering many more warheads on Soviet targets with the same number of missiles.

In the early 1960s two brothers who were both physicists at the Rand Corporation, Richard and Albert Latter, conceived the idea of using several warheads aboard American ICBMs as a way to overcome the problem of the Soviets having more available targets than America had missiles. At the same time, the American space program had developed a launch vehicle that could deploy a number of satellites in orbit while using just one rocket. Harold Brown, then serving as chief scientist in the Pentagon, fused these two ideas in 1964 and authorized the MK-12 warhead for American missiles. By 1965 McNamara had authorized research and development for two forms of MIRV—Minuteman III, which would carry three warheads aimed at three widely separated targets in the Soviet Union, and Poseidon, a successor to the Polaris missile and capable of delivering ten warheads to ten different locations.[6]

McNamara accepted the MIRV technology without examining its full implications because it met two critical needs. First, it offered him an ideal alternative to Nike-X. Instead of spending an estimated $10 billion to build an ABM system that could eventually be rendered useless by an increase in Soviet ICBMs, the United States could neutralize Galosh by spending less than $3 billion on Minuteman III and Poseidon. Not only was MIRV more cost effective, but from a scientific standpoint it was technically elegant compared to the complicated and unproven ABM technology. Second, MIRV gave McNamara an effective counter to the pressure from the air force to build more than 1,000 Minutemen in order to preserve an American lead in the face of the growing Soviet ICBM force. Instead of adding expensive missiles and silos, McNamara could offer the air force a way to triple the striking power of the existing 1,000 Minutemen without straining an already swollen defense budget.

MIRV had only one drawback: Unlike ABMs and ICBMs, a MIRV warhead could not be detected from a reconnaissance satellite. Once MIRVs became operational, it would be impossible to ban or to limit them by international agreement except with on-site inspection, a procedure the Soviet Union had always opposed. In his determination to thwart the army's insistence on deploying Nike-X, McNamara overlooked this critical shortcoming. At the same time, he kept the new technology highly classified, and thus the experts in arms control in both the State Department and the Arms Control and Disarmament Agency (ACDA) had no chance to object to MIRV in its early, critical stage of development.[7]

II

The American people first learned of the broad outlines of these new steps in the nuclear arms race in November 1966. After two trips to Texas to confer with LBJ on the fiscal year 1967 defense budget, McNamara held a press conference in Austin on November 9. Announcing that the United States had "considerable evidence" that the Soviets were building an ABM system around Moscow, the defense secretary confirmed widespread rumors about Galosh. The United States would respond, he revealed, with a greater offensive buildup that would overwhelm the Soviet ABM. He specifically cited the inclusion of $2 billion in the defense budget to equip submarines with the new Poseidon missiles. He did not mention Minuteman III nor make any reference to the still-secret MIRV concept, but the *New York Times* commented in vague terms about how American ICBMs would be equipped with new top-secret penetration aids that would offset the Soviet defensive system. McNamara parried questions about a U.S. ABM, saying it was still under consideration at the Pentagon, but he stressed his belief that Galosh would not affect the American strategic advantage. "There is absolutely no question," he declared flatly, "about our capability of penetrating the Soviet defenses with both our missiles and our aircraft."[8]

Although McNamara did his best to reassure the American people, he faced a stiff challenge from the Joint Chiefs of Staff. Through 1964 McNamara had been able to exploit differences between the three services over defense issues to maintain firm control over the Pentagon. But when Earle Wheeler replaced Maxwell Taylor as chairman of the Joint Chiefs, he outmaneuvered McNamara by insisting that the service chiefs hammer out their differences privately so that the JCS would always present the secretary of defense and the president with a unified position. "This united front," comments Lawrence Korb, "eventually paid dividends for the Joint Chiefs." With McNamara hesitant as a civilian to challenge the unanimous professional views of the military leaders, the Joint Chiefs entered the ABM debate in a strong position. McNamara knew there was a very real possibility that LBJ, on the defensive over Vietnam, would back the Joint Chiefs in any showdown with the secretary of defense.[9]

Given these considerations, McNamara was careful to stress areas of agreement with the Joint Chiefs in two memos he sent to Johnson just before the December 6 meeting in Austin. The secretary of defense, he wrote, concurred in the JCS recommendation to spend $705 million in fiscal 1968 to replace Polaris with Poseidon submarine-launched missiles. By 1972 the United States planned to have 31 Poseidon submarines, each capable of delivering 160 warheads against Soviet targets, thanks to MIRV, at a cost of $3.3 billion. He also endorsed the JCS recommendation to place MIRV warheads on 400 Minuteman III missiles at a total cost of $3.6 billion.

In supporting these moves to increase American offensive striking power, McNamara stressed his belief that the best way to counter both the Soviet ICBM buildup and ABM deployment was to make sure that the Russians knew that "we possess strategic nuclear forces so powerful as to be capable of absorbing a Soviet first strike and surviving with sufficient strength to impose unacceptable damage on them." This belief in "maximum assured destruction" made McNamara confident that there was nothing to fear from the latest Soviet nuclear moves; yet he seemed completely unaware of the possibility that the Johnson administration was overreacting to them. In a table accompanying his recommendation to the president, he showed that as a result of the Poseidon and Minuteman III recommendations, by 1976 the United States would be able to deliver 6,931 warheads on Soviet targets, more than four times the existing retaliatory capacity. In embracing the MIRV as the answer to the Soviet ABM challenge, McNamara was engaging in nuclear overkill.

Only in regard to deploying the ABM did McNamara take issue with the Joint Chiefs. They recommended including $800 million in the fiscal 1968 budget to begin deploying Nike-X to defend twenty-five American cities against a Soviet nuclear attack. The JCS estimated that the total cost would be $10 billion by 1976, and they also wanted the option of expanding the system to cover fifty cities for an additional $10 billion. They did not favor immediate deployment of a "thin" ABM system against the possible threat of Chinese ICBMs, claiming that such action could be deferred until a threat from China became a reality, probably in the late 1970s. McNamara concurred in this last recommendation, but he then argued that the United States could also wait another year before making the decision to deploy a "thick," anti-Soviet ABM system.

In presenting his case for deferring action on Nike-X, McNamara made three points to LBJ. First, he claimed that the ABM was technically suspect. It was not at all certain that the Spartan and Sprint missiles could destroy a significant proportion of incoming Soviet warheads, and the radar was still highly vulnerable. More important, however, was the simple fact that the ABM was not cost effective. The United States had already offset the Soviet ABM with the decision to deploy Poseidon and Minuteman III at a cost far below the $10 billion the JCS had budgeted for Nike-X. If LBJ went ahead with an American ABM, the Soviets could easily neutralize it in the same way—increasing their ICBM force proportionately. McNamara claimed that if the Soviets based their deterrent power on the ability to kill 22 million Americans in a retaliatory response, they would need to spend only one dollar for more missiles for every four dollars the U.S. spent on Nike-X. It would thus be far cheaper to deter an enemy attack by upgrading our offensive forces to maintain a capability of "assured destruction" of the Soviet Union.

The crucial consideration, McNamara told the president, was to avoid an unnecessary escalation of the nuclear arms race. The two superpowers were about to engage in yet another upward spiral in the deadly competition. Each would spend billions to deploy an ABM and the offensive missiles to overcome the opponent's system "without any gain in real security to either side." The only way to prevent this folly would be for LBJ to have the courage to resist political pressure and show restraint. The secretary of defense pleaded with Johnson to make the effort to educate the American people on the realities of the nuclear age by explaining to them why it was unnecessary for the United States to match the Soviet ABM system. It would take courage to rebut the inevitable argument that the Johnson administration wanted "to place dollars before lives," but McNamara felt the American people had to learn the true nature of deterrence in the nuclear age. "It is our ability to destroy the attacker as a viable 20th century nation that provides the deterrent,'' he argued, ''not the ability to limit damage to ourselves.''[10]

Although LBJ apparently was impressed with McNamara's arguments, he called for the meeting on December 6 in Austin to allow the JCS to make their case for the ABM. General Wheeler painted a grim picture of Soviet strategic behavior. He linked the Soviet ABM buildup, mentioning both Galosh and the more questionable Tallinn system, with the ''accelerated rate'' of the ICBM buildup, including the massive SS-9 missiles. Wheeler was not certain whether the Soviet goal was parity or nuclear superiority, but he feared that taken together these twin steps ''could reduce our assured destruction capability.'' At the very least, the result would enhance the Kremlin's ability ''to pursue aims short of nuclear war.''

Wheeler rested the case for an ABM on the need to save American lives in the event of an enemy attack. If America did not deploy an ABM, ''we would be denying to many of our own people a chance to survive a nuclear exchange,'' he argued, estimating that ''30–50 million lives might be saved by NIKE-X.'' Army Chief Harold Johnson backed up Wheeler: ''The critical question was U.S. casualties,'' he asserted; an ABM would cut American losses substantially in case of Soviet attack.

When McNamara countered that Nike-X would not save American lives because the Soviets would simply deploy enough ICBMs to overwhelm it, the Joint Chiefs fell back on their ultimate argument. An exclusive Soviet ABM might not change the actual strategic balance of power, they conceded, but it would give the Soviets a powerful psychological advantage. Walt Rostow, who kept the minutes, noted that Wheeler said that ''deterrence was not only technology, it was a state of mind.'' Our refusal to deploy an ABM would persuade the Russians that ''the U.S. was not willing to pay to maintain its present nuclear superiority.'' It was essential, Wheeler argued, for the United States, ''to maintain the kind of favorable power environment which helped us during the Cuban missile crisis.'' Air Force Chief of Staff Gen. John P. McConnell put the credibility argument in the most elemental terms, saying that he could not forget ''that we are dealing with the descendants of Genghis Khan. They only understand force.''

Lyndon Johnson followed the exchanges closely. When he asked Wheeler if the United States would be better off with Nike-X, assuming that the Russians did not increase their ICBMs in response, McNamara jumped in to say such a Russian move would be ''inconceivable.'' The secretary of defense again admitted that Johnson would "face a most difficult time politically and psychologically" if he did not match the Soviet ABM; but he burst out, "Their defenses are not worth a damn," adding that we should not follow their "error in deploying ABMs." Growing tired of the bickering, LBJ kept asking if there was any possible compromise, "any middle ground in this debate."

McNamara then came forward with two alternatives. First, he suggested a limited ABM system designed to meet four objectives—protect Minuteman silos, guard against a Chinese ICBM attack after 1975, ensure against the accidental launch of a hostile missile, and prevent a small Soviet blackmail attack. Such a thin ABM would not offer the false assurance of protecting the American people against an all-out Soviet strike. The second possibility would be to proceed with production of Nike-X components, some of which had lead times of over a year, while the State Department sounded out the Soviets on a possible freeze on all ABMs.

McNamara had presented these options to the president during their November meetings at LBJ's Texas ranch. The second alternative would permit spending $375 million in fiscal 1968 for ABM production but defer the actual deployment decision pending a diplomatic agreement with the Soviet Union. The president indicated his preference for this solution when he said he "wondered if the best opportunity for agreement among us would not be a decision to move ahead on a limited basis and to see what we can negotiate with the Soviet Union."[11]

There was no hint of the compromise solution to the ABM issue in the press conference following the meeting; the Joint Chiefs kept silent while McNamara and Johnson spoke only in generalities. Pressed by reporters, McNamara again took refuge in citing the decision to go ahead with Poseidon and Minuteman III, claiming that this guaranteed the viability of "assured destruction" for the foreseeable future by maintaining the American strategic advantage.[12]

At the president's request, National Security Adviser Walt Rostow polled leading Soviet experts in the State Department, as well as Donald Hornig, the presidential science adviser, on the likely Soviet response to American ABM deployment. They replied that they were certain the Russians would continue building up both their ABM and ICBM forces. Nicholas Katzenbach, the acting secretary of state in Dean Rusk's absence, and Llewellyn T. Thompson, American ambassador to the Soviet Union, urged a diplomatic initiative; pointing to the heavy costs of an escalating arms race, Thompson thought that there was "a good chance of negotiating an ABM, ICBM

freeze." Rostow concurred, but he warned LBJ that it would be difficult for the Soviets to accept "a freeze which appears to lock them
into permanent nuclear inferiority."[13]

Before he approved of a diplomatic approach to the Soviets,
Johnson sought final reassurance on the question of deferring Nike-
X deployment. On January 4, 1967, a half-dozen distinguished scientists—the former science advisers to Eisenhower and Kennedy and
the previous directors of research and engineering in the Pentagon—
met with Johnson at the White House. Just before this hurriedly
called meeting (one scientist was brought back from a Caribbean va-
cation by an air force jet), the group met in Donald Hornig's office
and discovered that they were all opposed to ABM deployment. They
then moved to the cabinet room to meet with the president, McNamara, and the Joint Chiefs of Staff. Asked a simple question about
Nike-X, "Would it work and should it be deployed?" the answer was
a unanimous no to a thick, anti-Soviet system and a qualified no to a
thin, anti-Chinese deployment.[14]

The judgment of this distinguished scientific panel confirmed
Johnson in his decision to delay final action on Nike-X while seeking an agreement with the Soviet Union to limit all ABM deployment, a solution that appealed to Johnson's highly developed political instincts. Releasing several hundred million dollars to begin
producing elements of Nike-X would satisfy hawks such as Sen.
Richard Russell and prevent the Republicans from charging Johnson
with endangering national security; at the same time, a diplomatic
initiative would please congressional doves who were critical of
Johnson's Vietnam policy. Above all, the compromise that McNamara had offered permitted Johnson to keep his options open. Instead of blocking the ABM, the president had merely deferred a deployment decision while he searched for a diplomatic solution. If
the Russians refused to compromise, then he could move ahead with
Nike-X well before the 1968 election. LBJ could hardly ask for
more.[15]

III

The diplomatic overture to the Soviet Union began in January
1967. Early in the month, Secretary of State Dean Rusk sounded out
Soviet ambassador Anatoly Dobrynin on the idea of the two superpowers entering into talks to limit ABM deployment. Dobrynin was
noncommittal, saying only that he would relay the American request to Moscow.[16]

The administration proceeded cautiously while waiting for the Kremlin's reply. In his annual State of the Union address on January 10, the president took note of the continuing Soviet ICBM buildup and the "limited antimissile defense" around Moscow. Without giving any details, Johnson stated his intention of consulting Congress about "the possibilities of international agreements bearing directly upon this problem." Privately, the State Department informed the NATO allies of Johnson's intention of announcing the plan to delay ABM deployment while seeking arms-control talks with the Soviets in his budget message in late January. At the same time, Rusk and McNamara persuaded LBJ not to make a public statement drafted by Walt Rostow that would explain the administration's ABM position to the American people; they thought it would be unwise to risk presidential involvement until it was clear whether or not the Soviets would cooperate.[17]

Ambassador Dobrynin informed the State Department on January 18 that his government was receptive to an American overture on arms control, provided such talks included offensive as well as defensive missiles. Although Rusk felt that the Soviet reply was "somewhat equivocal," he advised LBJ to proceed as planned since the United States was also interested in broadening arms talks to include ICBMs.[18]

On January 24 Johnson formally announced the decision to delay deployment of an American ABM while the United States sought to deal with this issue by direct negotiation with the Soviet Union. Faithful to the bargain McNamara had struck with the Joint Chiefs, the president asked Congress to appropriate $375 million in fiscal 1968 to fund components for Nike-X, suggesting that the ABM might be needed in the future for "the defense of our offensive weapon systems." LBJ made no specific references to MIRV in this budget message, but he did pledge to Congress his determination to "maintain our decisive strategic superiority" by deploying Poseidon submarine missiles and by improving the striking power of American ICBMs.[19]

Ambassador Llewellyn Thompson made the formal American approach to the Soviet Union on January 27, 1967. First, he presented Foreign Minister Andrei Gromyko with a personal message from President Johnson to Alexsei Kosygin, chairman of the council of ministers. The president stated that he believed it was "a matter of first priority" for the United States and the Soviet Union to enter into negotiations aimed at "reaching an understanding between us which would curb the strategic arms race." Citing the great pressure he faced from Congress and public opinion to match the Soviet ABM with both an American antimissile system and greater offensive weaponry, LBJ warned that the result could be only to escalate the nuclear arms race. Echoing McNamara's arguments, Johnson concluded, "We would thus have incurred on both sides colossal costs without substantially enhancing the security of our own people."[20]

In an accompanying oral statement, Thompson accepted the Soviet proviso that the talks cover offensive as well as defensive missiles. The American ambassador noted that each side had the ability "to inflict terrible destruction upon the other, even after having received an initial attack," making such an assault "not rational." He also made a concession on the key issue of verification, agreeing to unilateral means (presumably by reconnaissance satellite) "without requiring inspection on either party's territory." The point was crucial; American insistence on on-site inspection had blocked many earlier efforts at nuclear disarmament. But at the same time, Thompson made a veiled threat. Reminding the Russians of deliberate American restraint in the face of both the Soviet ICBM and ABM buildups, he said that unless there was rapid agreement on arms control, "we will be forced to increase our offensive forces and perhaps start to deploy an anti-ballistic missile system."[21]

The administration's hopes for prompt Soviet agreement to enter into discussions that eventually became known as SALT soon began to dim.* In early February, when Kosygin visited England, Dean Rusk urged the British prime minster to "prod" the Soviet leader, impressing upon him a sense of urgency for SALT. To the intense disappointment of American officials, however, Kosygin defended the Soviet ABM deployment, telling a London press conference on February 9 that it was not "a cause of the arms race" as Johnson claimed but was aimed simply at preventing "an attack involving the killing of enormous numbers of people." Although Soviet experts in the State Department had warned the secretary of the traditional Russian fondness for defensive systems, Rusk felt that Kosygin's remarks reflected "the naivete of the first look."[22]

Robert McNamara was appalled by the initial Soviet response. When Deputy Undersecretary of State Foy Kohler explained that Kosygin's statement was "perfectly predictable," McNamara agreed

---

*Robert Martin, a State Department official, coined the phrase in spring 1968 and despite opposition from ACDA and State Department colleagues, Martin's acronym became standard American usage at the insistence of the CIA, which already had adopted SALT in its filing system (see Newhouse, *Cold Dawn*, pp. 53–54).

but then expressed his doubt that "the Russians really understood what our offensive build-up would be like." To help educate them, he deliberately went public with MIRV.* In January he spoke candidly of the purpose of spending $400 million on Minuteman III, telling a Senate committee that it would cost the Soviets several times that amount to counter the American offensive innovation. At a press conference in mid-February, he likened MIRV to a bomber, saying it would enable each American missile to deliver several warheads to widely separated Soviet targets with no loss in accuracy. He also let the Kremlin know that American patience was not limitless; the United States might soon feel compelled to deploy its own ABM not to defend cities, which was impossible, but "for protection of our offensive weapons system, for possible protection of the Minuteman silos."[23]

Neither the threat of MIRV nor of an ABM designed to guarantee America's ability to achieve the "assured destruction" of the Soviet Union seemed to faze the Kremlin. On February 18 Ambassador Thompson found Kosygin noncommittal on SALT following his return from England; he promised to send a reply to Johnson's January message "soon." In an effort to encourage a favorable Soviet response, Thompson again stated that the United States was willing to rely on unilateral means of verification "without on-site inspections." In the expectation that Kosygin would urge broadening arms talks to include substantial reduction in nuclear weapons, Thompson was instructed to point out that anything more than a simple freeze might require on-site inspection. He was to tell Kosygin that the United States wanted to move one step at a time, claiming that it was necessary to "learn to walk before we can run."[24]

On February 28 Gromyko finally handed Thompson the long-awaited Soviet response. Kosygin did raise the issue of possible deep reductions in nuclear arms, but the rest of his message to President Johnson was surprisingly vague. The Soviet Union, he indicated, was willing to enter into arms negotiations but without specifying when and where the talks would take place. Submitting the text to the president, Rostow commented, "In short, they are willing to talk; but leave the ball in our court for the first move."

Johnson's advisers were in a quandary. McNamara asked Rostow to place this issue on the agenda for the next Tuesday lunch, where LBJ regularly discussed critical foreign policy issues with Rusk and

---

*The first public reference to MIRV appeared in the *Washington Post* on January 29, 1967 (see Newhouse, *Cold Dawn*, p. 9).

McNamara. One of Rostow's aides stressed that the Russians viewed ABM as a legitimate move to protect their people from attack and warned that they were unlikely to give up Galosh unless the United States reciprocated by reducing its ICBM advantage, a move he was certain the Pentagon would oppose.[25]

The president's primary concern was American public opinion. When Thompson had asked Gromyko if the Soviets planned to make their response public, the Soviet diplomat said no but then added, "what we [America] did was up to us." On March 2 LBJ opened a press conference with a simple and deceptive statement. Chairman Kosygin, he announced, had replied to the president's January message, voicing his "willingness" to enter into arms talks covering both offensive and defensive missiles. "This exchange of views," the president continued, "is expected to lead to further discussions of this subject in Moscow and with our allies." When reporters pressed for details, Johnson was forced to admit that the Soviets had not set a time for the talks, adding that he favored "the earliest possible date." LBJ admitted that he had proposed limiting only defensive weapons and that it was the Soviets who insisted on including offensive missiles. Further questioning compelled him to state that there was no sign that the Russians were halting work on Galosh and consequently the United States would continue with research and development of Nike-X. When a reporter asked if LBJ planned a summit meeting with Kosygin soon, the president curtly replied, "I see nothing in this that would indicate that now."[26]

Unable to convince skeptical journalists that the Russians were ready to engage in meaningful arms negotiations, the administration tried again to pin down the Kremlin. On March 17 Thompson presented Gromyko with a proposal calling for arms talks to begin in Moscow on April 12 at the working level. If the Russians agreed, Washington would send a team of experts to join with Thompson in exploring the outstanding issues with their Soviet counterparts. Anticipating a Soviet response stressing a reduction of weapons rather than a freeze, Thompson said his government wanted to search for "a way to 'level off' strategic offensive and defensive forces." If this first effort were successful, then they could move on to actual cuts in weaponry in future talks.

In the accompanying instructions to Thompson, Secretary Rusk explained that the United States had deliberately refrained from making a specific negotiating proposal. Commenting on the "reserved and suspicious attitude" of the Kremlin toward the question of the strategic balance of power, Rusk felt it would be better to take a flexible approach, one aimed simply at opening a dialogue aimed at a modest "leveling-off" arrangement. Then, the secretary concluded, even if they did not reach specific agreements, "the dialogue may assist each side to make better unilateral decisions and to hold down the arms race."[27]

Even this modest American approach proved abortive. As the April 12 date approached, Thompson received no response to his inquiry about Soviet willingness to meet with "appropriate senior representatives" from the United States. Finally in mid-May Johnson made one more effort to secure Russian cooperation. Noting the progress that American and Soviet negotiators were making on a draft nonproliferation treaty (NPT) designed to halt the spread of nuclear weapons to nations that did not yet possess them, he asked Kosygin "to respond positively" to the American proposal "to enter into serious discussions on the ABM and ICBM problem." Such a meeting, he told the Russian leader, would greatly ease "our task of persuading the non-nuclear powers to accept a non-proliferation treaty" by showing "our will and ability to begin to bring the nuclear arms race under better control."[28]

By early June Johnson had all but given up on the SALT initiative when events abroad suddenly provided a new opportunity. The Six Day War between Israel and its Arab neighbors led to urgent discussions with the Soviets over the Hot Line that stressed the need of the superpowers to cooperate in limiting world tension. The Chinese detonation of their first thermonuclear weapon in mid-June made both the Soviet Union and the United States more aware of their common interest in controlling the arms race. Finally, a Soviet announcement that Chairman Kosygin would come to New York to address the United Nations on the aftermath of the Six Day War led Johnson and Rusk to arrange for the two leaders to meet on hastily arranged neutral ground at Glassboro, New Jersey, in late June.[29]

Johnson and Kosygin had many issues to discuss at Glassboro, ranging from the Vietnam War to the still tense Middle East situation. But for the president, SALT took priority. When Walt Rostow suggested that the Soviets might have already made their decision about arms talks, Johnson jumped at the opportunity to seek that information from Kosygin in person. LBJ even allowed the State Department to brief him "to the gills" on the ABM issue.

In their first meeting on June 23 the president gave Kosygin what Dean Rusk termed "the Johnson treatment" on SALT. Repeating carefully prepared arguments about the need to halt the spiraling cost of the arms race, LBJ pressed Kosygin for a date and time to begin ABM negotiations. At one point he told the Soviet leader, "I'll have Robert McNamara in Moscow next Wednesday morning at nine o'clock. Will you see him?'' When Kosygin refused to commit himself, Johnson arranged for McNamara himself to make the case for limiting nuclear arms during the luncheon break.

It was to no avail. "When I have trouble sleeping,'' Kosygin told McNamara, "it's because of your offensive missiles, not your defensive missiles.'' The American leaders finally realized that Kosygin had come to Glassboro without any instructions on the ABM issue. Presumably, strong resistance within the Kremlin, especially from the military leaders who were bent on overcoming the American strategic advantage, had prevented the Soviet leadership from reaching a final decision on SALT. Reluctantly Johnson gave up his efforts to convince Kosygin when they met again on June 25; the final communique at the end of the Glassboro summit did not refer to the ABM issue and said simply that Rusk and Gromyko would continue to discuss outstanding issues during the current UN session in New York.[30]

Glassboro marked the end of Johnson's willingness to postpone action on Nike-X while seeking arms talks with the Soviets. Although Dean Rusk still believed that the Russians were on the verge of approving SALT, the president ordered Secretary of Defense McNamara to proceed with ABM deployment. Although he left the timing and manner of the public announcement to McNamara's discretion, Johnson felt he could no longer resist the growing public and political pressure to match the Soviet Galosh with the American Nike-X. He had made a series of concessions to the Soviets—including offensive as well as defensive missiles, accepting unilateral means of verification, beginning talks at the working level rather than at the top. He had received in return only a grudging acceptance of the general concept of negotiations accompanied by a deliberate refusal to set the date and place for the talks. Worried that the Soviet tactics reflected a desire to postpone negotiations until the USSR had achieved strategic parity and fearful of mounting Republican criticism, Johnson felt he had no choice but to go ahead with ABM deployment. He had accepted McNamara's compromise in good faith in December; six months later, it was time to protect himself politically by deploying Nike-X in conformity with the wishes of the Joint Chiefs of Staff.[31]

IV

Johnson's decision to go ahead with an American ABM placed Robert McNamara in a difficult position. Convinced that Nike-X could never achieve its goal of protecting the American people against an all-out Soviet attack, he came forth with a much more limited objective for a scaled-down ABM. When McNamara announced this development in a speech in mid-September, his own reservations made the president's decision appear to be, in the words of one historian, "irrational and certainly illogical."[32]

McNamara began the process of developing a new rationale for Nike-X in early July. He outlined his views to Morton Halperin, a Harvard political scientist to whom Assistant Secretary of Defense for International Security Affairs Paul Warnke had delegated working responsibility for arms-control efforts. Halperin listened approvingly as the secretary of defense outlined a speech that would reiterate his objections to a full-scale ABM but then was stunned when McNamara said he wanted to end with an announcement of American plans to deploy an ABM designed to protect against a Chinese ICBM attack. "Are you sure you want the last section in?" Halperin, who would draft the speech, asked. McNamara replied curtly, "Yes."

Halperin told Warnke, who saw McNamara later the same day and asked, "China bomb, Bob?" The secretary of defense looked down and muttered, "What else am I going to blame it on?" Actually, McNamara had been considering the possibility of deploying a thin Nike-X system against China since 1965 but had thought it unnecessary, believing that the vast American advantage in ICBMs would make a Chinese attack unthinkable. Still, he had retained the idea as a strategic alternative to a heavy, anti-Soviet ABM deployment. One attractive feature of a light ABM system would be to include defense of the Minuteman silos in the Midwest, an idea that Air Force Chief of Staff McConnell found attractive. By opting for the light ABM, McNamara could placate the Joint Chiefs, who would interpret it as a step toward the full, anti-Soviet system they wanted, and yet keep alive the possibility of reaching some form of arms-control arrangement with the Soviets. A final advantage in the anti-Chinese deployment was cost—a light ABM was budgeted at $5.5 billion, compared to a total expenditure as high as $40 billion for a full anti-Soviet system.[33]

On August 2 McNamara informed National Security adviser Walt Rostow of his plan for a Chinese-oriented ABM, asking only for presidential permission to delay the announcement until mid-September, when he was scheduled to speak to a group of newspaper editors in San Francisco. McNamara confessed he still had reservations about even a thin ABM, but if given the time to work out some "loose ends," he would support it publicly. Rostow advised Johnson to accept McNamara's proposal, pointing out that the thin system "would also have a capacity to protect to a significant degree our MINUTEMAN against Soviet attack." He thought it would be well for LBJ to manage the public relations aspect of the decision personally, with an eye to avoiding any sense of panic over the possibility of a Chinese attack in the future.[34]

McNamara sent Johnson a copy of the speech that Halperin had drafted on August 19, noting that the key point was the announcement at the end that the United States planned to go ahead with "a Chinese-oriented ABM deployment." The secretary of defense said he opposed a State Department suggestion that he stop short of calling for actual deployment of Nike-X and say only that the administration was contemplating such a system. McNamara felt that anything less than a full disclosure of Johnson's decision to go ahead with an ABM would allow critics to charge the president with deception; he would be receptive, however, to refinements the White House suggested for the final form of his San Francisco speech.

The president indicated his approval with a scrawled "L," but he did allow his advisers to suggest several key changes in the speech draft. Joseph Califano, worried about liberals in Congress opposed to high defense spending, wanted McNamara to make clear the much lower cost of the anti-China system. Spurgeon Keeny, Rostow's expert on arms control, wanted two major changes. First, he advised dropping a reference to a four-to-one American advantage in nuclear missiles; it could serve only as a red flag both to those in Congress opposed to heavy defense spending and to the Russians, who were likely to refuse to enter into arms talks in the face of such "tremendous military superiority." His second objection was to a reference to the light ABM serving the additional purpose of defending Minuteman silos. A proper defense of our ICBMs, he pointed out, would require many more short-range Sprint ABMs then were planned in the anti-Chinese deployment mode.[35]

When Rostow presented these issues to Johnson, he approved the suggested changes, along with a proposal by the arms-control agency to give the Soviets advance notice of the anti-Chinese ABM decision. Accordingly, Rusk instructed Ambassador Thompson to inform Foreign Minister Gromyko of McNamara's speech a week in advance, stressing the limited nature of the American ABM. "It will not provide, and will not attempt to provide," Thompson told Gromyko on September 12, "defense against [a] large-scale strategic missile attack of [the] kind which Soviet Union is capable of launching." There is no such thing as an ABM system that would protect against all-out nuclear assault, Thompson told Gromyko; he insisted that the American action should not be interpreted as an escalation of the arms race. Arguing that the only solution was meaningful arms control, Thompson concluded his statement by urging the Soviets to set the date for the opening of the long-deferred talks.[36]

McNamara also sought to prepare the American people for his forthcoming announcement. Three days before he was to deliver the San Francisco speech, he and his press spokesman met with a handful of distinguished journalists to explain that McNamara had not reversed his stand on the ABM. He still opposed a full Nike-X deployment designed to protect the American people from a Soviet attack; the thin, anti-Chinese system was one that he had been contemplating for a long time.

Despite this careful preparation, McNamara's San Francisco speech stunned both the audience of newspaper editors and the general public. The main body of the address was a sober critique of the ''mad momentum'' of nuclear escalation as the secretary of defense decried the ''action-reaction phenomenon that fuels an arms race.'' Yet after spending twenty minutes attacking the idea of adding new weaponry, he concluded by announcing the administration's decision to begin construction of a ''Chinese-oriented'' ABM system, Sentinel, before the end of 1967. Such a light ABM system, he added, would have two additional benefits—it would protect American cities against the accidental launch of an enemy missile and would provide ''further defense of our Minuteman sites against Soviet attack.''[37]

Rather than clearing up the confusion stemming from his San Francisco speech, McNamara simply muddied the waters further in an interview published in *Life* in late September. There he made explicit his belief that the proper American response to the Soviet ABM lay in the MIRV warheads on Poseidon and Minuteman III missiles. Citing the four-to-one American strategic advantage that the White House had told him to delete from his speech, the secretary of defense said the multiple independently targeted warheads aboard these new missiles would guarantee continued nuclear superiority for the United States in the foreseeable future. Admitting that the Soviet buildup of large ICBMs might soon enable the USSR to match the U.S. in megatonnage, McNamara declared, ''The number of targets each side can destroy is the important thing, not the total megatons each side can deliver.''

Aware that this assertion of American strategic superiority undercut his argument in behalf of Sentinel, McNamara told *Life* that in addition to protecting against a possible Chinese attack, the

American ABM would provide a "terminal defense" of our "underground Minutemen." Despite White House attempts to have this feature played down, for the sound reason that Sentinel called for Spartan missiles to be placed around major American cities rather than Sprint missiles near the Minuteman silos in the lightly populated Great Plains region, McNamara continued to insist that the American system included what the experts called "point defense" of the ICBMs. Warning Walt Rostow that the ensuing public debate meant that "we are operating in a glass bowl on this one," Spurgeon Keeny could only conclude, "Confusion reigns supreme."[38]

Despite the turmoil stirred up by McNamara's speech, several points were clear. Lyndon Johnson had decided that he could no longer wait for the Soviets to respond to the SALT initiative even though he still hoped that arms talks could be held. McNamara had offered him an attractive alternative. By focusing on China rather than on the Soviet Union, McNamara left open the possibility of reaching agreement with the Russian leaders on keeping ABM deployment at a low level in both countries. At the same time, the new Sentinel system promised to pay dividends at home; it pleased both the doves and the hawks, allowing each group to find in the light ABM system the advantages they wanted. ABM opponents were happy to avoid the heavy expenditures of a thick system; the Joint Chiefs and other supporters believed that Sentinel was but the first step toward their true objective of protecting the American people against a Soviet first strike.

Most important from Johnson's standpoint, Sentinel protected him from a Republican attempt to exploit the ABM issue for partisan advantage in an election year. In February the Republican National Committee had begun distributing a fifty-five-page booklet on the ABM issue subtitled, "Is LBJ Right?" Strange as McNamara's San Francisco speech may have seemed to many listeners, it had the effect of removing the ABM question from the 1968 campaign. As historian Ernest J. Yanarella comments, McNamara's Chinese-oriented Sentinel could be "more aptly described as a 'Republican-oriented' ABM system."[39]

V

The Sentinel decision did not end the American quest for an arms-control agreement with the Soviet Union, but it did require a major rethinking of the American goal in such negotiations. As a result of McNamara's speech, the Johnson administration began a reconsideration of its SALT negotiating proposal that involved intensive bureaucratic maneuvering in which the Joint Chiefs of Staff again played a key role.

The Arms Control and Disarmament Agency developed the initial American SALT proposal in the early months of 1967. Adrian Fisher, ACDA deputy director, set forth the basic concept of a freeze agreement that would cover both ABMs and ICBMs as well as shorter-range land missiles. Instead of seeking absolute strategic symmetry, the ACDA proposed achieving nuclear stability by letting each side retain its current area of superiority. Such an arrangement would give the Soviets an advantage in ABMs and intermediate- and medium-range ballistic missiles that would be offset by corresponding American leads in the number of ICBMs and Polaris-type submarine missiles. In effect, the fact that the Soviets alone would have an ABM system would be offset by larger numbers of American offensive missiles capable of reaching the Soviet Union.

The most significant feature of the ACDA proposal was what it did not include. The draft agreement, which was to rely exclusively on national means of verification, deliberately excluded any attempt to ban the modification or improvement of existing missile forces. Specifically, this omission meant that the United States would be able to continue expanding the number of warheads aimed at Soviet targets, thus neutralizing the Galosh and, if upgraded, the Tallinn ABM systems. The ACDA proposal singled out Poseidon for special treatment, urging that American negotiators resist an expected Soviet proposal to ban replacing Polaris submarines with ones having MIRV capability. Poseidon, ACDA argued, would serve as a ''major hedge'' against either unforeseen uncertainties or ''the possibility that an ABM freeze might be terminated.''[40]

Most surprising was the willingness of the advocates of arms control to exempt MIRV from their effort to limit the arms race. A major factor was a realization that a ban on MIRV simply could not be verified without on-site inspection, a condition the Soviets would never accept. Equally important was the need for the ACDA to win the support of the Joint Chiefs. The military leaders were to be asked to give up their preference for on-site inspection as well as to concede an exclusive Soviet ABM; at the very least, the JCS was bound to insist on MIRV to ensure continued American strategic superiority. Scientists found MIRV to be a simple and effective weapons system, ''technically sweet'' in comparison with the cumbersome and dubious ABM technology, thus making it much easier for the administration to base future American security on Minuteman III and

Poseidon. The fact that the public debate had already begun to center on ABM while MIRV remained cloaked in secrecy was a final consideration shaping the nature of the American SALT proposal.[41]

On March 14, 1967, Adrian Fisher presented the ACDA proposal to the Committee of Principals, the high-level administration group charged with overseeing arms-control policy. The committee, which consisted of Rusk, McNamara, Rostow, CIA director Richard Helms, ACDA director William Foster, and Gen. Earle Wheeler, chairman of the Joint Chiefs of Staff, gave the proposal a cool reception. Even Rusk, though strongly supportive of arms control, thought it conceded too much to the Soviets at the outset, especially by not demanding on-site inspection. Helms agreed, saying that he felt "queasy" about relying exclusively on national means of verification.

It was Wheeler, however, who expressed the strongest objections to the SALT proposal. Speaking for a unanimous JCS, he opposed doing anything to jeopardize the current American strategic advantage over the Soviet Union. The Joint Chiefs insisted that any agreement be in the form of a treaty requiring a two-thirds vote of the Senate rather than the kind of informal agreement favored by ACDA. He expressed the traditional JCS preference for on-site inspection although he did agree that it was possible to rely on reconnaissance satellites to verify certain categories of weapons, such as ICBM silos. His strongest objection, however, was to allowing the Soviets to have an exclusive ABM system; the JCS were unlikely to approve a SALT arrangement that did not permit the United States its own antimissile deployment.[42]

Despite the Soviet refusal to enter into the SALT process at Glassboro, the Johnson administration decided to make another effort to win over the JCS in September 1967. The decision to deploy Sentinel overcame one key objection and at the same time necessitated a revision of the original ACDA proposal to allow for an American ABM system. A working group of arms-control experts from both State and Defense began working out a compromise position based on two assumptions: an expected Soviet refusal to accept on-site inspection and the deployment of Sentinel.

There were two key features in the new American SALT proposal. The first was to permit each side to build a maximum of 1,000 ABM launchers. This high number would cover both Galosh and Tallinn on the Soviet side while permitting the United States to go ahead with some 600 Spartan and Sprint missiles for the Sentinel system. The expectation was that in return for this concession, the

Joint Chiefs would agree to give up their demand for on-site inspection.

The other major aspect was a freeze on offensive missiles. The Soviets would be permitted to complete an estimated 400 ICBMs under construction, along with three additional missile-launching submarines, but they would still lag behind the United States slightly in ICBMs, 925 to 1,054, and substantially in SLBMs, with about 150 compared to 656 Polaris missiles. Figuring in approximately 700 Soviet medium- and intermediate-range ballistic land-based missiles (the United States had none in this category), the result would be rough strategic parity, with each side possessing between 1,700 and 1,800 launchers.

The new proposal would continue to exclude MIRV from the SALT process, thereby offering the United States a way to maintain its strategic superiority despite accepting equality in the overall number of missiles. Responding to JCS pressure, McNamara dropped a proposal to reduce the American ICBM advantage in return for corresponding Soviet cuts in shorter-range missiles. Paul Nitze, an ardent cold warrior who had become deputy secretary for defense in summer 1967, suggested the United States should be allowed more missiles to offset the heavier megatonnage of the Soviet warheads. McNamara rejected this idea, claiming that MIRV and the greater accuracy of American missiles more than balanced the superior Soviet throw weight.[43]

Continued refusal by the Kremlin to enter into SALT made it unnecessary for the Johnson administration to reach final agreement on a negotiating position. The changes made in September 1967, particularly the provision allowing for equality in ABM systems, increased the likelihood that the Joint Chiefs would no longer be adamantly opposed to an arms-control agreement. Yet the resignation of Robert McNamara as secretary of defense, announced in fall 1967, made the outlook for SALT much dimmer. McNamara had used his authority to keep the Joint Chiefs from disrupting the arms-control process; his successor, Clark Clifford, lacked McNamara's personal commitment to arms control and was fully engaged with Vietnam issues. Any further progress on the American side would now rest with Dean Rusk, a man who wanted to curb the arms race but whose reticence made him an unlikely leader for such a difficult cause.[44]

Despite his preoccupation with Vietnam, President Johnson seemed most determined to keep the hopes for arms control alive in 1968. On January 22 he once again sent a personal message to Chairman Kosygin urging a prompt beginning of strategic-arms negotiations. Linking SALT to the progress being made on a nonproliferation treaty, the president said the United States and the Soviet Union needed to prove their good faith in asking other countries to limit nuclear weapons. As it was, both sides were spending "enormous resources" that resulted in an "ever-widening spiral of armament" that did not provide either nation with "any greater security." Ambassador Thompson was told to make it clear to the Soviets in an accompanying oral statement that Johnson was not seeking "military advantage." "On the contrary," Thompson's instructions read, "he seeks a solution through a limitation on arms based upon full appreciation by each side of the national interests and security of the other."[45]

Despite a perfunctory reply from Kosygin, Johnson refused to give up his quest for SALT. At the end of a National Security Council (NSC) meeting in late February, he asked Dean Rusk to consider taking additional steps to get arms-control talks started. The State Department sounded out the Soviets through diplomatic channels; by early April, conversations with Ambassador Dobrynin in Washington and with Foreign Minister Gromyko in Moscow suggested that a specific American negotiating proposal would help the Russians leaders overcome internal resistance to SALT.[46]

Accordingly, on April 3 Rusk proposed sending a new message to the Kremlin setting forth a detailed American proposal. The draft cable opened with a statement of two principles on which the talks would be based. First, any agreement would have to cover offensive and defensive weapons and "must provide balanced strategic postures acceptable to both sides." The second principle restated McNamara's axiom of mutual assured destruction. Claiming it would be futile to try to define "superiority" or "parity" in nuclear weapons, the United States sought an agreement in which "both sides should be confident of a reasonable second-strike deterrent force." In effect, the Johnson administration was willing to give up traditional American assertions of nuclear superiority; it now claimed that true security lay in the ability of each superpower to "inflict unacceptable damage" on the other.

The draft message then outlined a specific American proposal that had emerged in February as the result of intensive bargaining among ACDA, the State Department, and the Pentagon. It differed from the September 1967 draft proposal in one vital respect—it dropped submarine-based missiles such as the Polaris from the agreement on the grounds that such weapons required more than unilateral inspection. Thus the new terms were limited to land-based missiles. The United States proposed a freeze on all ICBMs and IRBMs, permitting the Soviets to complete those already under construction; the result would be virtual equality in this vital offensive category. In regard to the ABM, the American proposal called for an equal but unspecified number of launchers for both nations, allowing the Russians to have Galosh and Tallinn and leaving the United States free to complete the Sentinel anti-Chinese system. Finally, the United States would be willing to rely exclusively on national means of verification.[47]

Rusk, supported by Soviet expert Charles (Chip) Bohlen, pushed hard for this new, specific approach to SALT, but they met resistance from the two extremes within the bureaucracy. ACDA director William Foster was opposed to sending the Russians this specific proposal on the grounds that it was too favorable to the American position. The Kremlin, he argued, was bound to reject a plan that neither banned MIRVs nor covered submarine-launched missiles, a category in which the U.S. had a substantial advantage. Foster suggested simply outlining the two principles in an effort to secure Soviet agreement to enter into talks.

Gen. Earle Wheeler, speaking for a united Joint Chiefs of Staff, was even more adamantly opposed, but for the opposite reason; he objected to any agreement in which the United States surrendered either its qualitative or quantitative nuclear superiority. The JCS wanted to preserve the right to build more ICBMs as well as to place multiple warheads on those already deployed. The Joint Chiefs also continued to resist the idea of relying solely on national means of verification although they had already conceded that the CIA had "a high degree of confidence" in the ability of American satellites to detect land-based ABM and ICBM installations. Paul Warnke, who along with Morton Halperin and Alain Enthoven had convinced Clark Clifford that the draft plan did not endanger national security, voiced his frustrations with the JCS to the new secretary of defense. Wheeler's insistence on preserving an American nuclear advantage doomed any reasonable proposal for arms control. "We must face the fact," Warnke told Clifford, "that no agreement with the Soviet Union can be expected to maintain U.S. superiority."[48]

Once again Johnson had to decide whether to override the Joint Chiefs of Staff. Rusk had won over Foster to the idea of making a specific proposal to the Soviets, but Clifford had not been able to overcome the opposition of the Joint Chiefs to anything more than a message outlining basic principles. In presenting the issues to the president, Walt Rostow sided with Rusk and Clifford, suggesting that a specific proposal might well persuade the Russians that our insistence on SALT reflected a genuine desire to limit the arms race. Rusk was even more direct, rebutting Wheeler's claim that the negotiating proposal involved "extreme risks" for American security. Pointing out that the Soviets had built nearly 400 ICBMs in 1967 and now had nearly as many as the United States, Rusk argued that SALT, by freezing land-based offensive missiles, would guard against a future Soviet advantage.

Despite his personal desire for early negotiations, the president sided with the Joint Chiefs. On May 2 he sent a long message to Kosygin dealing with both the Middle East and SALT. Once more he stressed the need for prompt action to halt the spiraling arms race, referring obliquely to MIRV by noting that "technical" considerations were making it increasingly "difficult" to reach agreement. He then linked SALT to the nuclear nonproliferation treaty, urging the Soviets to agree to a joint announcement during current UN discussions of the NPT of a specific date for arms-control talks to begin.[49]

Johnson's refusal to present the Soviets with a specific American negotiating proposal or even with a broad statement of principles reflected his unwillingness to challenge the authority of the Joint Chiefs. He was now a lame-duck president, having announced on March 31 his decision not to seek reelection, and he still needed the full support of the JCS as he tried to wind down the Vietnam War. With McNamara gone, neither Rusk nor Clifford had the ability or the inclination to take on the Joint Chiefs in an all-out confrontation. Until the military leaders could be persuaded that American security could be better served by the limitation rather than the escalation of the arms race, there was little chance for SALT even if the Soviets finally came to the bargaining table.

VI

The long-awaited diplomatic breakthrough on SALT came quickly in summer 1968. On June 21 Kosygin finally responded to Johnson's January and May messages. Although the Russian leader still did not set a time and place for SALT, he said he hoped it would soon be possible "more concretely to exchange views." The next day LBJ proposed that the United States and the Soviets should announce jointly their intention of entering into strategic talks at the forthcoming signing of the nonproliferation treaty. On June 27 Kosygin agreed to this procedure, proposing language that spoke of talks dealing with the "limitation and reduction of both offensive strategic nuclear delivery systems and systems of defense against ballistic missiles."[50]

On July 1 Johnson signed the nonproliferation treaty in an elaborate ceremony in the East Room of the White House. Then he made the formal announcement of SALT, following the wording suggested by Kosygin. These negotiations, he added, "will not be easy," but he pledged that the United States would make every effort to reach "the day when the world moves out of the night of war into the light of sanity and security."[51]

With the opening of talks imminent, the question of the position of the Joint Chiefs on SALT became a crucial concern for the Johnson administration. A Pentagon team headed by Morton Halperin worked hard over the Fourth of July holiday preparing a revised draft of the American SALT proposal for a meeting of the Committee of Principals scheduled for July 8. In preparing for this session, Halperin and Warnke gave Clifford detailed advice on how to approach the JCS. Rather than seeking quick agreement on a negotiating position, they urged Clifford to give the Joint Chiefs at least a month to study and reflect on the issues at stake in order to avoid "a premature hardening of positions in opposition to the proposal." Clifford approved of these tactics, agreeing to consult with General Wheeler in a leisurely fashion to prevent the JCS from taking a position that was "premature and unproductive."[52]

The Halperin draft offered a cautious approach to the complex issue of arms control—one designed above all else to win the approval of the JCS. It included a freeze on ICBMs, with the Soviets permitted to complete any missiles under construction as of August 1, 1968, within a ceiling of 1,100. The United States had 1,054 ICBMs and was not planning any increase; the Soviets had 900 completed and 150 more under construction. The American proposal also called for a freeze on missile-launching submarines, maintaining a substantial American advantage, 656 Polaris/Poseidon missiles compared to an estimated 300 to 350 Soviet SLBMs. This U.S. advantage would be balanced by allowing the Russians to keep but not increase their force of some 700 IRBMs.

In regard to ABMs, the negotiating position called for each side to have a set and equal number, probably somewhere between 100 and 1,000 apiece. The Soviet Galosh system consisted of 65 launchers, and their Tallinn network, possibly capable of being upgraded to ABM status, added another 400 to 600. The United States planned to deploy 672 launchers for the Chinese-oriented Sentinel; a top limit of 1,000 would allow for a hard point defense of the Minuteman silos. The American draft proposal exempted bombers from the agreement and specifically prohibited each side from deploying mobile land-missiles that could not be detected by national means of verification. Finally, the draft explicitly excluded MIRV by ruling out any restrictions on technological improvements to missiles already deployed.[53]

The draft proposal was a clear attempt to maintain American nuclear superiority in the face of a determined Soviet arms buildup. A Pentagon analysis concluded that without SALT, by the mid-1970s the Soviets would have balanced the U.S. advantage in missile-launching submarines and would have nearly 1,500 ICBMs. If the Soviets accepted the American proposal, they would be limited to 1,725 warheads by the mid-1970s compared to an American strategic force that with MIRV would be capable of delivering 8,573 nuclear warheads on Soviet targets. It was hard to see how the Joint Chiefs could object to an arms-control agreement that allowed them to continue building an American ABM, maintained numerical equality in the number of missile launchers, and ensured a five to one advantage in deliverable warheads (see Table 8.1).[54]

Despite the clear strategic advantage inherent in the American proposal, the Committee of Principals was reluctant to give its approval when it met on July 8. Rusk opened the meeting by stressing President Johnson's desire to have a simple, clear negotiating proposal to offer the Soviets. Having spent eighteen months jockeying to get the Russian leaders to the bargaining table, LBJ wanted no further delays in reaching agreement on the American position. Yet the Pentagon representatives expressed reservations on several issues. Clifford opposed offering a detailed proposal that the Soviets would see as a chance to force further concessions; he favored a more general statement of principles designed to test Russian sincerity. Paul Nitze worried that a simple freeze of ICBMs would leave the Russians with a great advantage in throw weight since their warheads were so much bigger.

The most heated debate came over the issue of verification. Chairman Wheeler of the JCS objected to relying solely on national means, but ACDA director Foster, Undersecretary of State Chip Bohlen, and Dean Rusk pointed out that from the beginning the United States had assured the Russians that it was ready to reach agreements based on national means of verification. With McNamara gone, it fell to Rusk to become the champion of arms control. He did so with surprising force, telling the military leaders that the

TABLE 8.1. Comparison of Nuclear Warheads under SALT Proposal

Warheads	United States	Soviet Union
ICBMs	1,975	1,100
SLBMs	3,968	325
Bombs	2,630	300
Total	8,573	1,725

cost of nuclear weapons was becoming ''ruinous'' and that it was ''imperative'' to bring the arms race under control. Atomic Energy Commission (AEC) chairman Glenn Seaborg finally suggested a compromise—the United States would try to get the Soviets to agree to some form of on-site inspection but would accept national means of verification as a fallback position. The committee then agreed to allow a working group of deputies, headed by Adrian Fisher of ACDA, to attempt to hammer out an acceptable negotiating proposal.[55]

Rusk's fervent advocacy and the knowledge that the president put a high priority on reaching internal agreement led to a quick resolution of the debate over the American SALT position. The working group submitted a slightly modified draft to the full Committee of Principals on July 31; a week later the committee sent it to the White House for presidential approval. Meanwhile Clifford consulted with the Joint Chiefs while Halperin gradually convinced representatives of each of the armed services that the SALT proposal did not threaten any of their interests. Finally Clifford was able to submit a draft presidential memorandum to LBJ with the unanimous consent of the Joint Chiefs. It necessitated only one minor change in the ABM section of the American SALT proposal to which Johnson gave his formal approval on August 27.[56]

This negotiating document embodied the essence of the original Halperin draft of July 4. It provided for a freeze on ICBMs, with the ceiling raised from 1,100 to 1,200, and on SLBMs, including those under construction; ABMs were to be limited to an unspecified but equal number on each side. On the inspection issue, the Pentagon gave way and accepted national means of verification, but at the same time MIRV was specifically exempted from any limitation.[57]

In essence, the effort to win over the JCS by making certain that the American negotiating proposal satisfied their major concerns ensured final agreement on a document that had little chance of winning Soviet acceptance. As the product of a bureaucratic compromise, the Johnson administration's SALT proposal virtually guaranteed a continuing American nuclear advantage for the indefinite future. The key lay in the refusal to negotiate on MIRV. Although Morton Halperin and the ACDA wanted the Pentagon to delay tests of both Poseidon and Minuteman III planned for mid-August, the Joint Chiefs refused. When Ambassador Dobrynin asked about MIRV tests on August 15, Dean Rusk explained that they had been planned for a long time and the fact that they were taking place "was not connected in any way with the timing of discussions." Yet as Glenn Seaborg noted, "an ominous limitation" of the American SALT proposal was its failure to include MIRV. "Thus," he wrote, "while the number of missile launchers might be held steady, the number of warheads could increase significantly." In effect, the United States was willing to concede apparent numerical equality in missiles with the Soviet Union, confident that MIRV provided a way to ensure continued strategic superiority.[58]

VII

While the United States was putting the finishing touches on its SALT proposal, the Soviet Union seemed ready to make the final commitment to arms-control negotiations. On July 25 Kosygin sent LBJ a message proposing that SALT begin in Geneva in "a month to a month and a half." The president's advisers favored a later date out of a desire not to conflict with the Democratic convention in late August, and Johnson himself preferred to travel to the Soviet Union. Nevertheless, on July 31 Rusk handed Ambassador Dobrynin a response in which LBJ informed Kosygin that the United States was ready to meet in Geneva "at the level of Chiefs of Government, Foreign Ministers, or heads of special delegations." The president confirmed his eagerness to halt the escalating arms race by telling reporters on July 31 that he expected to reveal the place and date for SALT "in a matter of a reasonably short time." Stressing the importance of the issue, he said that although he could not speak, for the Russians, "our side is ready, willing and waiting."[59]

The waiting came to an end on Monday evening, August 19, when Ambassador Dobrynin interrupted a party Dean Rusk was holding on board the *Honey Fitz*, the presidential yacht. He handed the secretary of state a handwritten message with the text of a proposed public announcement stating that President Johnson would visit the Soviet Union during the first ten days of October "for the exchange of opinions with the leading figures of the USSR on the questions of mutual interest.'' Rusk quickly arranged for the message to be typed and sent to LBJ, who was returning from a Detroit speaking engagement on board Air Force One. Rostow and Rusk met with Johnson in his White House bedroom later that evening to draft the American letter of acceptance. They alerted Press Secretary George Christian of the plan to make the formal SALT announcement on Wednesday morning, August 21.[60]

At the regular Tuesday lunch on August 20, the president poured a glass of sherry for each of the advisers and said, ''Gentlemen, let us drink to a summit conference in the Soviet Union in October.'' ''He was as excited as I had ever seen him,'' Clifford commented. Although they spent a few minutes discussing the forthcoming arms-control negotiations, most of the session was devoted to a consideration of possible Soviet action against Czechoslovakia, where Alexander Dubcek had been carrying out liberal reforms that threatened to undermine the Soviet domination of Eastern Europe. Though opinion was divided on what the Soviets were likely to do, none of the participants thought that the Kremlin would take overt action that would doom the upcoming SALT negotiations.[61]

The message that Ambassador Dobrynin then delivered personally to President Johnson at the White House later that same Tuesday came as a shock. Reading from a longhand text, Dobrynin announced that the Soviet Union had just begun an invasion of Czechoslovakia in order to defend the ''vital interests'' of the Soviet Union. This action, he added, should not in any way ''harm the Soviet-American relations to the development of which the Soviet Government as before attaches great importance.''

While Dobrynin went to Rostow's office in the White House basement to have this message typed, the president convened an emergency meeting of the National Security Council to decide on the American response. After Rusk admitted that the Soviet action had caught him by surprise, Johnson spoke wistfully of the possibility of still going ahead with SALT. But when he mentioned the danger of appearing to condone Soviet aggression, his advisers agreed that it was impossible for the United States to conduct SALT as scheduled. Joint Chiefs Chairman Wheeler called the Soviet action ''an insult to the United States''; Johnson agreed and instructed Rusk to deliver the American reply to Dobrynin that evening. The secretary of state was to express American astonishment at the invasion of Czechoslovakia and inform the ambassador that the United States felt this was not ''the opportune time'' to announce the plans for SALT and was therefore calling off the next day's scheduled public statement.[62]

The next morning UN ambassador George Ball came to the White House as Press Secretary George Christian read a relatively mild statement taking exception to the Soviet invasion of Czechoslovakia, instead of the planned SALT announcement. Then Johnson told Ball to give the Russians hell at the United Nations. Ball thought Johnson was handling a difficult situation quite well, describing him as in a mood of "sardonic detachment." Other observers believed that Johnson had been devastated by the unexpected Soviet move. Clark Clifford said LBJ felt Kosygin had "double-crossed him." The president had been "as excited" about SALT "as anybody I ever saw," Clifford later recalled, but now he was "terribly disappointed." Rusk later told Dobrynin that the Czech invasion was "just like throwing a dead fish in the face of the President."[63]

No one could explain the Soviet behavior satisfactorily. When pressed, Dobrynin argued that the issues of Czechoslovakia and SALT were on separate tracks in the Kremlin and thus the Russian leaders had failed to understand that Americans would see them as intertwined. Rostow wondered if the Soviets had been too devious, hoping that by offering Johnson what he seemed to prize above all else, the opening of SALT, they could gain American acceptance of their action in Czechoslovakia.[64]

It is hard to believe that the Soviet leaders did not know that the use of force against Czechoslovakia was bound to doom SALT. They may not have been aware of just how much importance LBJ had placed on limiting the arms race as the final achievement of his administration, but they must have known that he could not appear to be giving the seal of approval to Soviet aggression. Perhaps they knew or suspected that the American negotiating proposal would simply prolong indefinitely the short end of the nuclear ratio that they had labored under since the end of World War II. Their action in Czechoslovakia indicates at the very least that they felt they had greater confidence in their own ability to redress the strategic balance by a continuing arms buildup than by entering into strategic arms limitation talks with the United States.

VIII

Incredibly, Johnson refused to give up on the possibility of beginning the SALT process before he left office. Throughout fall 1968, despite the continuing presence of Soviet troops in Czechoslovakia, he kept asking his advisers about the wisdom of meeting with the Russian leaders at least to begin serious arms-control negotiations. Driven both by the need for one final, constructive achievement and by a genuine desire to contain the nuclear arms race, LBJ met with inevitable failure in this quixotic effort.

The first attempt to revive SALT came in early September. Encouraged by a conversation between Ambassadors Thompson and Dobrynin in late August, Johnson asked the National Security Council on September 4 whether he should approve low-level talks on arms control. Thompson voiced his belief that ''the Soviets will be eager to reach agreement on something,'' and the State Department prepared a draft cable sounding out the NATO countries on such a move. This initiative quickly died, however. Johnson decided against a low-level approach to SALT, telling Rostow that SALT could be conducted only at the summit and that there was too much political risk in such a meeting just then. Opposition from the Joint Chiefs ended any chance for talks at any level. General Wheeler informed Clifford on September 10 that the military leaders believed any attempt to begin SALT ''could be interpreted as approval of Soviet aggression in Czechoslovakia and would be divisive of NATO at a critical time.''[65]

Although the Soviets again signaled their willingness to begin SALT in early October, Johnson decided to avoid any further steps until after the presidential election. Richard Nixon's victory then added a new complication—any negotiation could be viewed only as beginning a process that the next administration would bring to a culmination. Further progress on SALT would thus require the approval of the president-elect as well as of the Joint Chiefs of Staff.

Johnson, however, still did not give up his search for at least a symbolic start to SALT. In early November he told Clifford he still dreamed of visiting the Soviet Union on behalf of SALT. Later in the month, after a successful meeting with Nixon over the transition, the president canvassed his advisers, along with prominent senators, on the wisdom of seeking a meeting with Kosygin to agree on the principles to guide future arms negotiations. Rusk was dubious, but both Rostow and Clifford favored going ahead. Rostow felt Nixon would be favorably inclined since it would ''virtually guarantee Soviet restraint on Berlin and Eastern Europe in the first phase of his Administration.'' Clifford saw virtue in avoiding a long delay in SALT while the new administration was getting itself organized. ''If we get the talks started,'' he said, then Nixon will ''have to continue it. We need the impetus of a start.''[66]

The president-elect feared precisely this kind of entrapment and asked Robert Murphy, a veteran diplomat, to consult with the Johnson administration on SALT. When LBJ proposed that Murphy accompany him to a summit, the Republican adviser commented disparagingly, "The thought of another Glassboro would be unappealing." When Murphy finally agreed to give the president-elect his qualified approval, LBJ said he did not want "to commit Mr. Nixon," but "we do want him to know of it."[67]

In late November the Johnson administration made a formal proposal to the Soviets for a summit meeting on SALT in Geneva on December 16 and 17. The plan was to reach "agreement on principles to guide missile talks," with the United States prepared to accept two broad propositions the Soviets had offered in early October. When there was no immediate response from the Kremlin, Rusk instructed Ambassador Thompson on December 9 to assure the Soviets of American seriousness: "I wish to emphasize that there is no interest here in a meeting merely for its own sake or for cosmetic purposes at the end of an administration." Given the momentum of weapons technology, Rusk asserted, "the missile race may not wait for another protracted period."[68]

Two days later the Soviets indicated to Thompson that there would be no summit meeting on SALT. Nixon and his newly designated national security adviser, Henry Kissinger, decided that they wanted to undertake a complete review of American policy before embarking on SALT. It was not simply that they resented being forced to continue policies begun by Johnson; they wanted to forge an entirely new approach to the Soviet Union, one that would link arms control with other issues such as Vietnam in order to achieve an overall lessening of Cold War tension. Détente, as the Nixon-Kissinger policy would soon become known, ruled out any chance for beginning SALT during the Johnson presidency.

In characteristically indirect fashion, Nixon avoided any public statement on SALT, instead instructing Kissinger to inform the Kremlin that the new administration would not honor any commitments made at a summit attended by Johnson. Caught in the middle, the Soviets sought a graceful way out of a meeting they had originally favored. Dobrynin informed Ambassador Thompson on December 11 that "if the President decided not to go ahead with the meeting," that would be understood in Moscow and there would be no hard feelings." When LBJ read this cable, he still refused to give up, scrawling on it, "I'm ready—are they?" Rostow finally convinced him that there was nothing more he could do on SALT, commenting that "it may also be a decision we shall regret more than any other in the years ahead." A saddened Johnson agreed, circling the words "we shall regret" and writing, "I agree."[69]

IX

Clifford was right. It was nearly a year later, November 1969, before the new administration finally opened strategic arms limitation talks with the Soviet Union. "I have always felt that year could have been spent in the best interests of the safety of this planet and all the people who inhabit it," Lyndon Johnson wrote in his memoirs. His closest advisers agreed. Dean Rusk, referring to the rapid deployment of MIRV, claimed that by the time SALT began in late 1969, "the horses had cleared the stable." Rostow expressed the same regret over the delay, calling it "a terrible year to lose."[70]

These feelings of a lost opportunity are understandable but unrealistic: Little was lost between 1968 and 1969 in terms of meaningful arms control. SALT I, finally completed in spring 1972, followed the original American negotiating proposal quite closely, providing for a limit of 200 ABMs for each side and for a five-year freeze on offensive missiles. Most important, like the plan approved by the JCS in August 1968, MIRV was specifically excluded, thereby ensuring an American strategic advantage for a few more years.

John Newhouse, who has written the most thorough study of SALT, argues that the Soviet invasion of Czechoslovakia, by delaying arms talks for a year, "may have erased whatever chance there was of blocking MIRV deployment." Yet by August 1968 the United States had already passed the point of no return on MIRV. The Joint Chiefs agreed to SALT in the first place only because MIRV was not included. Originally embraced by Robert McNamara as a convenient way to resist the army's demands for an American ABM, MIRV was, in the words of Ted Greenwood, "just too good. . . . It contributed to the solution of too many political problems of the Administration and the civilian authorities in the Pentagon," he contends. MIRV justified not only restraint on ABM deployment but offered a way to keep the air force from insisting on expanding the number of ICBMs to match the Russian buildup. It even allowed the Joint Chiefs to accept national means of verification for SALT; with on-site inspection ruled out, the Soviets could not demand that MIRV be included in the final SALT agreements.[71]

Glenn Seaborg offers one final regret. If only Lyndon Johnson had played a more active role in developing the original American

SALT proposal, Seaborg argues, then perhaps he could have exerted "a predominant influence" in blocking MIRV's development. It is difficult to see how LBJ could have persuaded McNamara and the Joint Chiefs to give up their dependence on MIRV, however, when both men together were unable to prevent the JCS from deploying an American ABM. The only time MIRV might have been halted was in 1967, before it had become public knowledge and before it had been tested. Given Johnson's predicament in Vietnam and his dependency on the Joint Chiefs, it is inconceivable that he would have even considered challenging them on a technological development that promised to increase American strategic forces at minimum cost.[72]

From the outset, SALT proved to be a flawed attempt at genuine control of the nuclear arms race. Triggered by concern over the Soviet ABM, it focused on the wrong issue all along. The ABM, as most scientists admitted, had little chance of altering the nature of the strategic balance. MIRV was the truly revolutionary form of technological advance that led to what Robert McNamara so aptly described as the "mad momentum" of the nuclear arms race. It was not the Soviet invasion of Czechoslovakia in August 1968 that doomed a meaningful effort at arms control; it was the successful testing of Poseidon and Minuteman III earlier that same month that ensured the continuation of the nuclear madness for at least two more decades.

Notes

1. B. Bruce-Briggs, *The Shield of Faith: A Chronicle of Strategic Defense from Zeppelins to Star Wars* (New York: Simon and Schuster, 1988), p. 282; John Prados, *Keepers of the Keys: A History of the National Security Council from Truman to Bush* (New York: William Morrow, 1991), pp. 190–91.

2. Dean Rusk, as told to Richard Rusk, *As I Saw It*, ed. Daniel S. Papp (New York: W. W. Norton, 1990), p. 240; Morton Halperin, "The Decision to Deploy the ABM: Bureaucratic and Domestic Politics in the Johnson Administration," *World Politics* 25 (October 1972): 74–76.

3. Roman Kolkowicz, Matthew P. Gallagher, and Benjamin Lambeth, *The Soviet Union and Arms Control: A Superpower Dilemma* (Baltimore: Johns Hopkins University Press, 1970), pp. 60–61, 203; John Prados, *The Soviet Estimate: U.S. Intelligence Analysis and Russian Military Strength* (New York: Dial Press, 1982), pp. 169, 191–93; Alain C. Enthoven and K. Wayne Smith, *How Much Is Enough?: Shaping the Defense Program, 1961–1969* (New York: Harper and Row, 1971), pp. 177–78; John Newhouse, *Cold Dawn: The Story of SALT* (Oxford, Eng.: Pergamon-Brassey's International Defense Publishers, 1989), p. 20.

4. Fred Kaplan, *Wizards of Armageddon* (New York: Simon and Schus-

ter, 1983), pp. 344–45; Bruce-Briggs, *Shield of Faith*, pp. 226–27; Glenn T. Seaborg and Benjamin S. Loeb, *Stemming the Tide: Arms Control in the Johnson Years* (Lexington, Mass.: D. C. Heath, 1987), pp. 413–14; Henry L. Trewhitt, *McNamara* (New York: Harper and Row, 1971), pp. 122–26.

5. Prados, *Soviet Estimate*, pp. 155–62; Ernest J. Yanarella, *The Missile Defense Controversy* (Lexington: University Press of Kentucky, 1977), p. 118.

6. Kaplan, *Wizards*, pp. 361–63; Prados, *Soviet Estimate*, pp. 204–5; Herbert F. York, *Making Weapons, Talking Peace: A Physicist's Odyssey from Hiroshima to Geneva* (New York: Basic Books, 1987), p. 224.

7. Ted Greenwood, *Making the MIRV: A Study of Defense Decision Making* (Cambridge, Mass.: Ballinger Publishing Company, 1975), pp. 49, 74, 76; Kaplan, *Wizards*, p. 363; Trewhitt, *McNamara*, pp. 126–27.

8. *New York Times*, November 11, 1966, pp. 1, 19; Chalmers Roberts, *The Nuclear Years: The Arms Race and Arms Control, 1945–70* (New York: Praeger, 1970), p. 81.

9. Lawrence Korb, *The Joint Chiefs of Staff: The First Twenty-Five Years* (Bloomington: Indiana University Press, 1976), pp. 115–16; Halperin, "ABM Decision," pp. 69, 72–73.

10. McNamara to Johnson, December 2 and 3, 1966, National Security File (NSF) Agency File, "Defense Dept. Budget for FY 1968," box 16, Lyndon B. Johnson Library (hereafter cited as LBJL), Austin, Texas. All manuscript and oral history citations, unless otherwise noted, are to materials in the Johnson Library. The folder title is included in the first reference to each file.

11. Rostow notes, December 10, 1966, of meeting with the JCS, December 6, 1966, NSF, Rostow Memos to the President, vol. 16, box 11; Prados, *Keepers of the Keys*, p. 190.

12. *Public Papers of the Presidents: Lyndon B. Johnson, 1966* (Washington, D.C.: Government Printing Office, 1967), 2:1433–35 (hereafter cited as *Public Papers*).

13. Katzenbach to Rostow, Foy Kohler to Rostow, Thompson to Rostow, Hornig to Rostow, and Rostow memo for the record, December 10, 1966, and Rostow to Johnson, December 11, 1966, NSF, Rostow Memos to the President, vol. 16, box 11.

14. Herbert York, *Race to Oblivion: A Participants's View of the Arms Race* (New York: Simon and Schuster, 1970), pp. 194–95; Ann Hessing Cahn, "American Scientists and the ABM: A Case Study in Controversy," in *Scientists and Public Affairs*, ed. Albert H. Teich (Cambridge, Mass.: MIT Press, 1974), pp. 49–50; W. Henry Lambright, *Presidential Management of Science and Technology: The Johnson Presidency* (Austin: University of Texas Press, 1985), p. 134; president's schedule, January 4, 1967, Diary Backup Files, box 52; Harold Brown Oral History Interview, January 17, 1969, by Dorothy Pierce, tape 1, p. 16.

15. Halperin, "ABM Decision," p. 85.

16. Rusk to Harlan Cleveland, March 4, 1967, NSF, Country File, France, vol. 11, box 173.

17. *Public Papers, 1967*, 1:10–11; Rusk to David Bruce, January 17, 1967, and Rostow to Johnson, January 15, 1967, NSF, Country File, USSR, "ABM Negotiations," box 231.

18. Rusk to Bruce, January 19, 1967, NSF, Country File, USSR, box 231; Rusk to Cleveland, March 4, 1967, NSF, Country File, France, vol. 11, box 173.

19. *Public Papers, 1967*, 1:48.

20. Johnson to Kosygin, January 21, 1967, NSF, Intelligence File, ''Arms Control Messages,'' box 11.

21. Rusk to Thompson, January 21, 1967, NSF, Country File, USSR, box 231.

22. Rusk to Bruce, February 3, 1967, and Soviet statements on ABM, February 10, 1967, NSF, Country File, USSR, box 231; Seaborg, *Stemming the Tide*, p. 416.

23. Kohler to Katzenbach, February 15, 1967, NSF, Country File, USSR, box 231; McNamara statement, January 23, 1967, NSF, Agency File, ''FY 68 Defense Budget,'' box 17; transcript of McNamara press conference, February 15, 1967, NSF, Agency File, Department of Defense (DOD), vol. 4, box 12.

24. Rusk to Cleveland, March 4, 1967, NSF, Country File, France, vol. 11, box 173; summary of U.S. statements to Russians, January 67–June 68, ''Kosygin Talks with Soviet Union,'' box 22, Clark Clifford Papers, LBJL.

25. Lyndon Baines Johnson, *The Vantage Point: Perspectives of the Presidency, 1963-1969* (New York: Holt, Rinehart and Winston, 1971), p. 480; Rostow to Johnson, February 28, 1967, NSF, Rostow File, ''Kosygin,'' box 10; Nathaniel Davis to Rostow, March 1, 1967, NSF, Country File, USSR, box 231.

26. Thompson to Rusk, February 28, 1967, NSF, Country File, USSR, box 231; *Public Papers, 1967*, 1:259–62.

27. Rusk to Thompson, March 17, 1967, NSC, Rostow Memos to the President, vol. 23, box 14.

28. Rusk to Thompson, April 4, 1967, NSF, Country File, USSR, vol. 15, box 223; Johnson to Kosygin, May 19, 1967, NSF, Intelligence File, box 11.

29. Johnson, *Vantage Point*, pp. 481–82; Seaborg, *Stemming the Tide*, p. 420; James Edward Katz, *Presidential Politics and Science Policy* (New York: Praeger, 1978), p. 176.

30. Position paper, June 1967, and talking points for meeting with Kosygin, undated, NSF, Country File, USSR, ''Hollybush (I),'' box 229; Rostow to Johnson, June 21, 1967, NSF, Country File, USSR, ''Hollybush (II),'' box 230; Rusk, *As I Saw It*, pp. 349–50; Johnson, *Vantage Point*, pp. 483–84; Kaplan, *Wizards*, p. 346; *Public Papers, 1967*, 1:650–52.

31. Rusk memorandum of conversations with Sir Patrick Dean, June 29, 1967, NSF, Country File, USSR, box 230; Morton Halperin, *Bureaucratic Politics and Foreign Policy* (Washington, D.C.: Brookings Institution, 1974), p. 302; Newhouse, *Cold Dawn*, p. 95.

32. Katz, *Presidential Politics*, p. 177.

33. Kaplan, *Wizards*, pp. 346–47; Halperin, ''ABM Decision,'' pp. 87–88; Strobe Talbott, *The Master of the Game: Paul Nitze and the Nuclear Peace* (New York: Alfred A. Knopf, 1988), p. 102; Phil G. Goulding, *Confirm or Deny: Informing the People on National Security* (New York: Harper and Row, 1970); Trewhitt, *McNamara*, p. 131.

34. Rostow to Johnson, August 2, 1967, NSF, Country File, USSR, box 231.

35. McNamara to Johnson, August 19, 1967, draft of McNamara speech, August 9, 1967, Califano to Rostow, August 27, 1967, and Keeny to Rostow, August 28, 1967, NSF, Agency File, DOD, vol. 5, box 12.

36. Rostow to Johnson, August 28, 1967, and Rusk to Thompson, September 5, 1967, NSF, Country File, USSR, box 231; summary of U.S. statements to Russians, January 1967–June 1968, box 22, Clifford Papers.

37. Goulding, Confirm or Deny, pp. 217–25; Trewhitt, McNamara, pp. 130–31.

38. Life, September 29, 1967, pp. 28A, 28B; Greenwood, Making the MIRV, p. 77; Keeny to Rostow, October 3, 1967, NSF, Country File, USSR, box 231.

39. W. W. Rostow, The Diffusion of Power: An Essay in Recent History (New York: Macmillan, 1972), pp. 387–88; Enthoven and Smith, How Much Is Enough? p. 193; Halperin, "ABM Decision," pp. 91–92; Yanarella, Missile Defense Controversy, pp. 125, 141.

40. Fisher memo to deputies of Committee of Principals, January 13, 1967, NSF, Rostow Files, "Strategic Missile Talks," box 11.

41. Cahn, "American Scientists and the ABM," p. 57; Greenwood, Making the MIRV, pp. 113–23.

42. Seaborg, Stemming the Tide, pp. 417–18; Keeny to Rostow, March 14, 1967, NSF, Agency File, "Joint Chiefs of Staff," box 30; Paul Nitze, From Hiroshima to Glasnost: At the Center of Decision (New York: Grove Weidenfeld, 1989), p. 288.

43. Nitze, From Hiroshima to Glasnost, p. 289; Garthoff to Keeny, September 8, 1967, and Keeny to Rostow, September 14, 1967, NSF, Country File, USSR, box 231.

44. Rusk, As I Saw It, p. 350.

45. Johnson to Kosygin, January 22, 1968, NSF, Intelligence File, box 11.

46. Paul Warnke to Clifford, February 27, 1968, box 22, Clifford Papers; U.S. Arms Control and Disarmament Agency (ACDA), "Strategic Arms Limitation, 1968," pp. 2–3, photocopy in Vertical File, LBJL.

47. Draft cables, Rusk to Thompson and Johnson to Kosygin, April 3, 1968, NSF, Rostow File, box 11; Paul Warnke to Paul Nitze, January 16, 1968, and draft oral statement, Thompson to Kosygin, February 27, 1968, box 22, Clifford Papers.

48. ADCA, "Strategic Arms Limitation, 1968," p. 3; Warnke to Clifford, April 23, 1968, box 22, Clifford Papers.

49. Rostow to Johnson, April 23, 1968, and Rusk to Johnson, April 26, 1968, NSF, Rostow Files, box 11; Warnke to Clifford, April 25, 1968, box 22, Clifford Papers; Johnson to Kosygin, May 2, 1968, NSF, Intelligence File, box 11.

50. Arms control messages, NSF, Intelligence File, box 11; Johnson, Vantage Point, p. 485; Ben Read to Clifford, June 27, 1968, "Soviet Union—Talks on Reduction of Strategic Nuclear Weapons," box 17, Clifford Papers.

51. Johnson, Vantage Point, p. 462; Public Papers, 1968, 2:765.

52. Halperin to Clifford, June 28, 1968, and Warnke to Clifford, July 4, 1968, box 22, Clifford Papers.

53. Basic position paper, July 4, 1968, box 22, Clifford Papers.

54. Morton Halperin, Analysis of Draft U.S. Proposal on Limiting Strategic Systems, July 4, 1958, box 22, Clifford Papers.

55. Newhouse, *Cold Dawn*, p. 103; minutes of meeting of the executive committee of the Committee of Principals, July 8, 1968, box 17, Clifford Papers; Seaborg, *Stemming the Tide*, pp. 433–35.

56. Fisher to executive committee of Committee of Principals, July 26, 1968, box 17, Clifford Papers; Seaborg, *Stemming the Tide*, p. 436; Nitze to Joint Chiefs, August 2, 1968, Warnke to Clifford, August 6, 1968, and Clifford to Johnson, August 24, 1968, box 22, Clifford Papers; ACDA, "Strategic Arms Limitation, 1968," pp. 23–25.

57. Strategic Missile Talks Proposal, August 24, 1968, box 22, Clifford Papers.

58. Greenwood, *Making the MIRV*, pp. 124–25; Rusk memo of August 15, 1968, conversation with Dobrynin, August 16, 1968, NSF, Rostow Files, box 11; Seaborg, *Stemming the Tide*, p. 437.

59. Clark Clifford, with Richard Holbook, *Counsel to the President: A Memoir* (New York: Random House, 1991), pp. 558–59; Johnson to Kosygin, July 30, 1968, NSF, Intelligence File, box 11; Bromley Smith to Johnson, July 31, 1968, NSF, Rostow Files, box 10; *Public Papers, 1968*, 2:862.

60. Roberts, *Nuclear Years*, p. 79; chronology, August 19, 1968, NSF, Rostow Files, box 11; George Christian, *A President Steps Down: A Personal Memoir of the Transfer of Power* (New York: Macmillan, 1970), p. 142.

61. Clifford, *Counsel*, p. 558; Tom Johnson's Notes of Meetings, August 20, 1968, box 3; Johnson, *Vantage Point*, p. 487.

62. Johnson, *Vantage Point*, p. 488; Tom Johnson's Notes of Meetings, August 20, 1968, box 3; Christian, *President Steps Down*, p. 142.

63. George Ball, *The Past Has Another Pattern: Memoirs* (New York: W. W. Norton, 1982), p. 440; Clifford, *Counsel*, p. 561; Clark Clifford Oral History Interview, December 15, 1969, by Joe F. Frantz, tape 5, pp. 17–18; John Leddy Oral History Interview, March 3, 1969, by Paige Mulhollan, p. 19.

64. Rusk, *As I Saw It*, p. 351; Seaborg, *Stemming the Tide*, p. 438.

65. Thompson memorandum of conversation with Dobrynin, August 27, 1968, and Rostow memo for the record, September 7, 1968, NSF, Rostow Files, box 11; summary notes of National Security Council (NSC) meeting, September 4, 1968, NSF, NSC Meetings File, box 2, draft cable, Rusk to Harlan Cleveland, September 6, 1968, and Wheeler to Clifford, September 10, 1968, box 22, Clifford Papers.

66. Rostow to LBJ, October 4, 1968, and November 20, 1968, NSC, Rostow Files, box 11; Clifford, *Counsel*, p. 594; Tom Johnson's Notes of Meetings, November 26, 1968, box 4.

67. Tom Johnson's Notes of Meetings, November 26, 1968, box 4.

68. Telephone call, Thompson to Rusk, November 29, 1968, NSF, Rostow Files, box 10, and Rusk to Thompson, December 9, 1968, ibid., box 11.

69. Henry Kissinger, *White House Years* (Boston: Little, Brown, 1979), pp. 49–50; Richard Nixon, *RN: The Memoirs of Richard Nixon* (New York: Grosset and Dunlap, 1978), pp. 345–46; Johnson, *Vantage Point*, p. 490; Rostow to Johnson, December 11, 1968, NSF, Rostow Files, Box 11.

70. Johnson, *Vantage Point*, p. 491; Seaborg, *Stemming the Tide*, p. 442.

71. Newhouse, *Cold Dawn*, p. 108; Greenwood, *Making the MIRV*, p. 139.

72. Seaborg, *Stemming the Tide*, p. 450.

About the Contributors

Robert A. Divine is the George W. Littlefield Professor in American History at the University of Texas at Austin, where he has taught since 1954. A specialist in American diplomatic history, his most recent book is *The Sputnik Challenge* (1993). He is the editor of two previous collections of essays on the Johnson administration.

Lloyd Gardner is the Charles and Mary Beard Professor of History at Rutgers University, where he has taught since 1963. His most recent book is *Spheres of Influence: The Great Powers Partition of Europe from Munich to Yalta* (1993). He is currently working on a study of the political rationale for the Vietnam War and its interaction with the conception of the Great Society.

Lewis L. Gould is the Eugene C. Barker Centennial Professor in American History at the University of Texas at Austin. His most recent book is *1968: The Election That Changed America* (1993). He is also the author of *Lady Bird Johnson and the Environment* (1988).

Susan M. Hartmann is Professor of History and Women's Studies at Ohio State University. Her publications include *The Home Front and Beyond: American Women in the 1940s* (1982) and *From Margin to Mainstream: American Women and Politics since 1960* (1989). At present she is writing a history of feminism in male-dominated organizations.

Lawrence S. Kaplan is University Professor Emeritus of History and Director Emeritus of the Lyman L. Lemnitzer Center for NATO Studies at Kent State University. He has written and edited many books on NATO's history, including *A Community of Interests: NATO and the Military Assistance Program*, *NATO and the United States: The Enduring Alliance*, and *NATO after Forty Years*.

Steven F. Lawson is Professor and Head of the History Department at the University of North Carolina at Greensboro. He received his Ph.D. from Columbia University in 1974 and is the author of *Run-*

ning for Freedom: Civil Rights and Black Politics since 1941. He is currently working on a study of race, anticommunism, and popular culture in the late 1950s and early 1960s.

Douglas Little is Associate Professor of History at Clark University, where he has taught since 1978. He received his Ph.D. from Cornell University and is the author of *Malevolent Neutrality: The United States, Great Britain, and the Origins of the Spanish Civil War* (1985). His current work focuses on American involvement in the Middle East from 1945 to 1970, with special emphasis on the Arab world. Among his most recent publications are articles in the *Journal of American History*, the *Middle East Journal*, and the *International Journal of Middle East Studies*.

Index